ORCS

FORGED FOR WAR

First Second

New York & London

Story copyright © 2011 by Stan Nicholls
Adaptation and illustrations copyright © 2011 by Joe Flood
Published by First Second
First Second is an imprint of Roaring Brook Press, a division of Holtzbrinck Publishing Holdings
Limited Partnership
175 Fifth Avenue, New York, New York 10010
All rights reserved

Distributed in the United Kingdom by Macmillan Children's Books, a division of Pan Macmillan.

Cataloging-in-Publication Data is available at the Library of Congress

First Second books are available for special promotions and premiums.
For details, contact: Director of Special Markets, Holtzbrinck Publishers.

First edition 2011
Book design by Colleen AF Venable
Printed in China

FIRST

EDITION

10 9 8 7 6 5 4 3 2 1

ORCS
FORGED FOR WAR

Story by **Stan Nicholls**
Adapted and Drawn by **Joe Flood**

First Second
New York & London

INTRODUCTION

by Stan Nicholls

This book might make you think about orcs in a different way.

Before we go any further, let's deal with the elephant in the room. My Orcs universe is not based on the works of J.R.R. Tolkien. I have enormous admiration for Tolkien and *The Lord of the Rings*, which was a seminal work for me when I was growing up. It's a terrific piece of fiction that couldn't possibly be improved upon, and any writer, myself included, would be insane to try.

I think a certain confusion has arisen from the mistaken belief that Tolkien invented orcs. In fact, orcs have featured in European folklore for hundreds of years, and they've appeared in various narratives from at least as early as the fifteenth century. When Tolkien needed a savage horde to personify evil, he pulled orcs out of mythology and refashioned them for his own purposes.

He popularized them, so to speak—in the same way Bram Stoker popularized vampires in *Dracula* and Anne McCaffrey had a new angle on dragons, though neither claimed to have invented those legendary creatures. Orcs are just one of the pantheon of fantasy creatures—elves, fairies, trolls, goblins, and all the rest—and as such are available to any writer who wants to play with them. All I'm doing is offering my own take on this particular fantasy race.

When I first started thinking about using orcs as protagonists, back in the late '90s, I played the "What if?" game. Quite a lot of speculative fiction comes from asking yourself "What if?" In this case the question I posed was, "What if orcs were heroes instead of villains?" Here in the real world it's the winners who get to write the history books, and they tend to demonize the losers. I got to wondering how it would be if that was what happened to orcs; that rather than being wicked fiends they simply had bad press. Suppose they were savage, peerless warriors, but not actually evil?

WAS A TIME WHEN YOU'D SEE A LOT MORE STARS, BEFORE THE HUMANS FOULED THE SKIES.
YOU REMEMBER THAT?
FROM WHEN I WAS A HATCHLING, THAT'S WHAT MY SIRE SAID, AND WHAT HIS TOLD HIM.

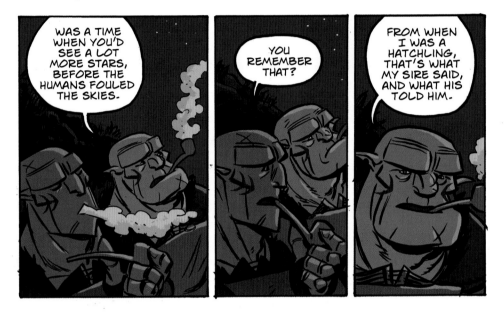

Why shouldn't orcs have hopes and dreams, a history, a culture, spiritual beliefs, and a code of honor? Part of my aim was to give them all that, to make them more rounded, and even to imbue them with a certain nobility. I wanted to write about them as sympathetic characters. Not a bunch you'd want to get into a fight with, admittedly, but a race capable of a certain rough compassion as much as of savagery. My orcs aren't mindless servants of evil. They have a well-earned reputation for ferocity in battle, but that isn't all there is to them. They're battling against the odds in the face of almost universal prejudice. They're outsiders, and I've always empathized with outsiders, misfits, and rebels. Because most of us feel like outsiders at times.

Of course, once you cast orcs as heroes you look around for the villains, and the logical choice is humans. So the concept's really quite simple: it's just a case of turning everything upside down.

All that "What if-ing?" led to the initial trilogy, Orcs: First Blood, and a subsequent trio of books with the series title Orcs: Bad Blood. As I am writing this, the novels have achieved worldwide sales of around one and a quarter million copies. Why not follow that success in prose with an experiment in a visual format? This graphic novel isn't an adaptation of any of the previous books. It's a totally new story written specifically for a visual medium. It might be useful, for those who are interested, to make clear at what point in the saga the story you're about to read sits, although this work stands on its own, and new readers should have no trouble following it.

Here's the bibliography:

The Taking (Short story; included in the *Orcs: First Blood Omnibus*)

Orcs: Forged for War (Graphic novel)

Orcs: First Blood trilogy:
    Bodyguard of Lightning
    Legion of Thunder
    Warriors of the Tempest

Orcs: Bad Blood trilogy:
    Bad Blood (Weapons of Magical Destruction in the UK)
    Army of Shadows
    Inferno

As I say, you don't have to be familiar with any of the above to get into this graphic novel. But if you are coming to my orcs universe for the first time, it could be helpful to know the context for this story…

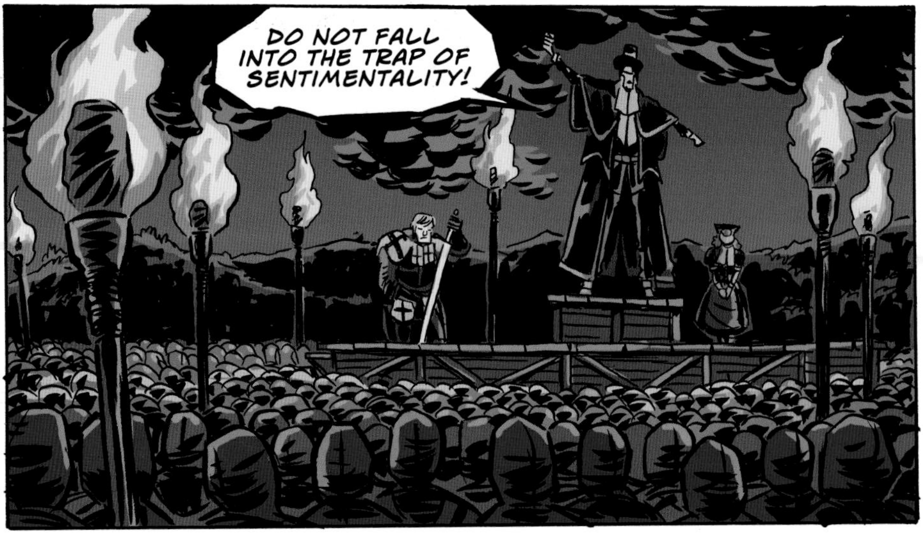
DO NOT FALL INTO THE TRAP OF SENTIMENTALITY!

Maras-Dantia is a land that for ages has been inhabited solely by a wide variety of exotic species, known collectively as the elder races. It wouldn't be true to say that all these races have coexisted peacefully; given such diversity some degree of conflict has been inevitable. But in general there has long been a measure of tolerance.

That balance is ruined by the coming of a new race. They are called humans and they have crossed inhospitable deserts to enter Maras-Dantia from the far south. A trickle at first, growing to a torrent as the years pass, these newcomers are contemptuous of the cultures they encounter, regarding the elder races as mere beasts or monsters. As the humans' numbers increase, so does the destruction they bring. They dam rivers, denude forests, raze villages, tear precious resources from the earth.

And they eat Maras-Dantia's magic.

Their rape of the land bleeds it of essential energies, weakening the magic the elder races took for granted. This distorts the climate and throws the seasons into chaos. Summers become autumnal. Winters lengthen, swallowing spring. An ice field begins advancing from the north.

This inevitably leads to war between the natives of Maras-Dantia and the humans.

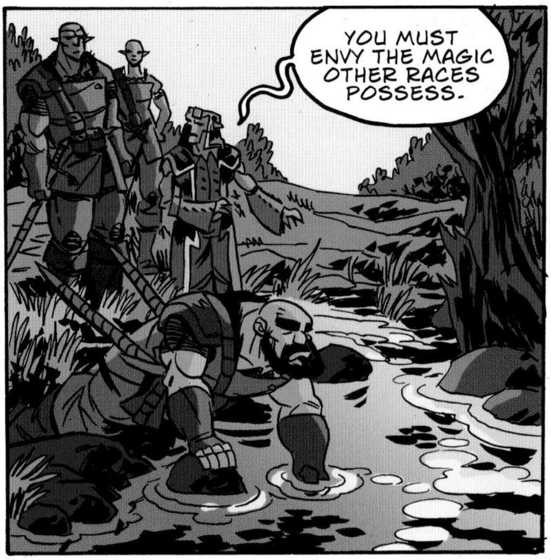
YOU MUST ENVY THE MAGIC OTHER RACES POSSESS.

Old rivalries divide the races, complicated by the actions of the notoriously opportunistic dwarf population. Many side with the humans and willingly undertake their dirty work. Others remain loyal to the elder races' cause.

But the humans are divided themselves, with most separated into two religious factions. The Followers of the Manifold Path, commonly termed Manis, pursue ancient pagan ways. Their rivals march under the banner of Unity. Known as Unis, they adhere to the younger cult of monotheism. Both groups are prone to fanaticism, but the more numerous Unis have the edge in bigotry and no shortage of demagogues.

Of all the elder races, orcs are the most warlike. One of the few races not possessed of magical powers, they make up for it with a fierce talent for combat, and are usually to be found in the eye of the storm.

By orc standards, Stryke is bright. He captains a thirty-strong warband called the Wolverines. Below Stryke are two sergeants, Haskeer and Jup. Haskeer is the most reckless and headstrong of the group; Jup is the only dwarf, indeed the only member who isn't an orc, and consequently the occasional object of suspicion. Below the sergeants are corporals Alfray and Coilla. Alfray is the oldest member and a healer, specializing in field surgery; Coilla is the sole female in the Wolverines, and a brilliant strategist. Below them are twenty-five grunts.

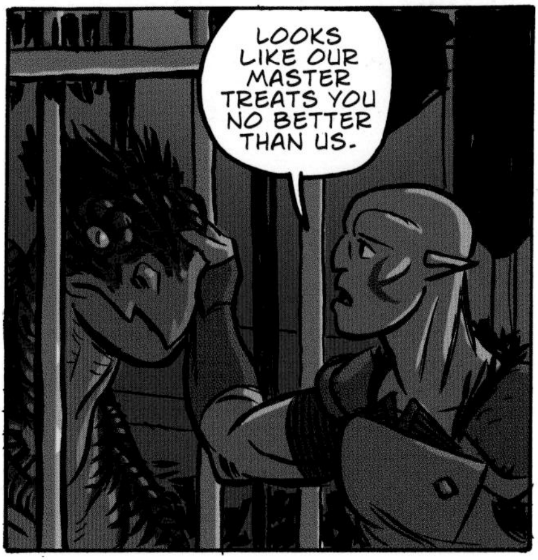
LOOKS LIKE OUR MASTER TREATS YOU NO BETTER THAN US.

The Wolverines are effectively enslaved to Jennesta, a despotic, self-styled Queen and commander of great magical powers who supports the Mani cause. A half human, half nyadd hybrid, her insatiable appetite for cruelty is infamous.

Under Stryke's leadership, the Wolverines are one of the most successful and feared warbands in Jennesta's horde. Consequently she has taken to using them for vital assignments. *Orcs: Forged for War* tells the story of one such mission.

I'm thrilled to see my version of the orcs so expertly depicted in another medium by the outstanding artistic talent of Joe Flood. And I'm indebted to the midwifery skills of our editor, Mark Siegel, and all the folk at First Second for bringing this particular baby, mottle-skinned and fractious as it may be, to life.

My hope is that all our efforts will enable you see the orcs in a new light.

Stan Nicholls
Warwickshire, UK
October 2011

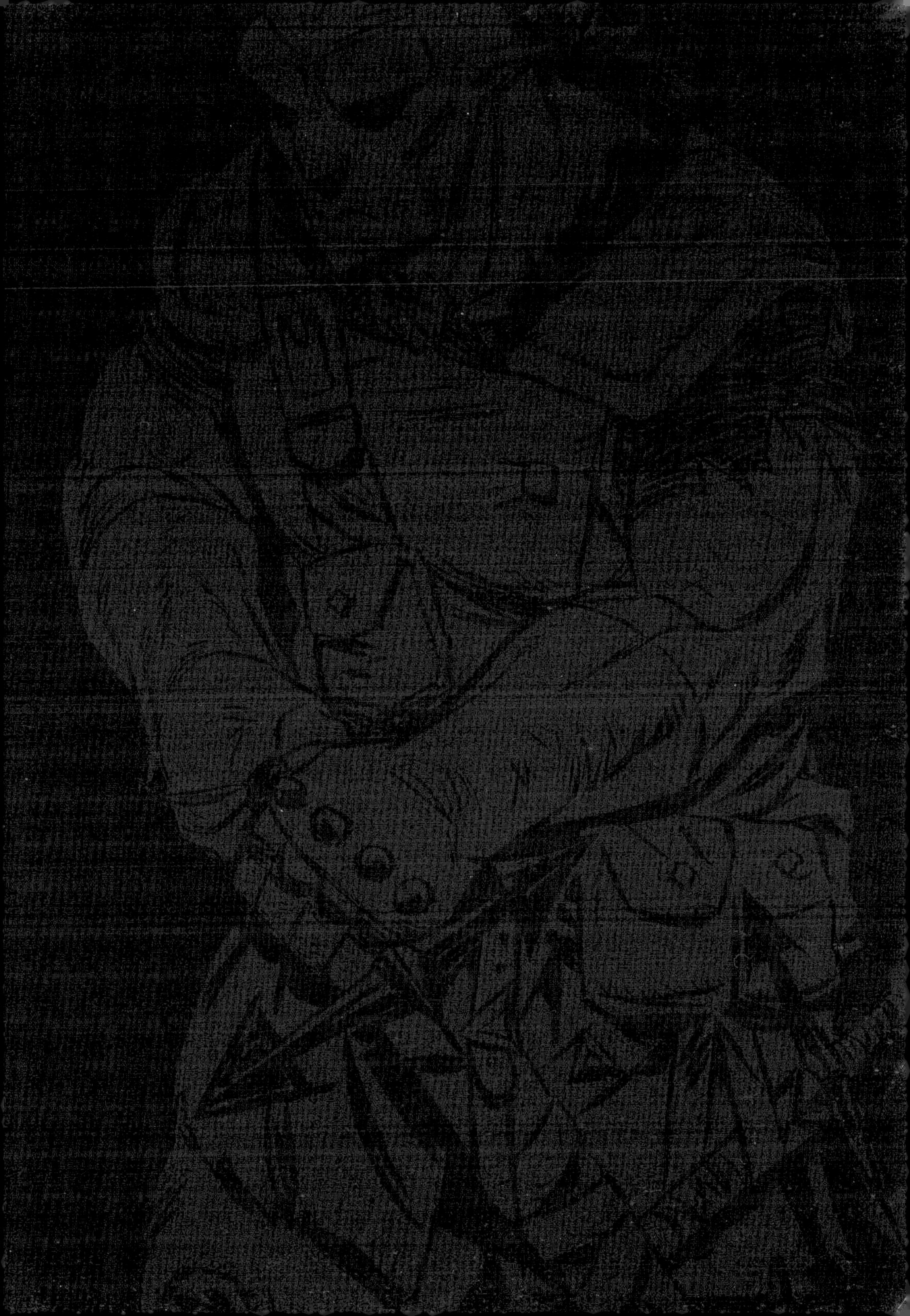

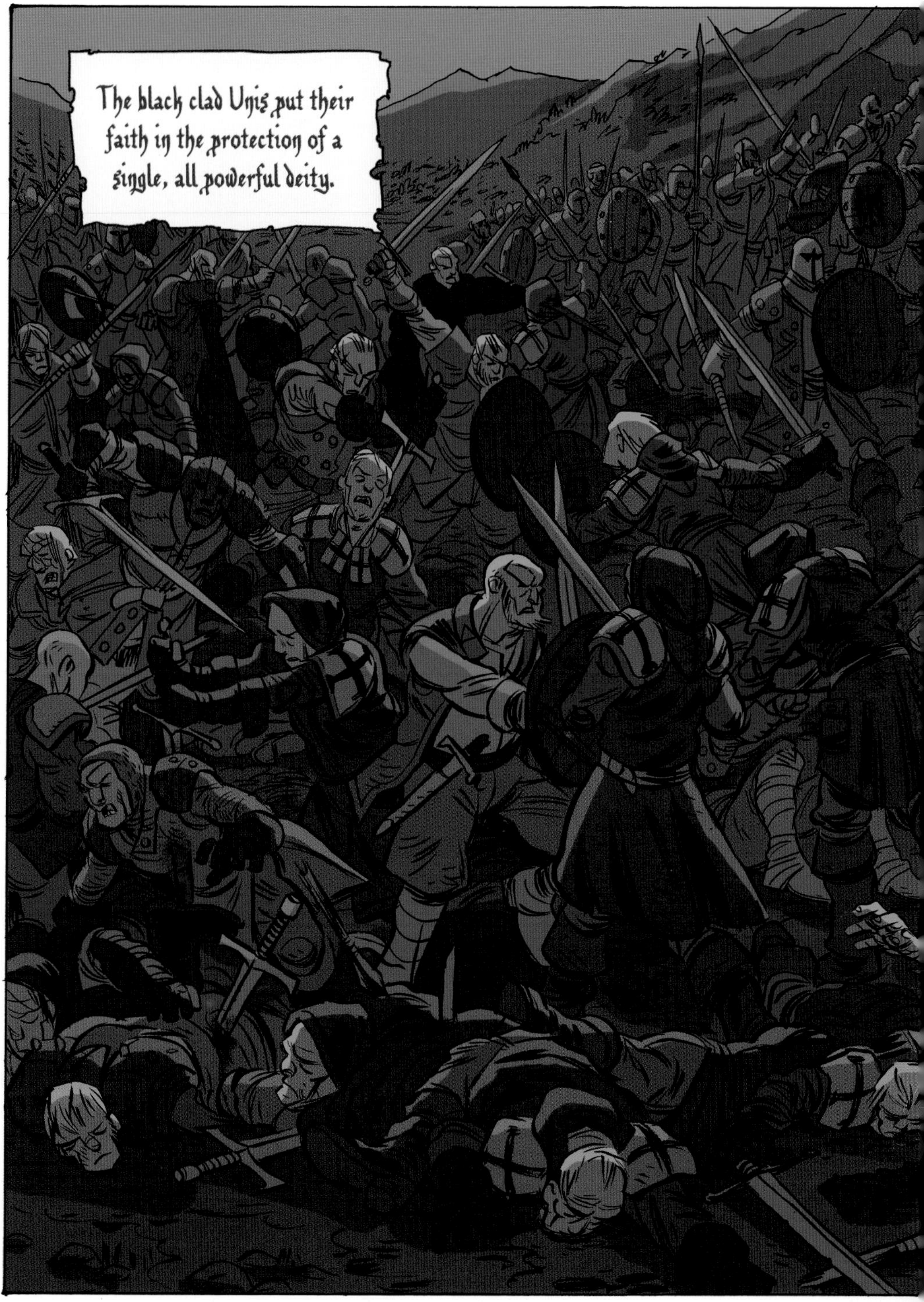
The black clad Unis put their faith in the protection of a single, all powerful deity.

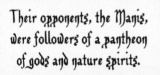

Their opponents, the Manis, were followers of a pantheon of gods and nature spirits.

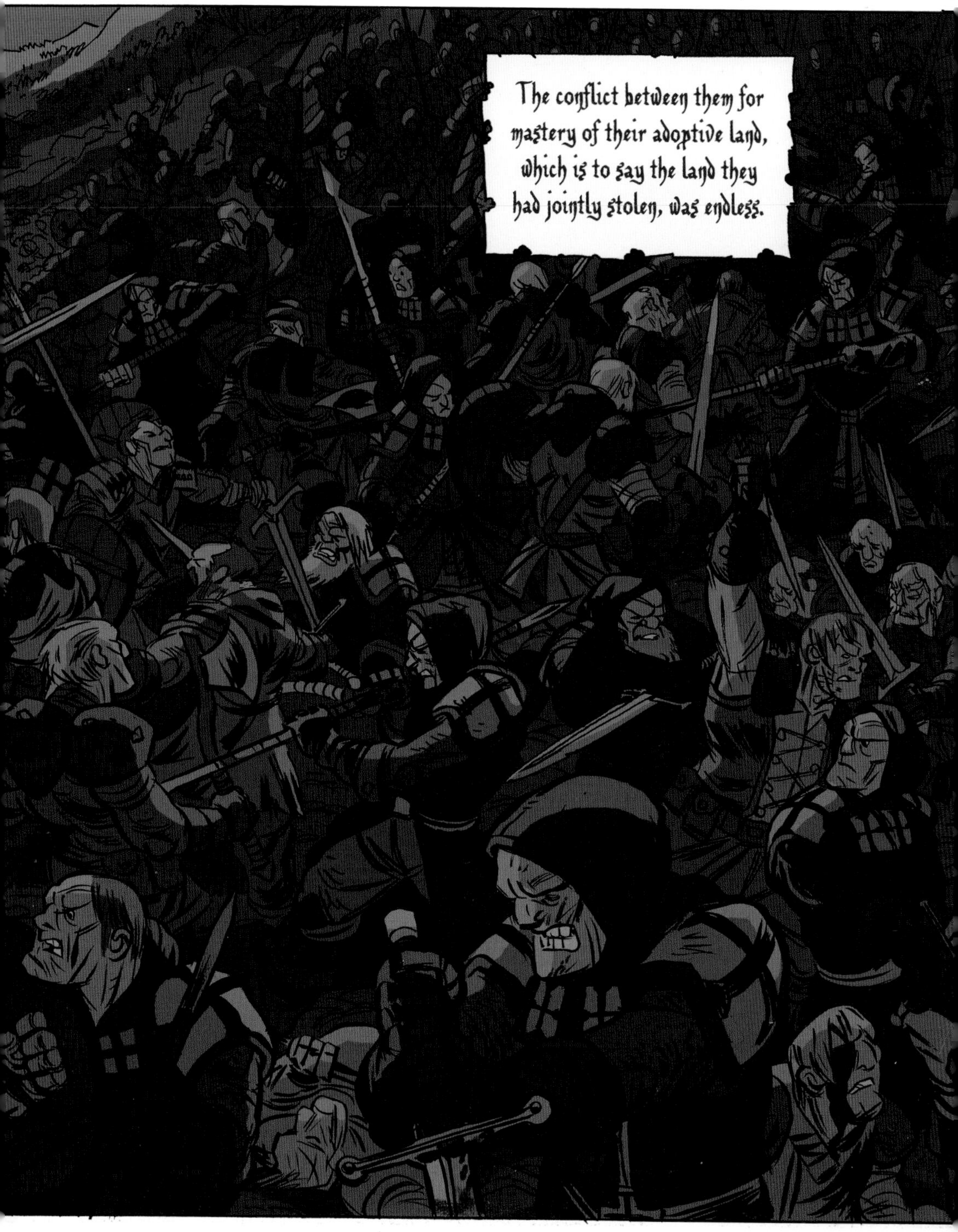
The conflict between them for mastery of their adoptive land, which is to say the land they had jointly stolen, was endless.

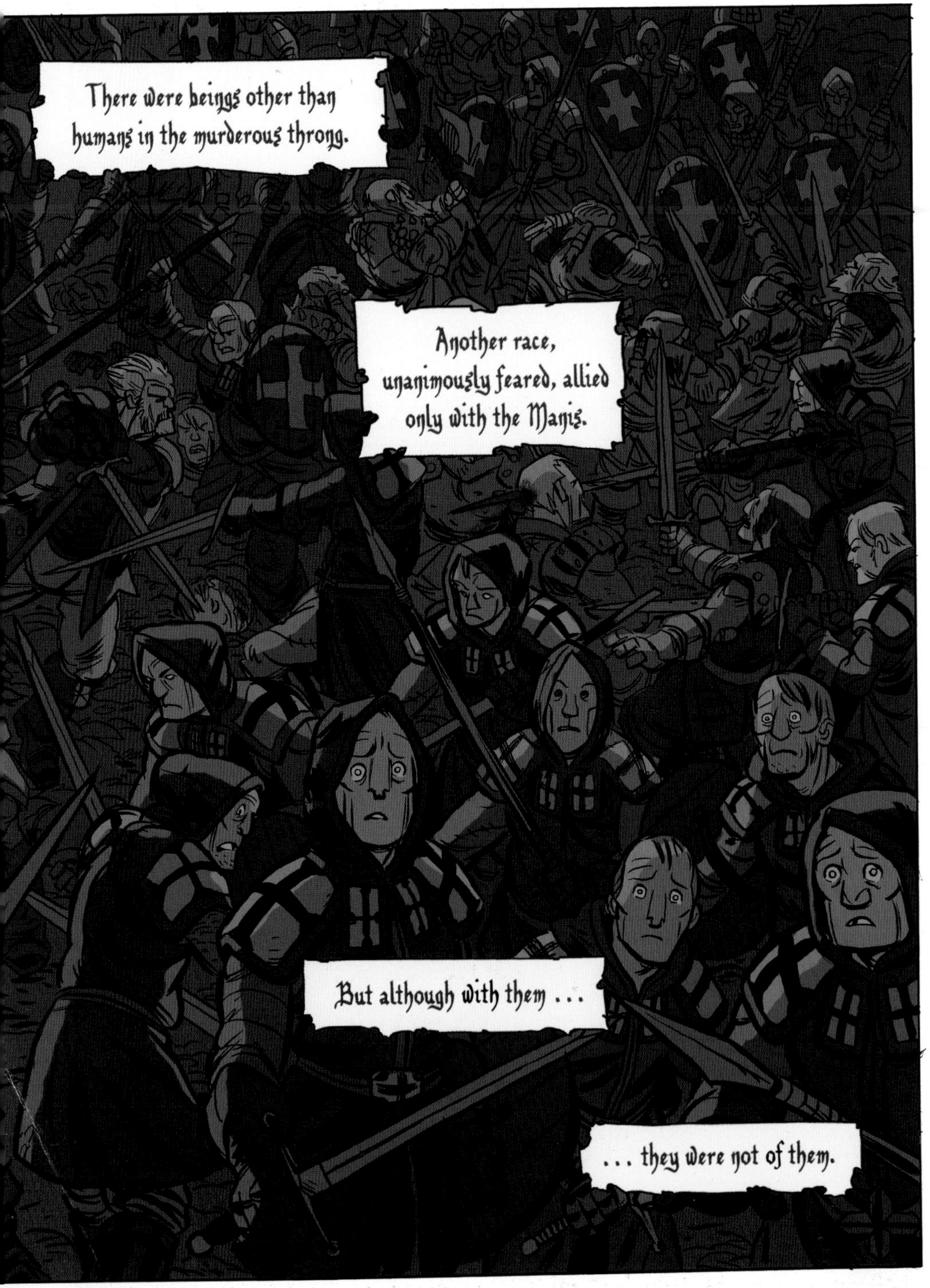
There were beings other than humans in the murderous throng.
Another race, unanimously feared, allied only with the Manis.
But although with them . . .
. . . they were not of them.

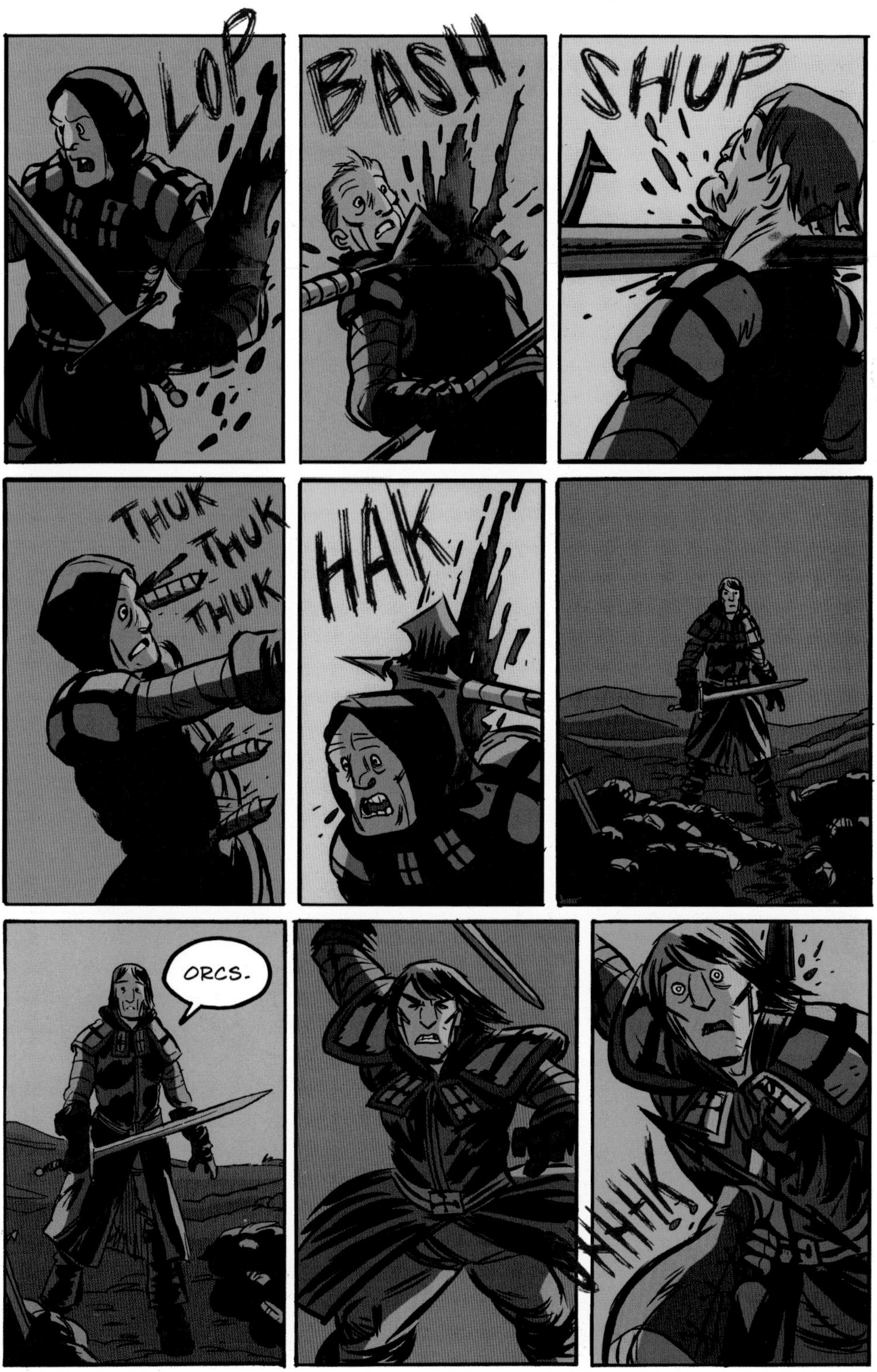
LOP
BASH
SHUP
THUK
THUK
THUK
HAK
ORCS.
SHHK

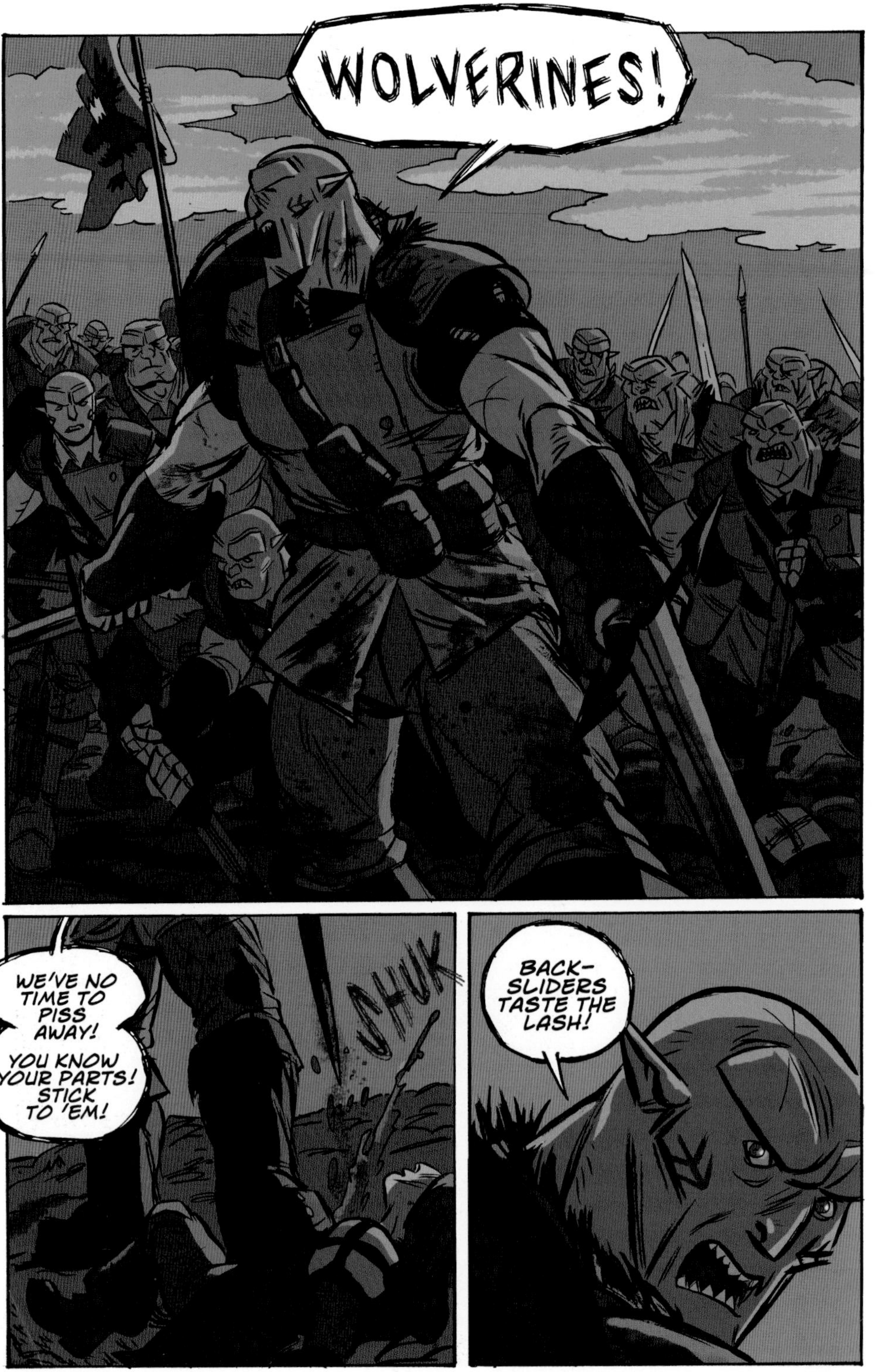
WOLVERINES!
WE'VE NO TIME TO PISS AWAY!
YOU KNOW YOUR PARTS! STICK TO 'EM!
SHUK
BACK-SLIDERS TASTE THE LASH!

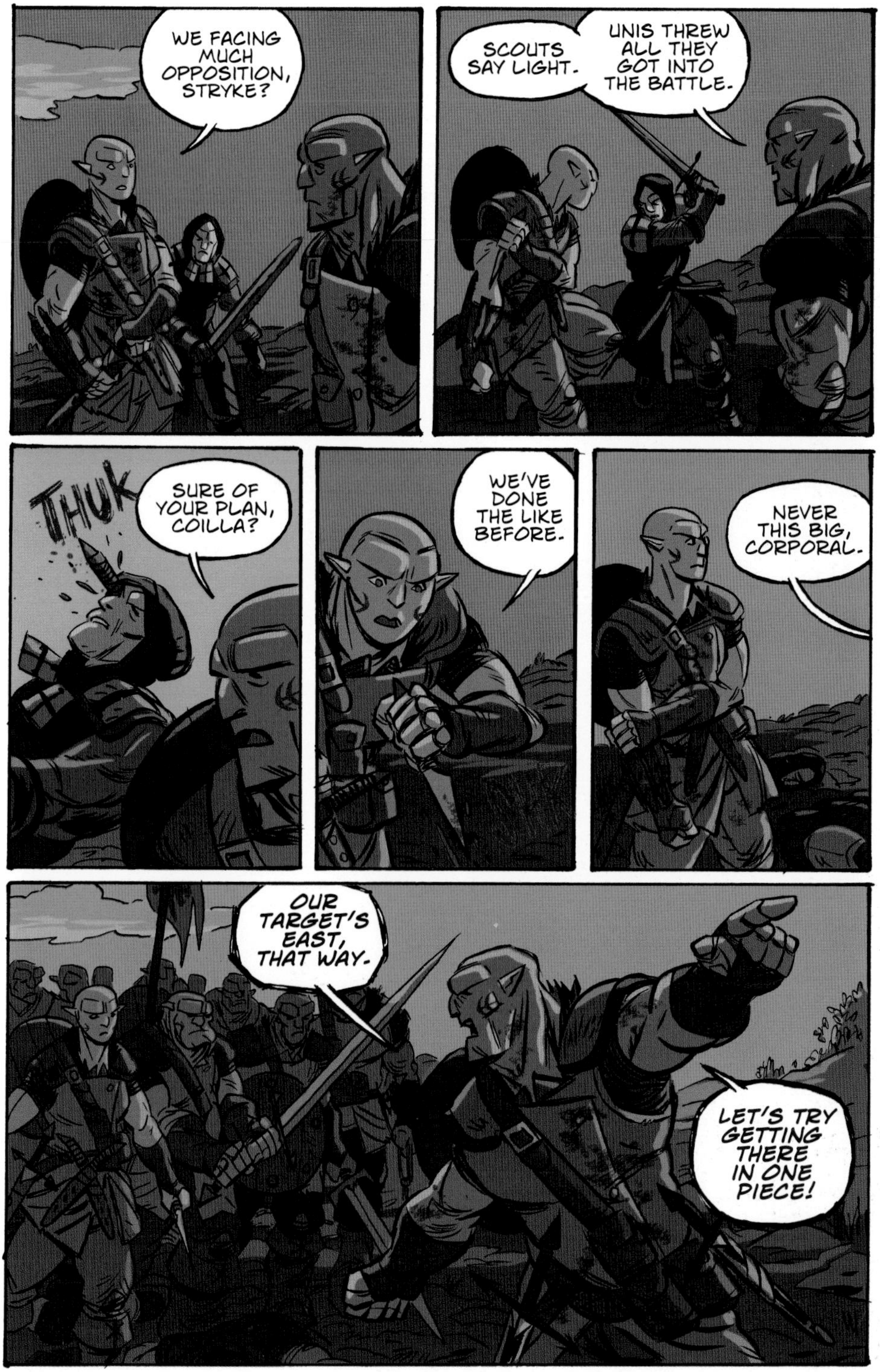
WE FACING MUCH OPPOSITION, STRYKE?
SCOUTS SAY LIGHT.
UNIS THREW ALL THEY GOT INTO THE BATTLE.
THUK
SURE OF YOUR PLAN, COILLA?
WE'VE DONE THE LIKE BEFORE.
NEVER THIS BIG, CORPORAL.
OUR TARGET'S EAST, THAT WAY.
LET'S TRY GETTING THERE IN ONE PIECE!

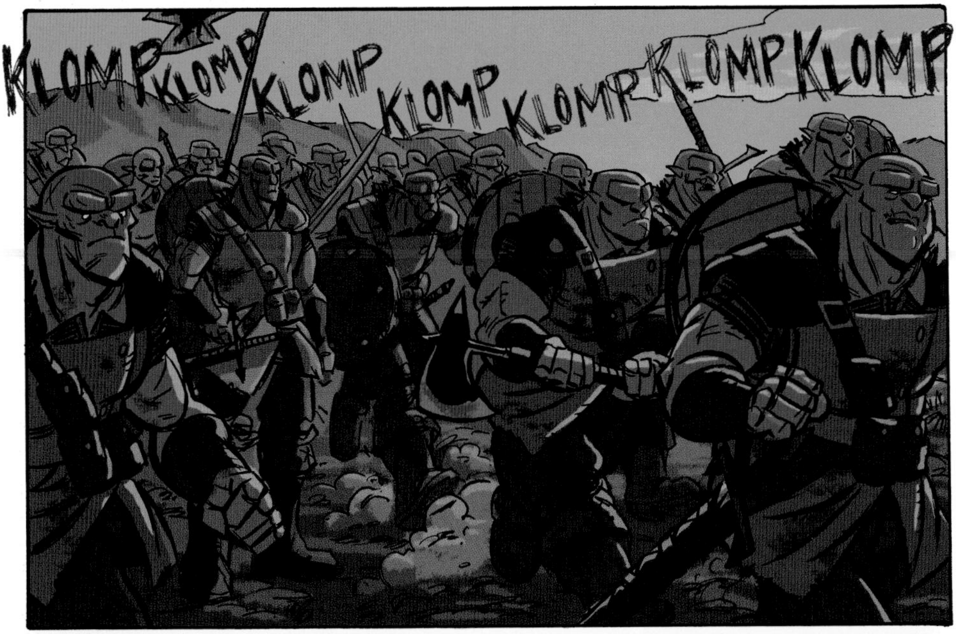
KLOMP KLOMP KLOMP KLOMP KLOMP KLOMP KLOMP

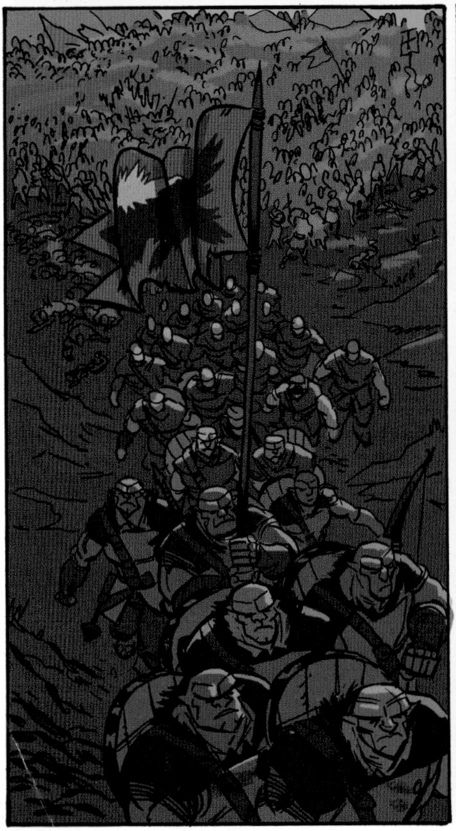

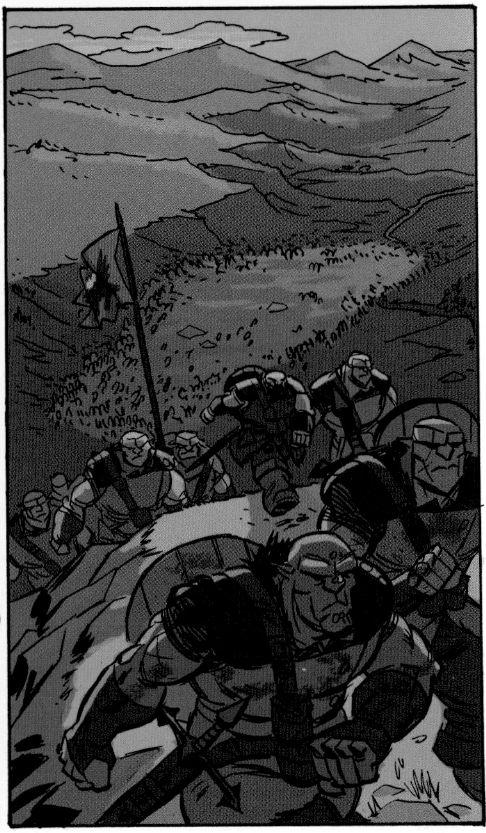

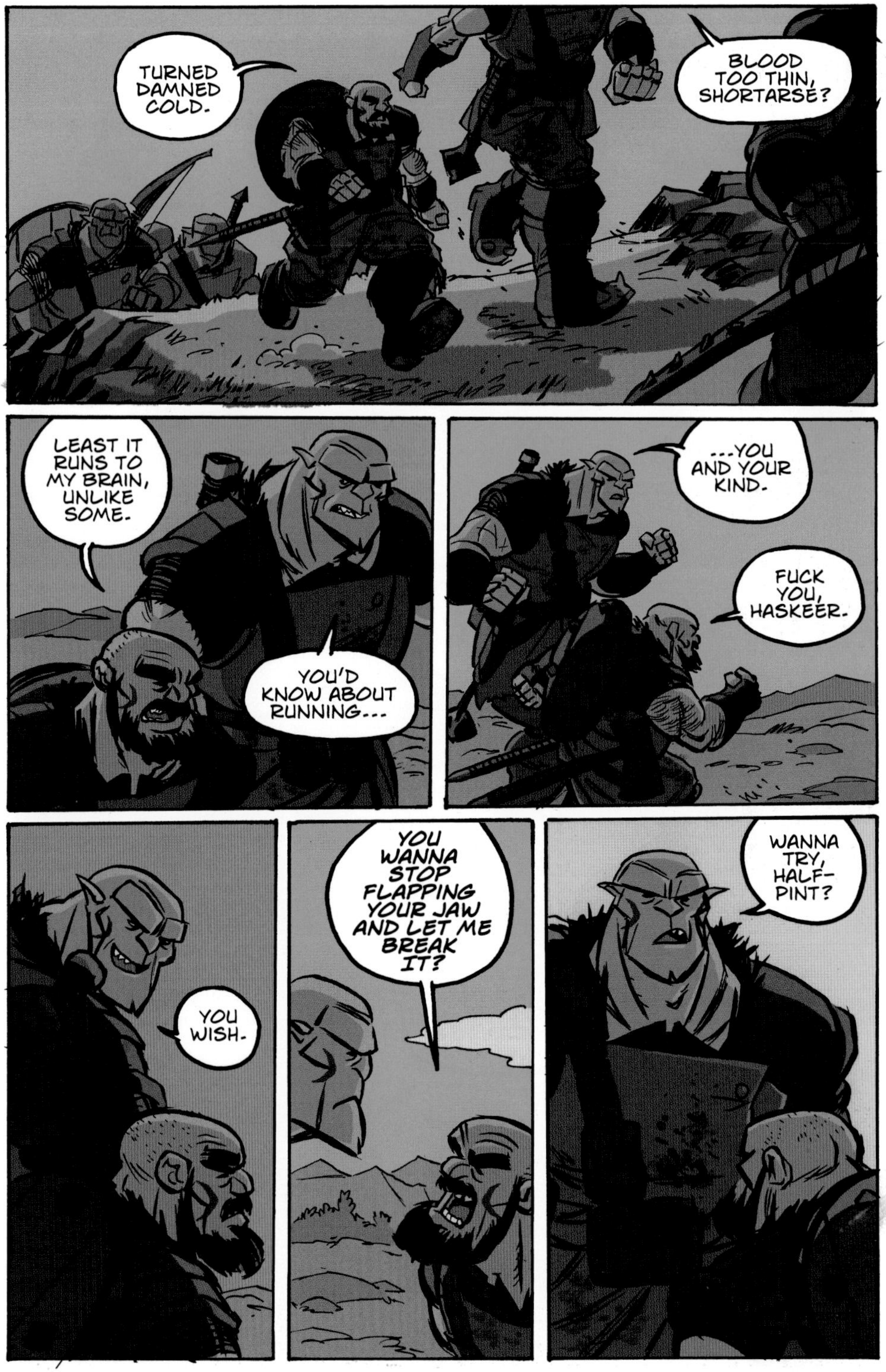
TURNED DAMNED COLD.
BLOOD TOO THIN, SHORTARSE?
LEAST IT RUNS TO MY BRAIN, UNLIKE SOME.
YOU'D KNOW ABOUT RUNNING...
...YOU AND YOUR KIND.
FUCK YOU, HASKEER.
YOU WISH.
YOU WANNA STOP FLAPPING YOUR JAW AND LET ME BREAK IT?
WANNA TRY, HALF-PINT?

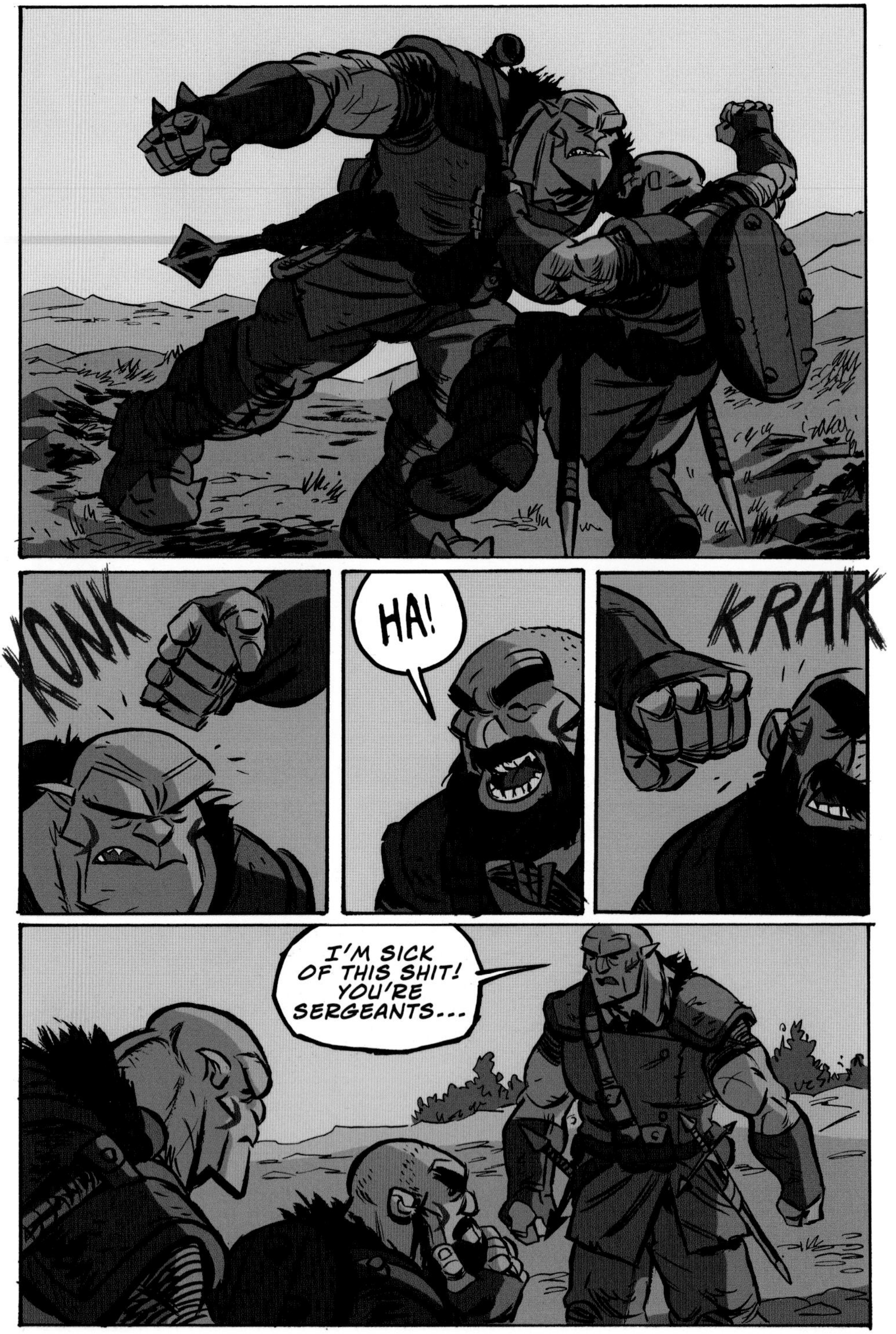
KONK
HA!
KRAK
I'M SICK OF THIS SHIT! YOU'RE SERGEANTS...

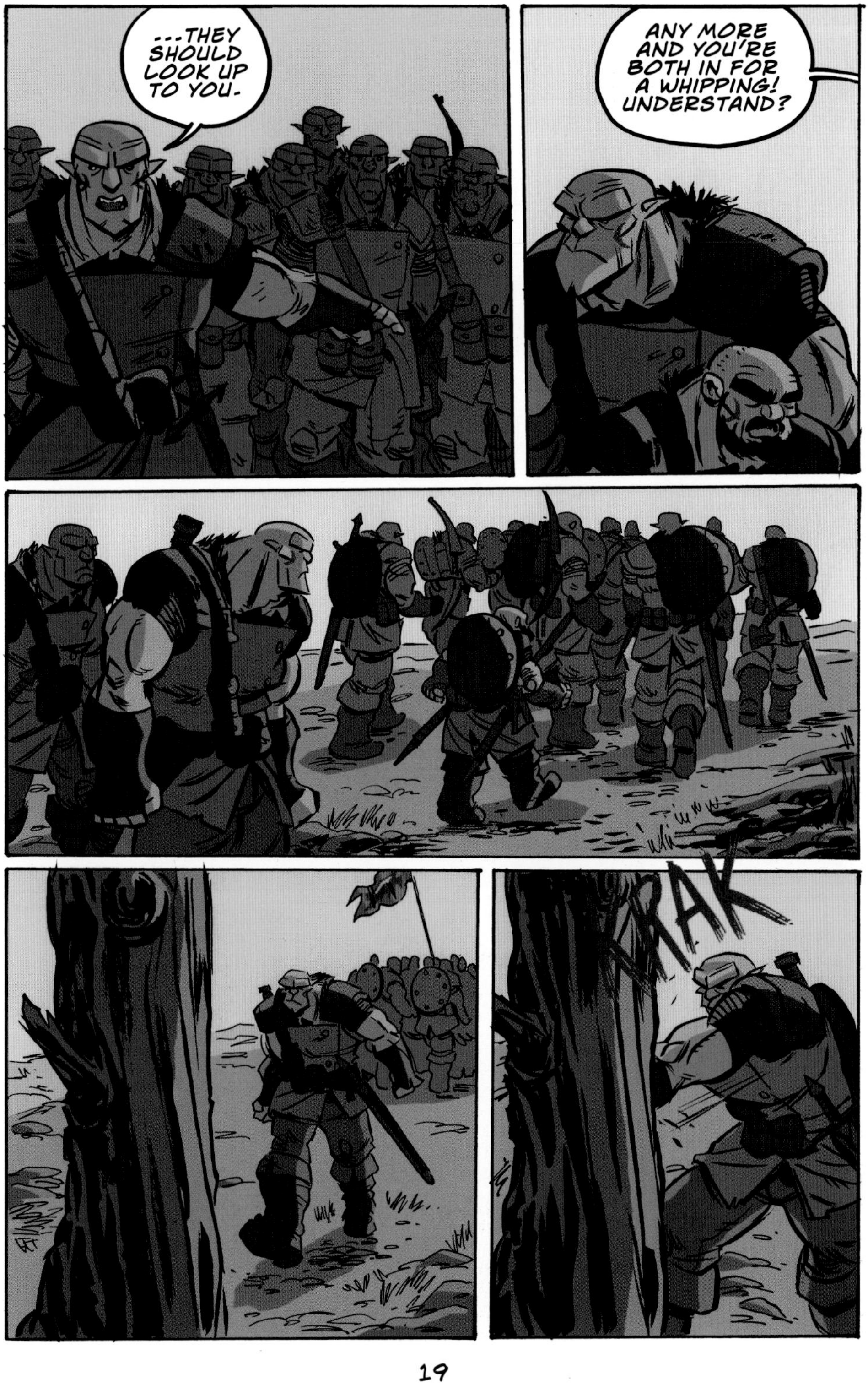
...THEY SHOULD LOOK UP TO YOU.
ANY MORE AND YOU'RE BOTH IN FOR A WHIPPING! UNDERSTAND?
KRAK

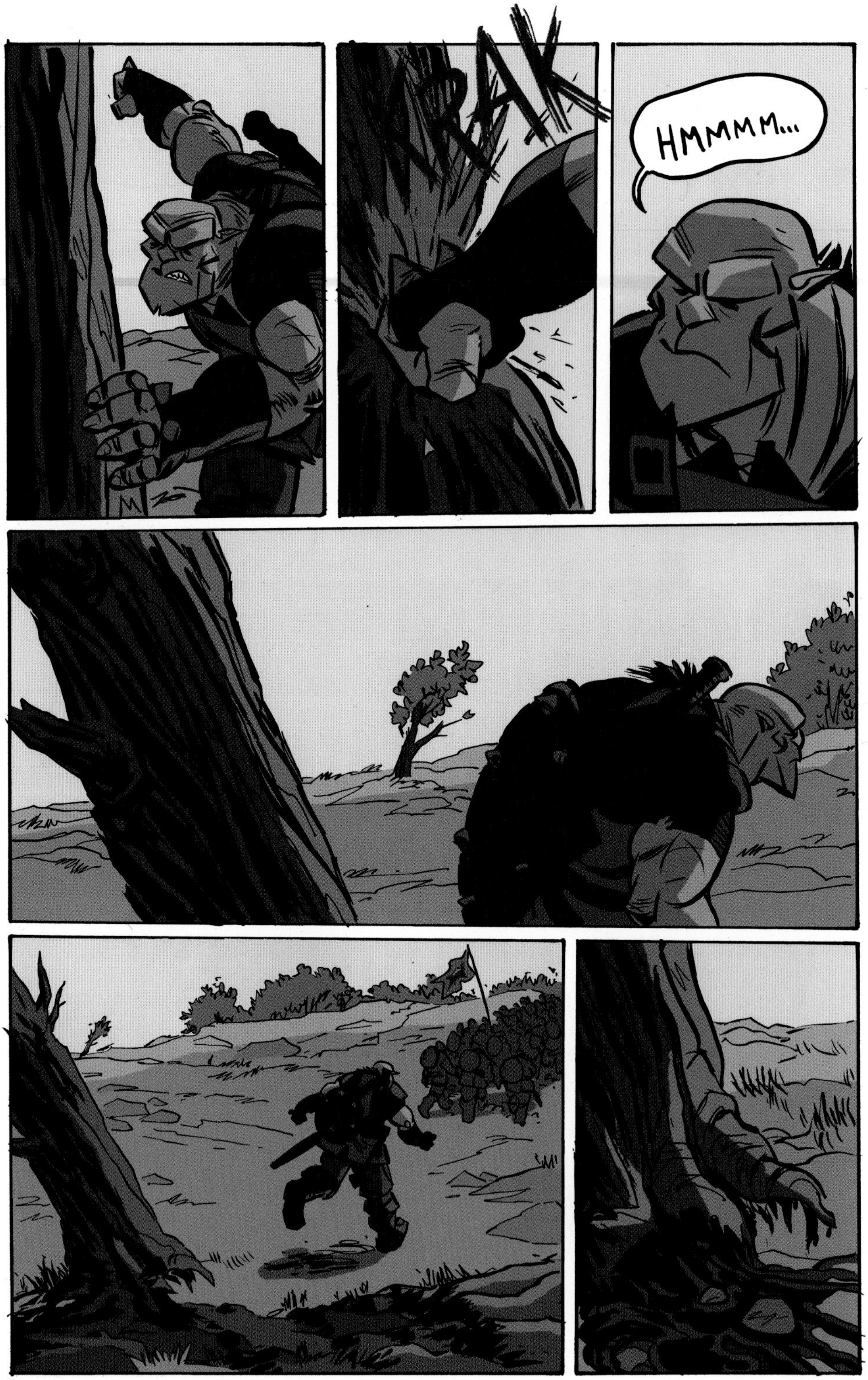
KRAK
HMMMM...

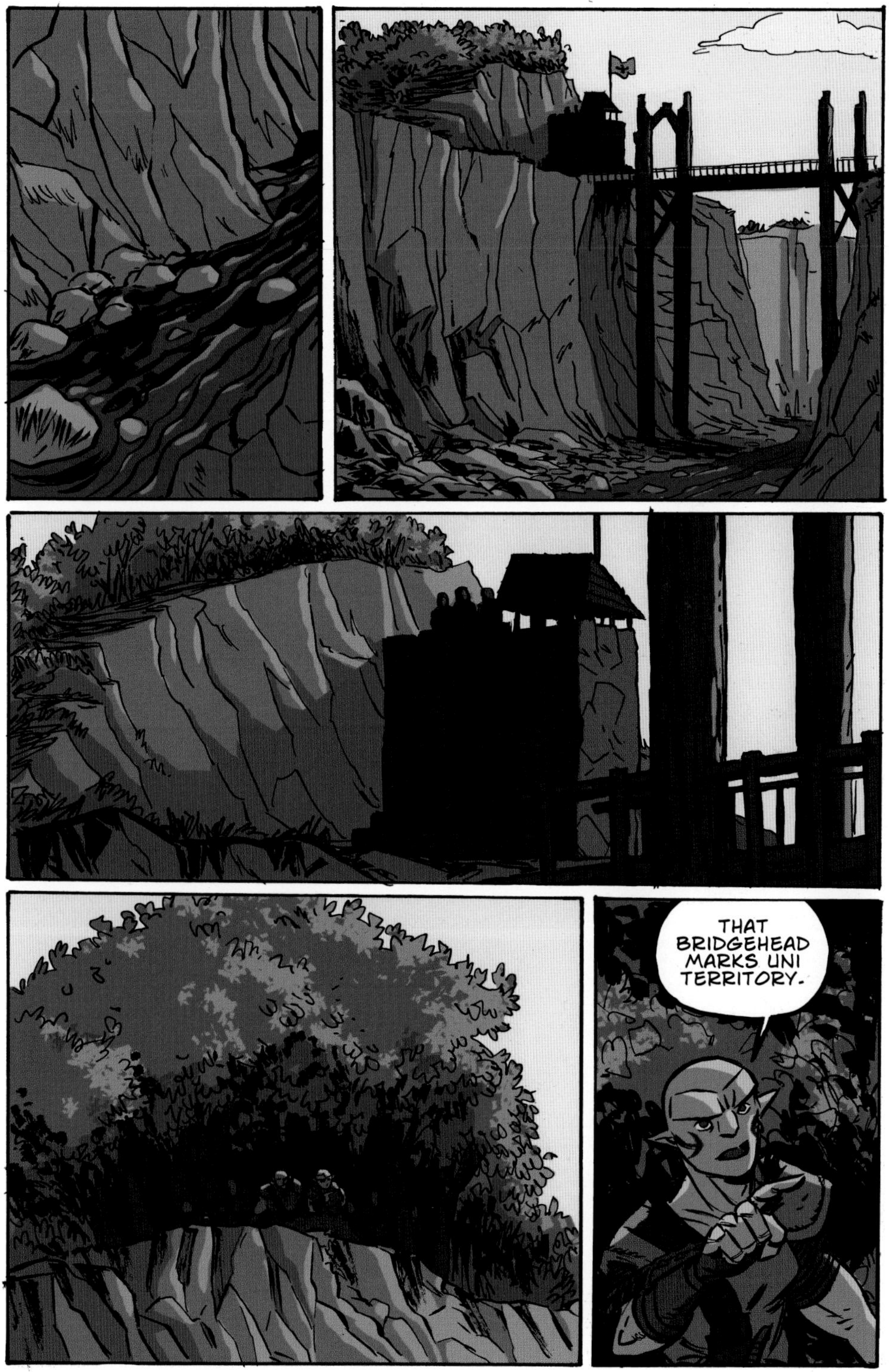
THAT BRIDGEHEAD MARKS UNI TERRITORY.

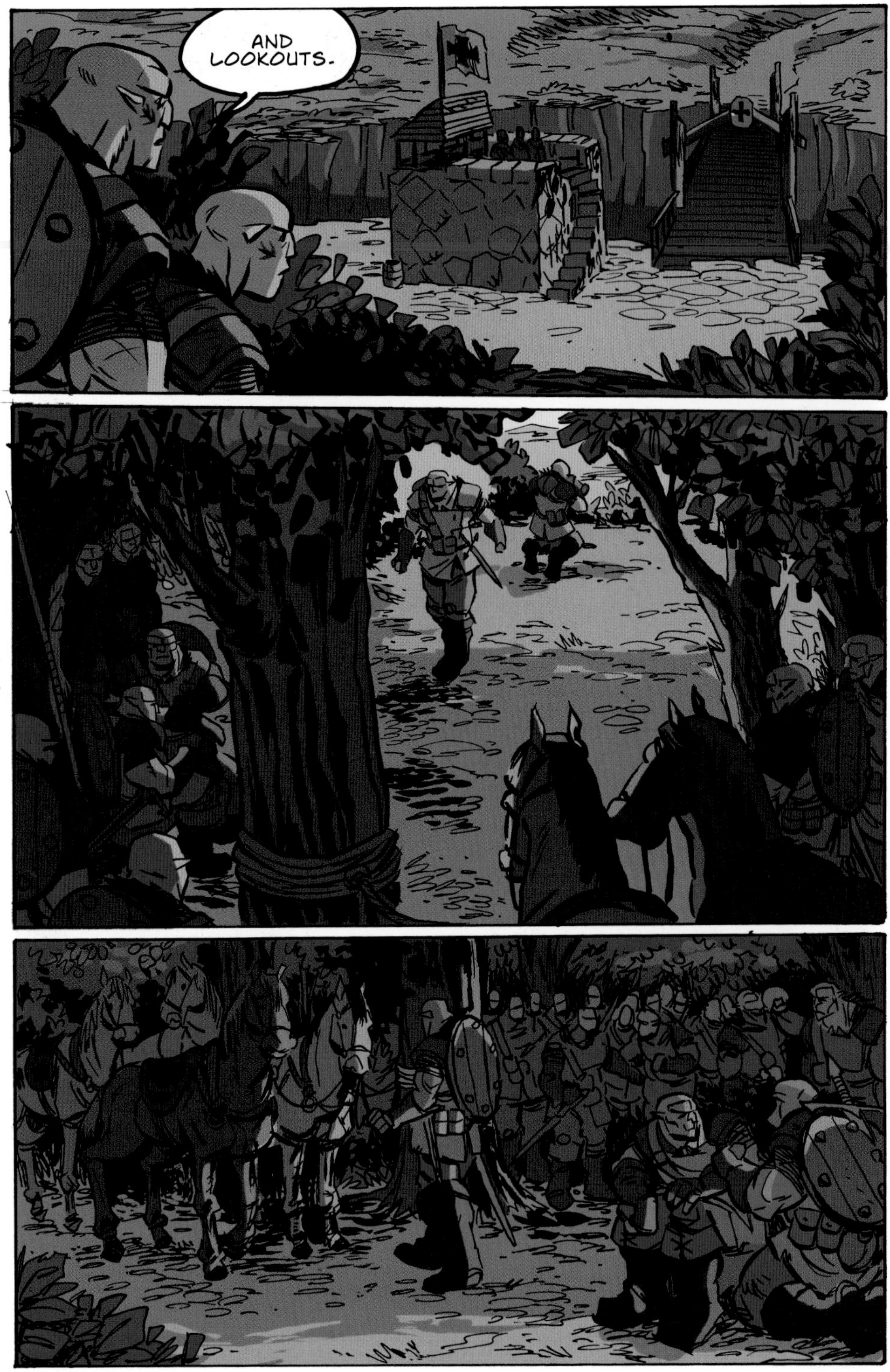
AND LOOKOUTS.

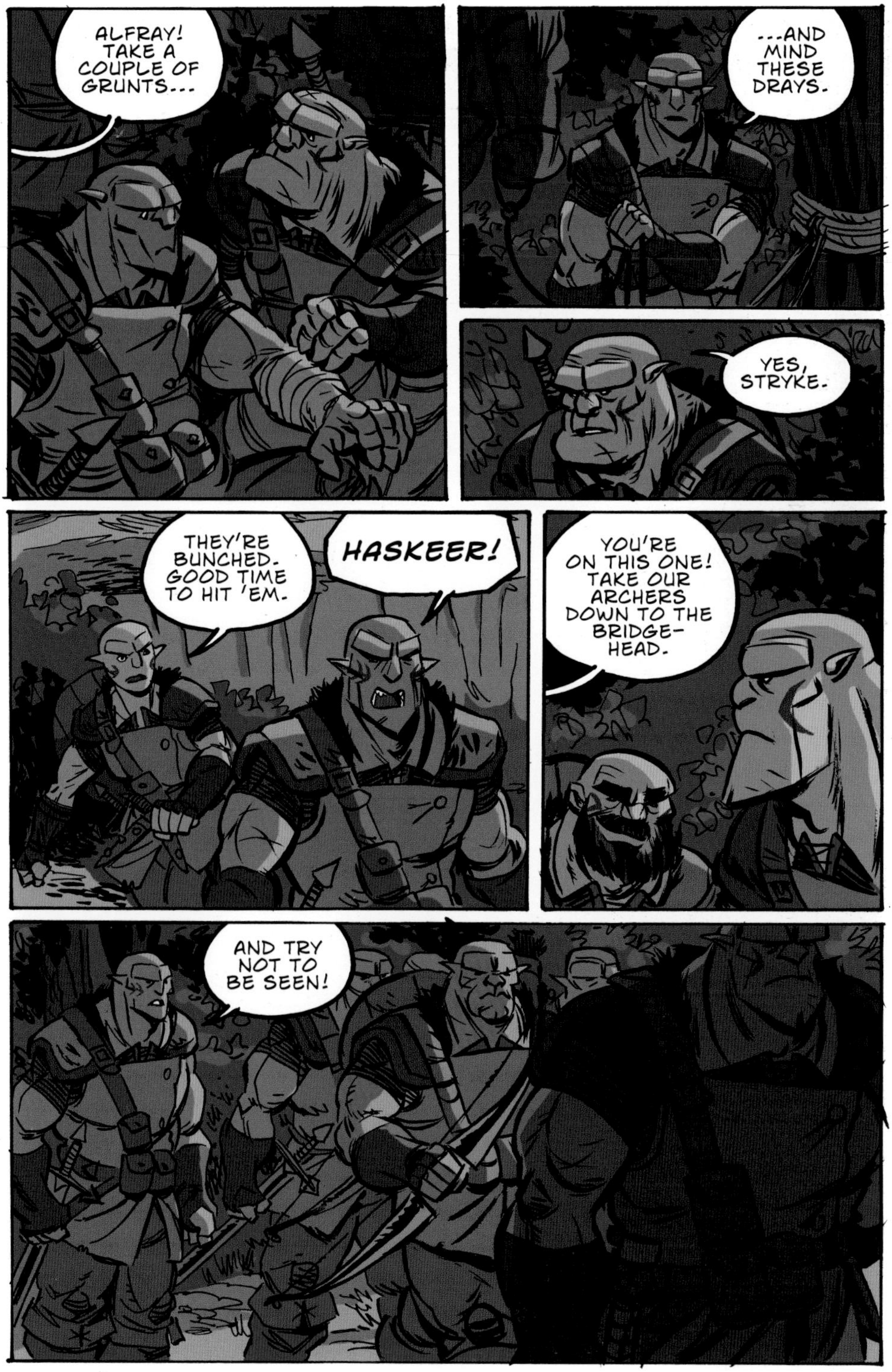
ALFRAY! TAKE A COUPLE OF GRUNTS...
...AND MIND THESE DRAYS.
YES, STRYKE.
THEY'RE BUNCHED. GOOD TIME TO HIT 'EM.
HASKEER!
YOU'RE ON THIS ONE! TAKE OUR ARCHERS DOWN TO THE BRIDGE-HEAD.
AND TRY NOT TO BE SEEN!

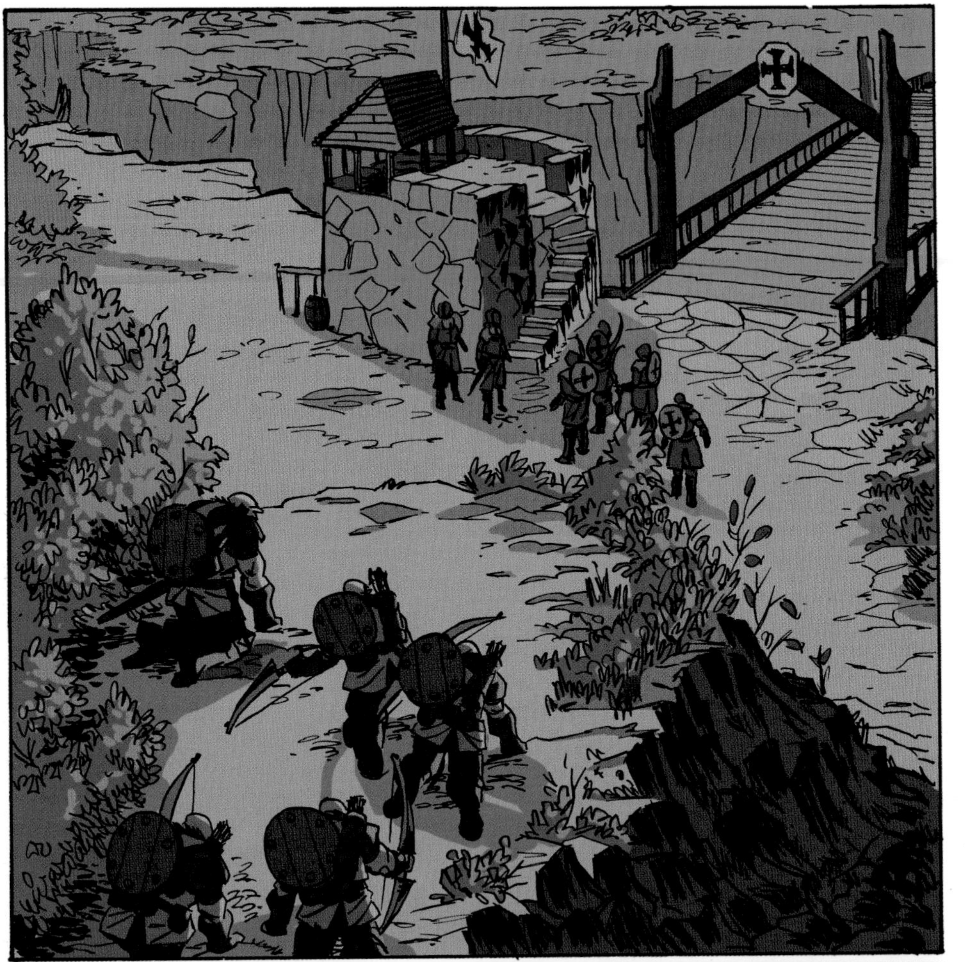
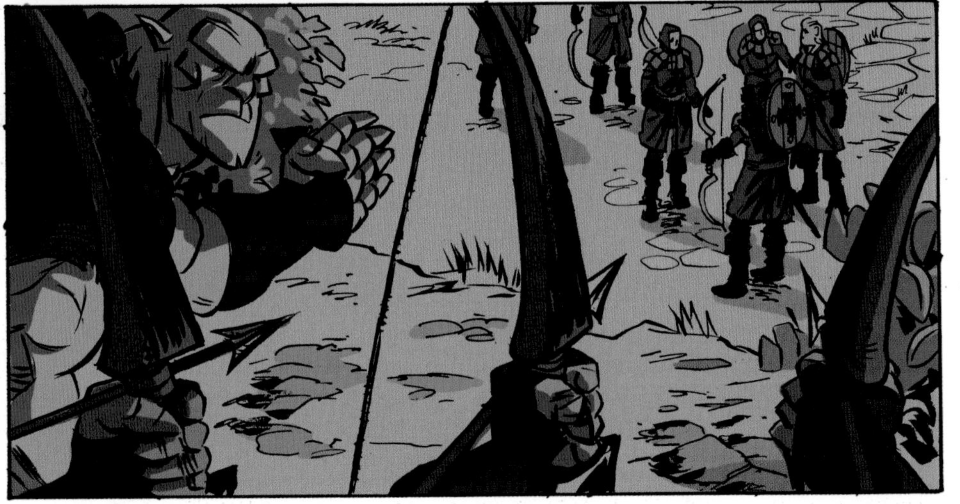

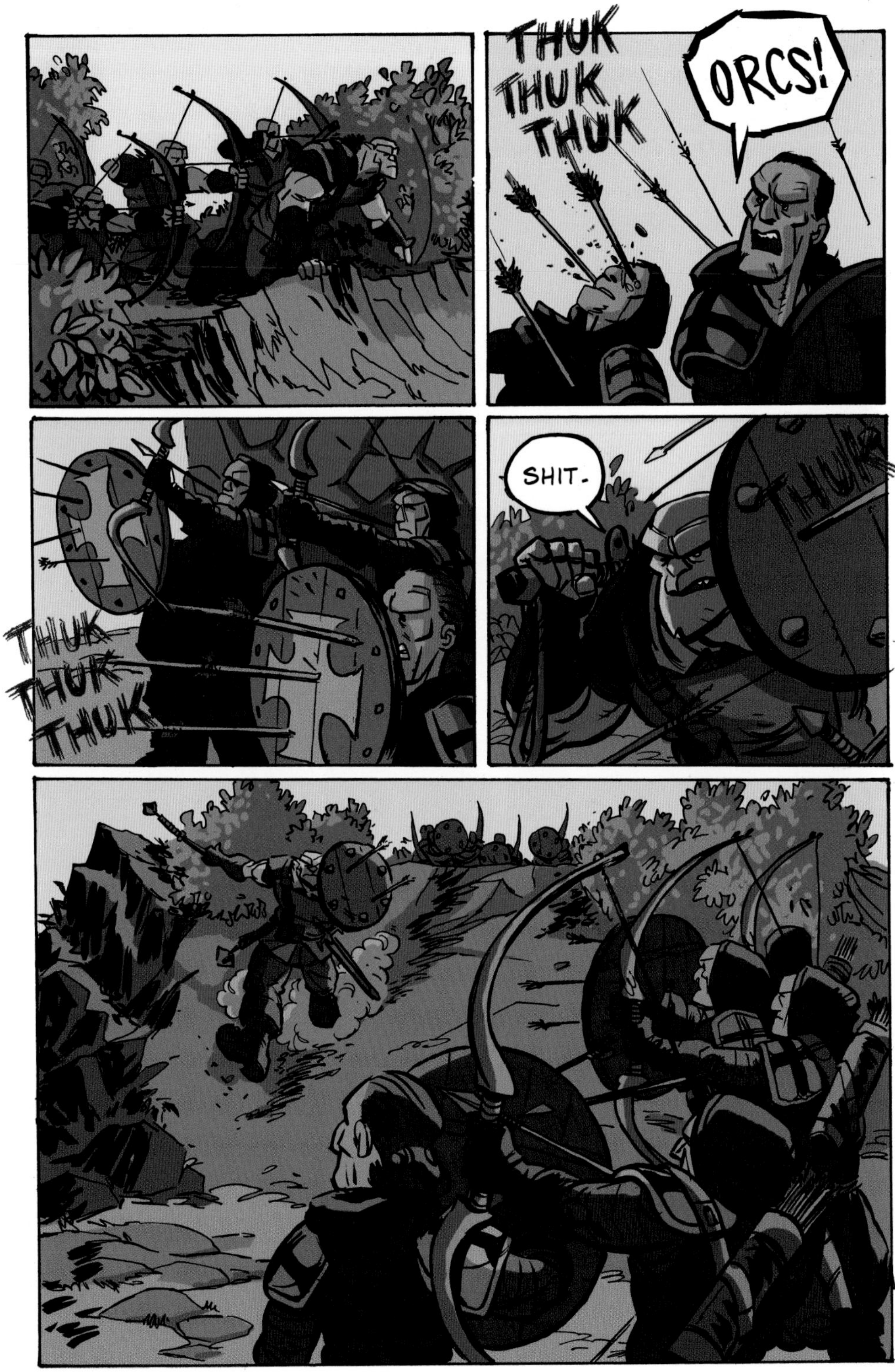
THUK
THUK
THUK
ORCS!
THUK
THUK
THUK
SHIT.
THUK

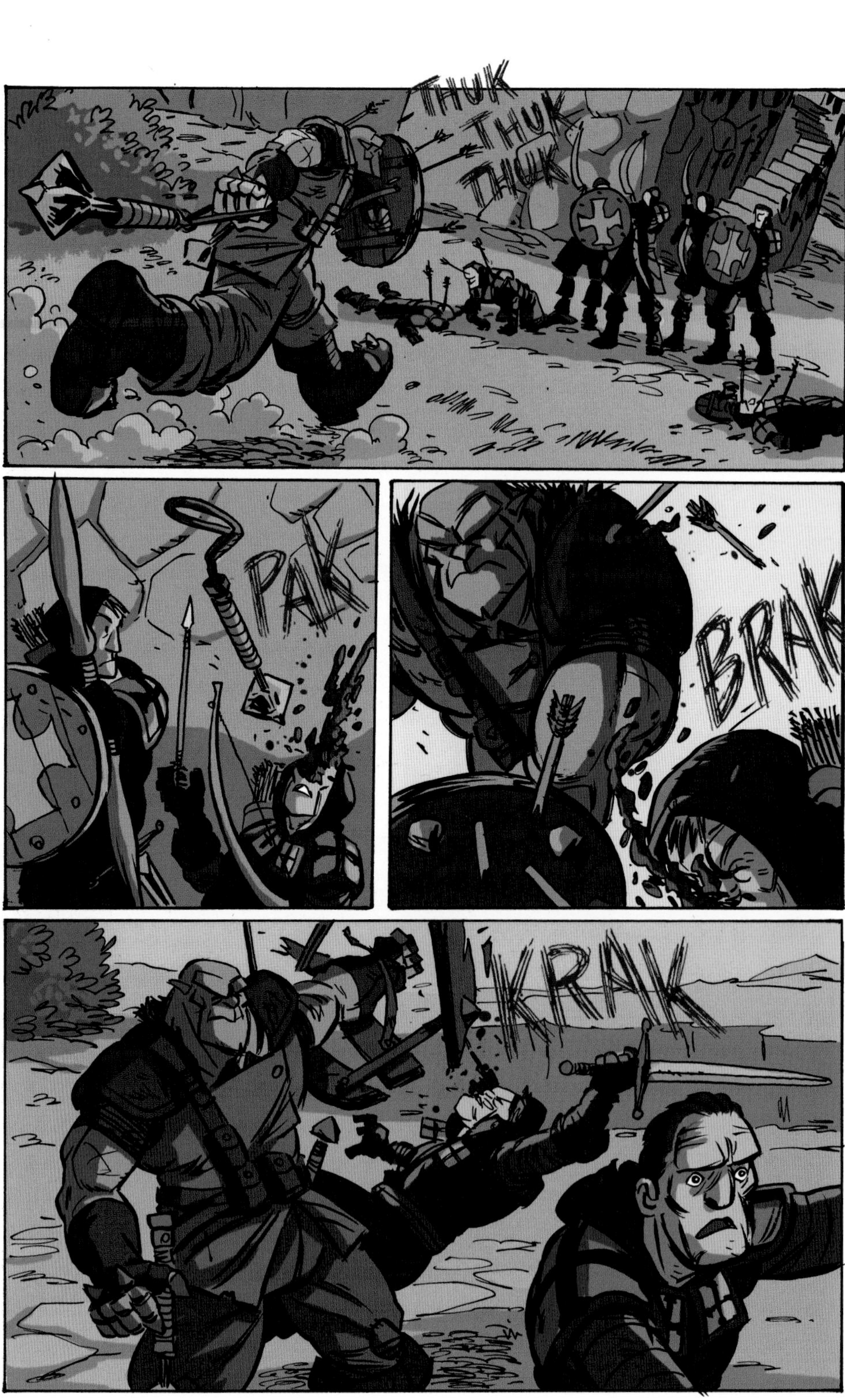
THUK
THUK
THUK
PAK
BRAK
KRAK

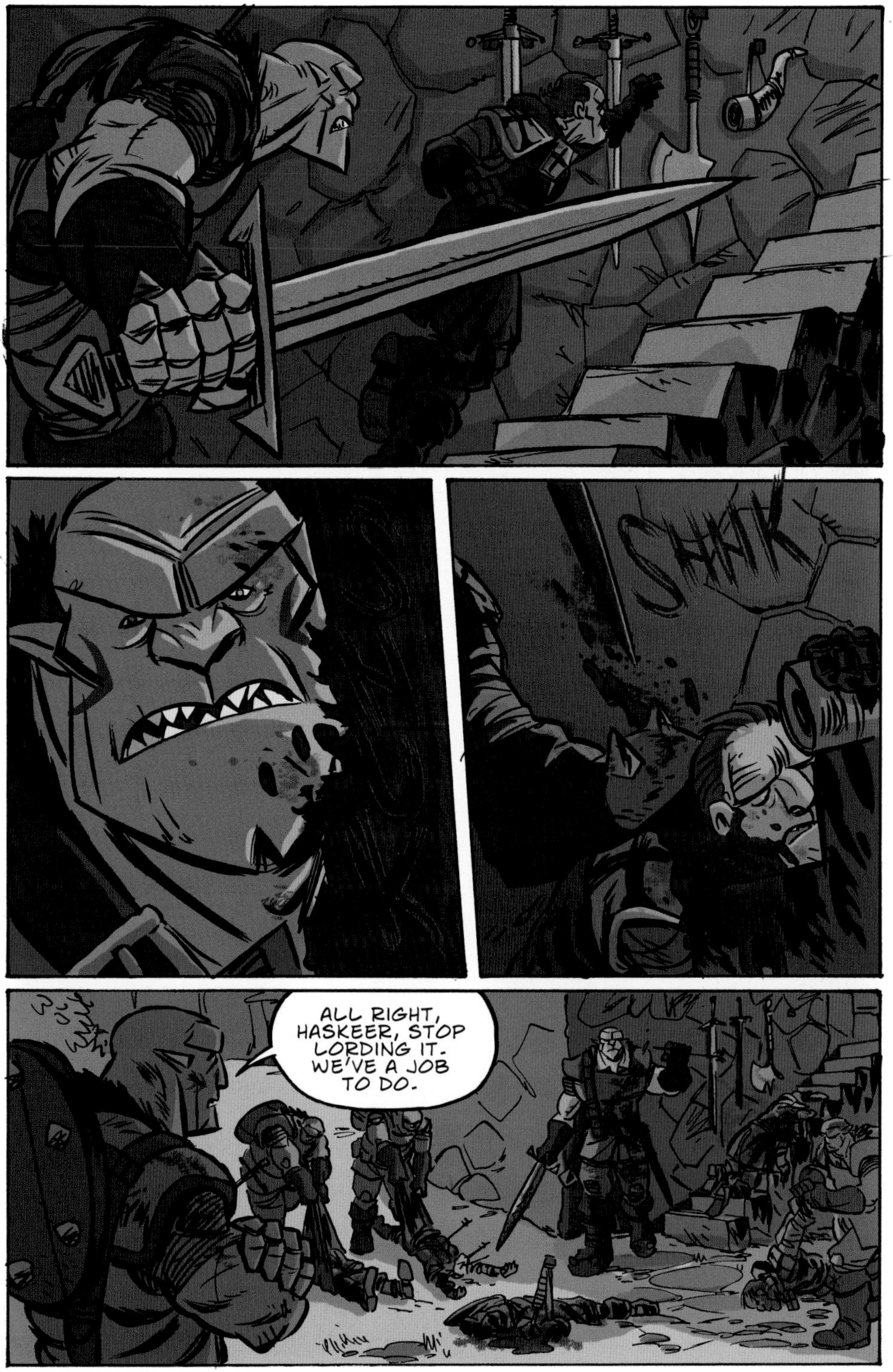
SHNK
ALL RIGHT, HASKEER, STOP LORDING IT. WE'VE A JOB TO DO.

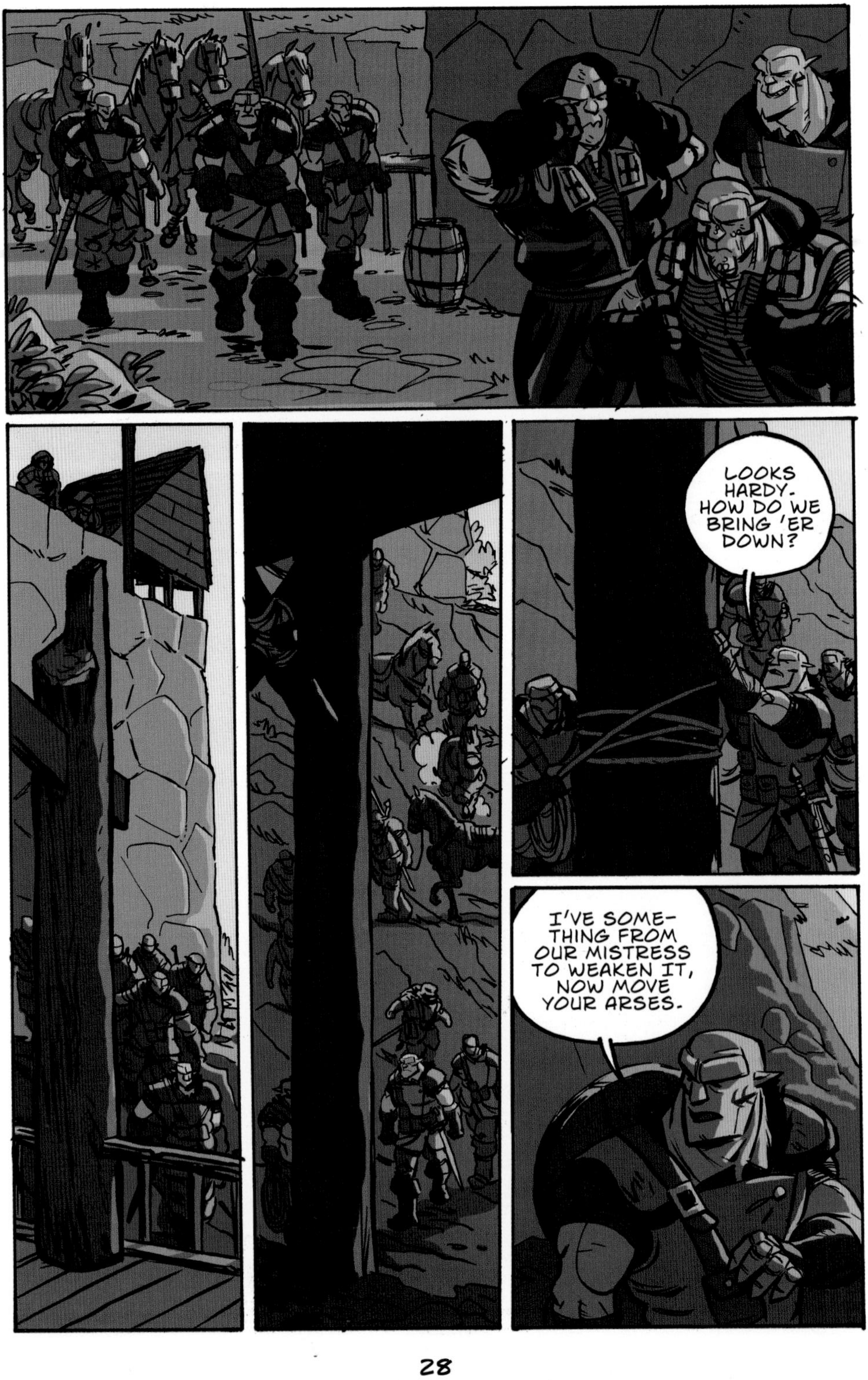
LOOKS HARDY. HOW DO WE BRING 'ER DOWN?
I'VE SOMETHING FROM OUR MISTRESS TO WEAKEN IT, NOW MOVE YOUR ARSES.

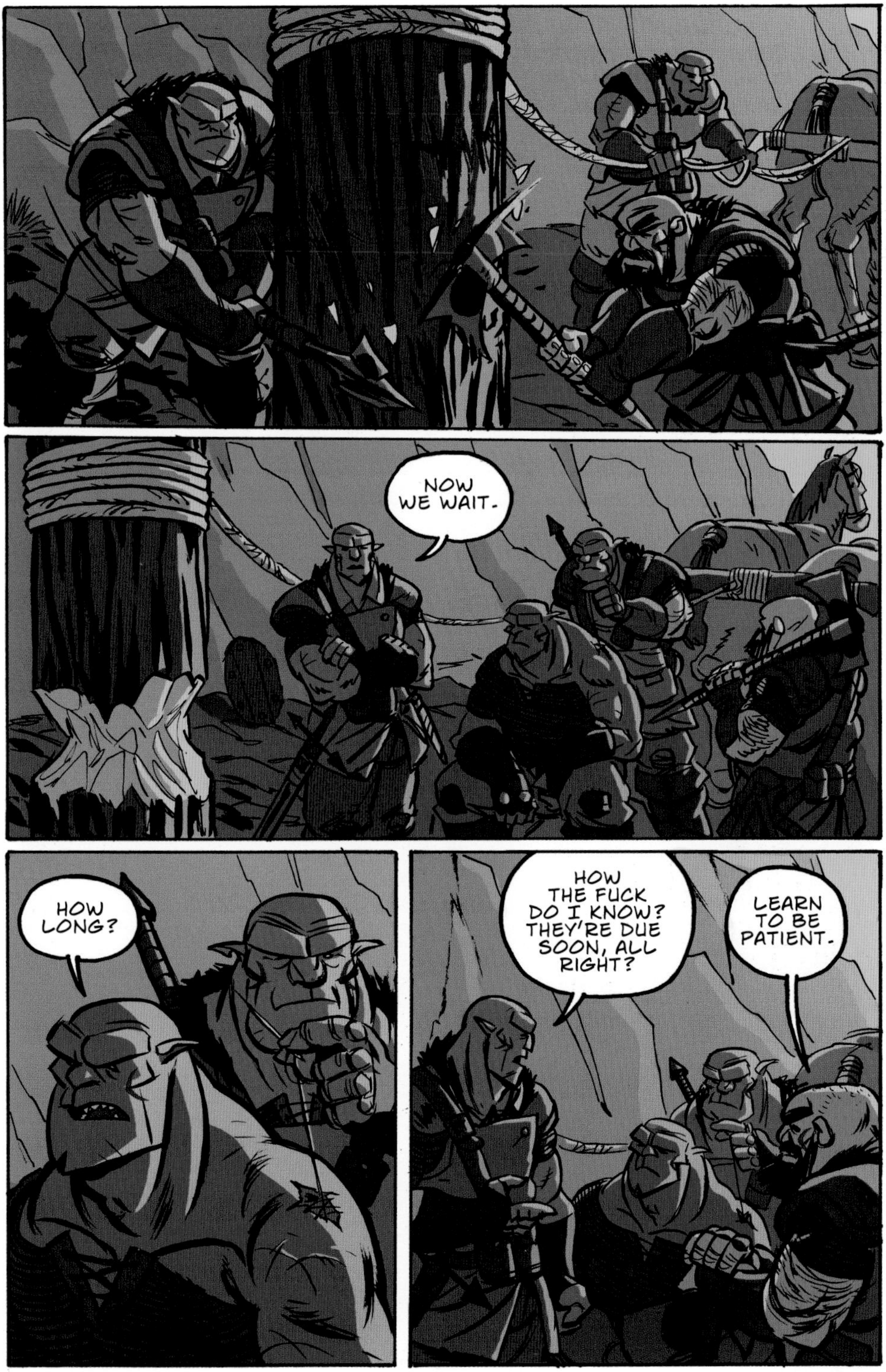
NOW WE WAIT.
HOW LONG?
HOW THE FUCK DO I KNOW? THEY'RE DUE SOON, ALL RIGHT?
LEARN TO BE PATIENT.

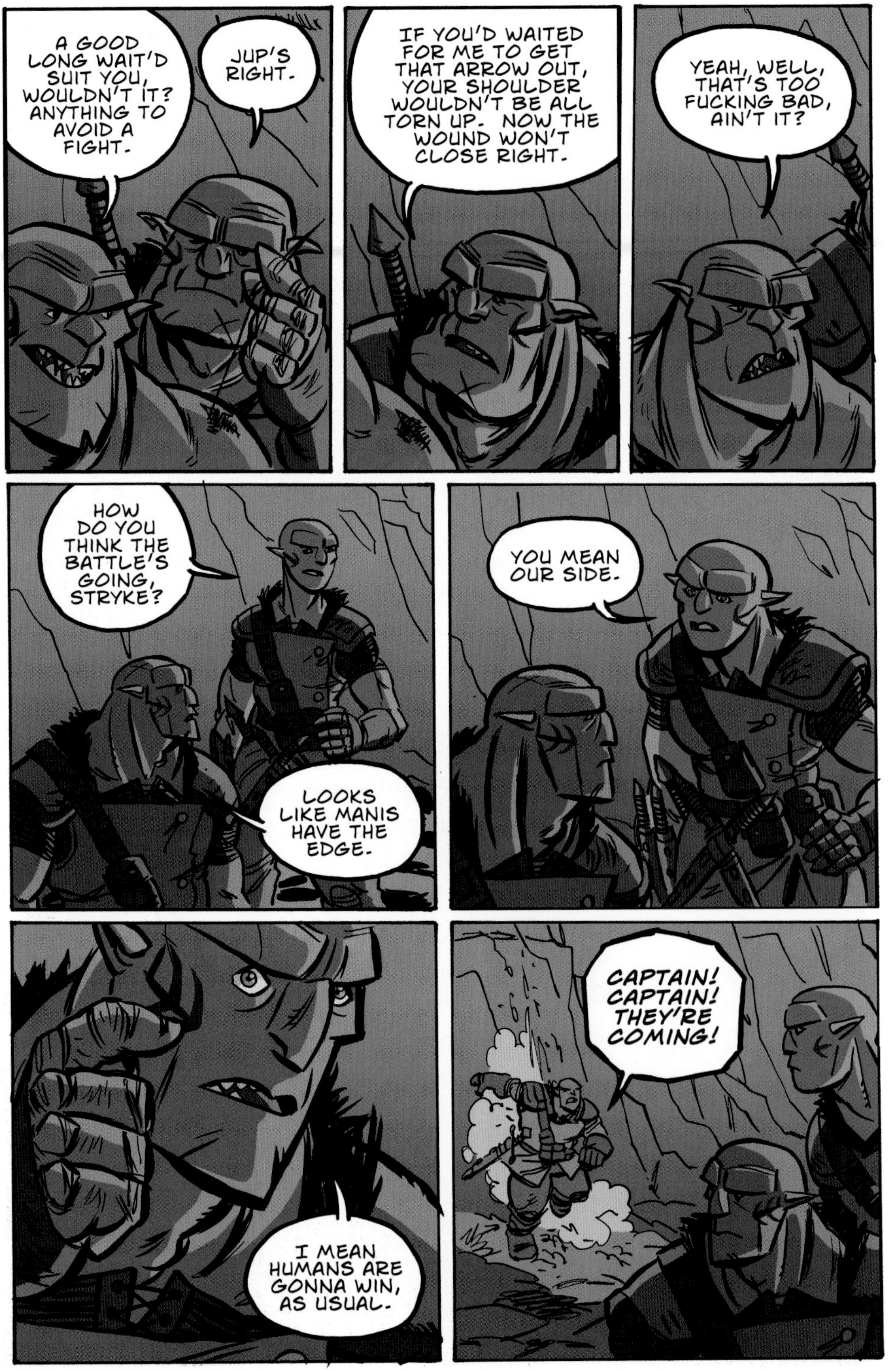
A GOOD LONG WAIT'D SUIT YOU, WOULDN'T IT? ANYTHING TO AVOID A FIGHT.
JUP'S RIGHT.
IF YOU'D WAITED FOR ME TO GET THAT ARROW OUT, YOUR SHOULDER WOULDN'T BE ALL TORN UP. NOW THE WOUND WON'T CLOSE RIGHT.
YEAH, WELL, THAT'S TOO FUCKING BAD, AIN'T IT?
HOW DO YOU THINK THE BATTLE'S GOING, STRYKE?
LOOKS LIKE MANIS HAVE THE EDGE.
YOU MEAN OUR SIDE.
I MEAN HUMANS ARE GONNA WIN, AS USUAL.
CAPTAIN! CAPTAIN! THEY'RE COMING!

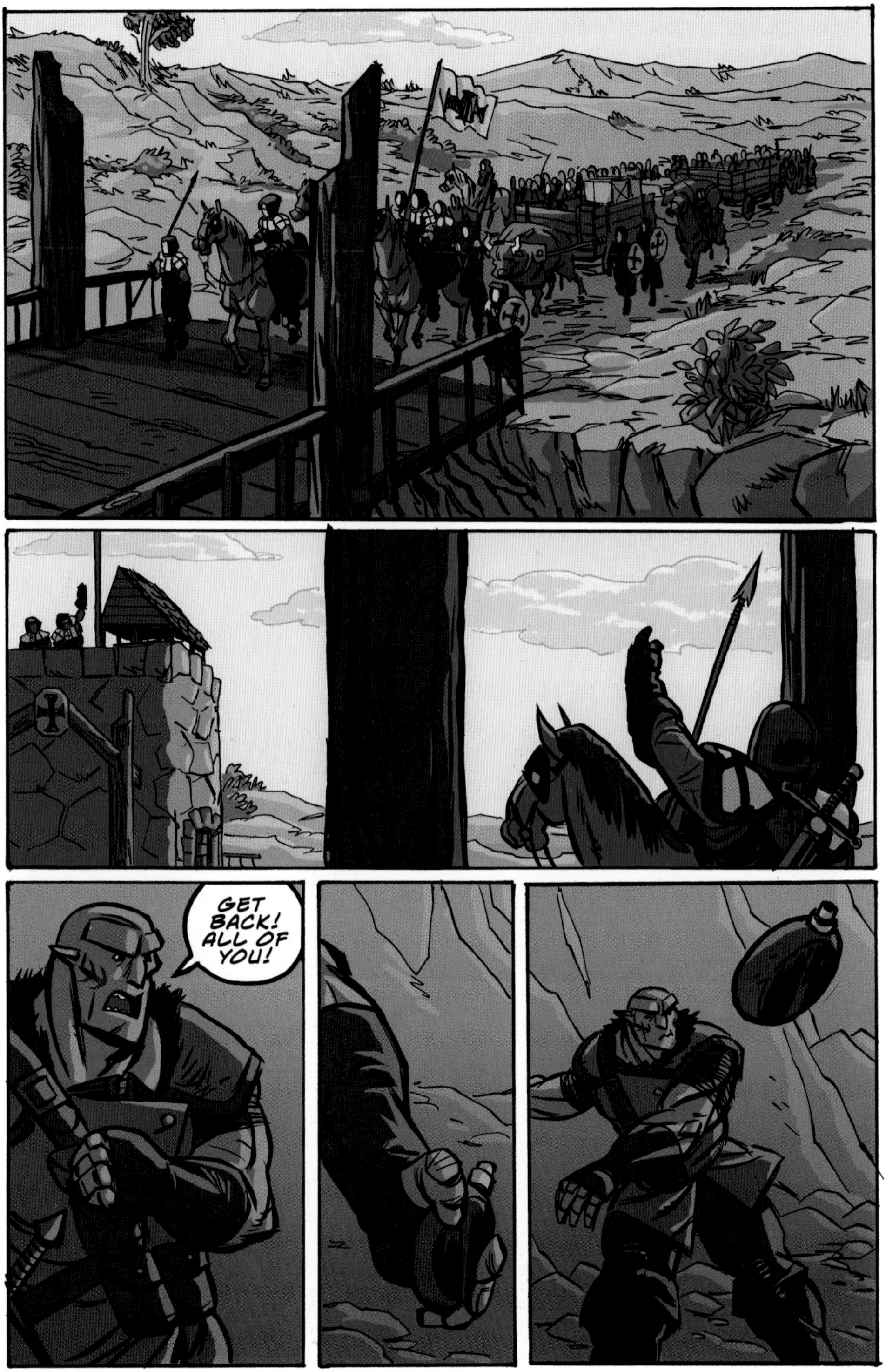
GET BACK! ALL OF YOU!

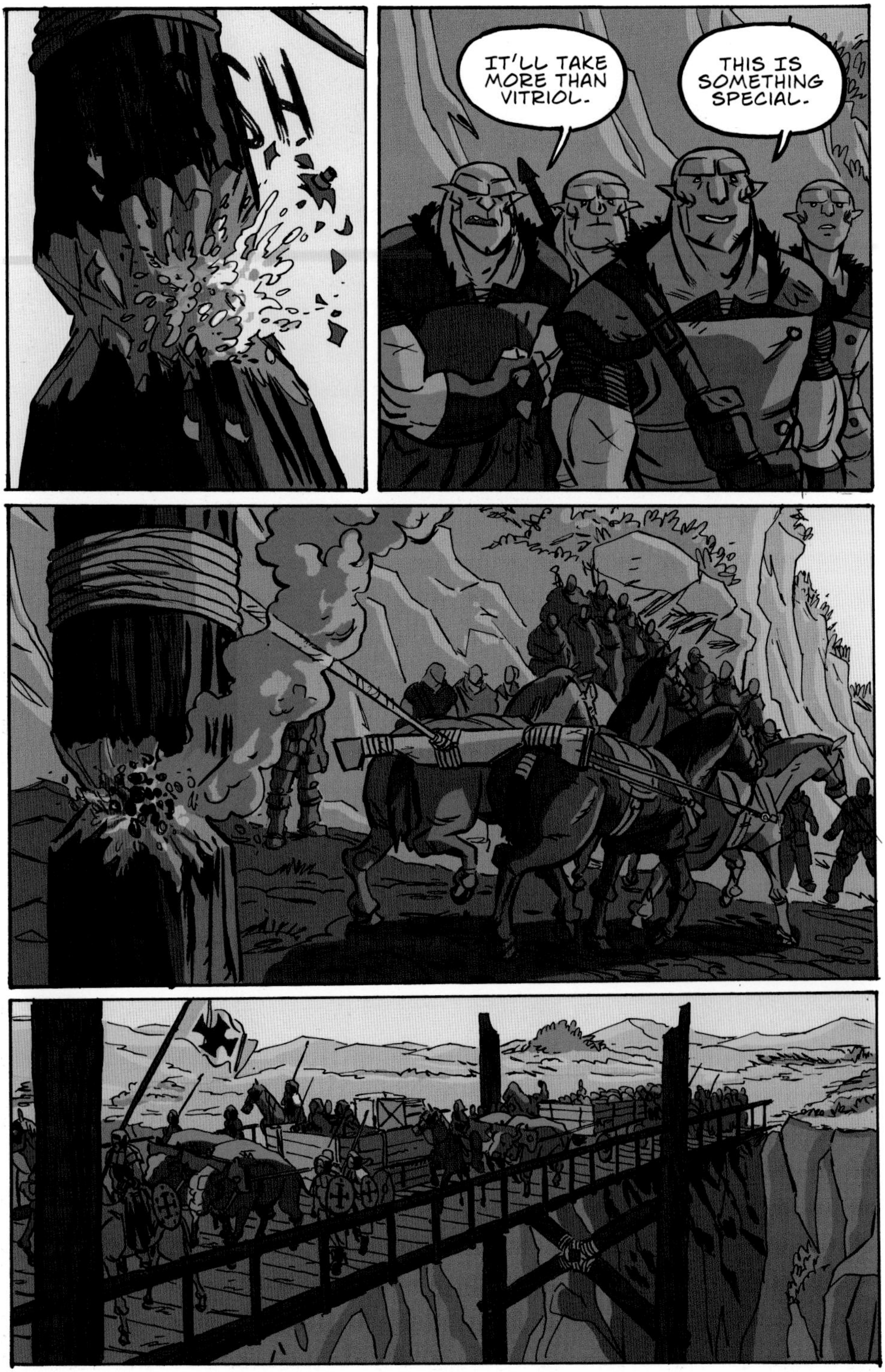
IT'LL TAKE MORE THAN VITRIOL.
THIS IS SOMETHING SPECIAL.

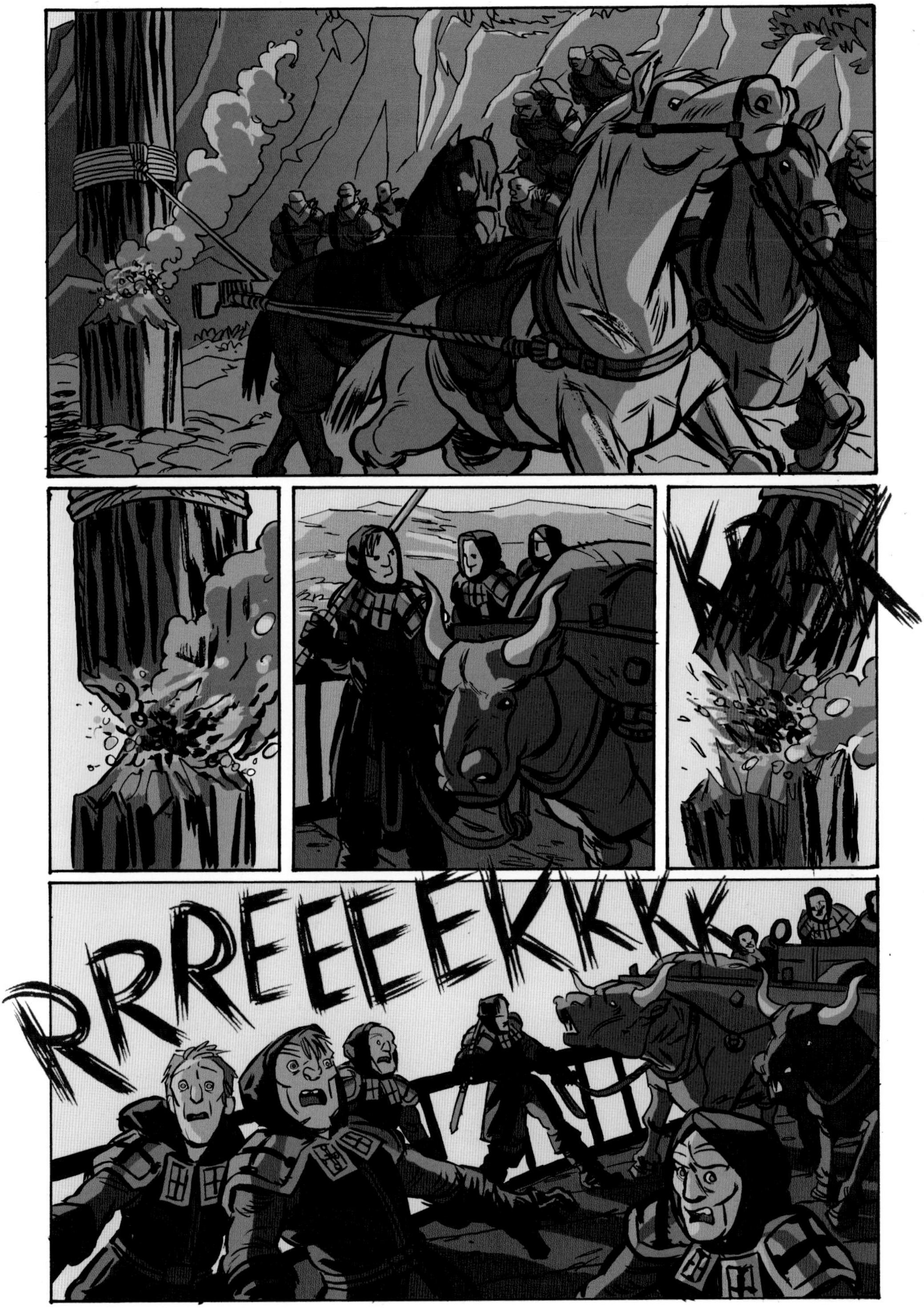
RRREEEEKKKK

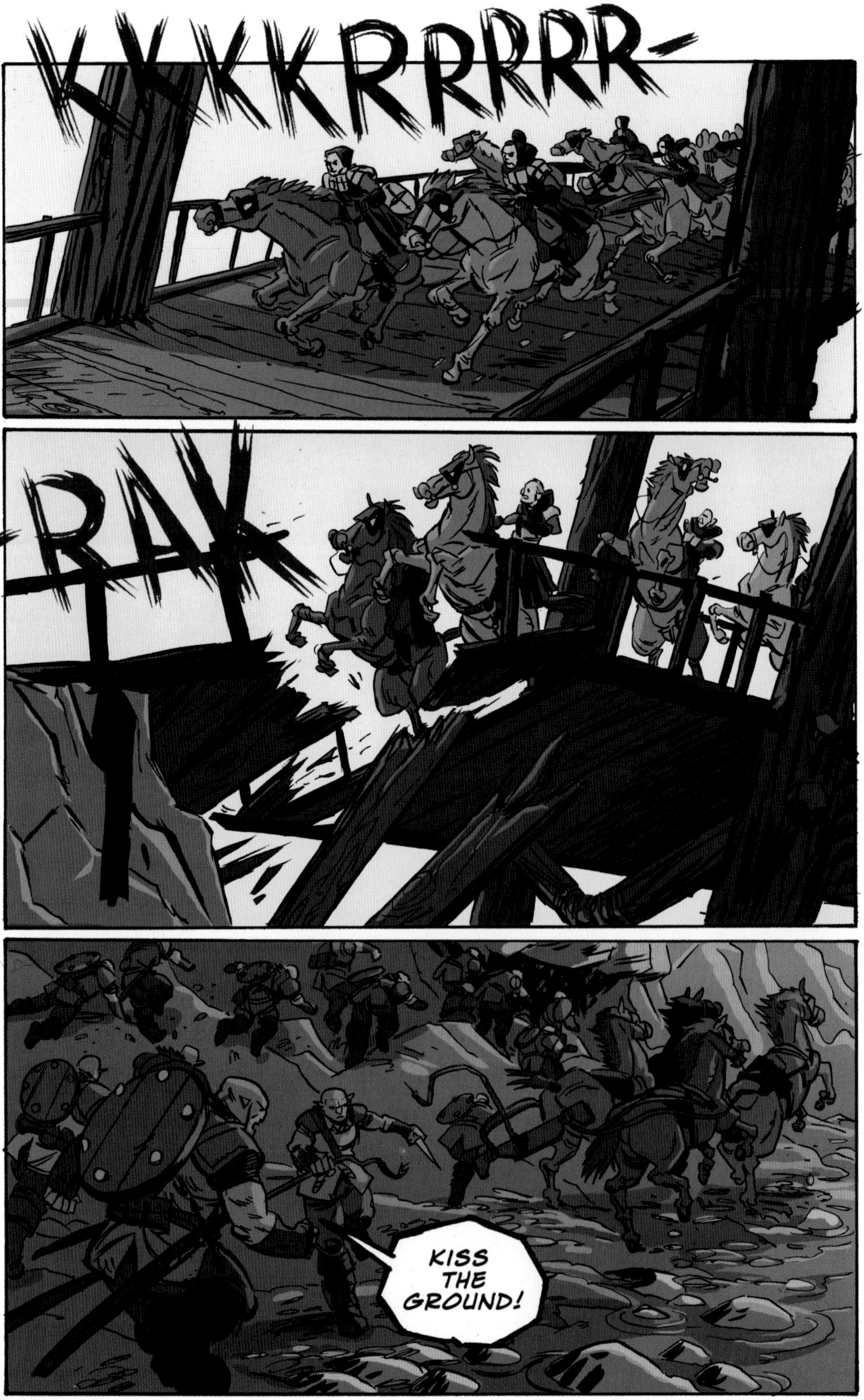
KKKKRRRRR-
-RAK
KISS THE GROUND!

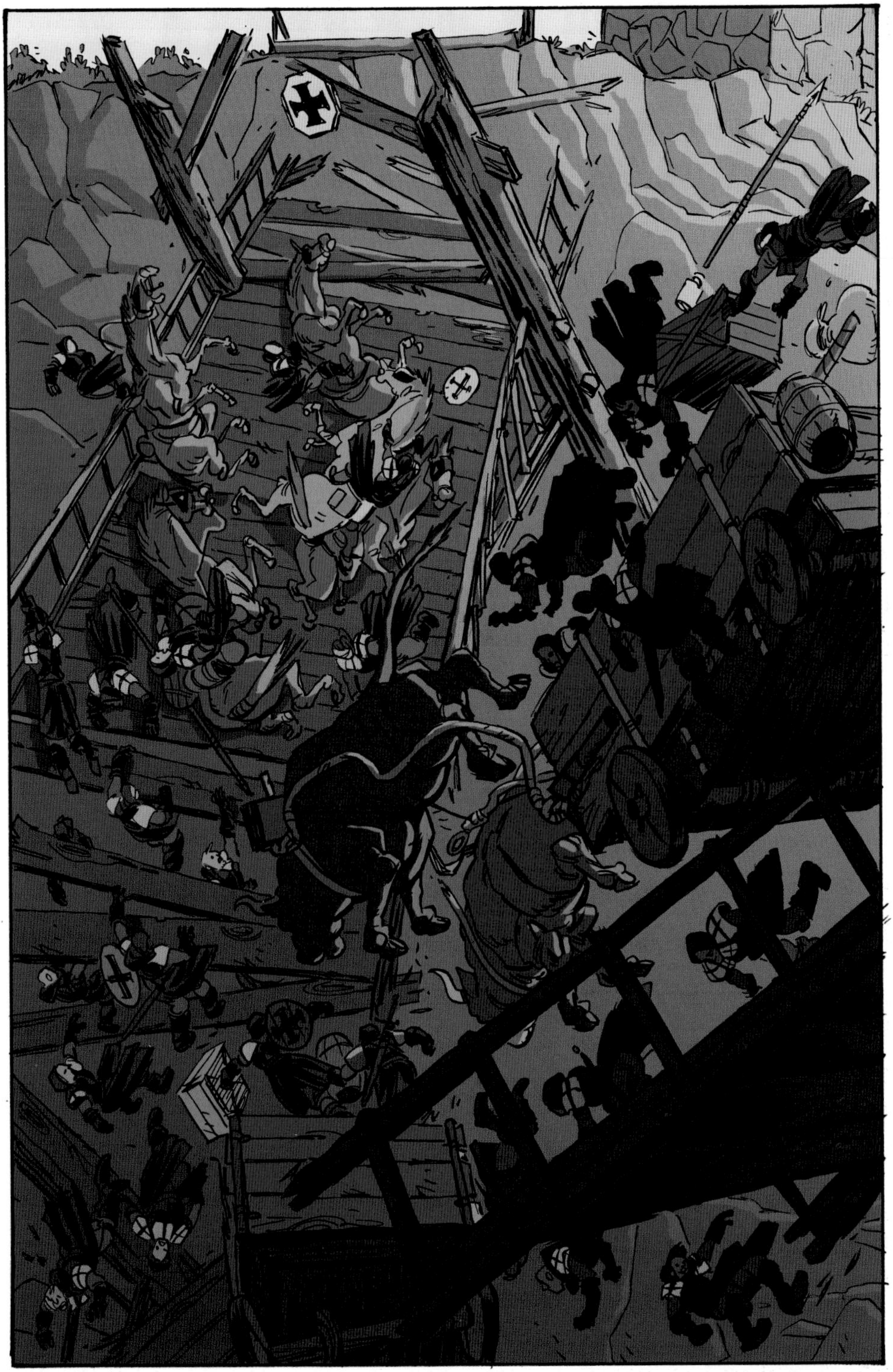

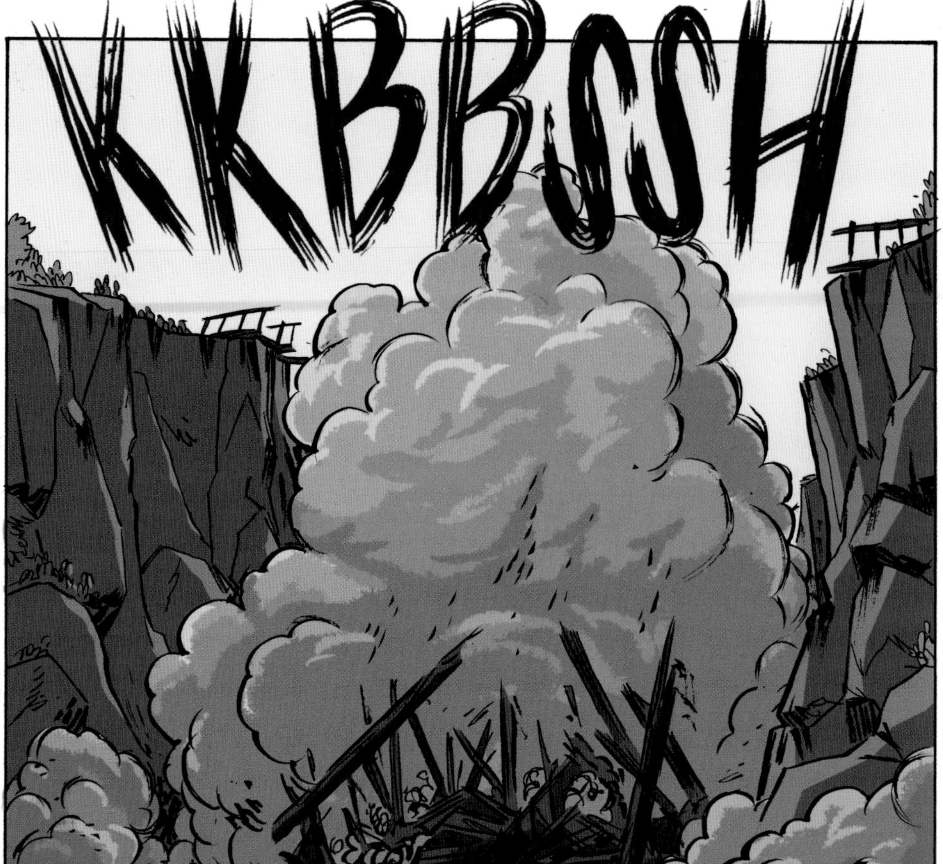
KKBBSSH

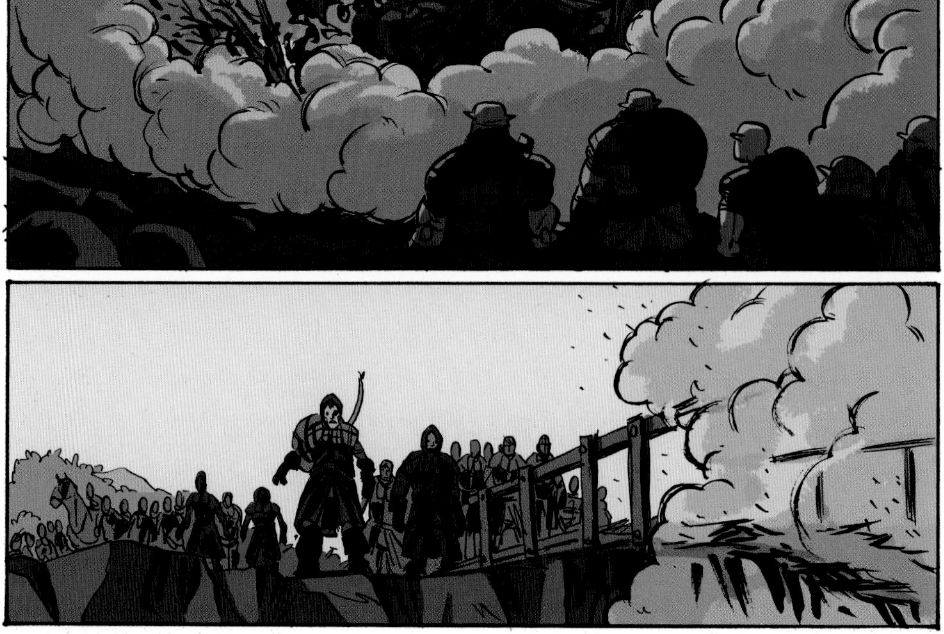

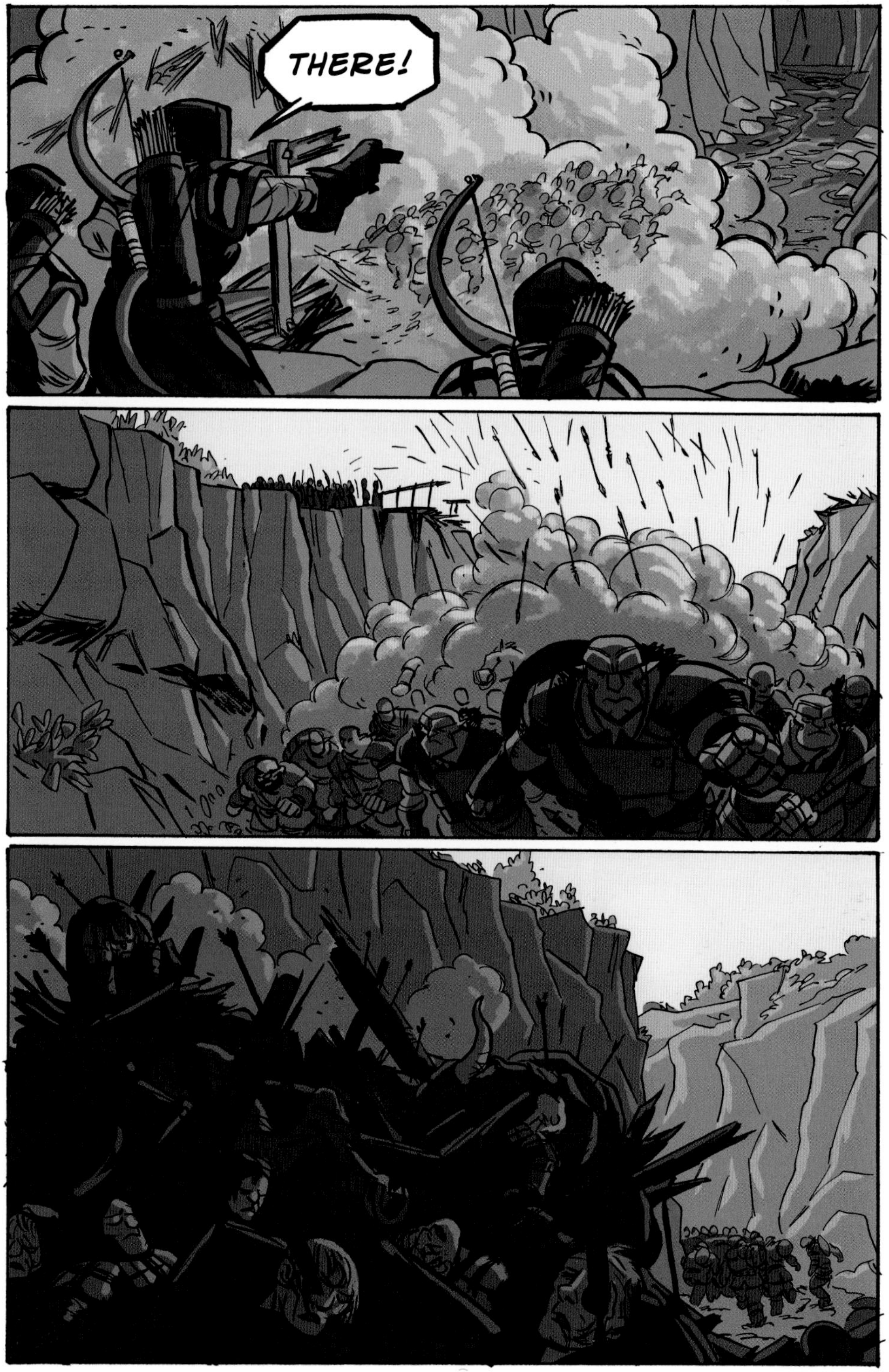
THERE!

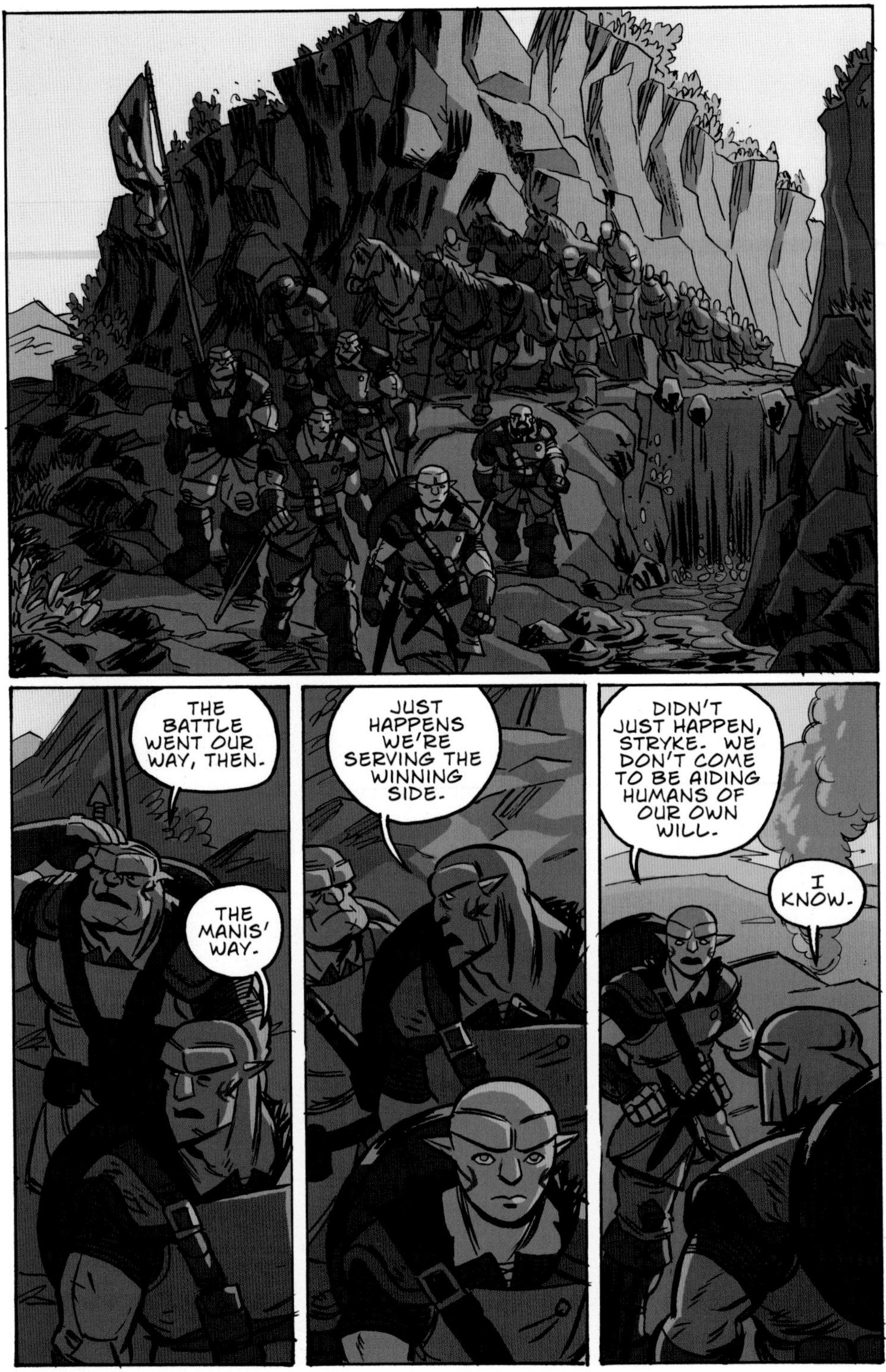
THE BATTLE WENT OUR WAY, THEN.
THE MANIS' WAY.
JUST HAPPENS WE'RE SERVING THE WINNING SIDE.
DIDN'T JUST HAPPEN, STRYKE. WE DON'T COME TO BE AIDING HUMANS OF OUR OWN WILL.
I KNOW.

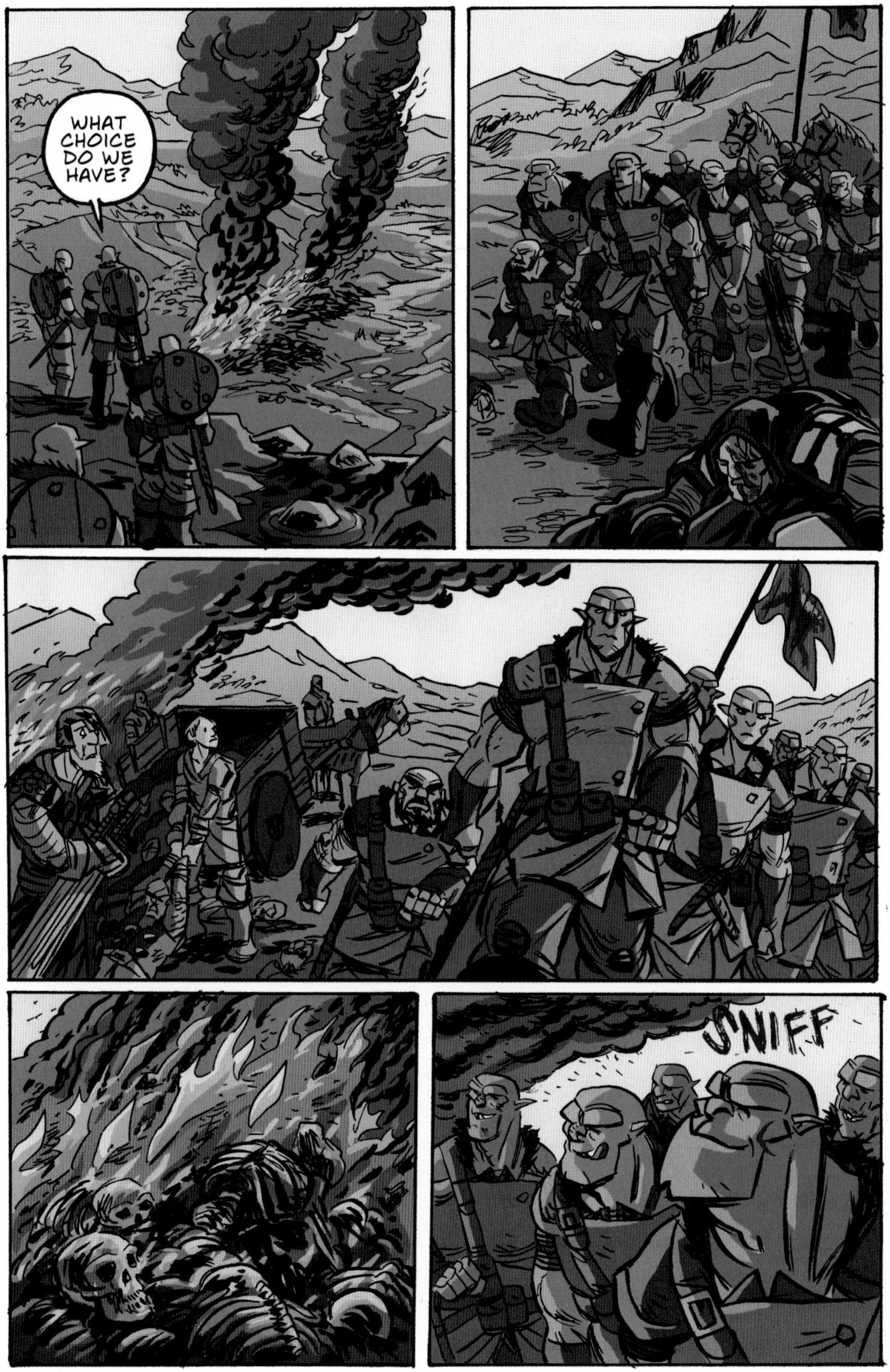
WHAT CHOICE DO WE HAVE?
SNIFF

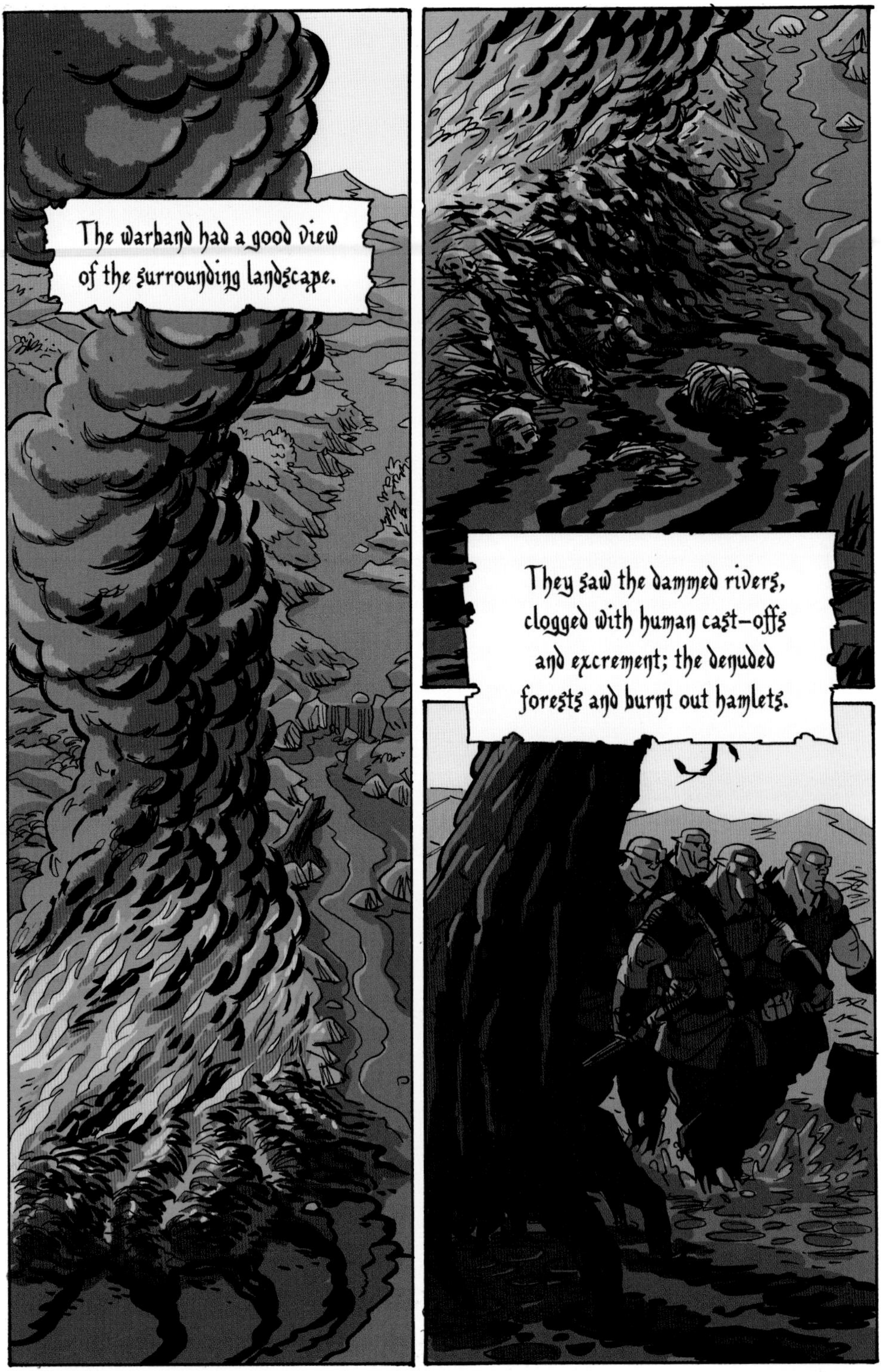
The warband had a good view of the surrounding landscape.
They saw the dammed rivers, clogged with human cast-offs and excrement; the denuded forests and burnt out hamlets.

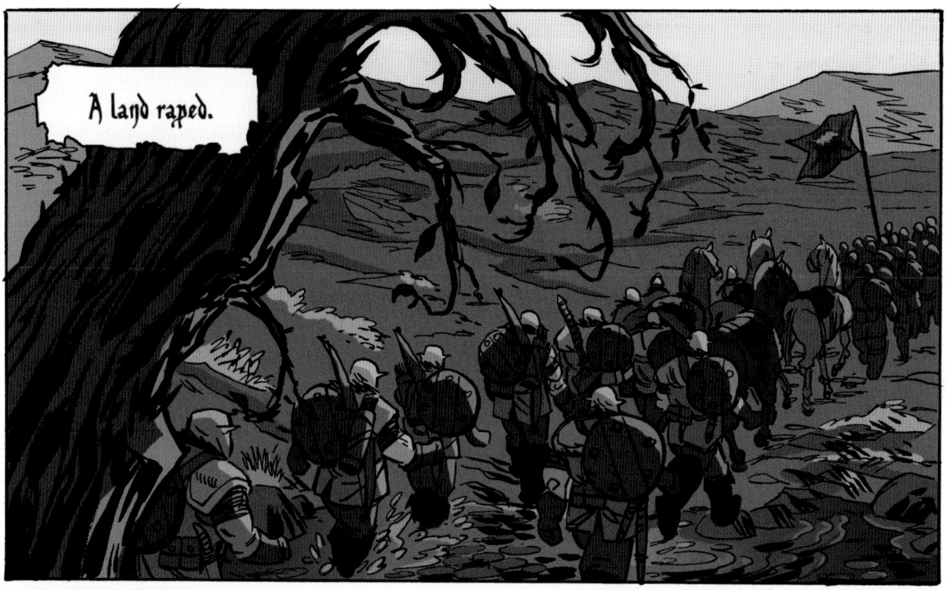
A land raped.

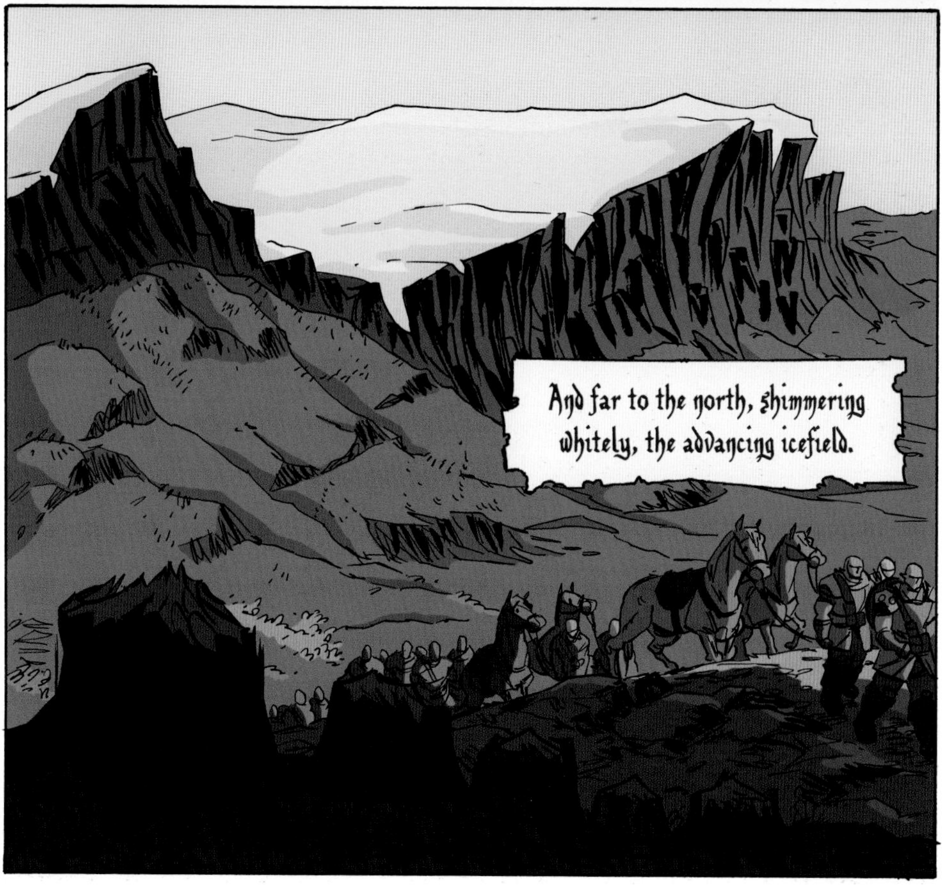
And far to the north, shimmering whitely, the advancing icefield.

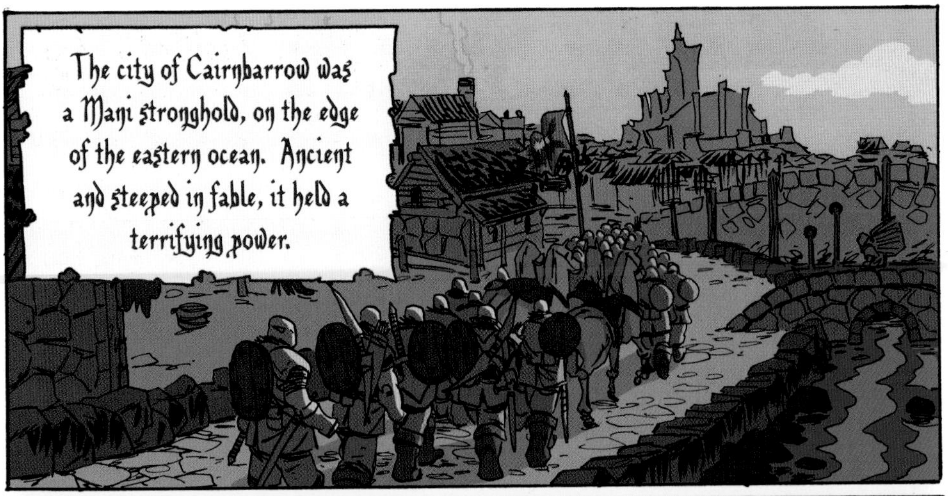
The city of Cairnbarrow was a Mani stronghold, on the edge of the eastern ocean. Ancient and steeped in fable, it held a terrifying power.

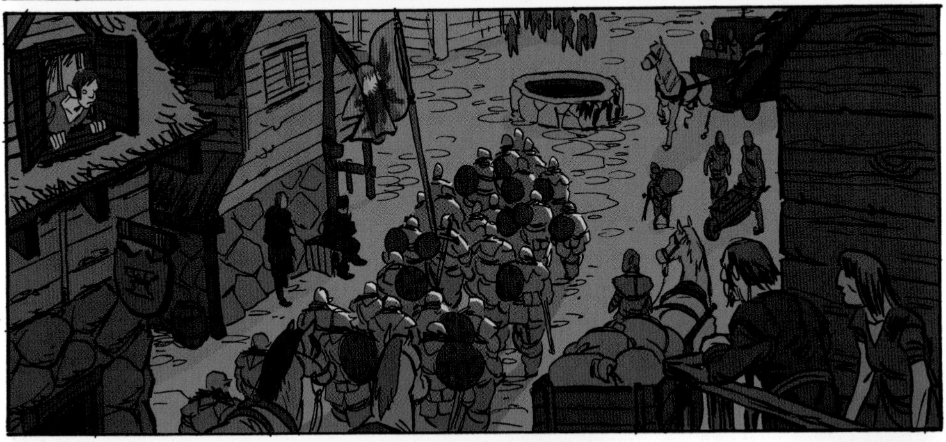

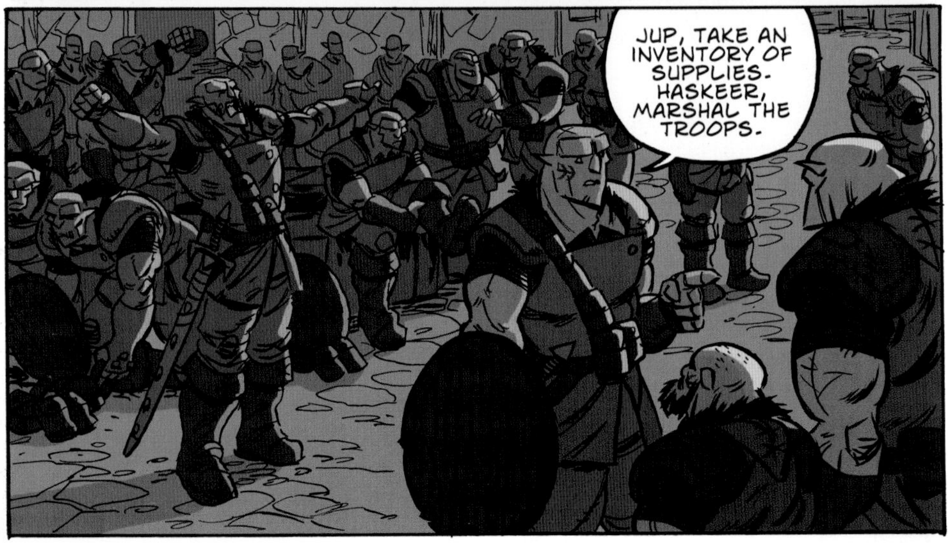
JUP, TAKE AN INVENTORY OF SUPPLIES. HASKEER, MARSHAL THE TROOPS.

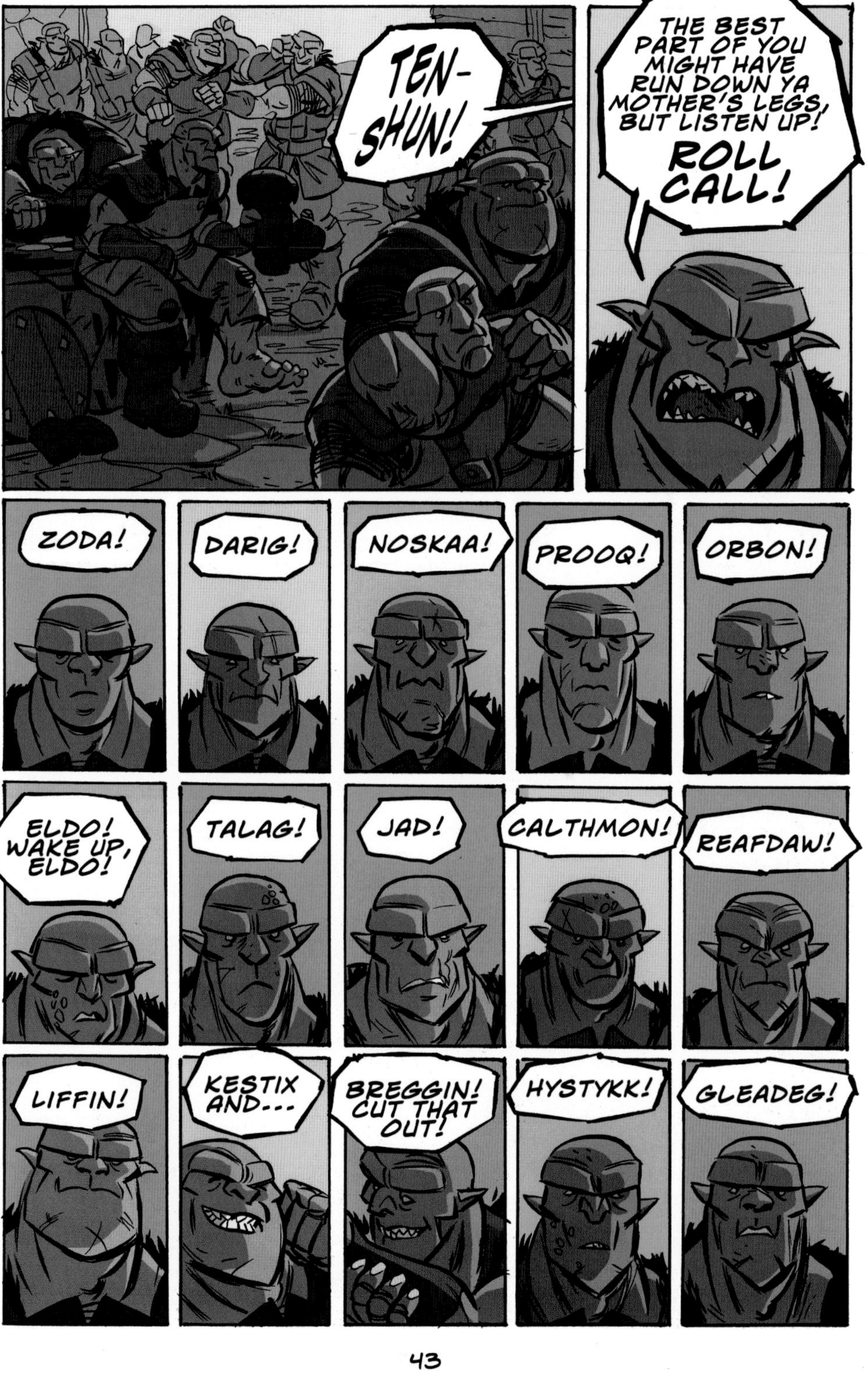
TEN-SHUN!
THE BEST PART OF YOU MIGHT HAVE RUN DOWN YA MOTHER'S LEGS, BUT LISTEN UP! ROLL CALL!
ZODA!
DARIG!
NOSKAA!
PROOQ!
ORBON!
ELDO! WAKE UP, ELDO!
TALAG!
JAD!
CALTHMON!
REAFDAW!
LIFFIN!
KESTIX AND...
BREGGIN! CUT THAT OUT!
HYSTYKK!
GLEADEG!

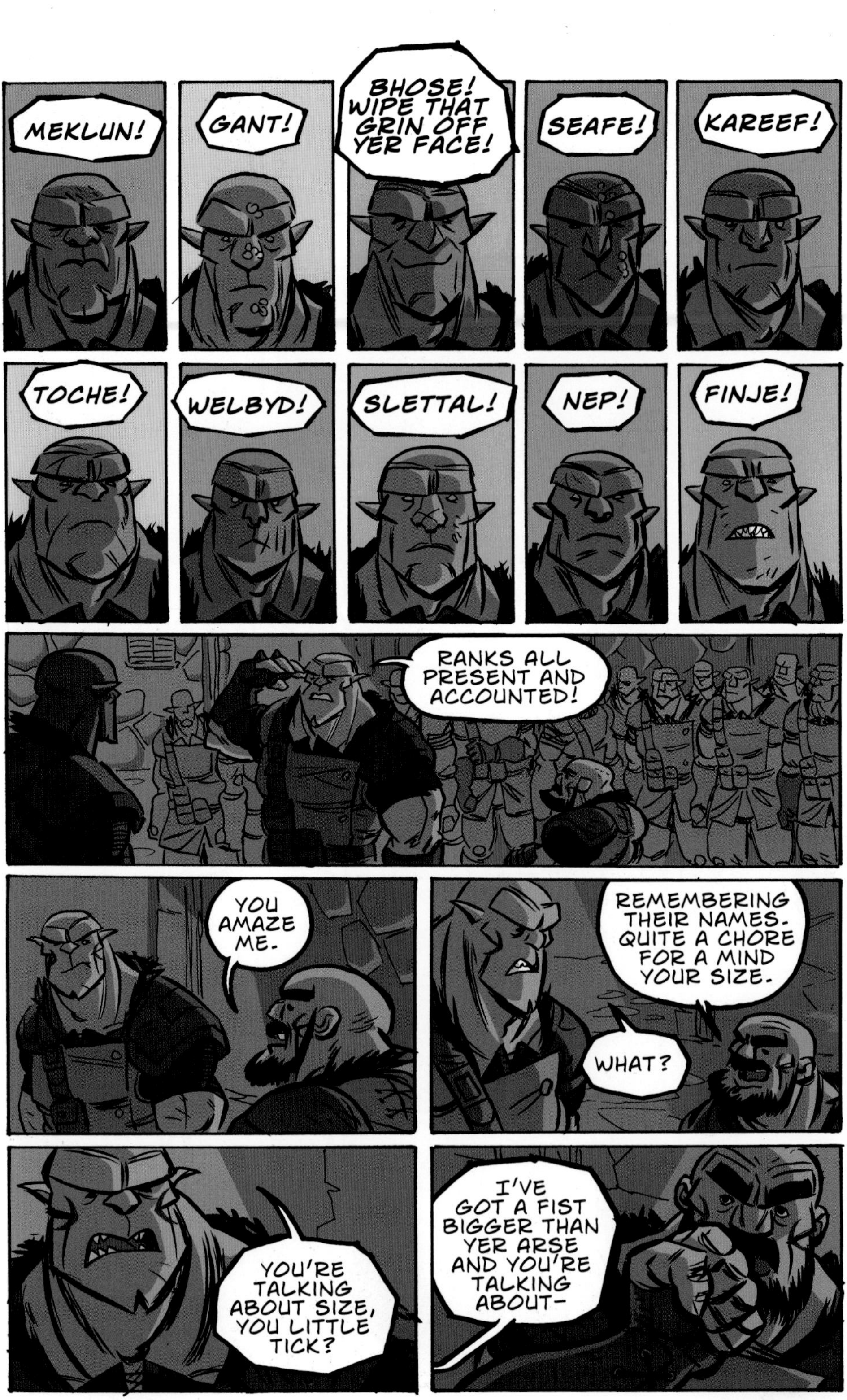
MEKLUN!
GANT!
BHOSE! WIPE THAT GRIN OFF YER FACE!
SEAFE!
KAREEF!
TOCHE!
WELBYD!
SLETTAL!
NEP!
FINJE!
RANKS ALL PRESENT AND ACCOUNTED!
YOU AMAZE ME.
REMEMBERING THEIR NAMES. QUITE A CHORE FOR A MIND YOUR SIZE.
WHAT?
YOU'RE TALKING ABOUT SIZE, YOU LITTLE TICK?
I'VE GOT A FIST BIGGER THAN YER ARSE AND YOU'RE TALKING ABOUT-

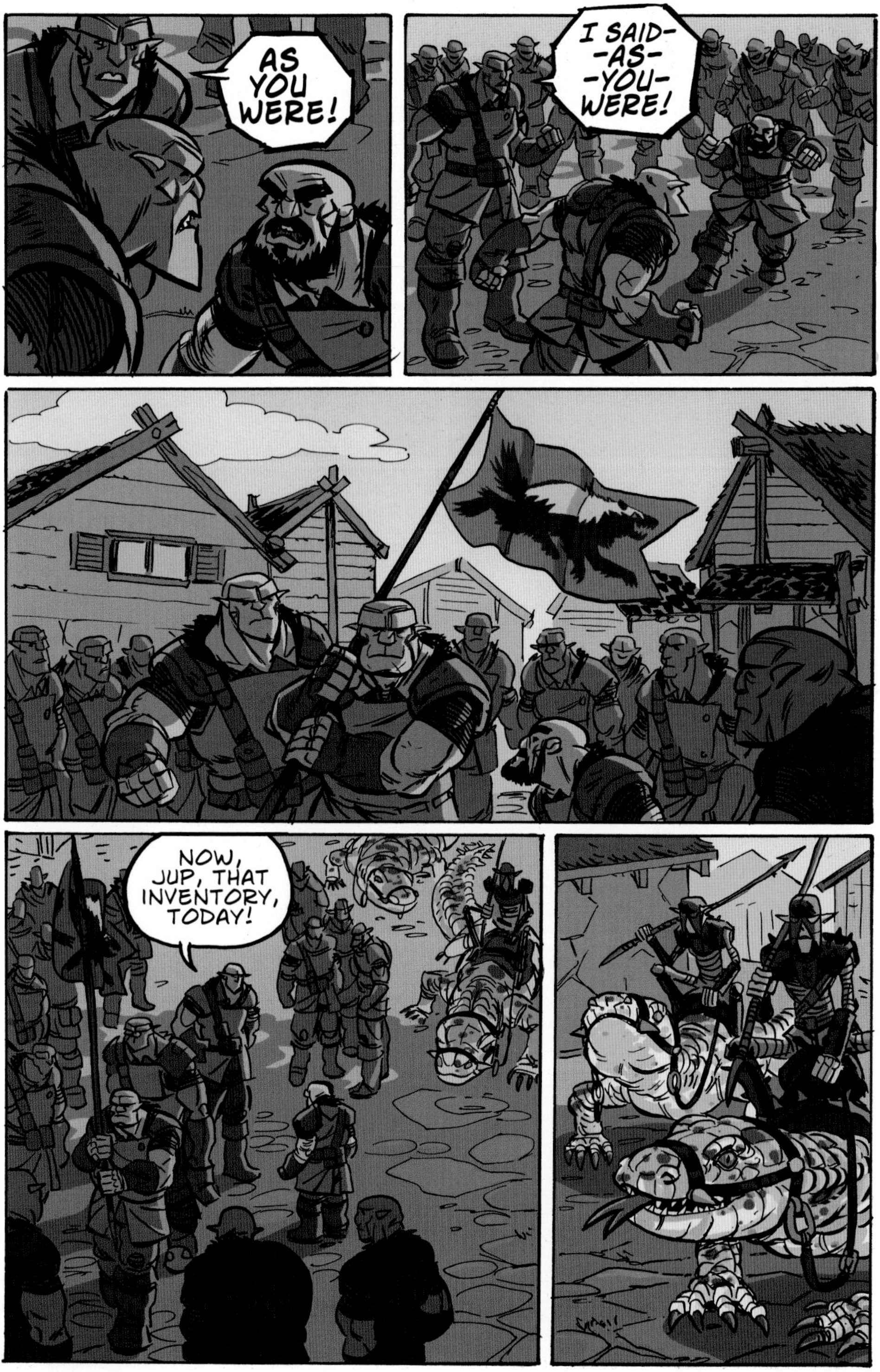
AS YOU WERE!
I SAID- -AS- -YOU- WERE!
NOW, JUP, THAT INVENTORY, TODAY!

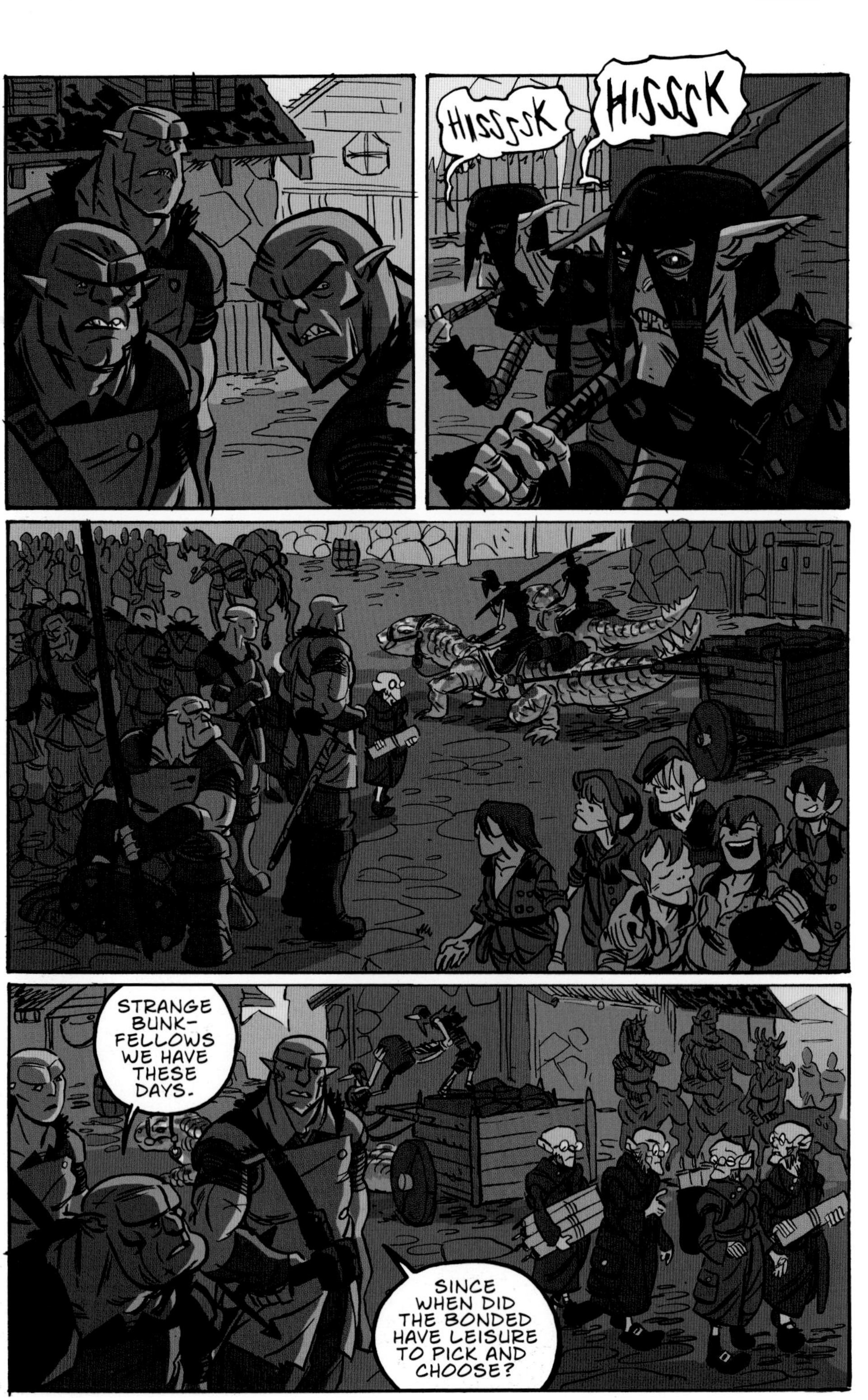
HISSSSK
HISSSK
STRANGE BUNK-FELLOWS WE HAVE THESE DAYS.
SINCE WHEN DID THE BONDED HAVE LEISURE TO PICK AND CHOOSE?

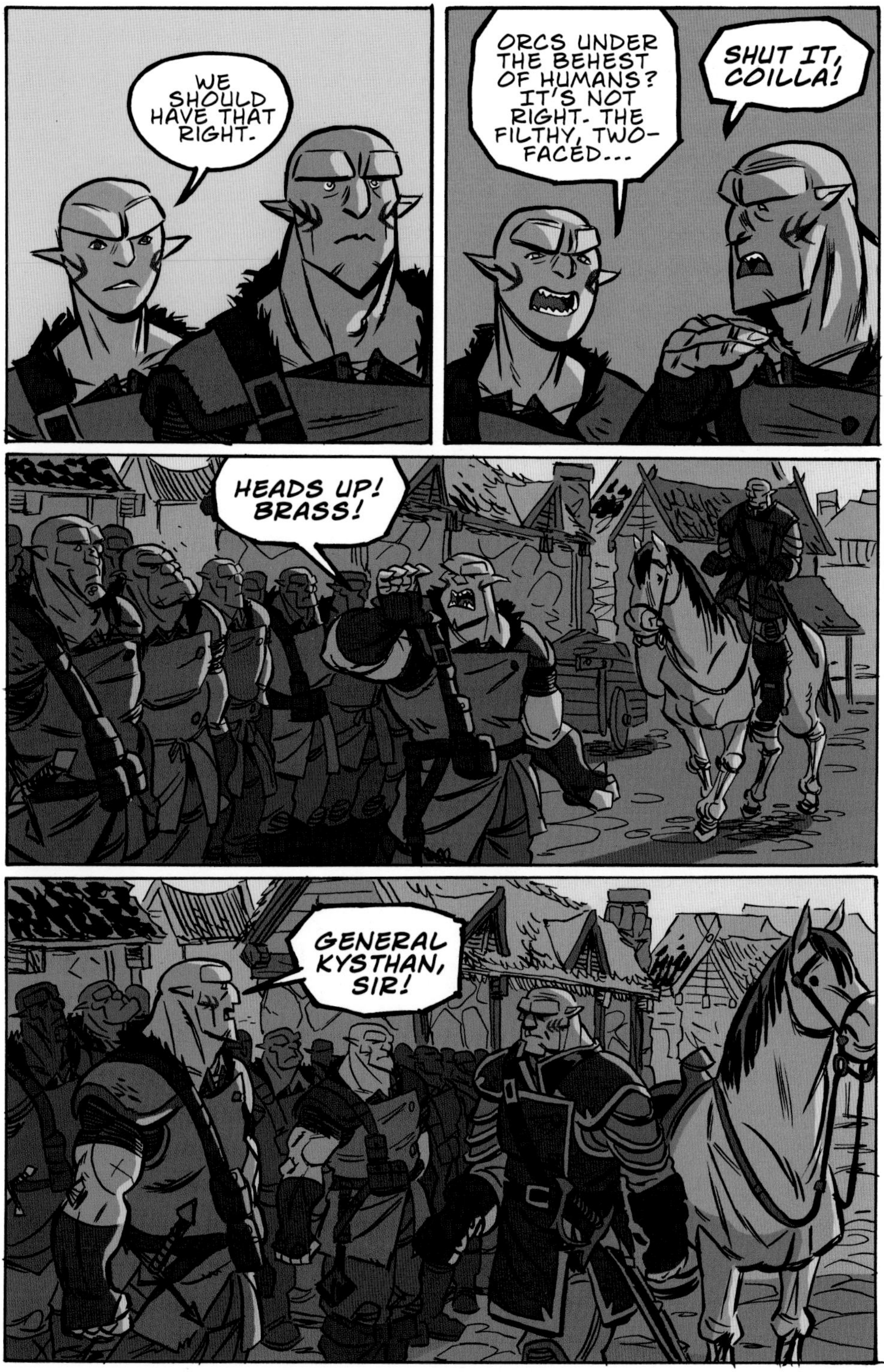
WE SHOULD HAVE THAT RIGHT.
ORCS UNDER THE BEHEST OF HUMANS? IT'S NOT RIGHT. THE FILTHY, TWO-FACED...
SHUT IT, COILLA!
HEADS UP! BRASS!
GENERAL KYSTHAN, SIR!

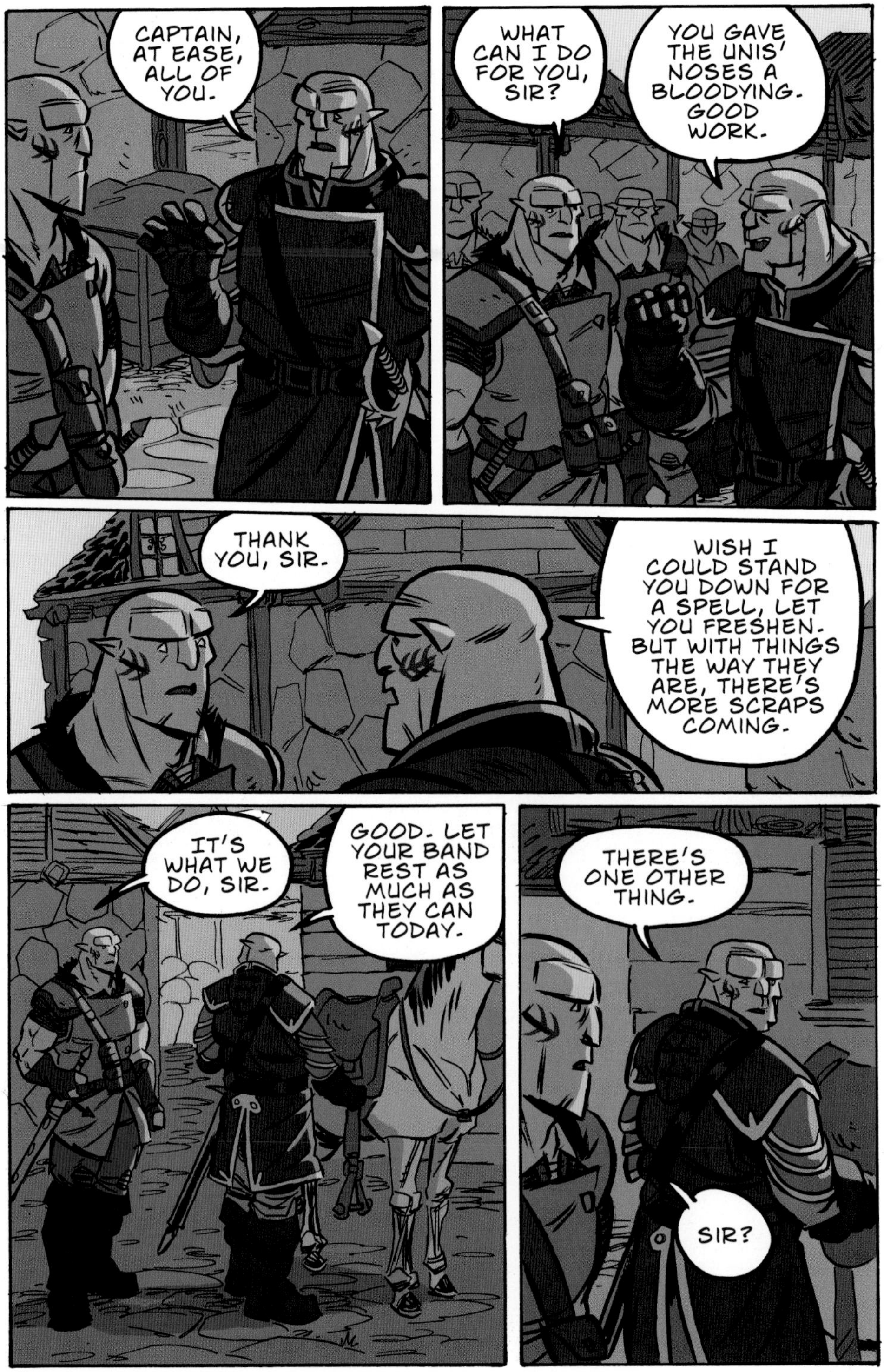
CAPTAIN, AT EASE, ALL OF YOU.
WHAT CAN I DO FOR YOU, SIR?
YOU GAVE THE UNIS' NOSES A BLOODYING. GOOD WORK.
THANK YOU, SIR.
WISH I COULD STAND YOU DOWN FOR A SPELL, LET YOU FRESHEN. BUT WITH THINGS THE WAY THEY ARE, THERE'S MORE SCRAPS COMING.
IT'S WHAT WE DO, SIR.
GOOD. LET YOUR BAND REST AS MUCH AS THEY CAN TODAY.
THERE'S ONE OTHER THING.
SIR?

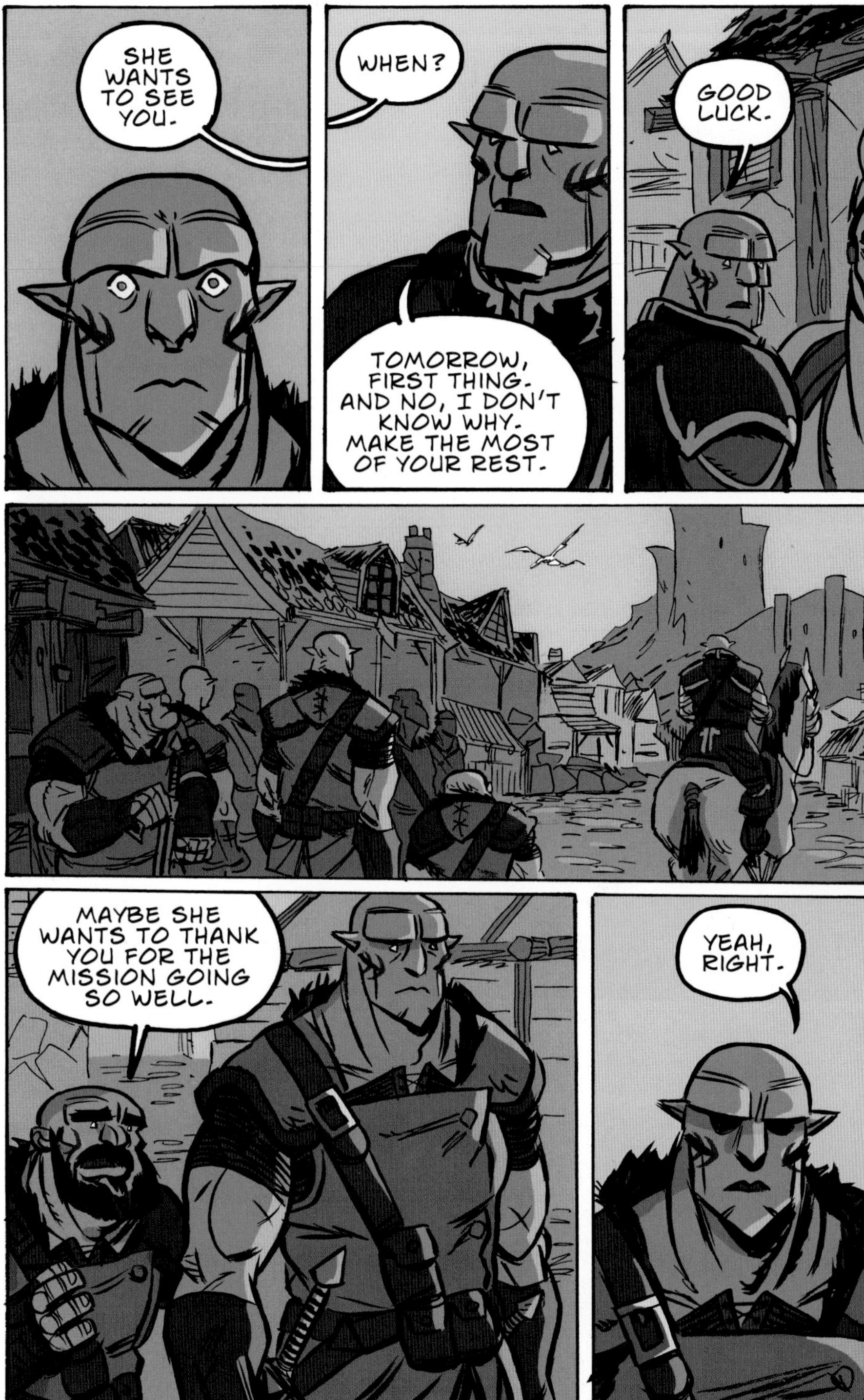
SHE WANTS TO SEE YOU.
WHEN?
TOMORROW, FIRST THING. AND NO, I DON'T KNOW WHY. MAKE THE MOST OF YOUR REST.
GOOD LUCK.
MAYBE SHE WANTS TO THANK YOU FOR THE MISSION GOING SO WELL.
YEAH, RIGHT.

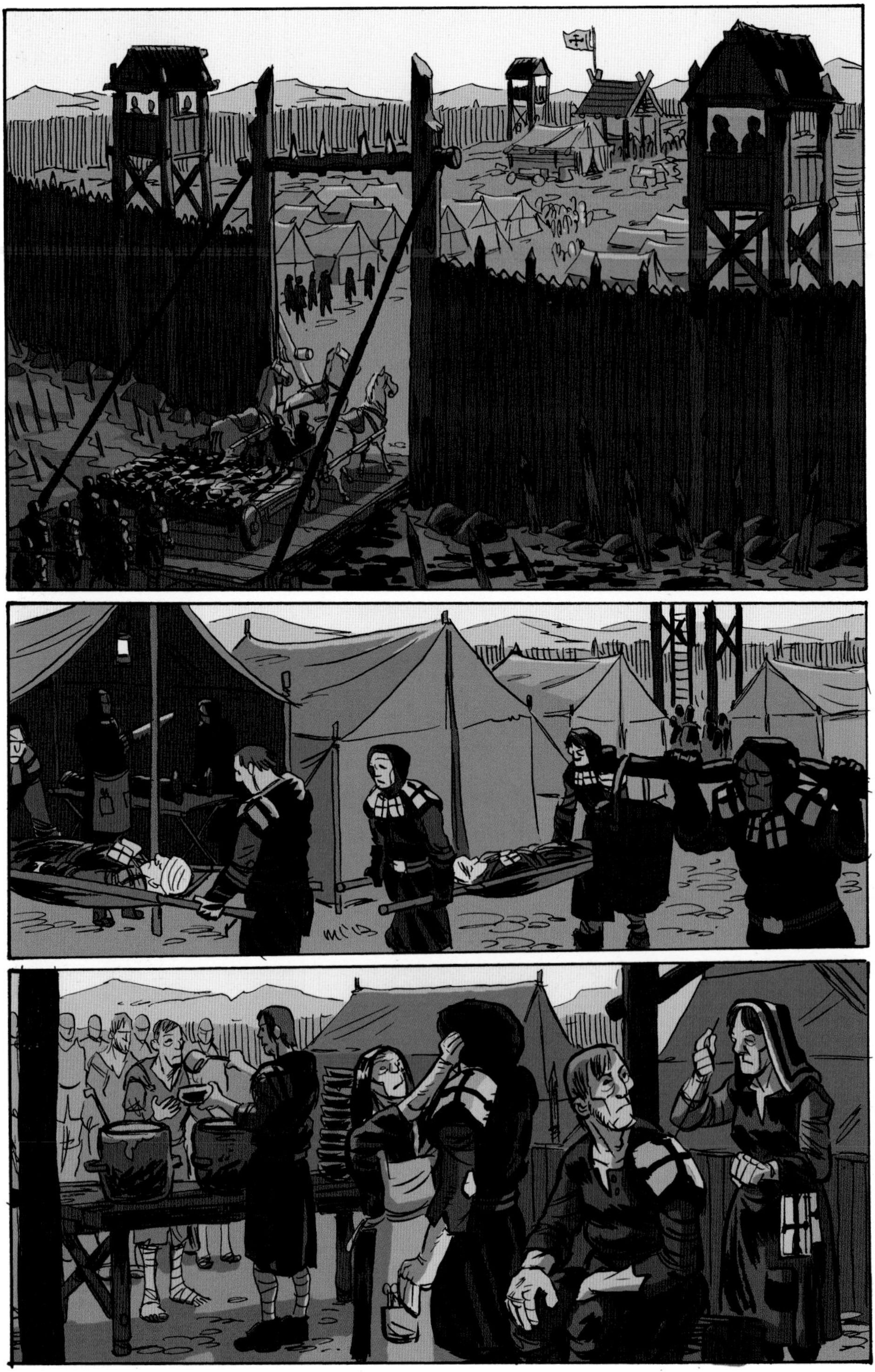

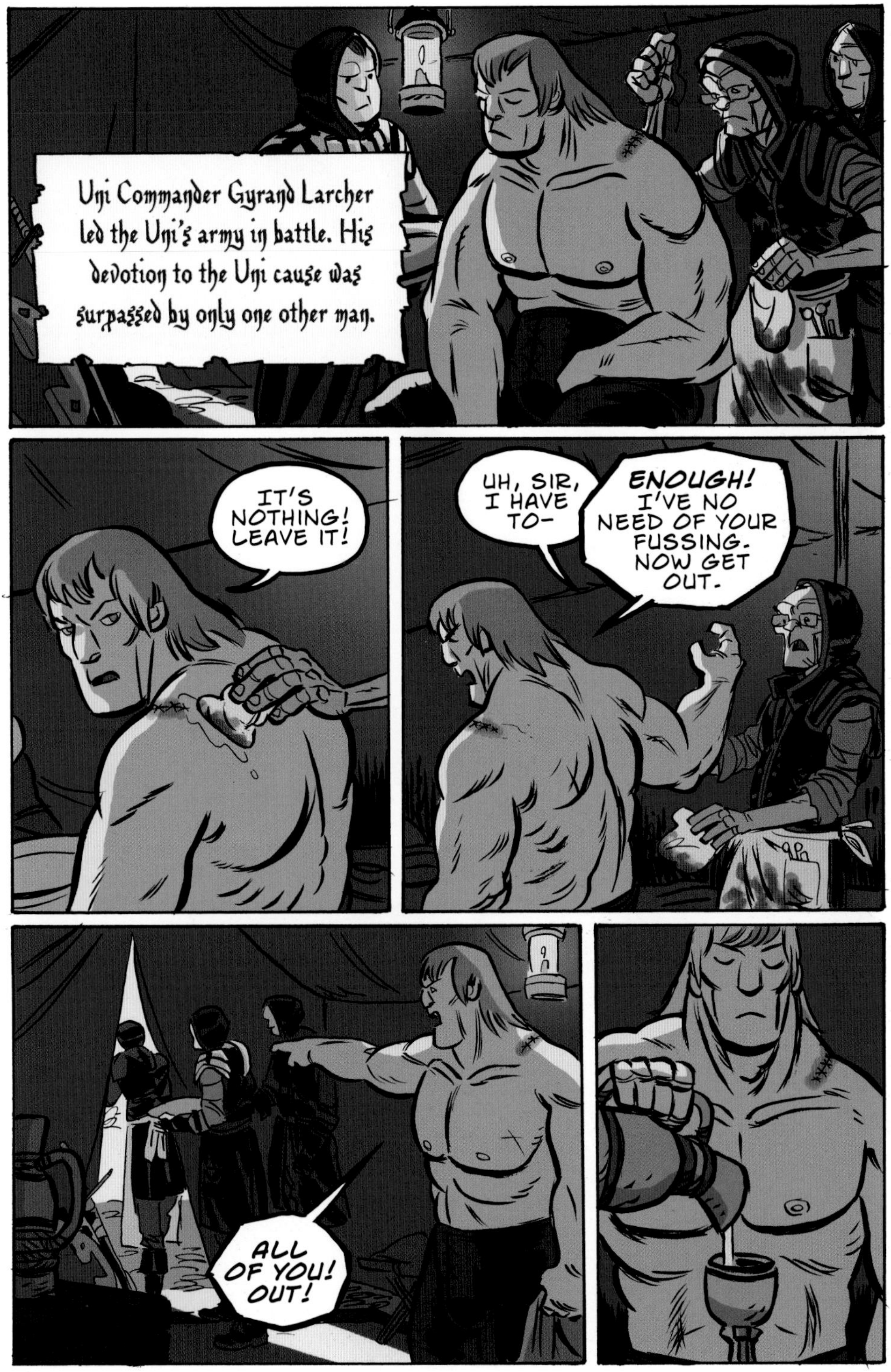
Uni Commander Gyrand Larcher led the Uni's army in battle. His devotion to the Uni cause was surpassed by only one other man.
IT'S NOTHING! LEAVE IT!
UH, SIR, I HAVE TO–
ENOUGH! I'VE NO NEED OF YOUR FUSSING. NOW GET OUT.
ALL OF YOU! OUT!

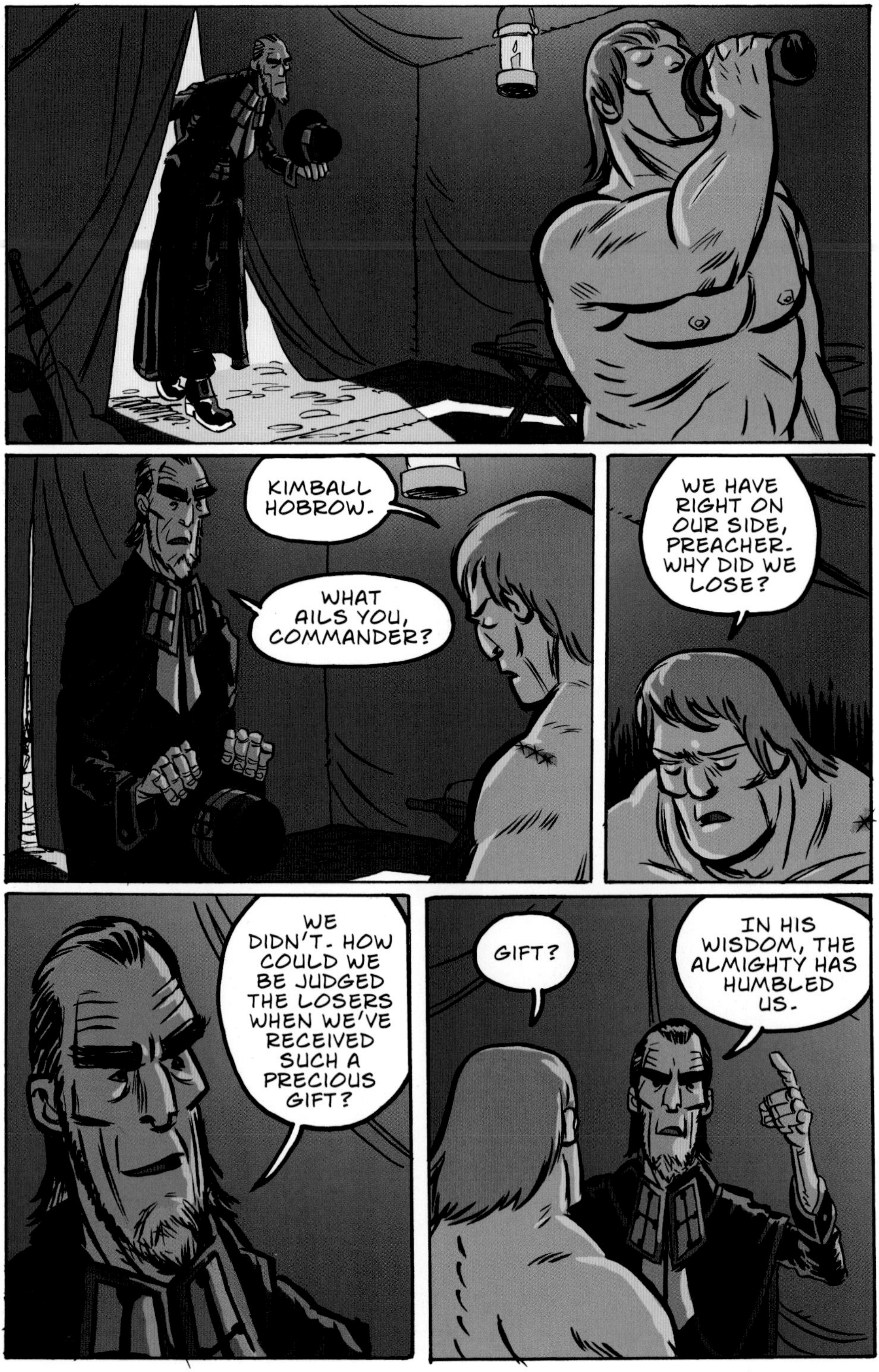
KIMBALL HOBROW.
WHAT AILS YOU, COMMANDER?
WE HAVE RIGHT ON OUR SIDE, PREACHER. WHY DID WE LOSE?
WE DIDN'T. HOW COULD WE BE JUDGED THE LOSERS WHEN WE'VE RECEIVED SUCH A PRECIOUS GIFT?
GIFT?
IN HIS WISDOM, THE ALMIGHTY HAS HUMBLED US.

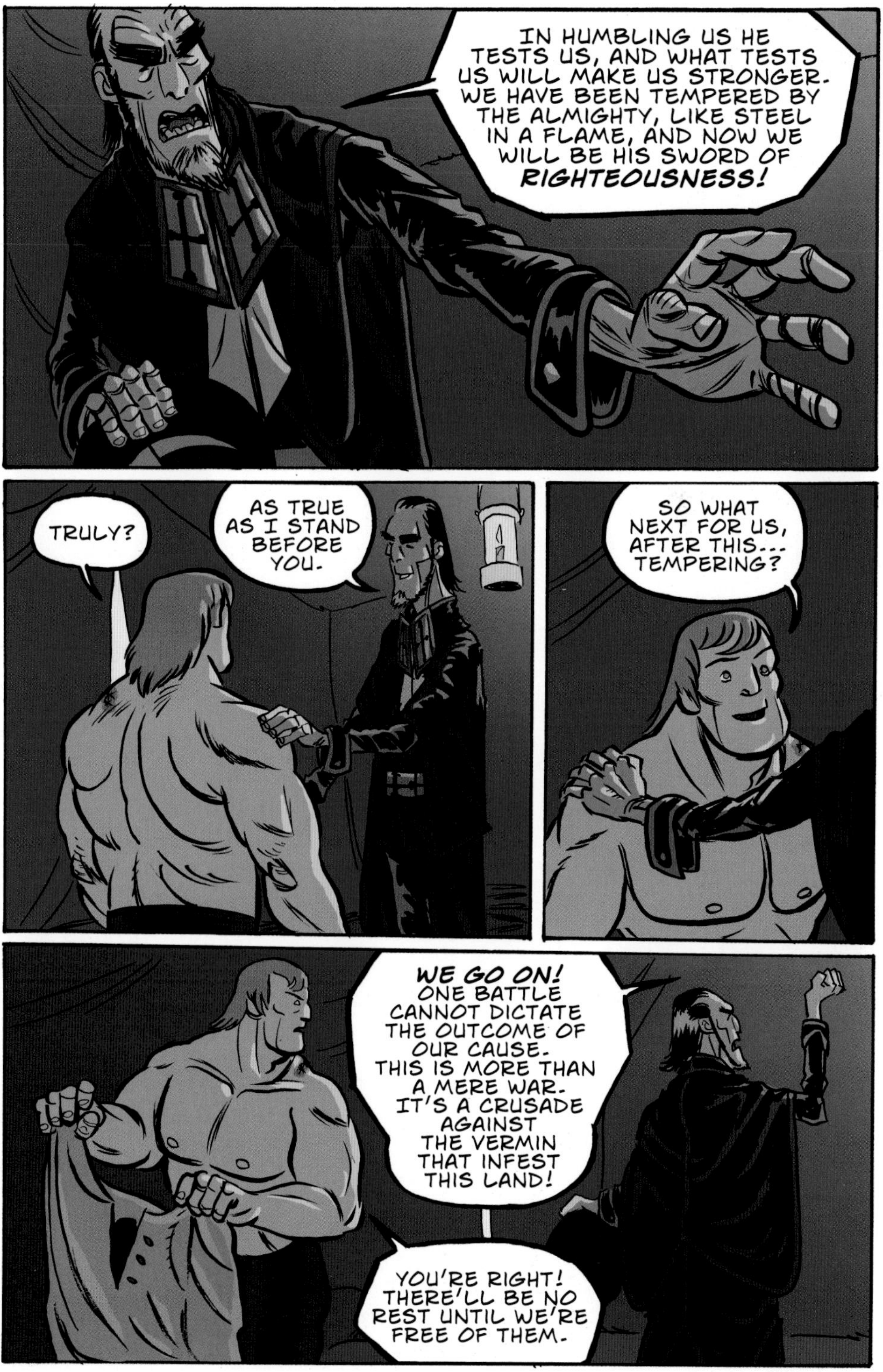

IN HUMBLING US HE TESTS US, AND WHAT TESTS US WILL MAKE US STRONGER. WE HAVE BEEN TEMPERED BY THE ALMIGHTY, LIKE STEEL IN A FLAME, AND NOW WE WILL BE HIS SWORD OF *RIGHTEOUSNESS!*
TRULY?
AS TRUE AS I STAND BEFORE YOU.
SO WHAT NEXT FOR US, AFTER THIS... TEMPERING?
WE GO ON! ONE BATTLE CANNOT DICTATE THE OUTCOME OF OUR CAUSE. THIS IS MORE THAN A MERE WAR. IT'S A CRUSADE AGAINST THE VERMIN THAT INFEST THIS LAND!
YOU'RE RIGHT! THERE'LL BE NO REST UNTIL WE'RE FREE OF THEM.

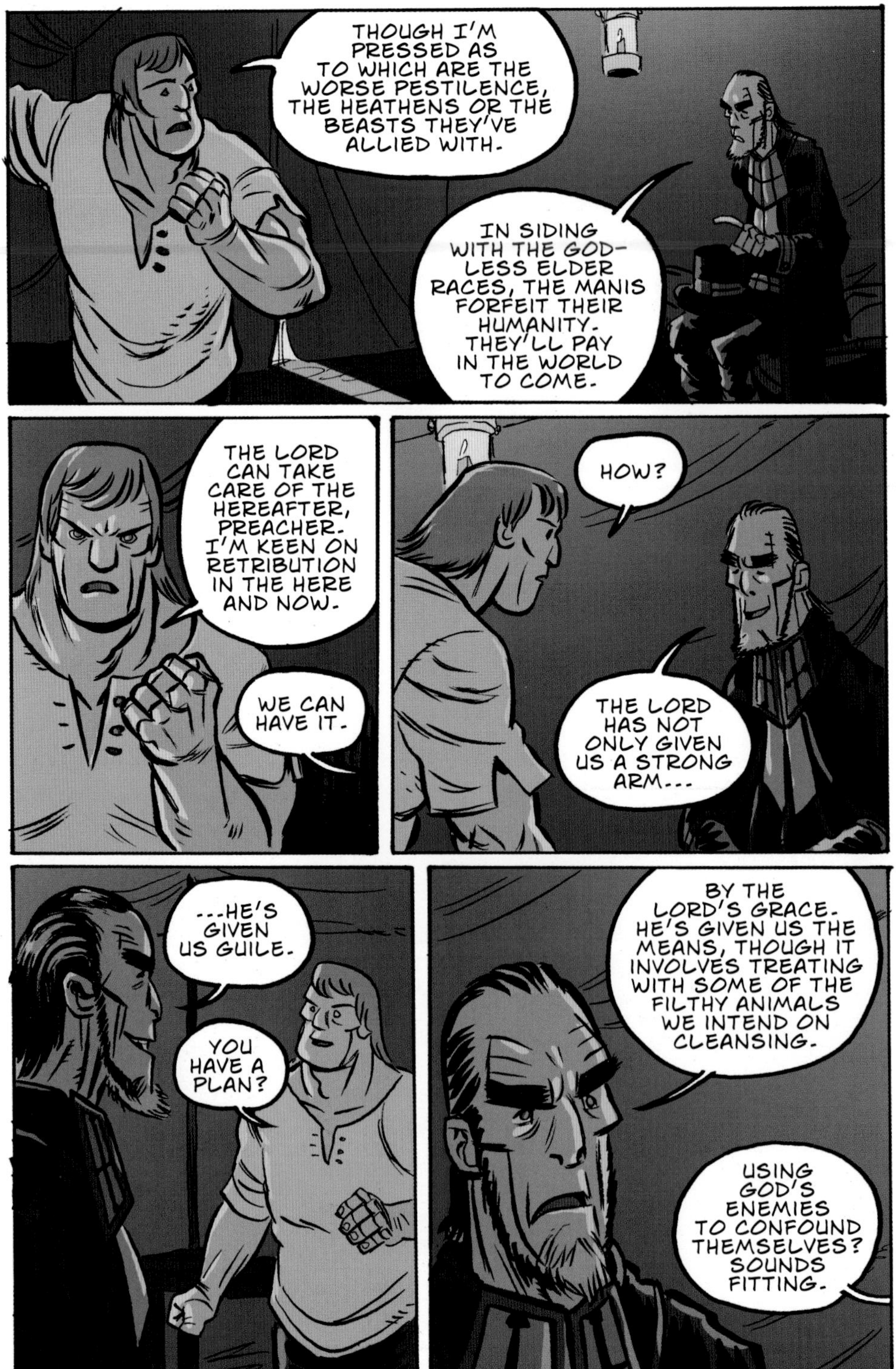
THOUGH I'M PRESSED AS TO WHICH ARE THE WORSE PESTILENCE, THE HEATHENS OR THE BEASTS THEY'VE ALLIED WITH.
IN SIDING WITH THE GOD-LESS ELDER RACES, THE MANIS FORFEIT THEIR HUMANITY. THEY'LL PAY IN THE WORLD TO COME.
THE LORD CAN TAKE CARE OF THE HEREAFTER, PREACHER. I'M KEEN ON RETRIBUTION IN THE HERE AND NOW.
WE CAN HAVE IT.
HOW?
THE LORD HAS NOT ONLY GIVEN US A STRONG ARM...
...HE'S GIVEN US GUILE.
YOU HAVE A PLAN?
BY THE LORD'S GRACE. HE'S GIVEN US THE MEANS, THOUGH IT INVOLVES TREATING WITH SOME OF THE FILTHY ANIMALS WE INTEND ON CLEANSING.
USING GOD'S ENEMIES TO CONFOUND THEMSELVES? SOUNDS FITTING.

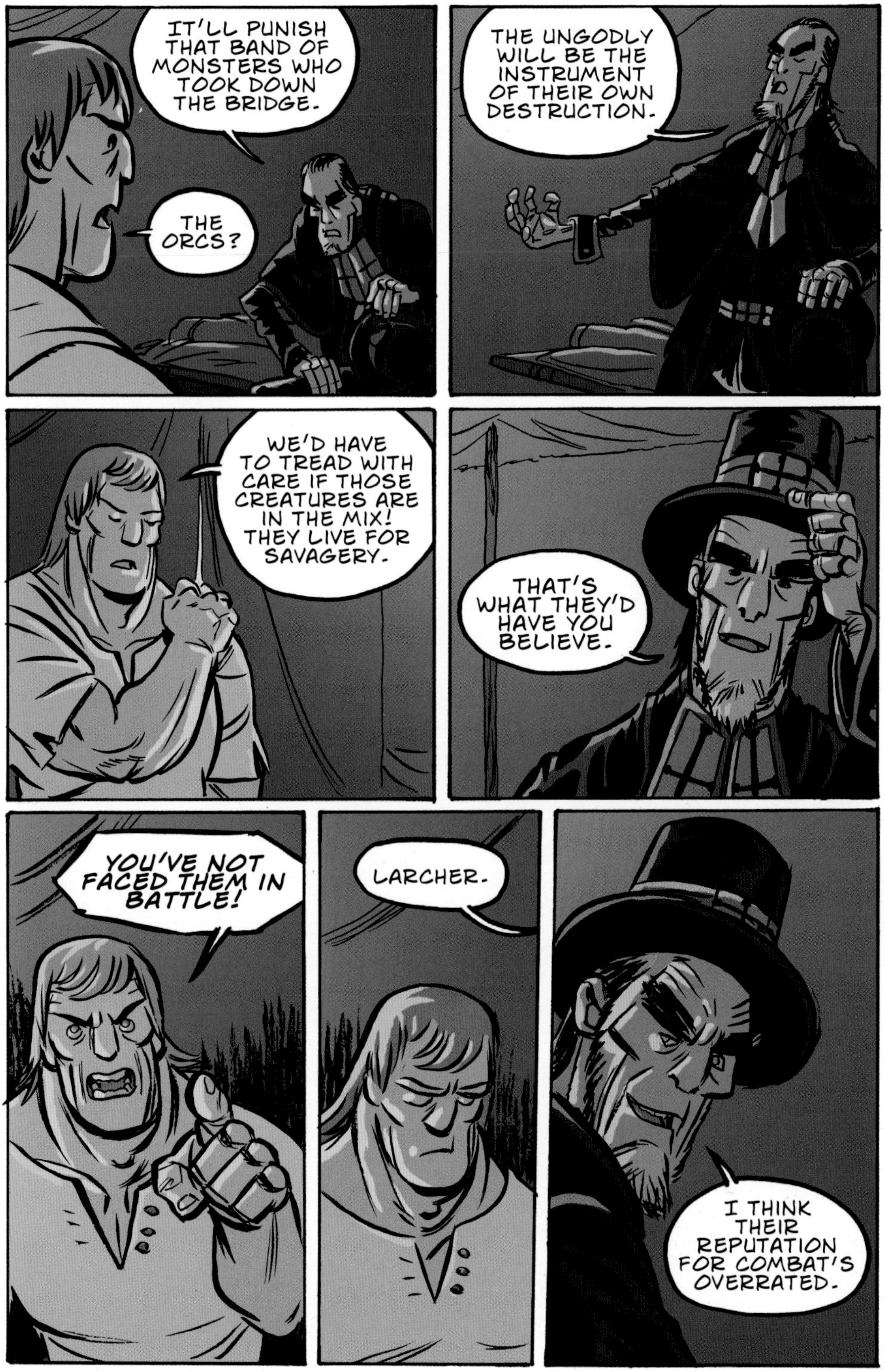
IT'LL PUNISH THAT BAND OF MONSTERS WHO TOOK DOWN THE BRIDGE.
THE ORCS?
THE UNGODLY WILL BE THE INSTRUMENT OF THEIR OWN DESTRUCTION.
WE'D HAVE TO TREAD WITH CARE IF THOSE CREATURES ARE IN THE MIX! THEY LIVE FOR SAVAGERY.
THAT'S WHAT THEY'D HAVE YOU BELIEVE.
YOU'VE NOT FACED THEM IN BATTLE!
LARCHER.
I THINK THEIR REPUTATION FOR COMBAT'S OVERRATED.

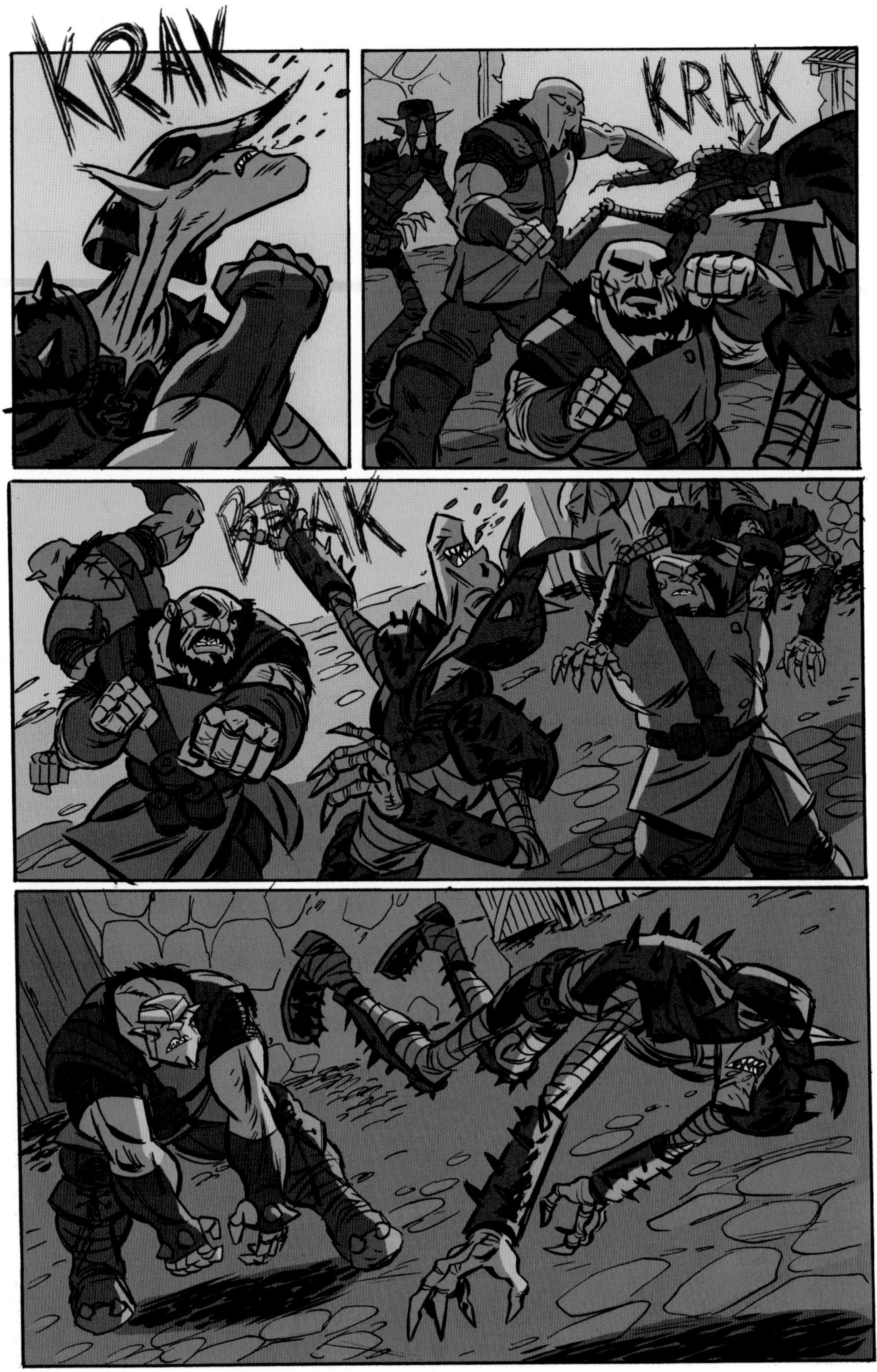
KRAK
KRAK
BRAK

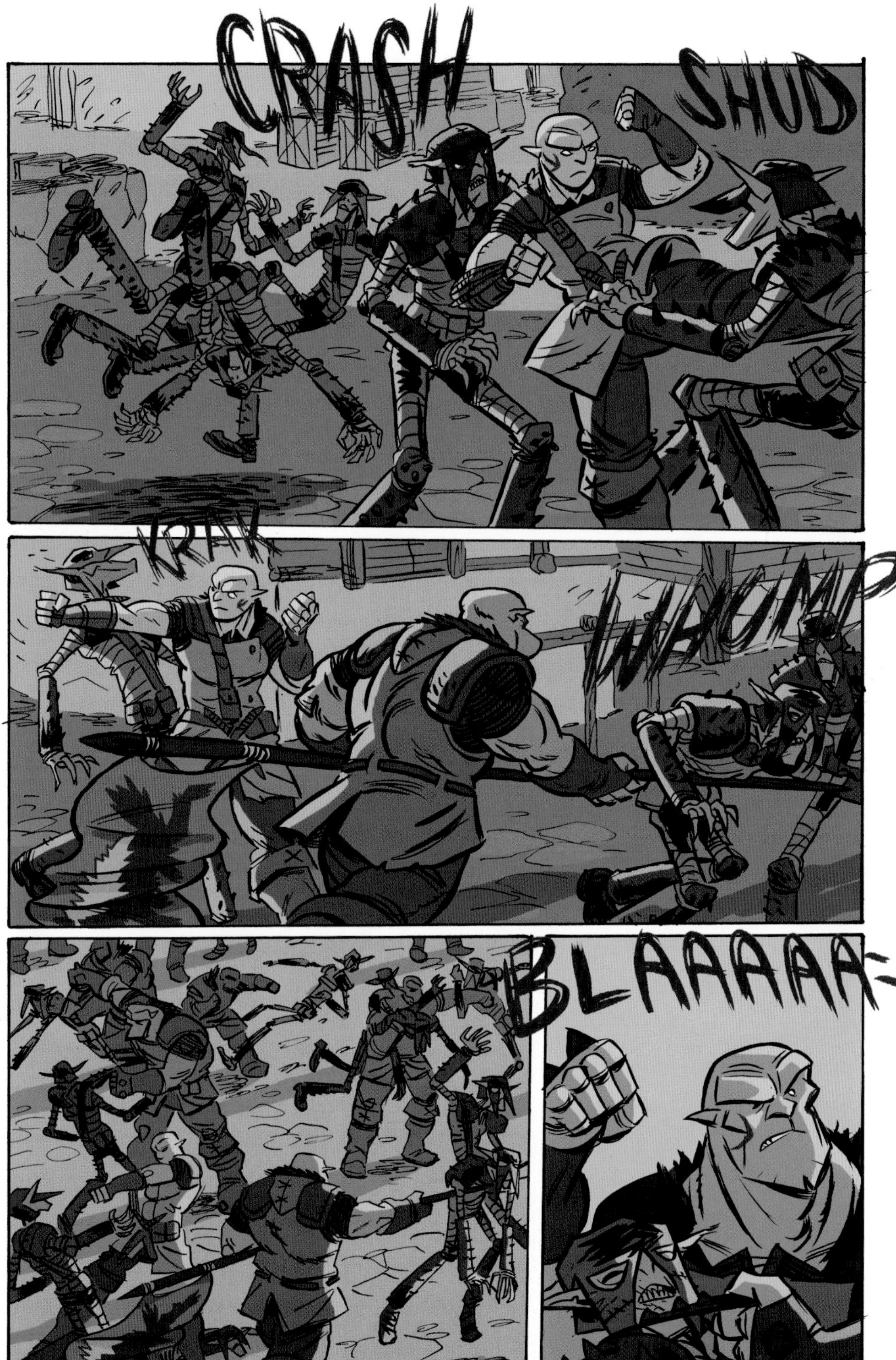
CRASH
SHUD
KRAK
WHUMP
BLAAAAA-

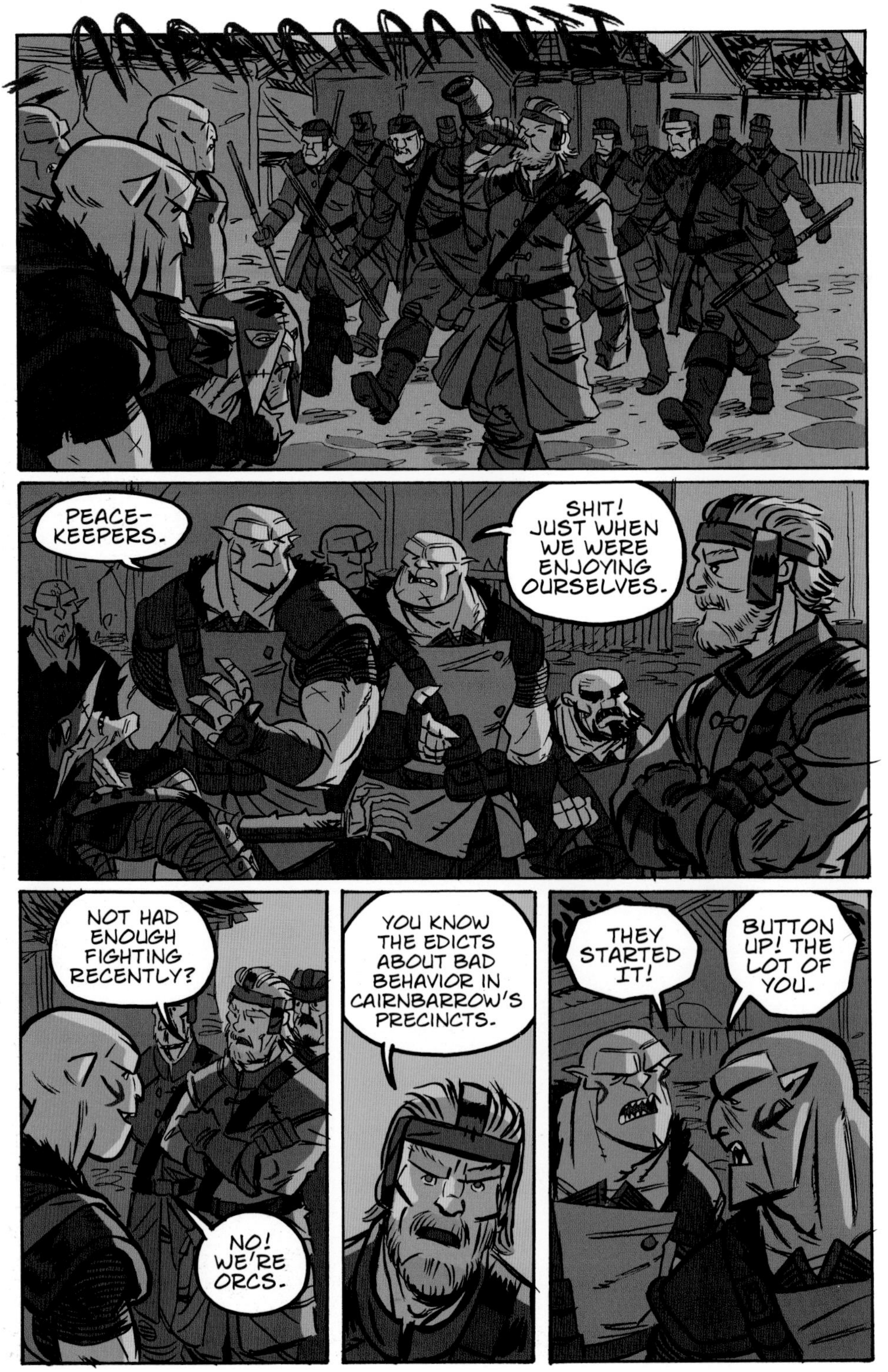
PEACE-KEEPERS.
SHIT! JUST WHEN WE WERE ENJOYING OURSELVES.
NOT HAD ENOUGH FIGHTING RECENTLY?
NO! WE'RE ORCS.
YOU KNOW THE EDICTS ABOUT BAD BEHAVIOR IN CAIRNBARROW'S PRECINCTS.
THEY STARTED IT!
BUTTON UP! THE LOT OF YOU.

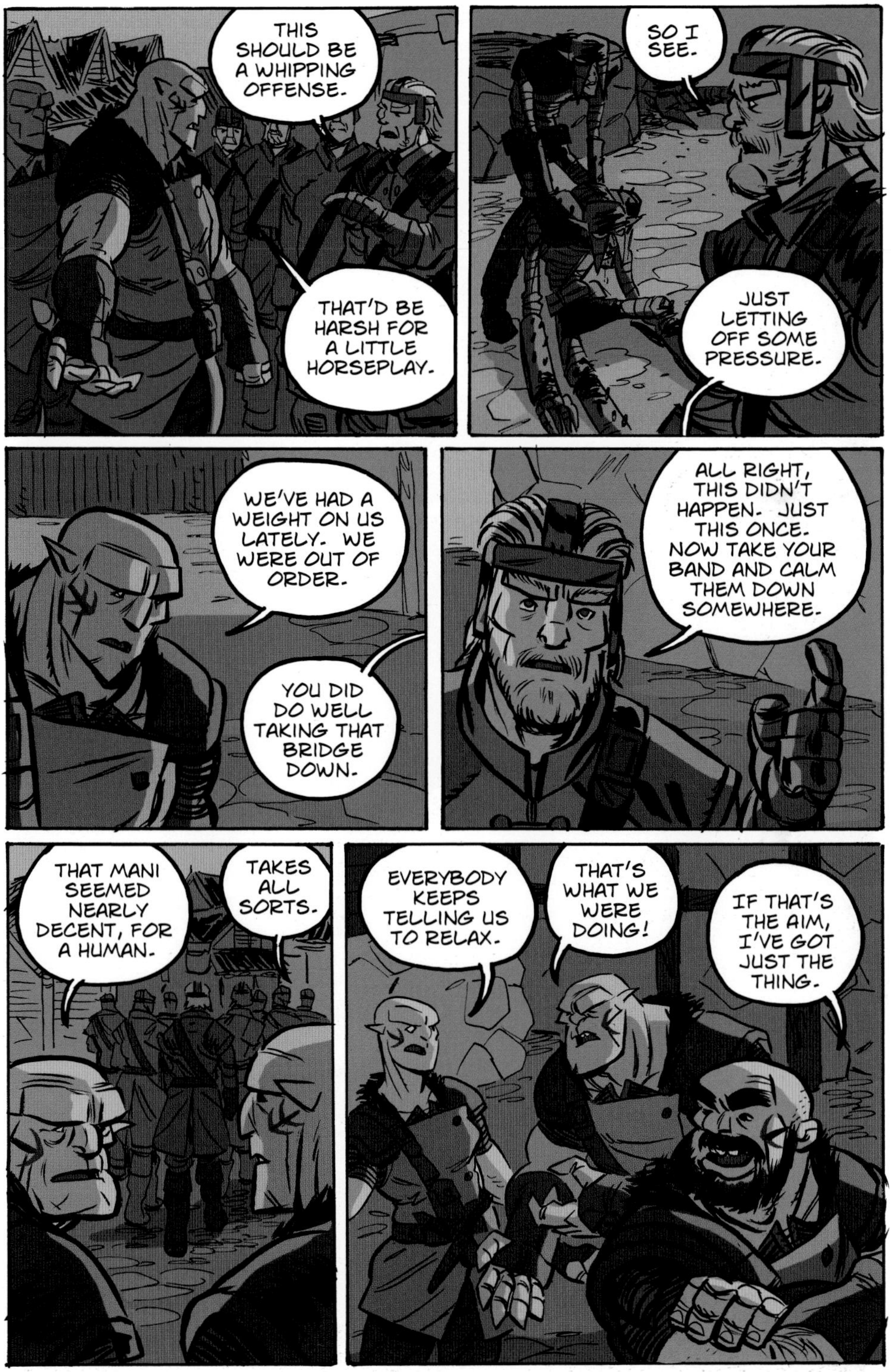
THIS SHOULD BE A WHIPPING OFFENSE.
THAT'D BE HARSH FOR A LITTLE HORSEPLAY.
SO I SEE.
JUST LETTING OFF SOME PRESSURE.
WE'VE HAD A WEIGHT ON US LATELY. WE WERE OUT OF ORDER.
YOU DID DO WELL TAKING THAT BRIDGE DOWN.
ALL RIGHT, THIS DIDN'T HAPPEN. JUST THIS ONCE. NOW TAKE YOUR BAND AND CALM THEM DOWN SOMEWHERE.
THAT MANI SEEMED NEARLY DECENT, FOR A HUMAN.
TAKES ALL SORTS.
EVERYBODY KEEPS TELLING US TO RELAX.
THAT'S WHAT WE WERE DOING!
IF THAT'S THE AIM, I'VE GOT JUST THE THING.

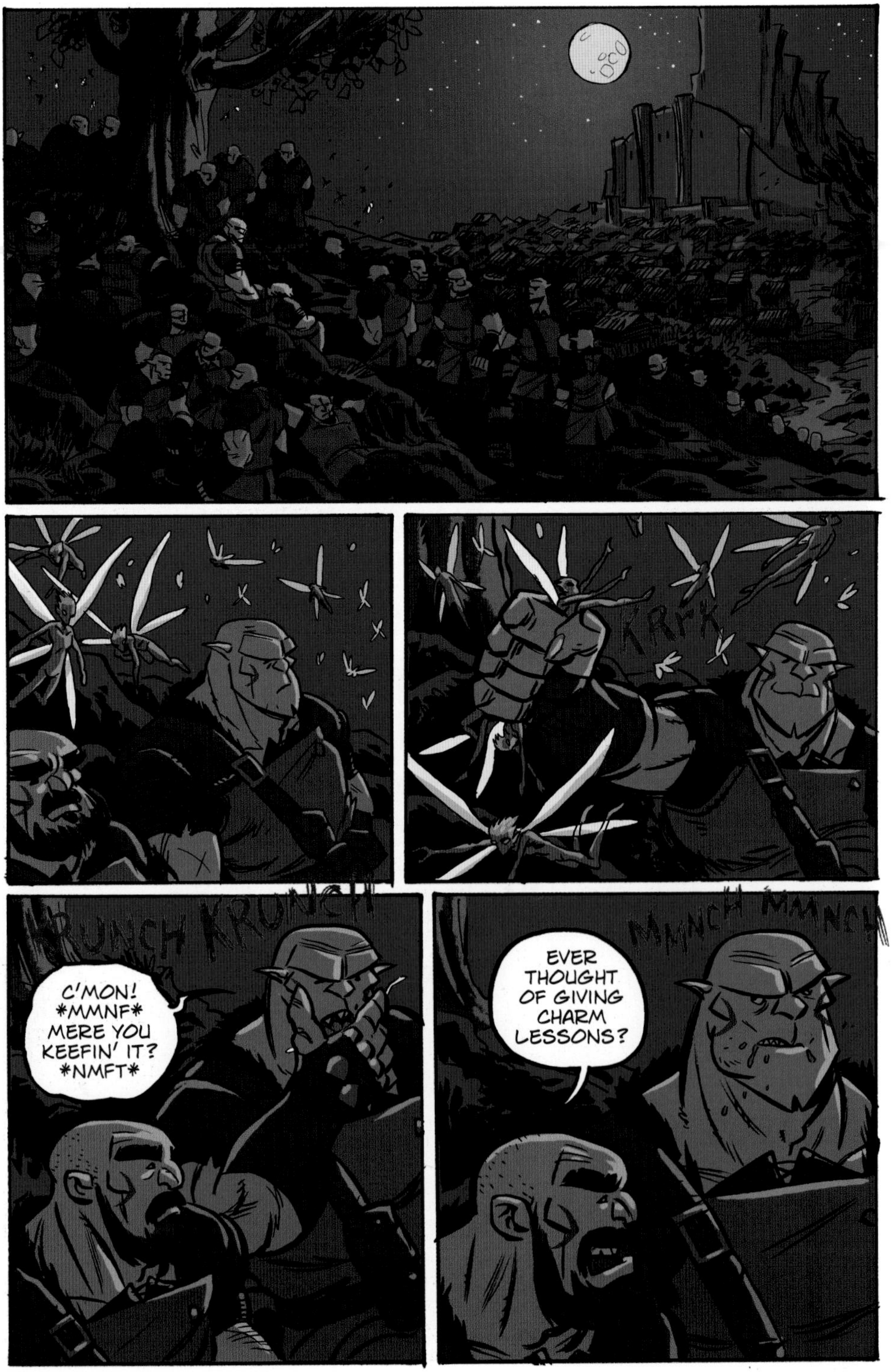
KRFK
KRUNCH KRUNCH
C'MON! *MMNF* MERE YOU KEEFIN' IT? *NMFT*
MMNCH MMNCH
EVER THOUGHT OF GIVING CHARM LESSONS?

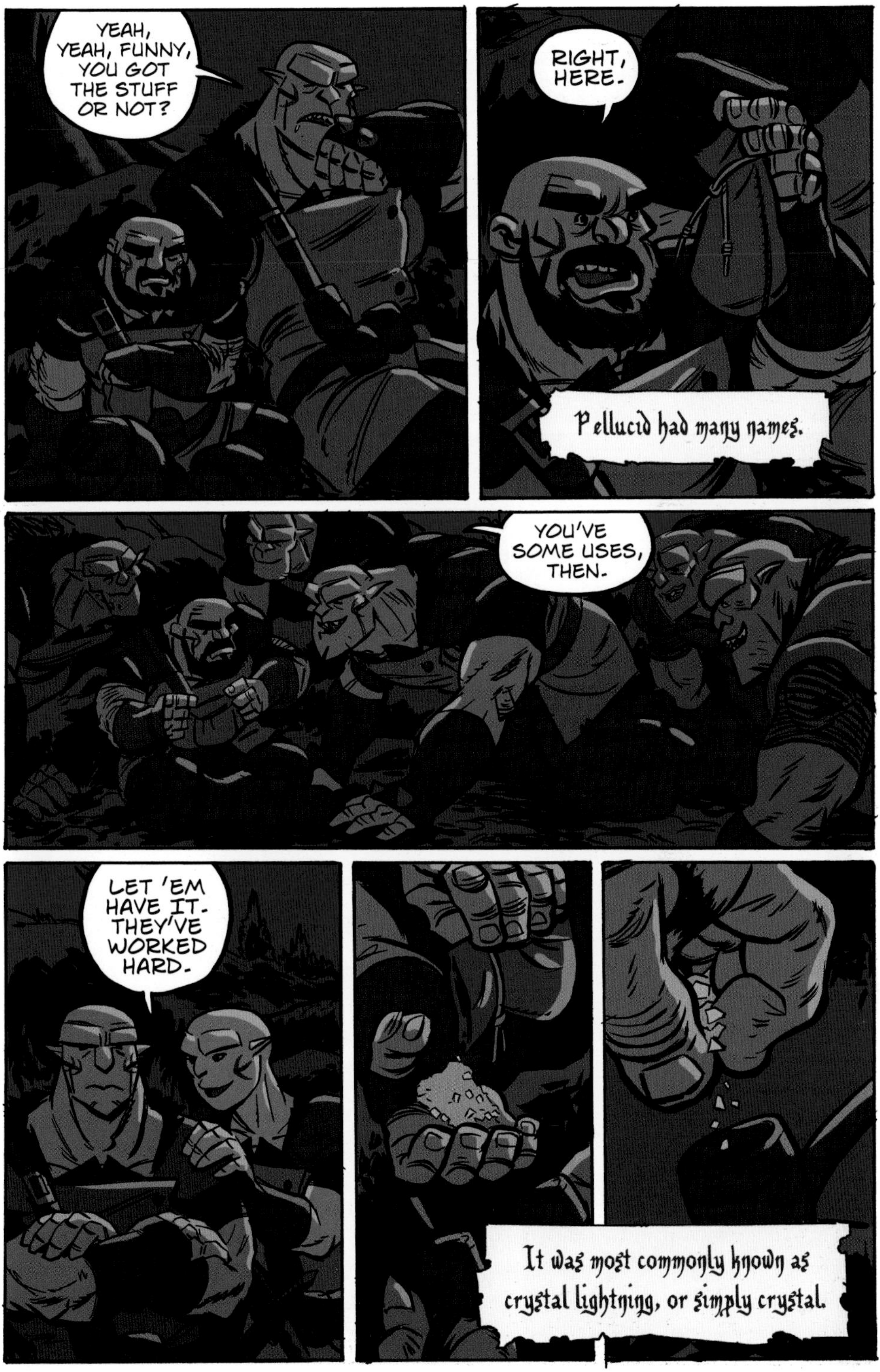

YEAH, YEAH, FUNNY, YOU GOT THE STUFF OR NOT?
RIGHT, HERE.
Pellucid had many names.
YOU'VE SOME USES, THEN.
LET 'EM HAVE IT. THEY'VE WORKED HARD.
It was most commonly known as crystal lightning, or simply crystal.

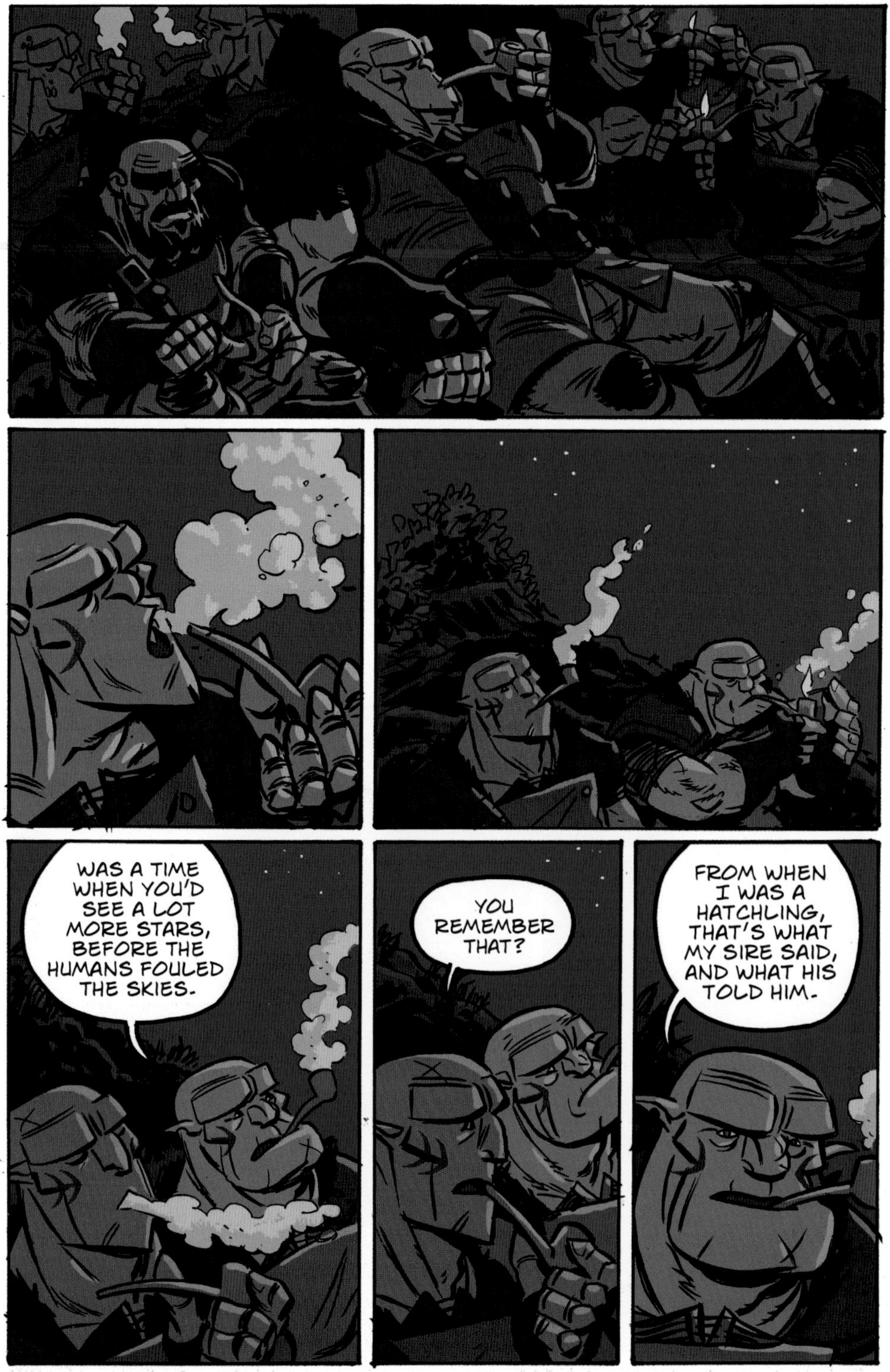
WAS A TIME WHEN YOU'D SEE A LOT MORE STARS, BEFORE THE HUMANS FOULED THE SKIES.
YOU REMEMBER THAT?
FROM WHEN I WAS A HATCHLING, THAT'S WHAT MY SIRE SAID, AND WHAT HIS TOLD HIM.

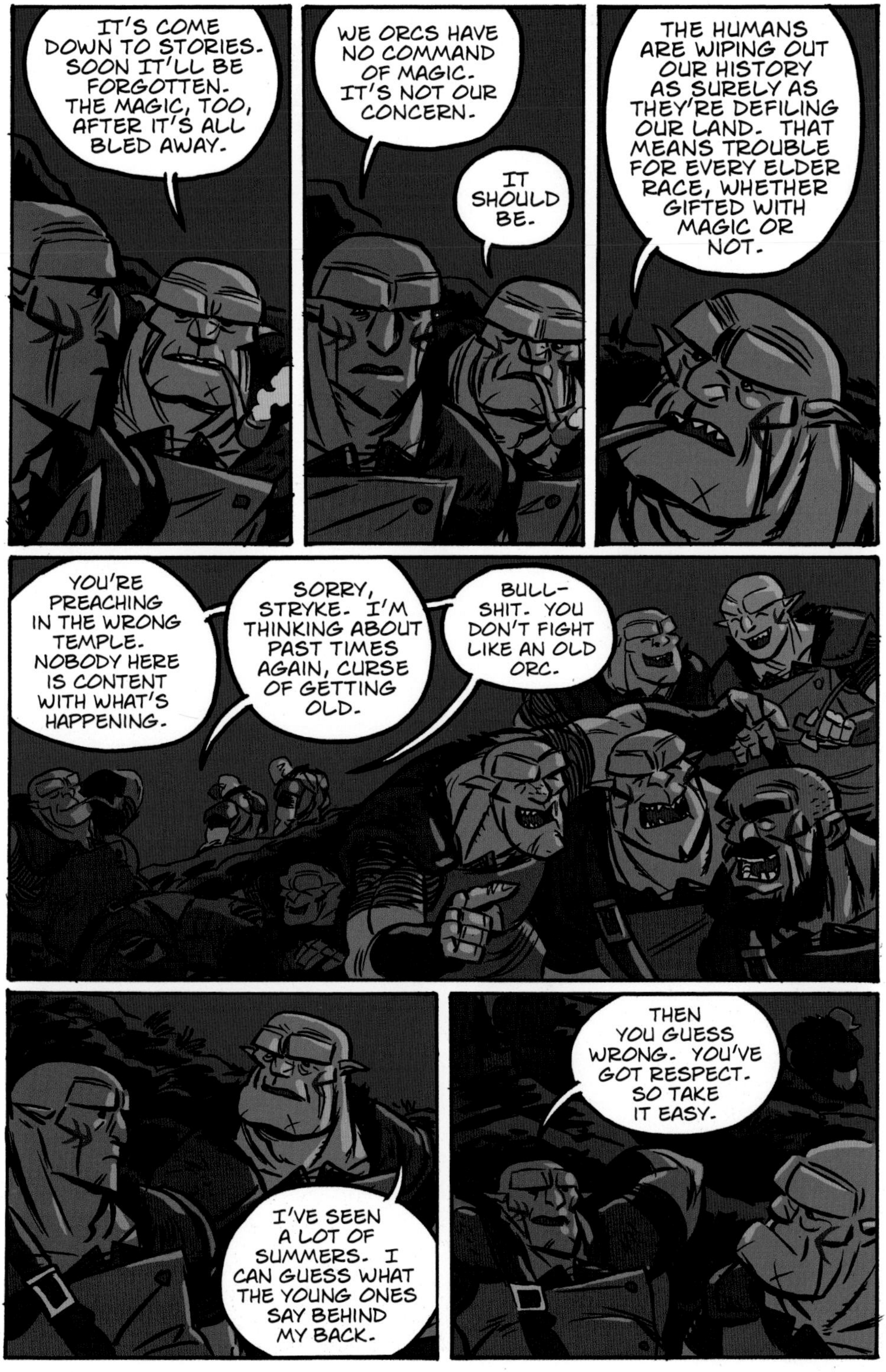
IT'S COME DOWN TO STORIES. SOON IT'LL BE FORGOTTEN. THE MAGIC, TOO, AFTER IT'S ALL BLED AWAY.
WE ORCS HAVE NO COMMAND OF MAGIC. IT'S NOT OUR CONCERN.
IT SHOULD BE.
THE HUMANS ARE WIPING OUT OUR HISTORY AS SURELY AS THEY'RE DEFILING OUR LAND. THAT MEANS TROUBLE FOR EVERY ELDER RACE, WHETHER GIFTED WITH MAGIC OR NOT.
YOU'RE PREACHING IN THE WRONG TEMPLE. NOBODY HERE IS CONTENT WITH WHAT'S HAPPENING.
SORRY, STRYKE. I'M THINKING ABOUT PAST TIMES AGAIN, CURSE OF GETTING OLD.
BULL-SHIT. YOU DON'T FIGHT LIKE AN OLD ORC.
I'VE SEEN A LOT OF SUMMERS. I CAN GUESS WHAT THE YOUNG ONES SAY BEHIND MY BACK.
THEN YOU GUESS WRONG. YOU'VE GOT RESPECT. SO TAKE IT EASY.

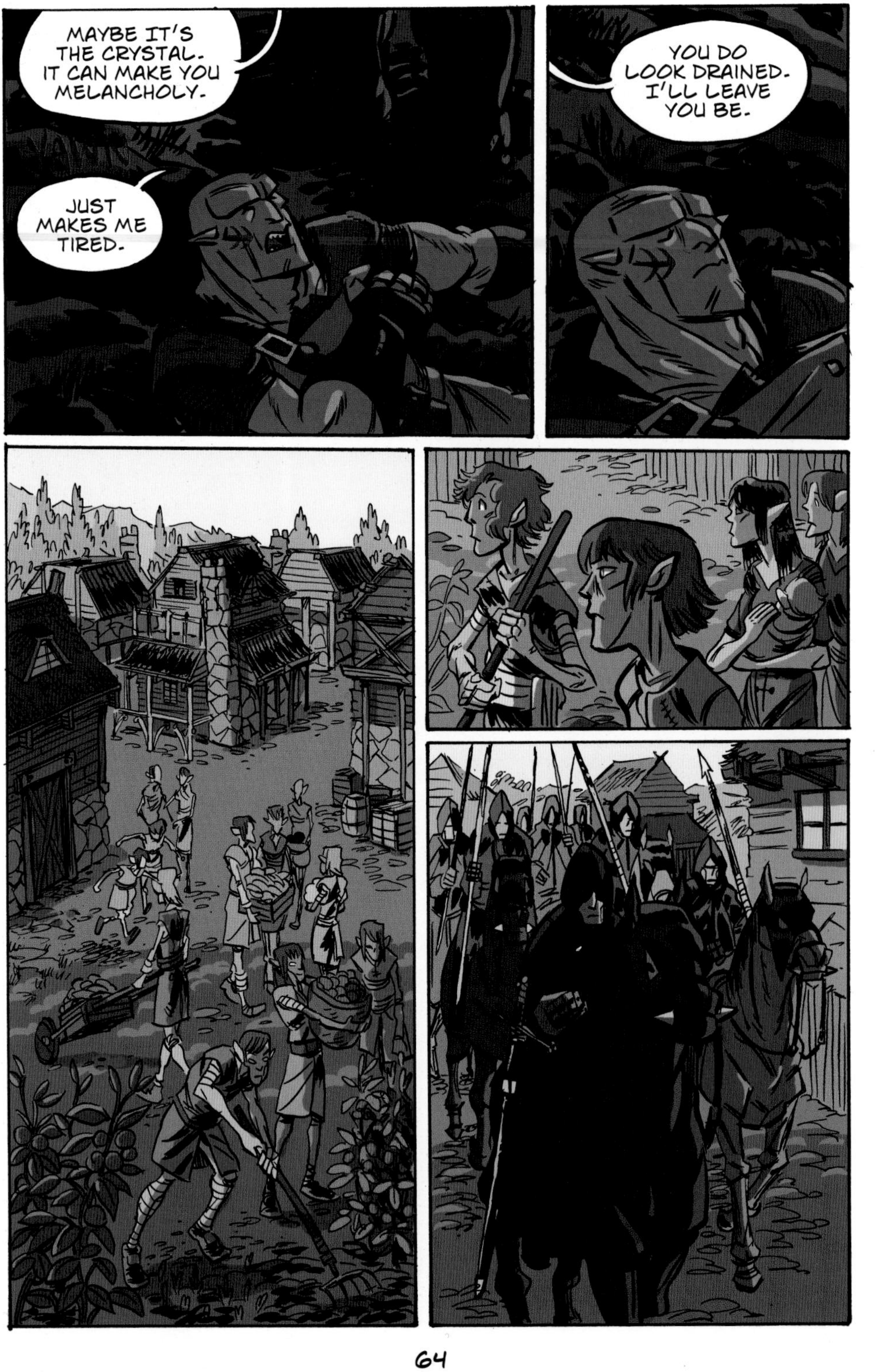
MAYBE IT'S THE CRYSTAL. IT CAN MAKE YOU MELANCHOLY.
JUST MAKES ME TIRED.
YOU DO LOOK DRAINED. I'LL LEAVE YOU BE.

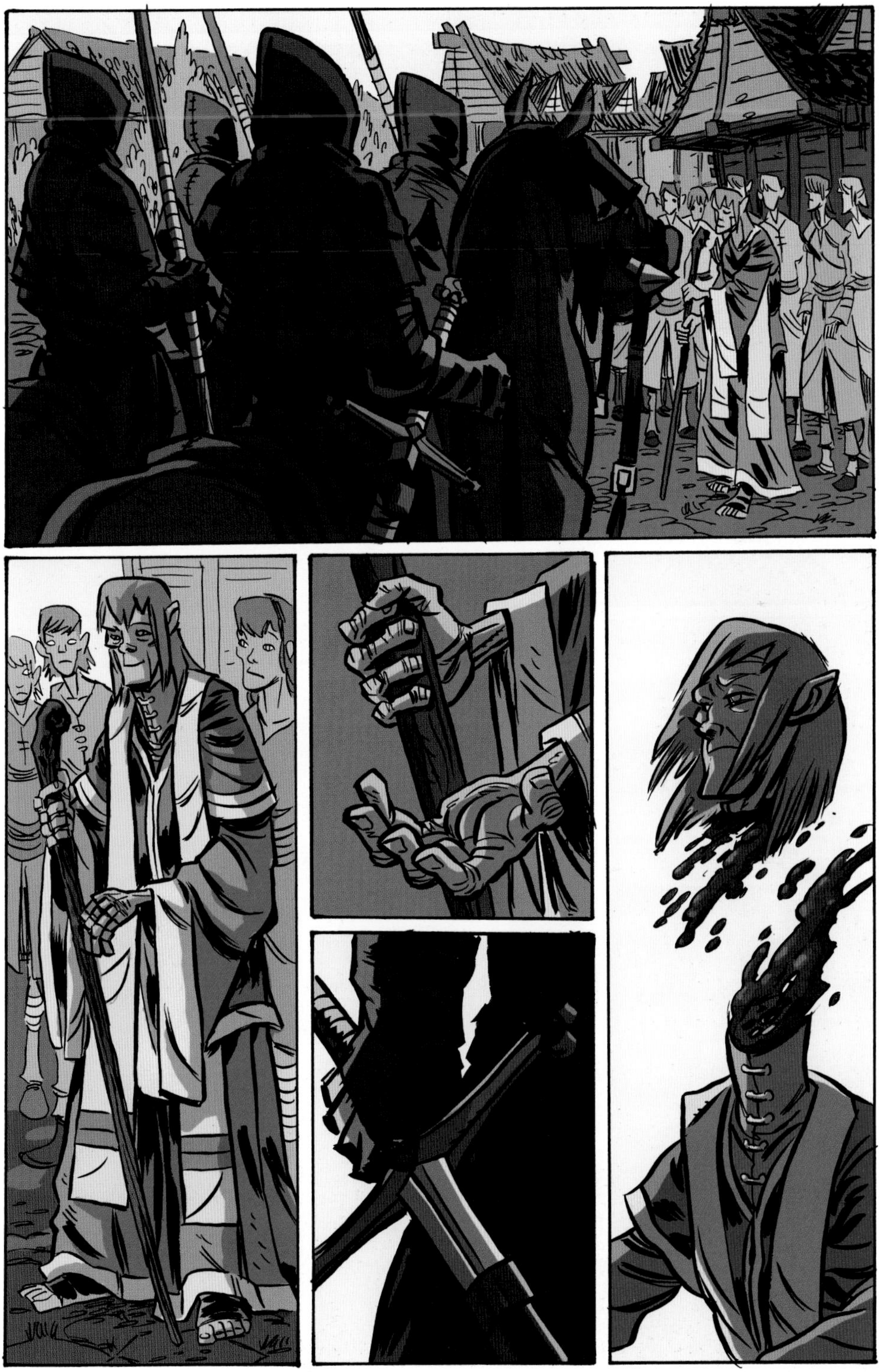

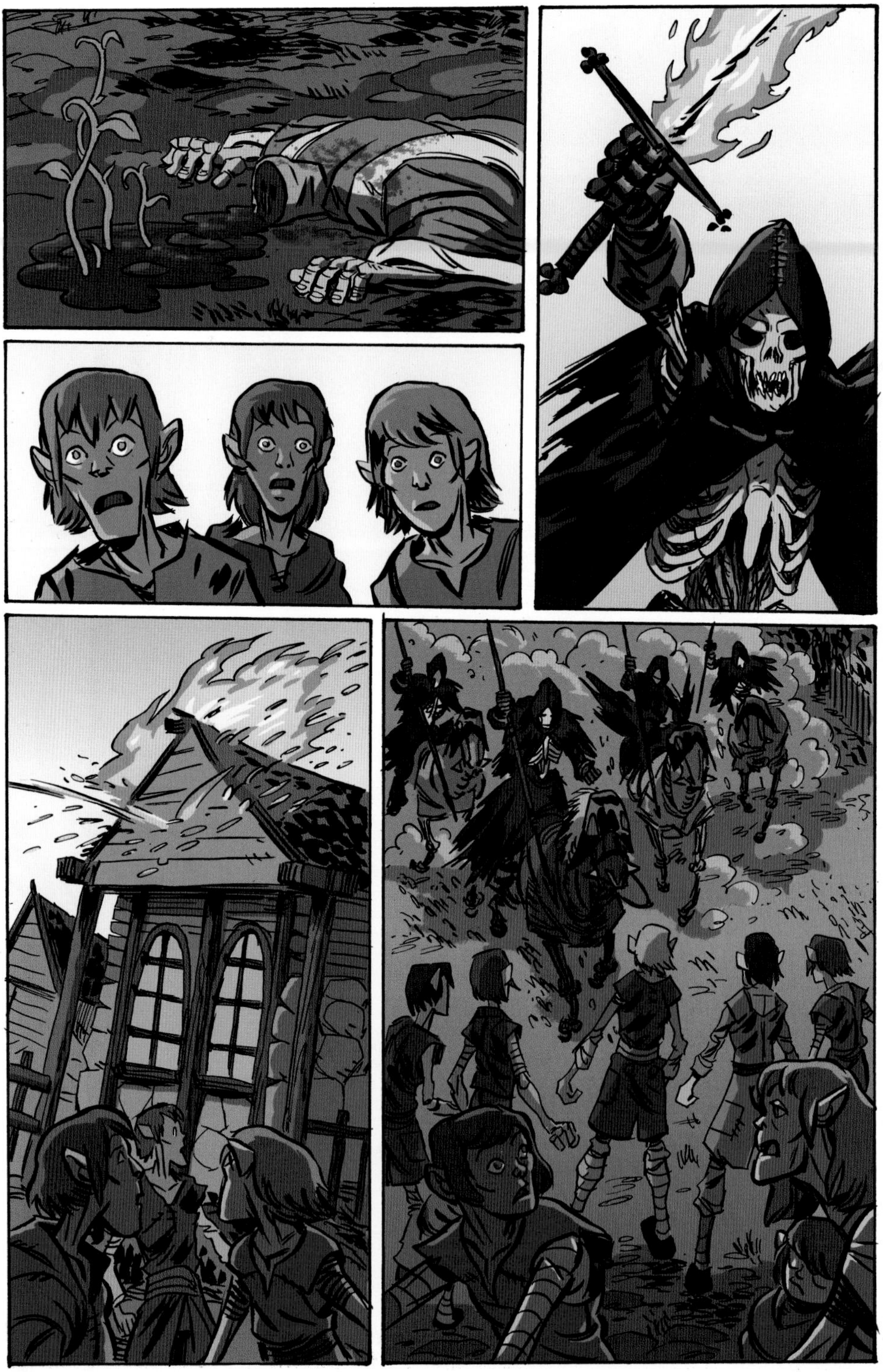

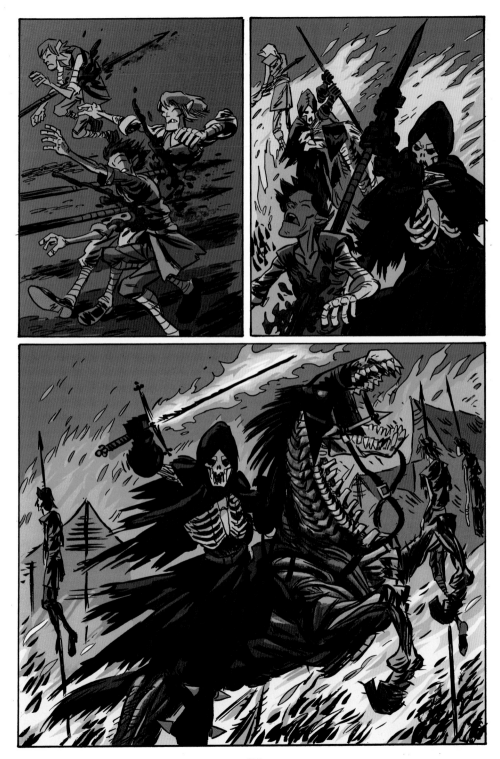

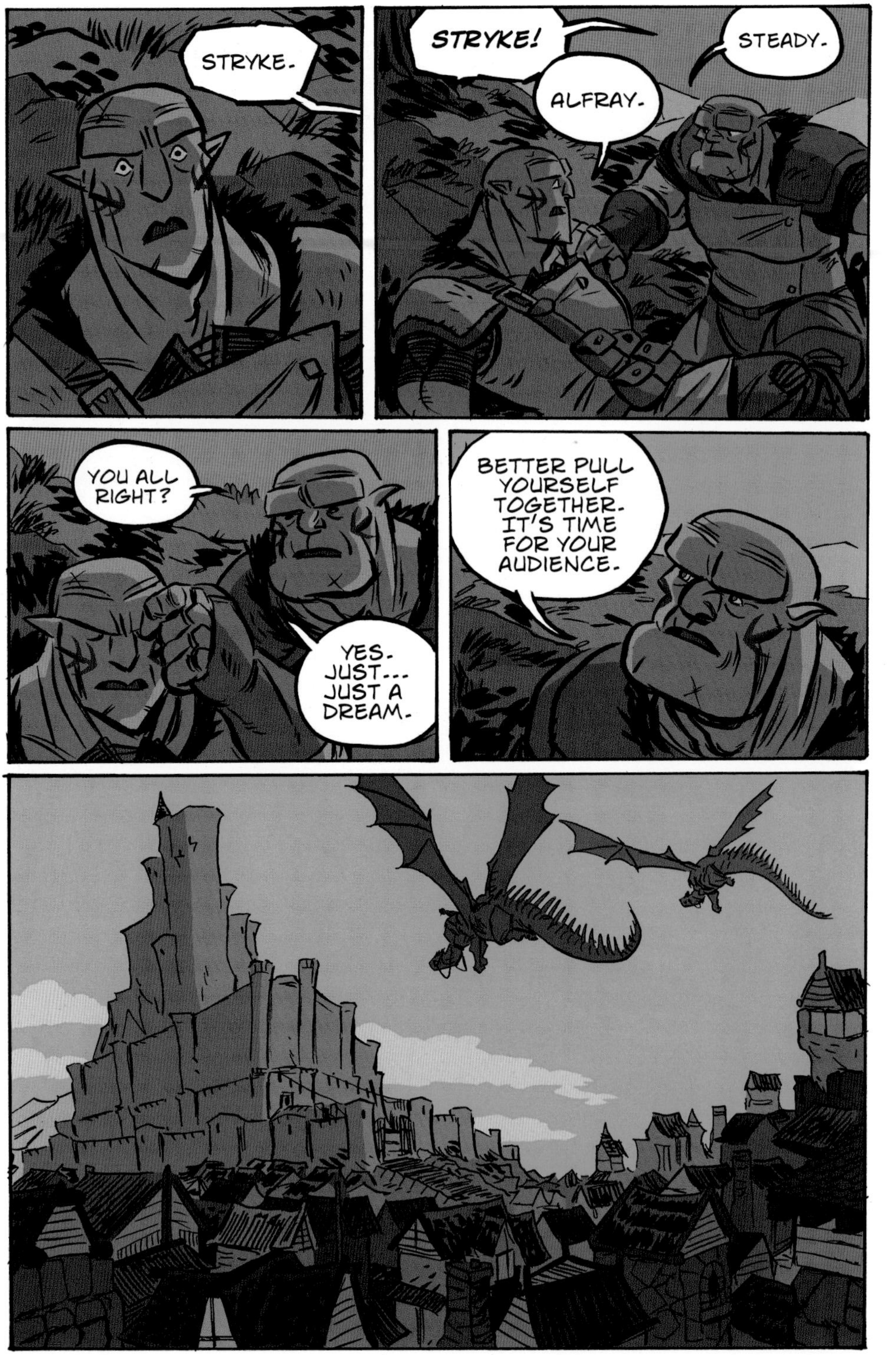
STRYKE.
STRYKE!
ALFRAY.
STEADY.
YOU ALL RIGHT?
YES. JUST... JUST A DREAM.
BETTER PULL YOURSELF TOGETHER. IT'S TIME FOR YOUR AUDIENCE.

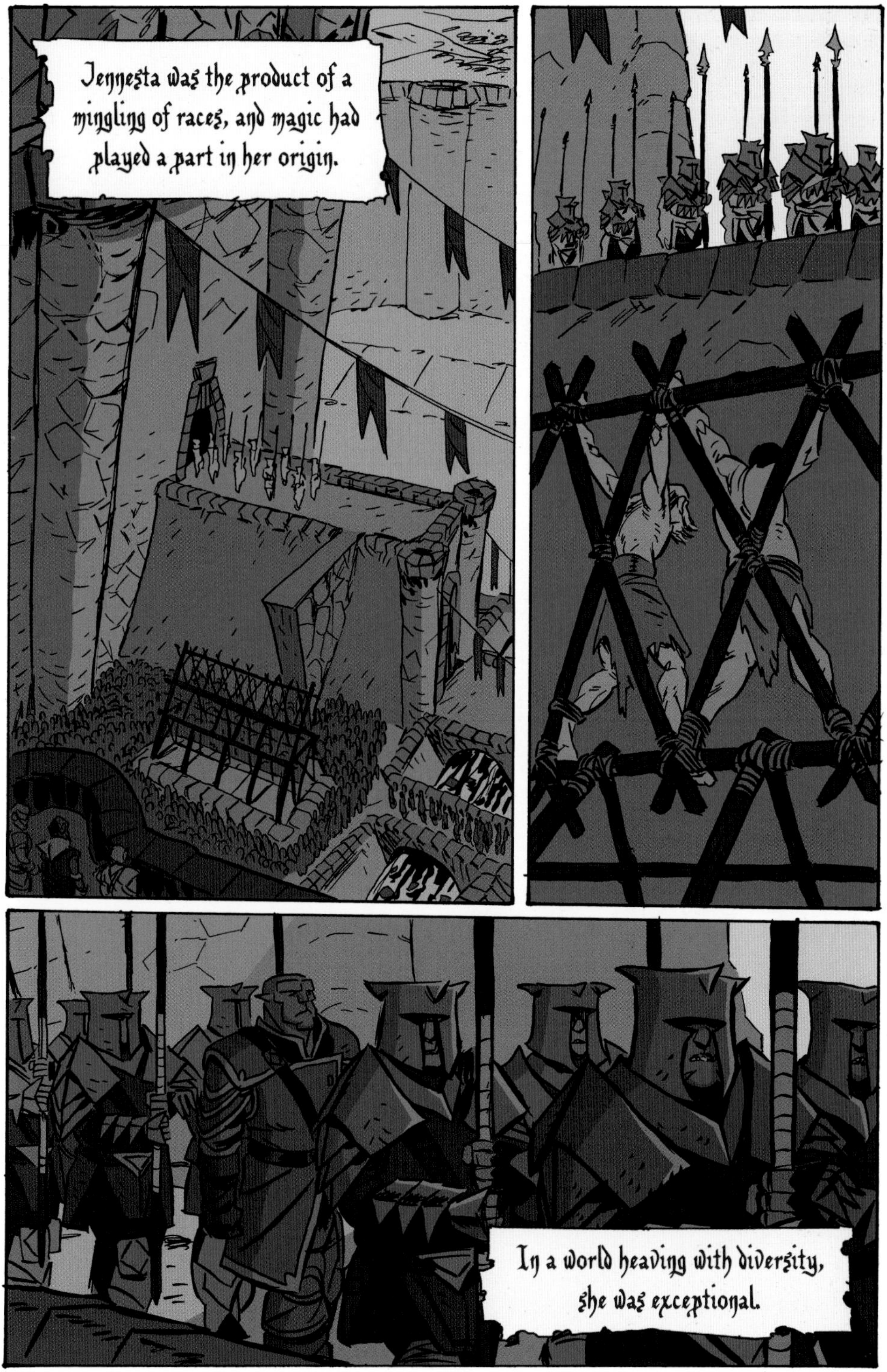
Jennesta was the product of a mingling of races, and magic had played a part in her origin.
In a world heaving with diversity, she was exceptional.

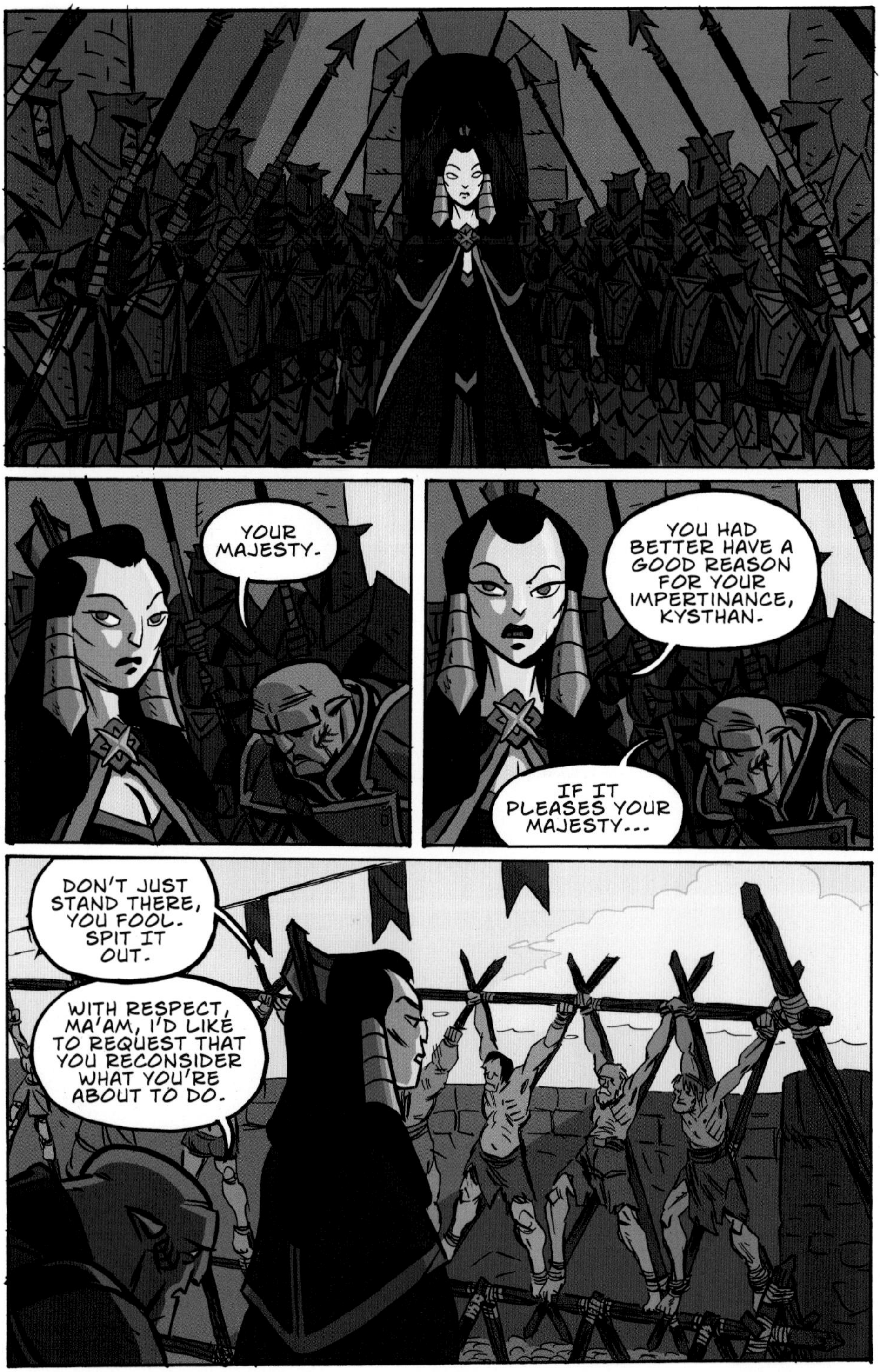
YOUR MAJESTY.
YOU HAD BETTER HAVE A GOOD REASON FOR YOUR IMPERTINANCE, KYSTHAN.
IF IT PLEASES YOUR MAJESTY...
DON'T JUST STAND THERE, YOU FOOL. SPIT IT OUT.
WITH RESPECT, MA'AM, I'D LIKE TO REQUEST THAT YOU RECONSIDER WHAT YOU'RE ABOUT TO DO.

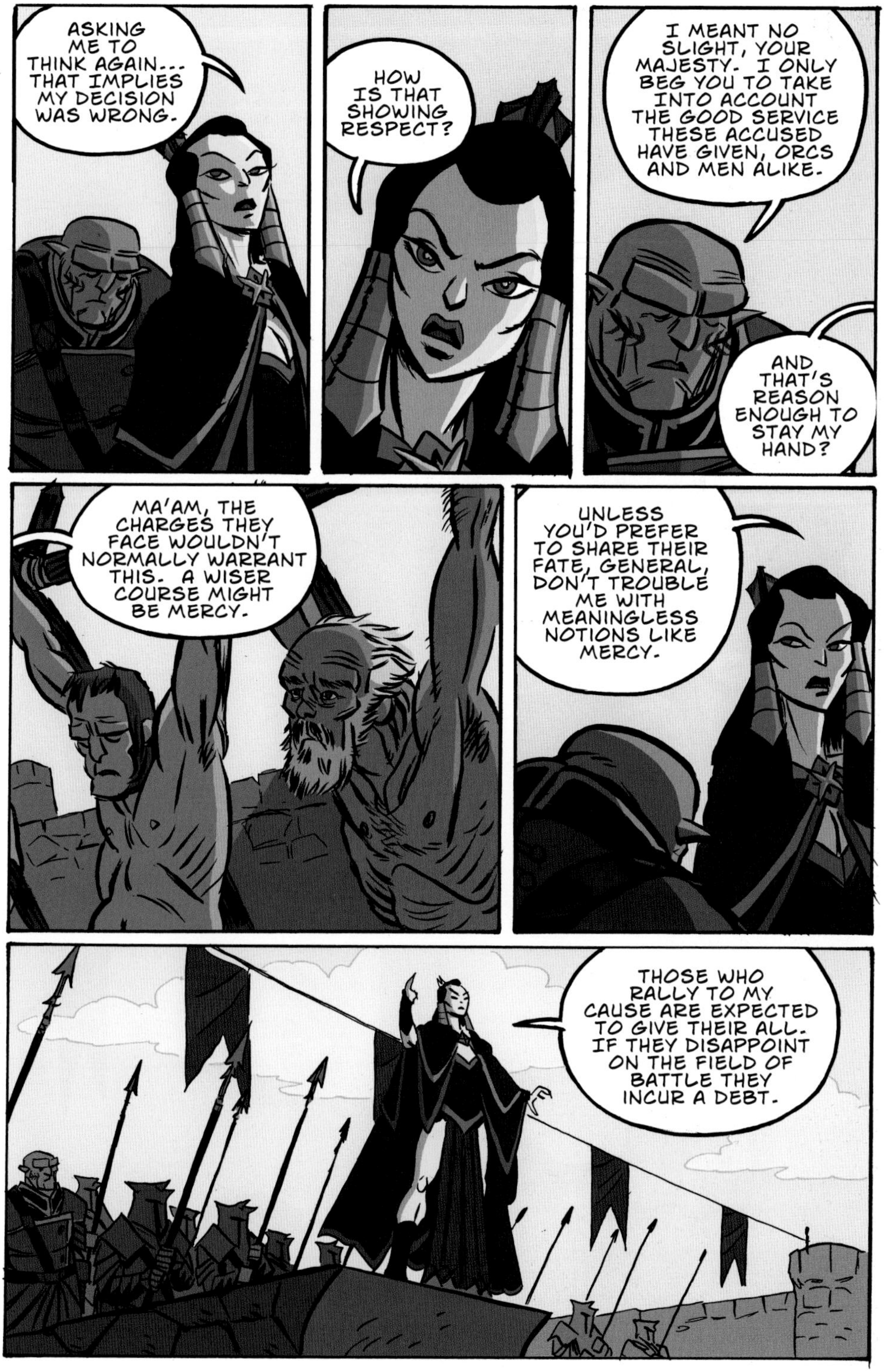
ASKING ME TO THINK AGAIN... THAT IMPLIES MY DECISION WAS WRONG.
HOW IS THAT SHOWING RESPECT?
I MEANT NO SLIGHT, YOUR MAJESTY. I ONLY BEG YOU TO TAKE INTO ACCOUNT THE GOOD SERVICE THESE ACCUSED HAVE GIVEN, ORCS AND MEN ALIKE.
AND THAT'S REASON ENOUGH TO STAY MY HAND?
MA'AM, THE CHARGES THEY FACE WOULDN'T NORMALLY WARRANT THIS. A WISER COURSE MIGHT BE MERCY.
UNLESS YOU'D PREFER TO SHARE THEIR FATE, GENERAL, DON'T TROUBLE ME WITH MEANINGLESS NOTIONS LIKE MERCY.
THOSE WHO RALLY TO MY CAUSE ARE EXPECTED TO GIVE THEIR ALL. IF THEY DISAPPOINT ON THE FIELD OF BATTLE THEY INCUR A DEBT.

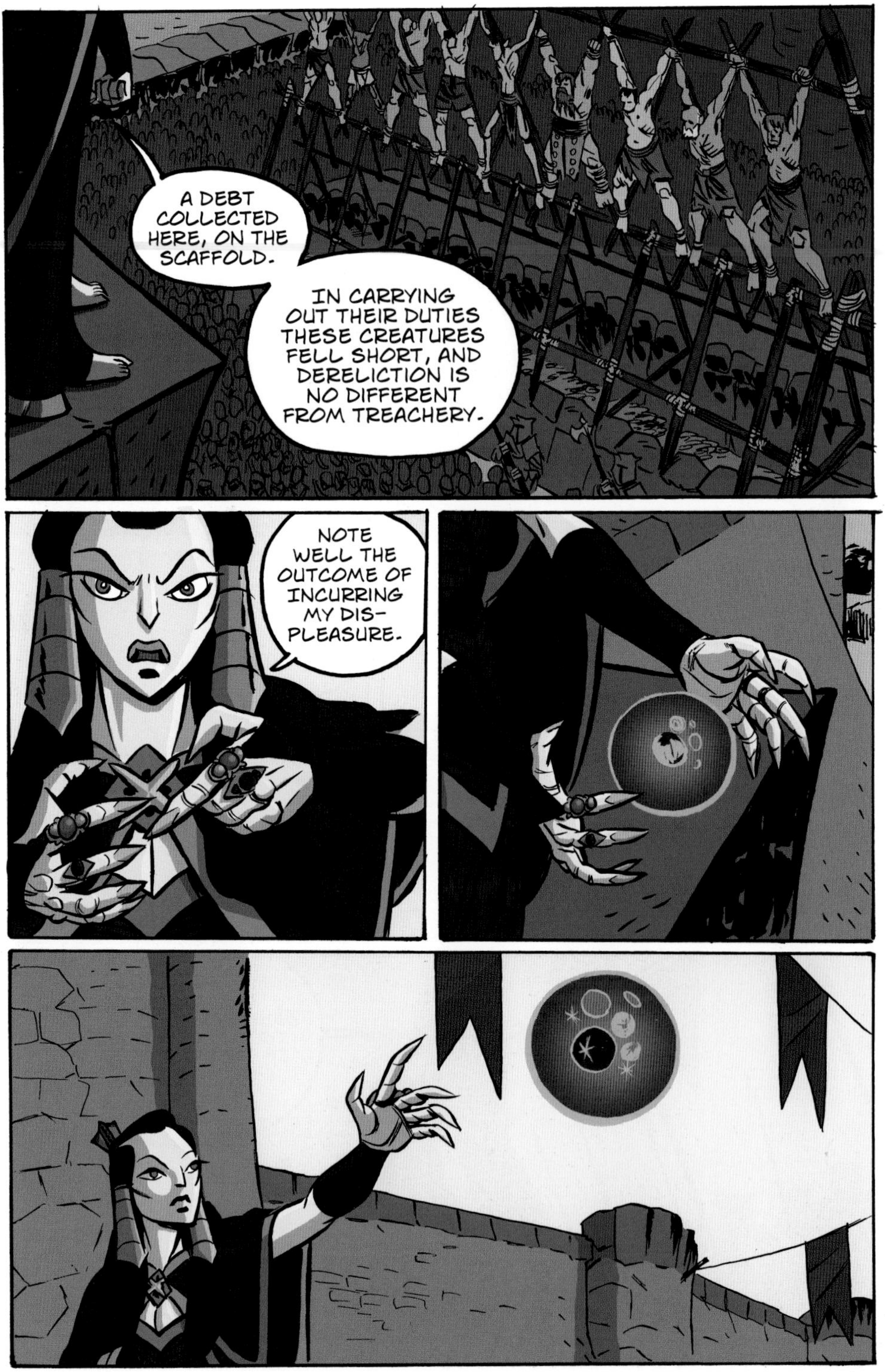
A DEBT COLLECTED HERE, ON THE SCAFFOLD.
IN CARRYING OUT THEIR DUTIES THESE CREATURES FELL SHORT, AND DERELICTION IS NO DIFFERENT FROM TREACHERY.
NOTE WELL THE OUTCOME OF INCURRING MY DIS- PLEASURE.

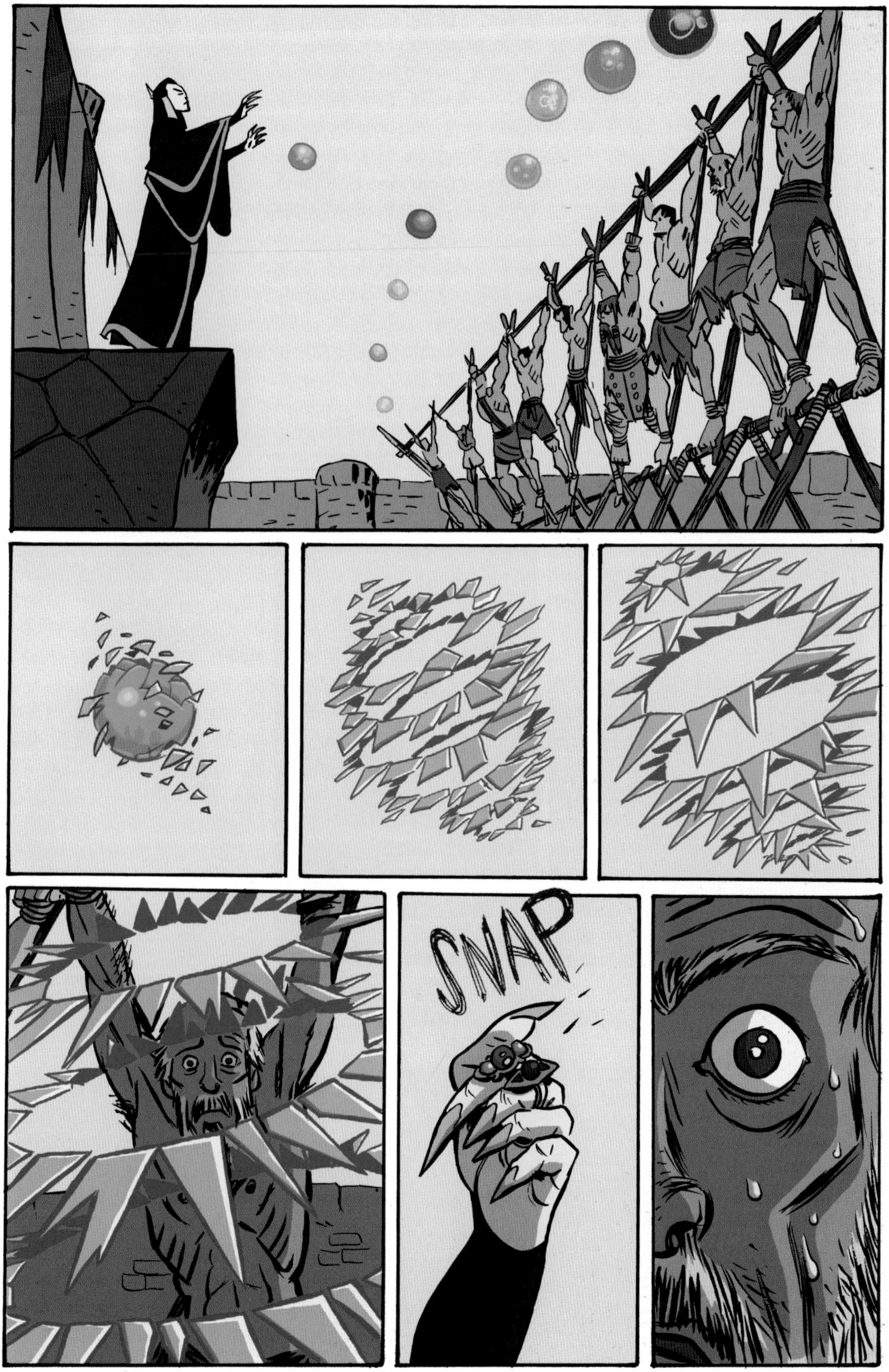
SNAP

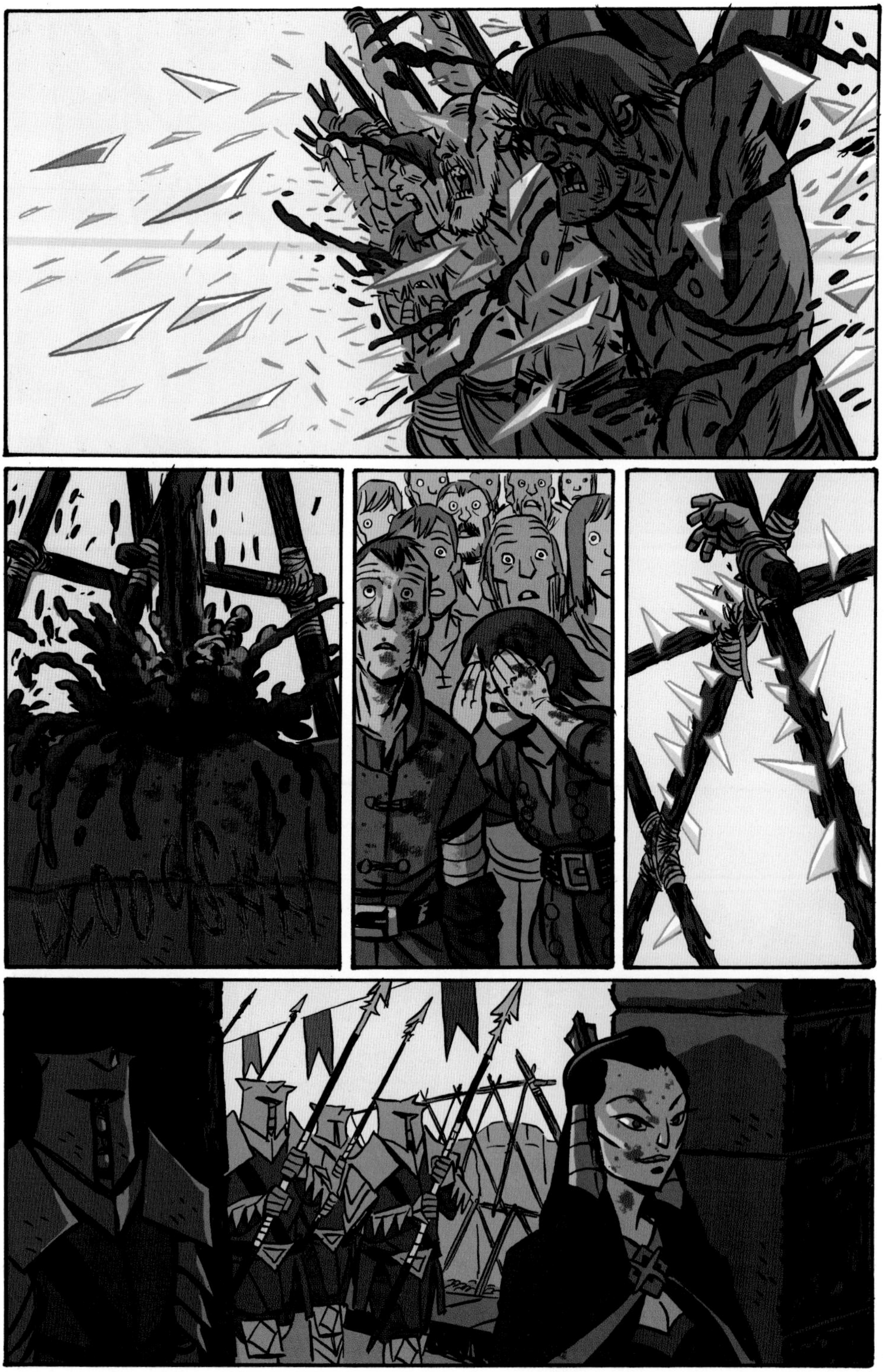

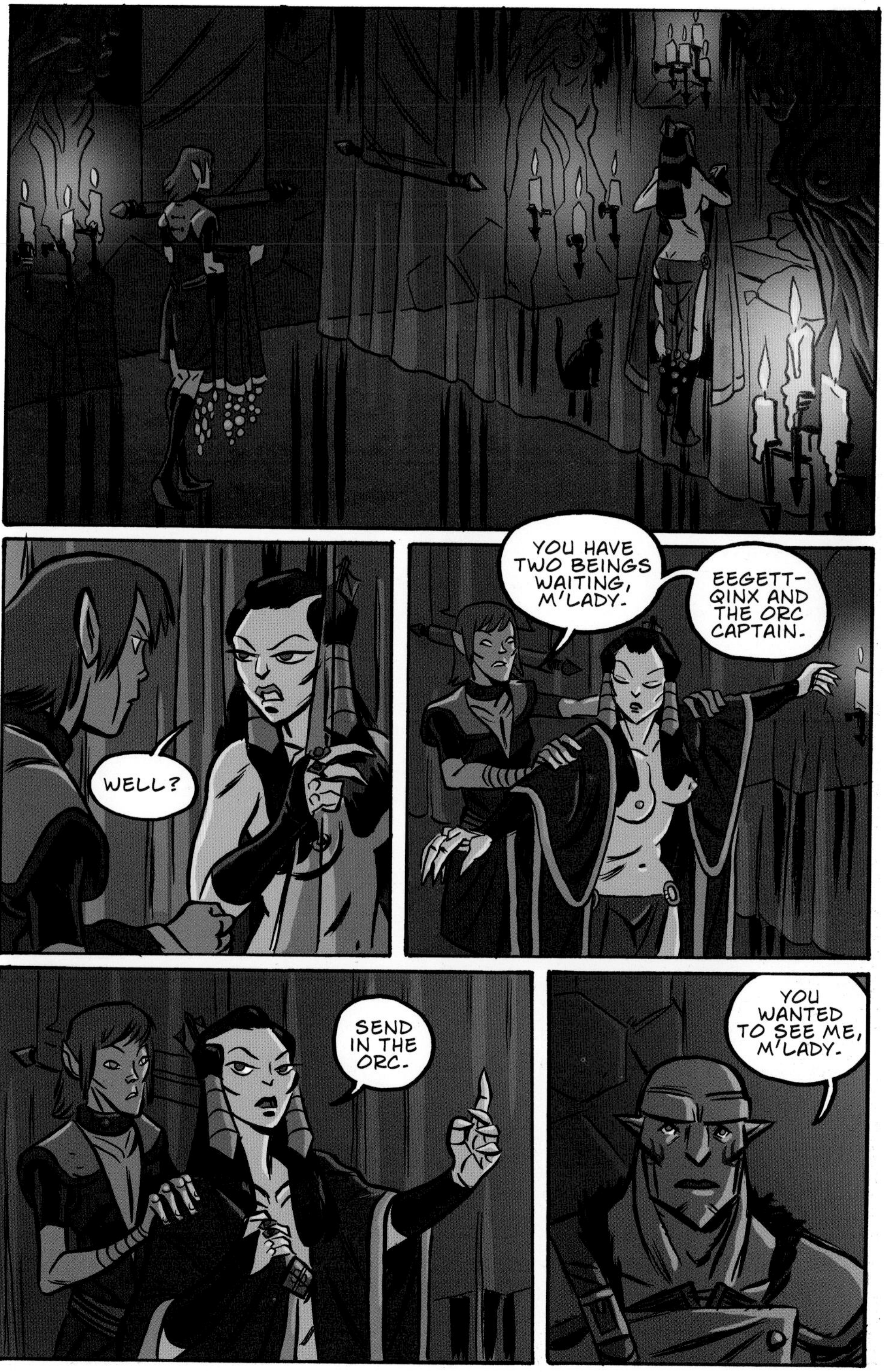
WELL?
YOU HAVE TWO BEINGS WAITING, M'LADY.
EEGETT-QINX AND THE ORC CAPTAIN.
SEND IN THE ORC.
YOU WANTED TO SEE ME, M'LADY.

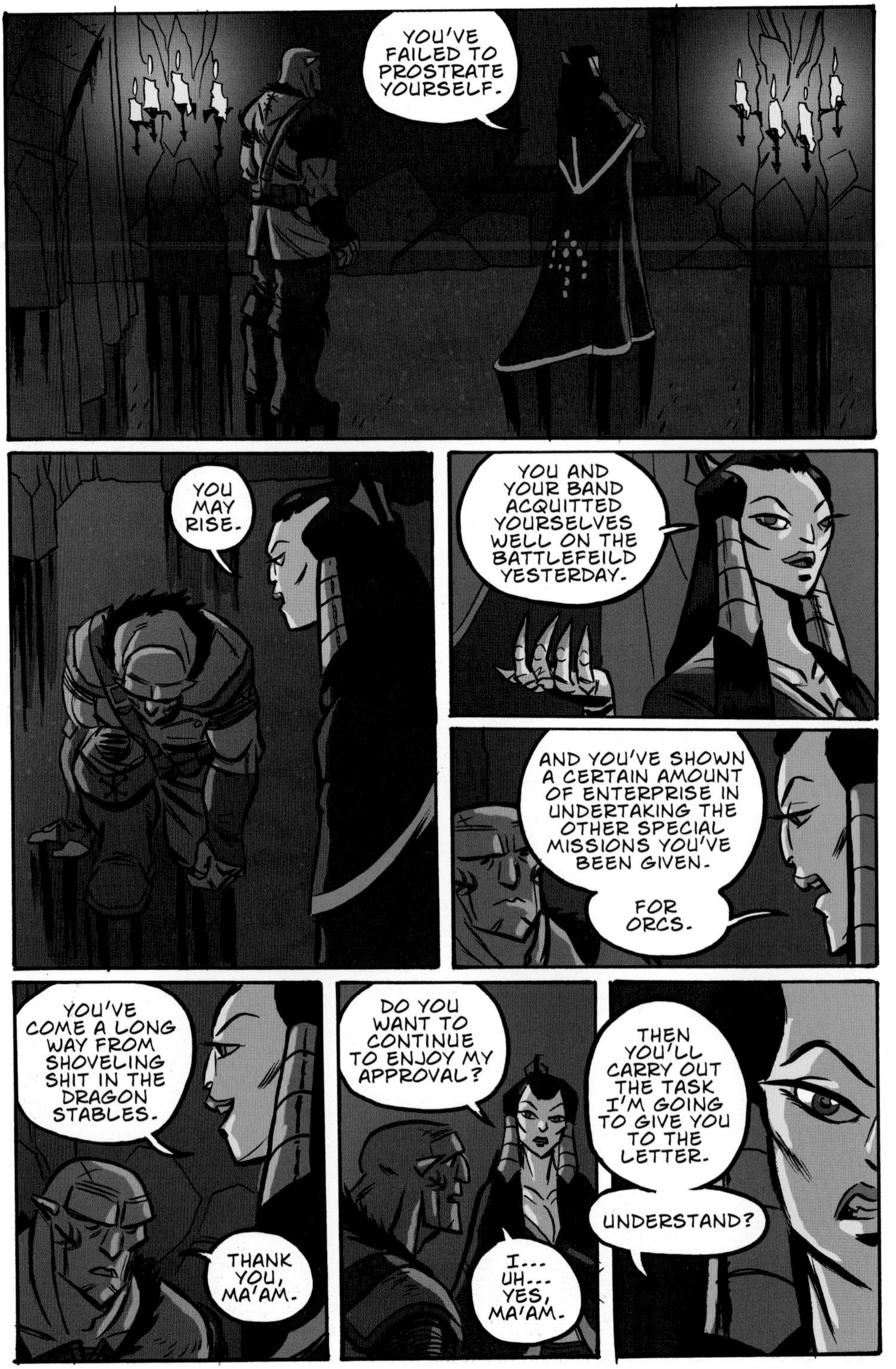
YOU'VE FAILED TO PROSTRATE YOURSELF.
YOU MAY RISE.
YOU AND YOUR BAND ACQUITTED YOURSELVES WELL ON THE BATTLEFEILD YESTERDAY.
AND YOU'VE SHOWN A CERTAIN AMOUNT OF ENTERPRISE IN UNDERTAKING THE OTHER SPECIAL MISSIONS YOU'VE BEEN GIVEN.
FOR ORCS.
YOU'VE COME A LONG WAY FROM SHOVELING SHIT IN THE DRAGON STABLES.
THANK YOU, MA'AM.
DO YOU WANT TO CONTINUE TO ENJOY MY APPROVAL?
I... UH... YES, MA'AM.
THEN YOU'LL CARRY OUT THE TASK I'M GOING TO GIVE YOU TO THE LETTER.
UNDERSTAND?

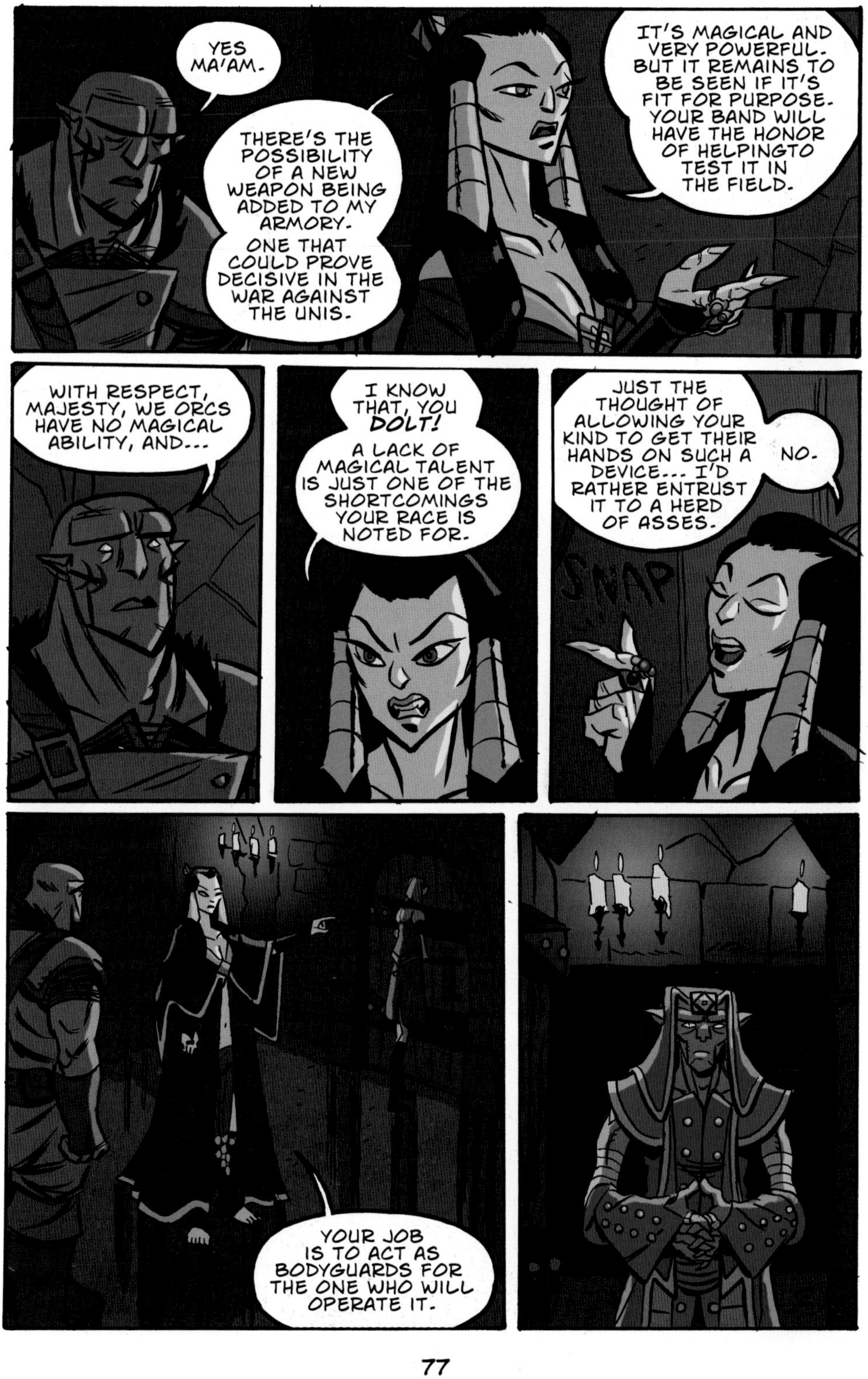
YES MA'AM.
THERE'S THE POSSIBILITY OF A NEW WEAPON BEING ADDED TO MY ARMORY.
ONE THAT COULD PROVE DECISIVE IN THE WAR AGAINST THE UNIS.
IT'S MAGICAL AND VERY POWERFUL. BUT IT REMAINS TO BE SEEN IF IT'S FIT FOR PURPOSE. YOUR BAND WILL HAVE THE HONOR OF HELPINGTO TEST IT IN THE FIELD.
WITH RESPECT, MAJESTY, WE ORCS HAVE NO MAGICAL ABILITY, AND...
I KNOW THAT, YOU DOLT!
A LACK OF MAGICAL TALENT IS JUST ONE OF THE SHORTCOMINGS YOUR RACE IS NOTED FOR.
JUST THE THOUGHT OF ALLOWING YOUR KIND TO GET THEIR HANDS ON SUCH A DEVICE... I'D RATHER ENTRUST IT TO A HERD OF ASSES.
NO.
SNAP
YOUR JOB IS TO ACT AS BODYGUARDS FOR THE ONE WHO WILL OPERATE IT.

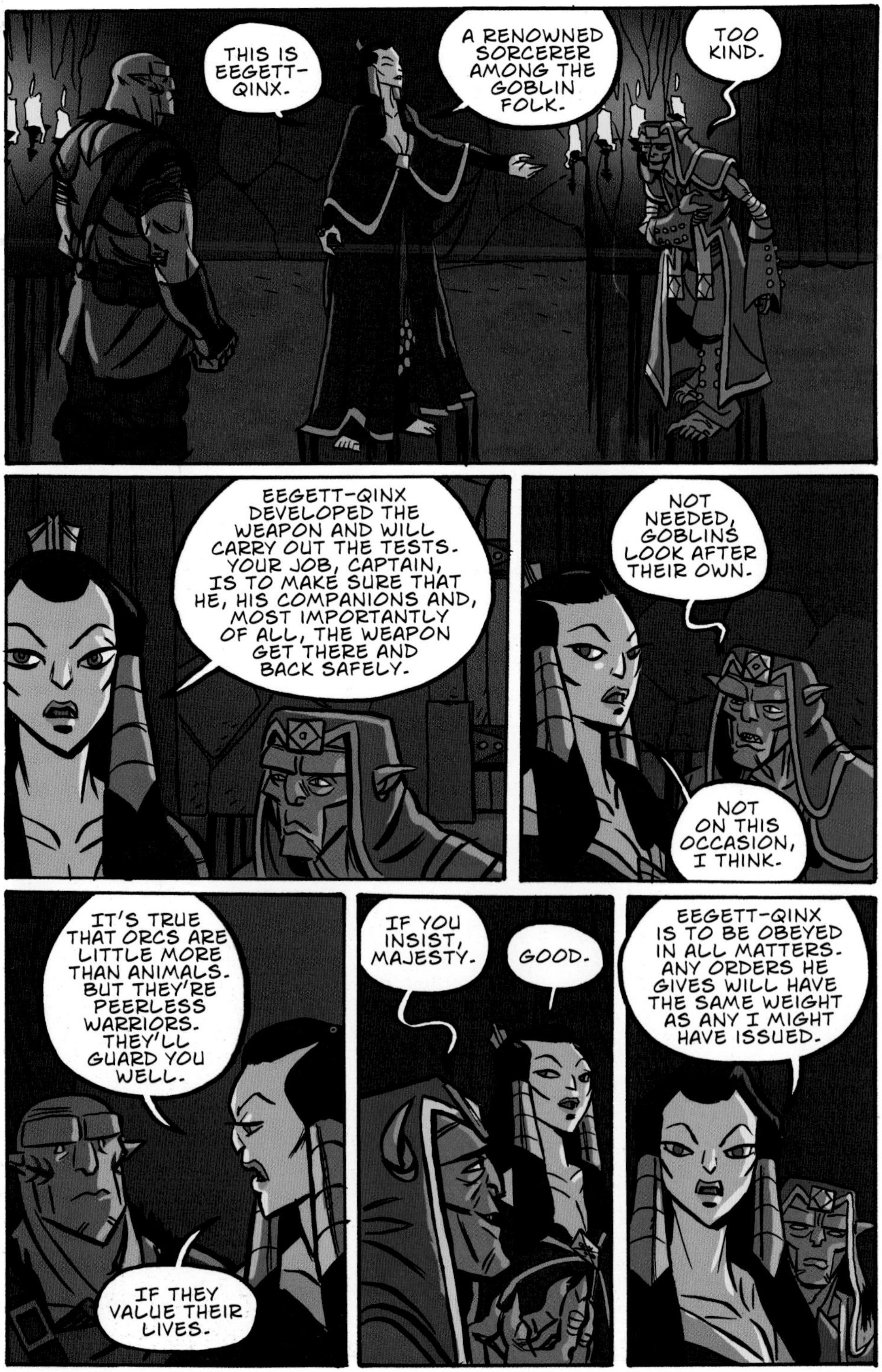
THIS IS EEGETT-QINX.
A RENOWNED SORCERER AMONG THE GOBLIN FOLK.
TOO KIND.
EEGETT-QINX DEVELOPED THE WEAPON AND WILL CARRY OUT THE TESTS. YOUR JOB, CAPTAIN, IS TO MAKE SURE THAT HE, HIS COMPANIONS AND, MOST IMPORTANTLY OF ALL, THE WEAPON GET THERE AND BACK SAFELY.
NOT NEEDED, GOBLINS LOOK AFTER THEIR OWN.
NOT ON THIS OCCASION, I THINK.
IT'S TRUE THAT ORCS ARE LITTLE MORE THAN ANIMALS. BUT THEY'RE PEERLESS WARRIORS. THEY'LL GUARD YOU WELL.
IF THEY VALUE THEIR LIVES.
IF YOU INSIST, MAJESTY.
GOOD.
EEGETT-QINX IS TO BE OBEYED IN ALL MATTERS. ANY ORDERS HE GIVES WILL HAVE THE SAME WEIGHT AS ANY I MIGHT HAVE ISSUED.

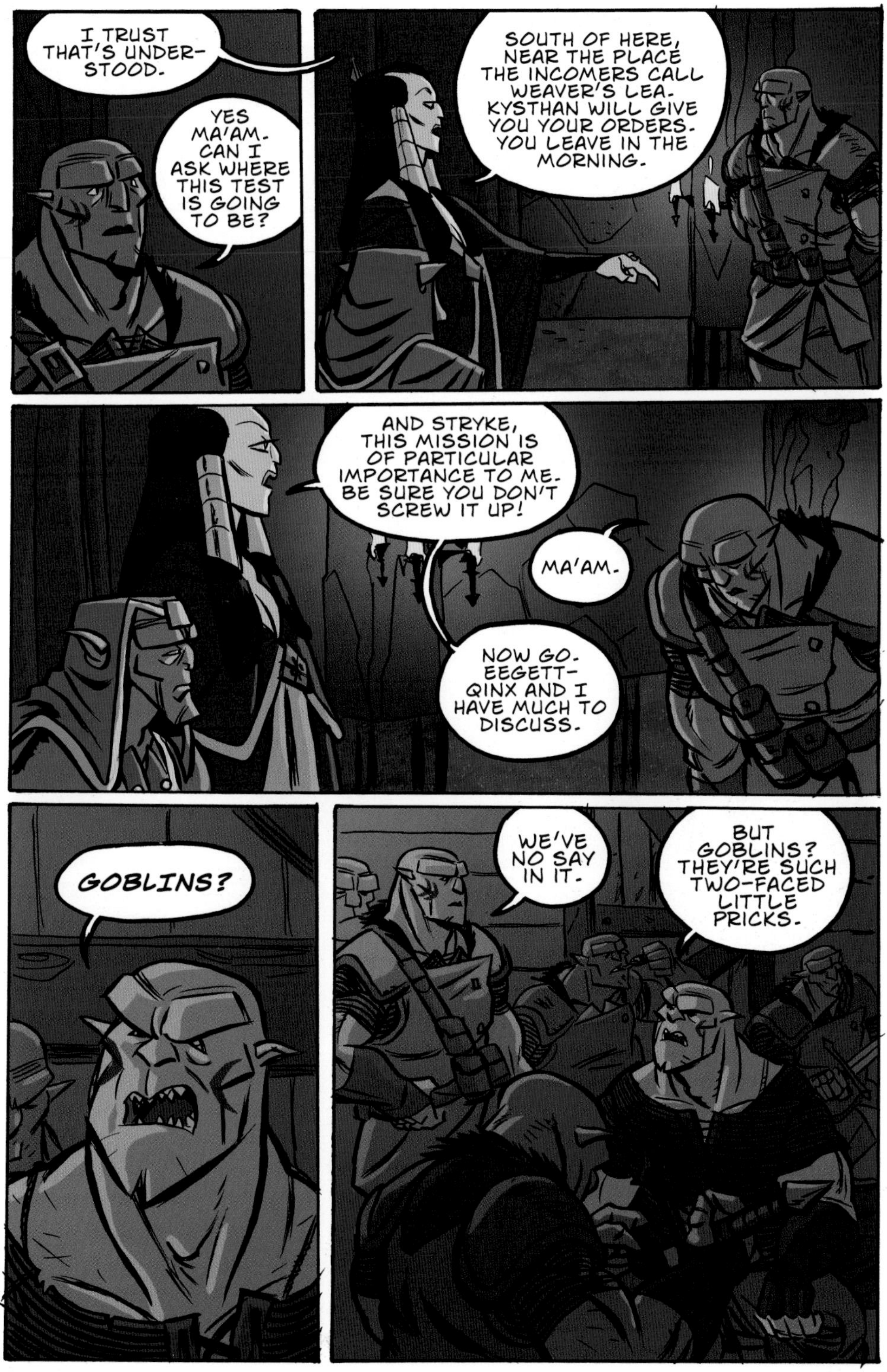
I TRUST THAT'S UNDER-STOOD.
YES MA'AM. CAN I ASK WHERE THIS TEST IS GOING TO BE?
SOUTH OF HERE, NEAR THE PLACE THE INCOMERS CALL WEAVER'S LEA. KYSTHAN WILL GIVE YOU YOUR ORDERS. YOU LEAVE IN THE MORNING.
AND STRYKE, THIS MISSION IS OF PARTICULAR IMPORTANCE TO ME. BE SURE YOU DON'T SCREW IT UP!
MA'AM.
NOW GO. EEGETT-QINX AND I HAVE MUCH TO DISCUSS.
GOBLINS?
WE'VE NO SAY IN IT.
BUT GOBLINS? THEY'RE SUCH TWO-FACED LITTLE PRICKS.

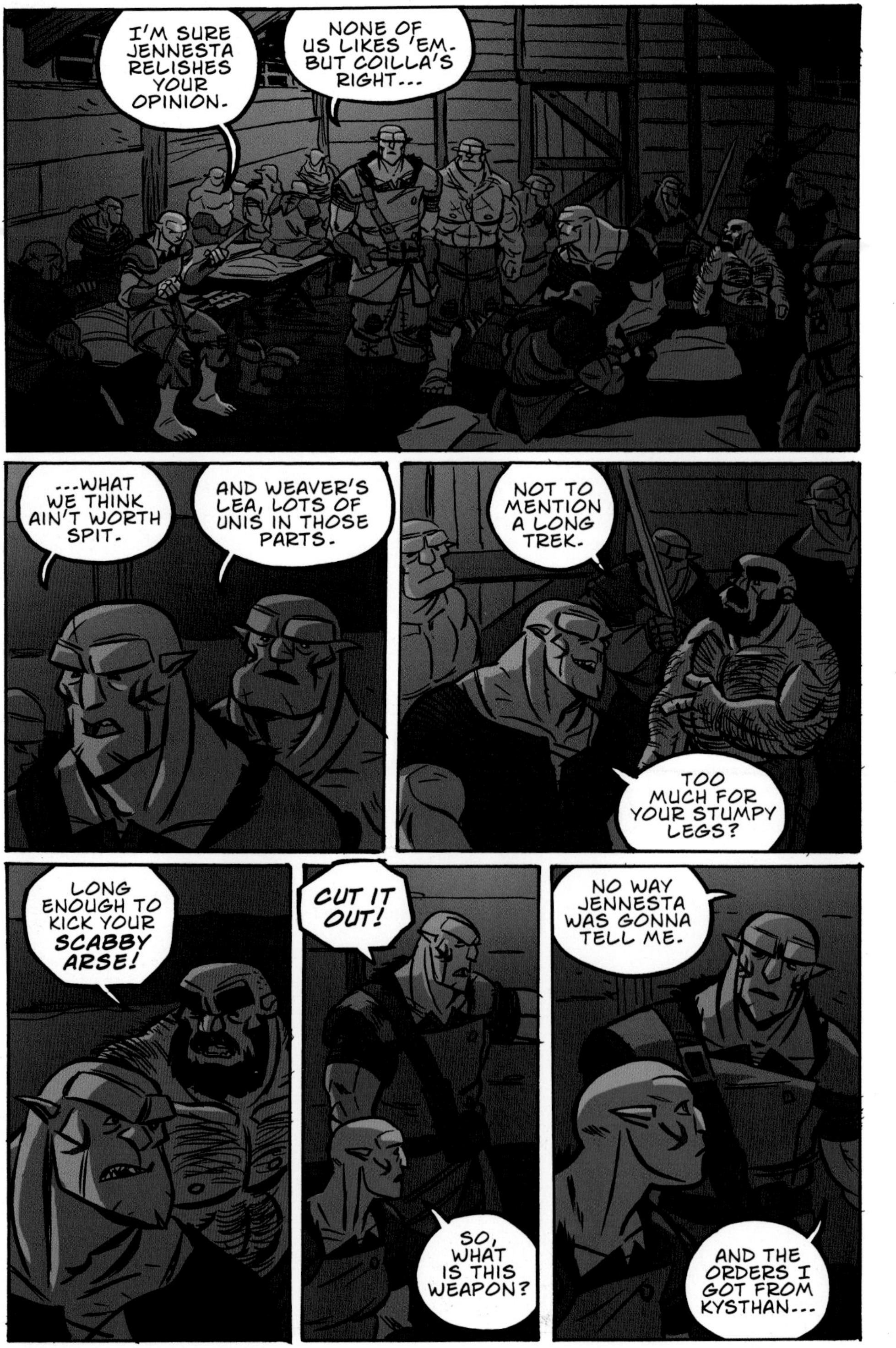
I'M SURE JENNESTA RELISHES YOUR OPINION.
NONE OF US LIKES 'EM. BUT COILLA'S RIGHT...
...WHAT WE THINK AIN'T WORTH SPIT.
AND WEAVER'S LEA, LOTS OF UNIS IN THOSE PARTS.
NOT TO MENTION A LONG TREK.
TOO MUCH FOR YOUR STUMPY LEGS?
LONG ENOUGH TO KICK YOUR SCABBY ARSE!
CUT IT OUT!
SO, WHAT IS THIS WEAPON?
NO WAY JENNESTA WAS GONNA TELL ME.
AND THE ORDERS I GOT FROM KYSTHAN...

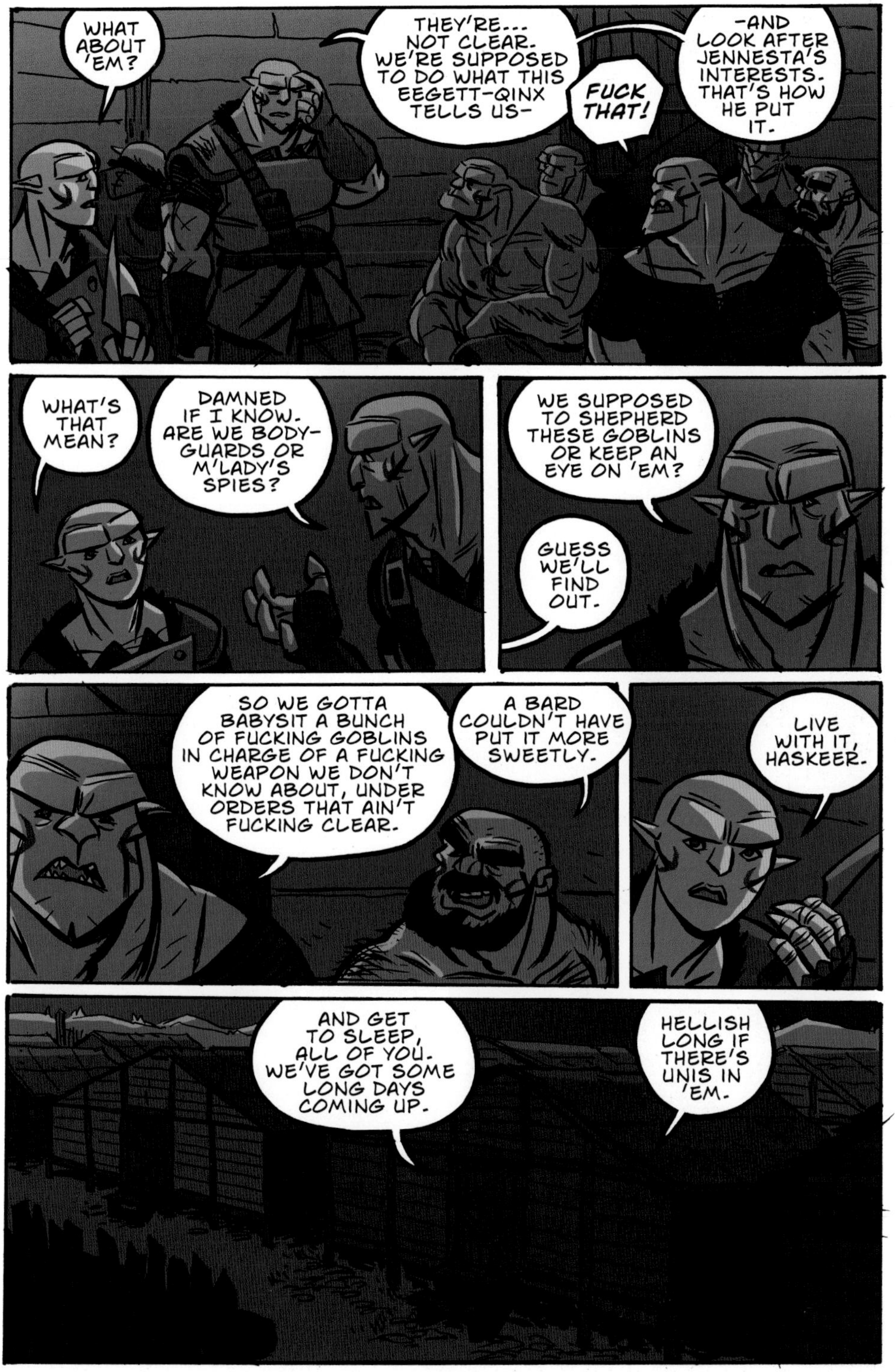
WHAT ABOUT 'EM?
THEY'RE... NOT CLEAR. WE'RE SUPPOSED TO DO WHAT THIS EEGETT-QINX TELLS US-
-AND LOOK AFTER JENNESTA'S INTERESTS. THAT'S HOW HE PUT IT.
FUCK THAT!
WHAT'S THAT MEAN?
DAMNED IF I KNOW. ARE WE BODY-GUARDS OR M'LADY'S SPIES?
WE SUPPOSED TO SHEPHERD THESE GOBLINS OR KEEP AN EYE ON 'EM?
GUESS WE'LL FIND OUT.
SO WE GOTTA BABYSIT A BUNCH OF FUCKING GOBLINS IN CHARGE OF A FUCKING WEAPON WE DON'T KNOW ABOUT, UNDER ORDERS THAT AIN'T FUCKING CLEAR.
A BARD COULDN'T HAVE PUT IT MORE SWEETLY.
LIVE WITH IT, HASKEER.
AND GET TO SLEEP, ALL OF YOU. WE'VE GOT SOME LONG DAYS COMING UP.
HELLISH LONG IF THERE'S UNIS IN 'EM.

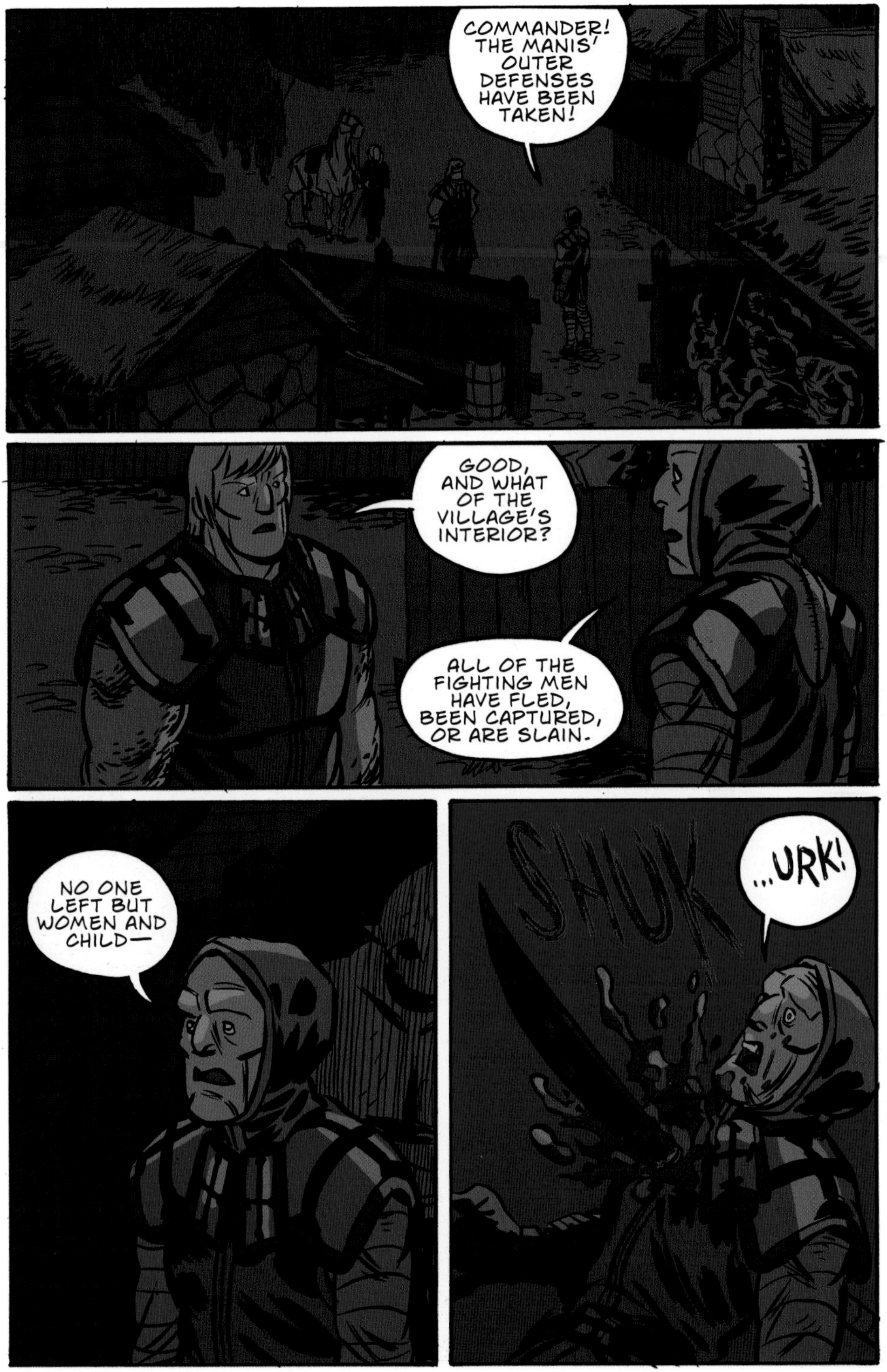
COMMANDER! THE MANIS' OUTER DEFENSES HAVE BEEN TAKEN!
GOOD, AND WHAT OF THE VILLAGE'S INTERIOR?
ALL OF THE FIGHTING MEN HAVE FLED, BEEN CAPTURED, OR ARE SLAIN.
NO ONE LEFT BUT WOMEN AND CHILD—
SHUK
...URK!

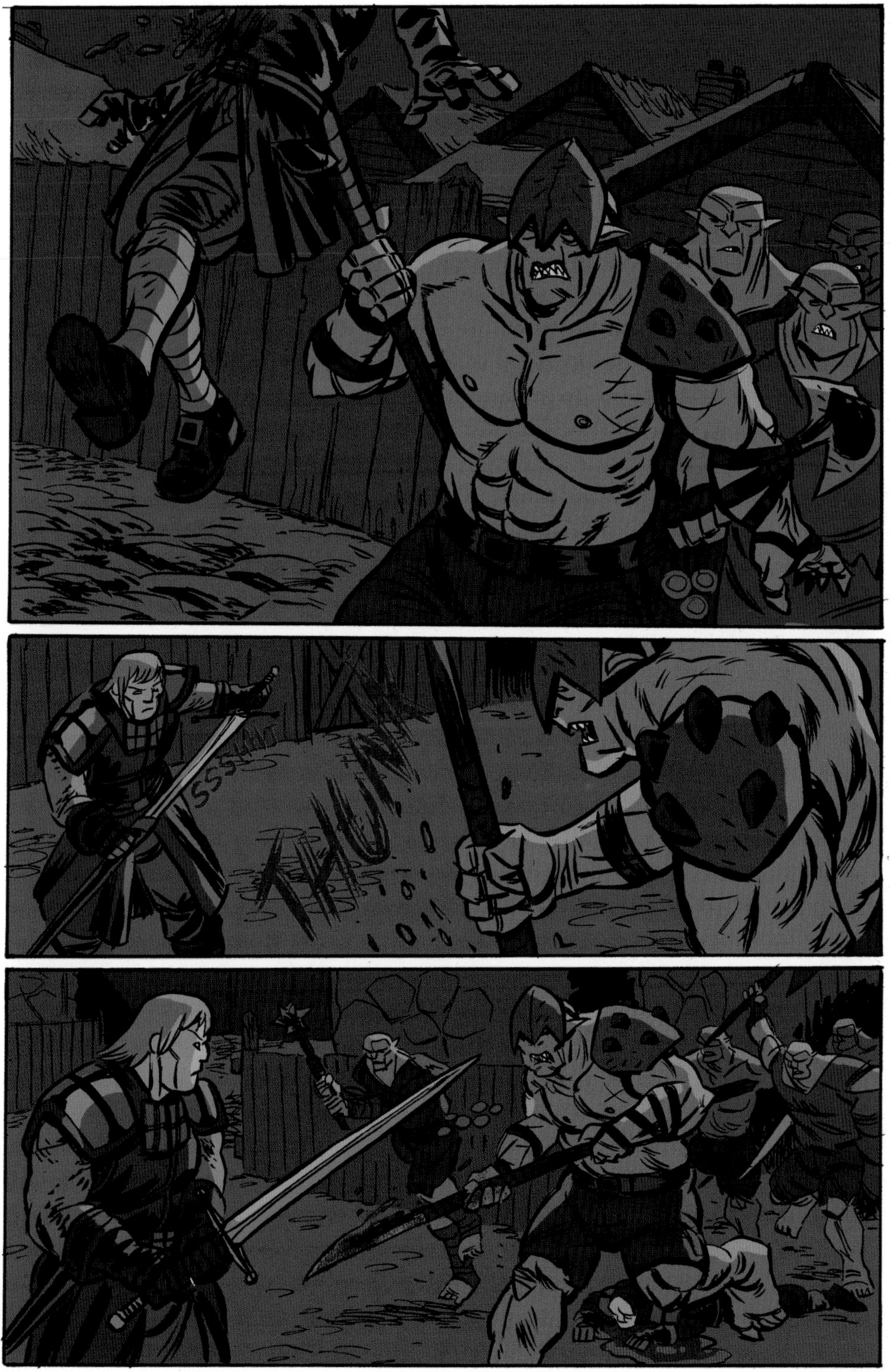
THUNK

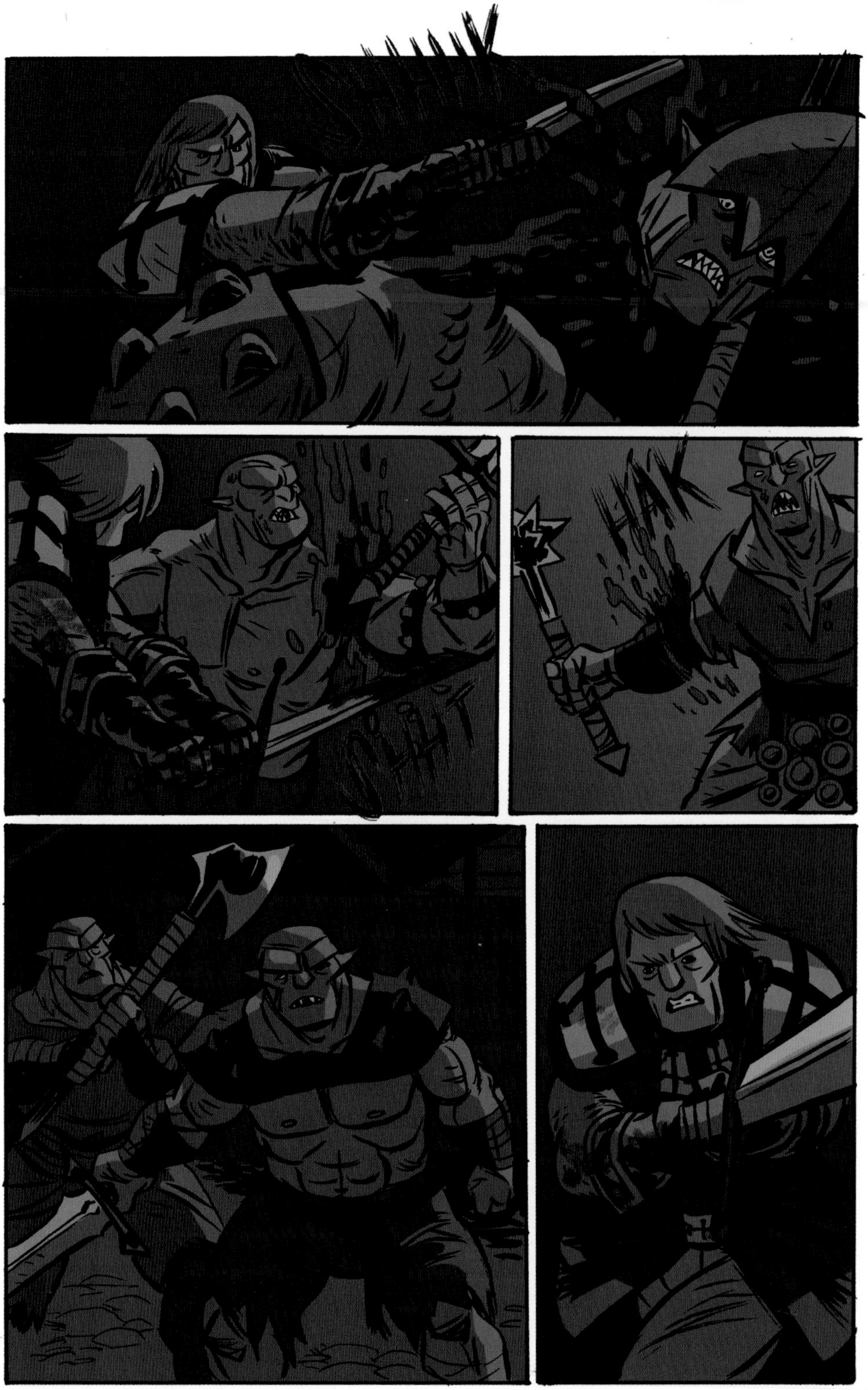
HAK

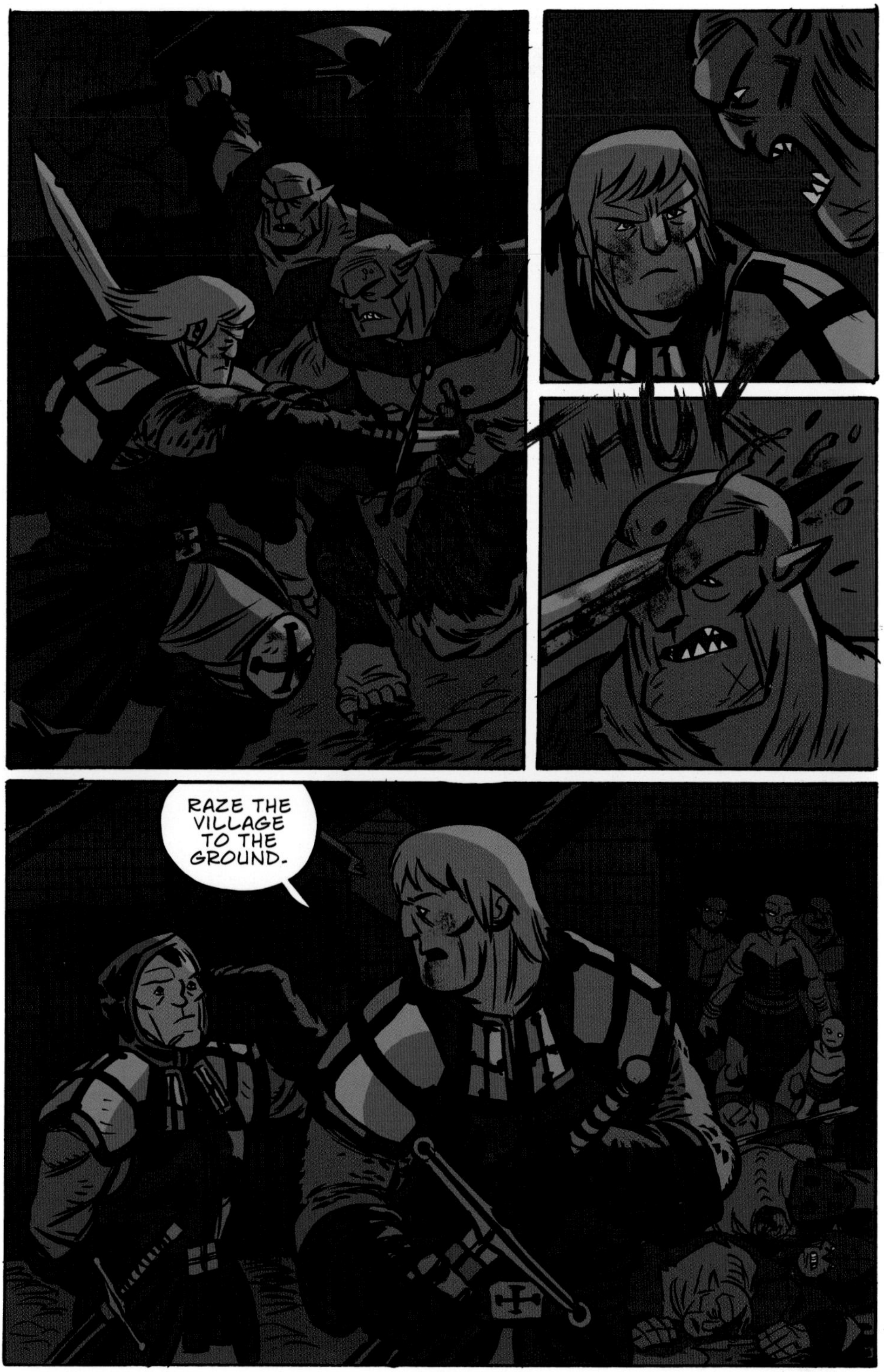
THUK
RAZE THE VILLAGE TO THE GROUND.

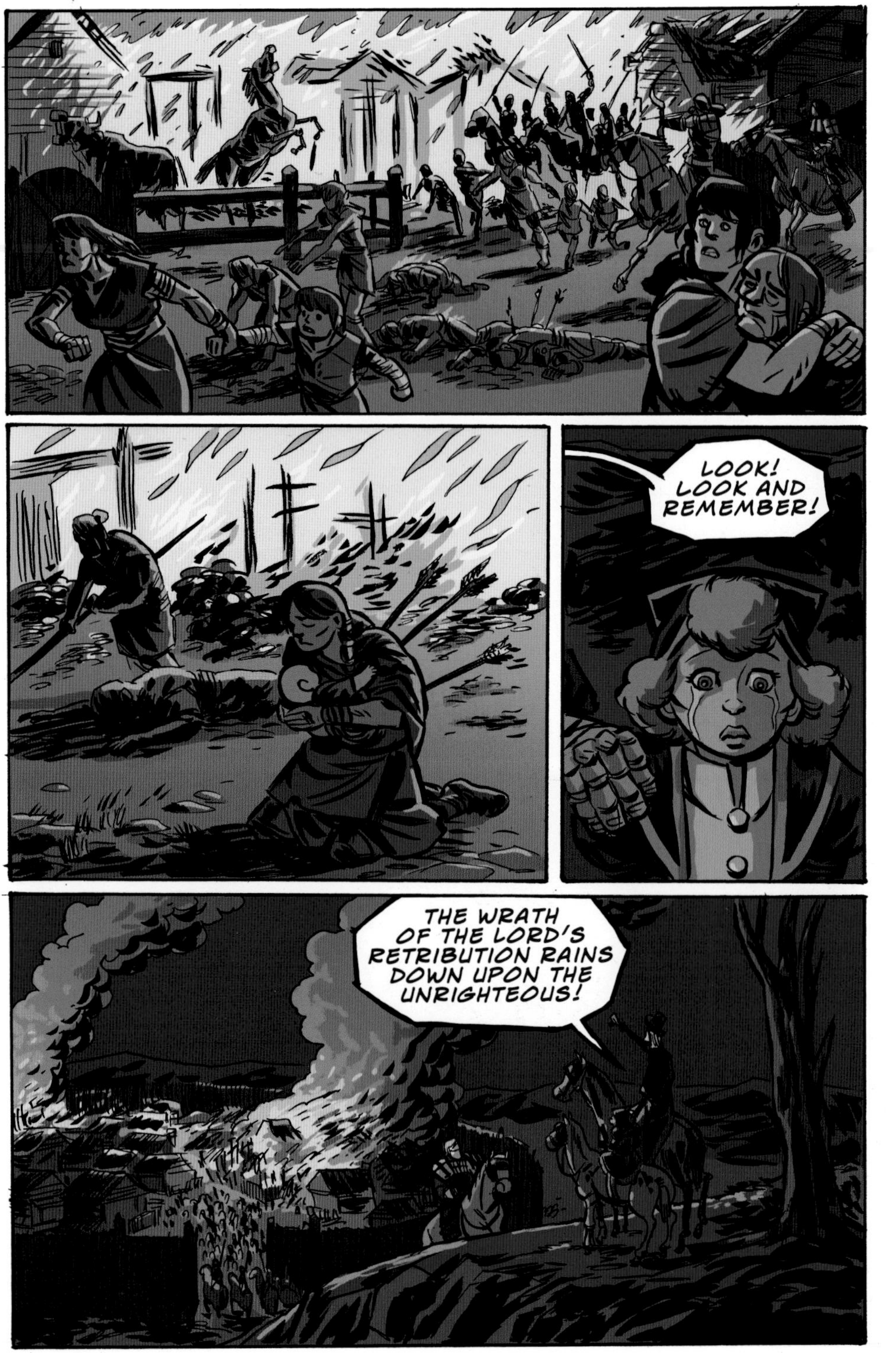
LOOK! LOOK AND REMEMBER!
THE WRATH OF THE LORD'S RETRIBUTION RAINS DOWN UPON THE UNRIGHTEOUS!

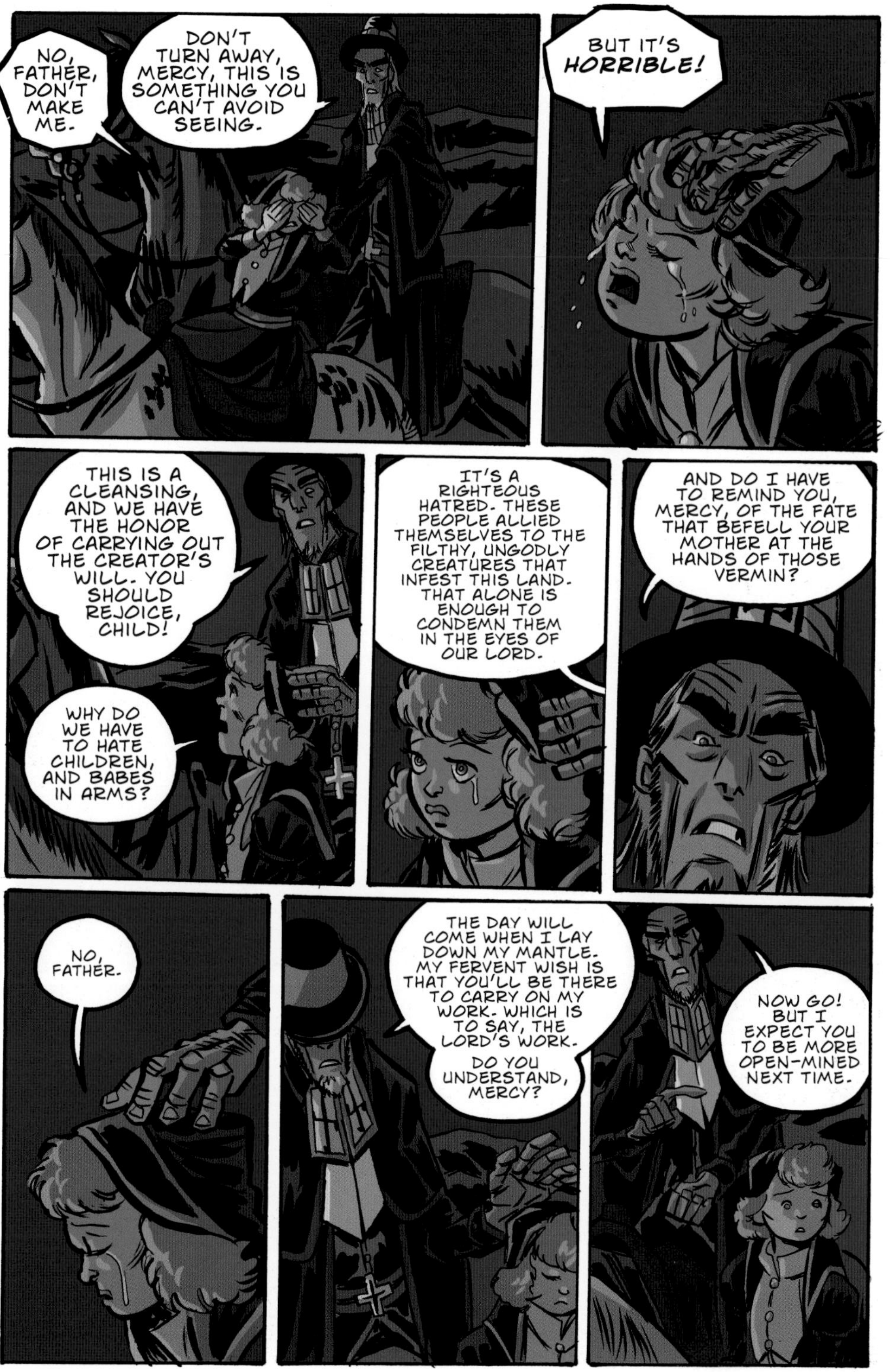
NO, FATHER, DON'T MAKE ME.
DON'T TURN AWAY, MERCY, THIS IS SOMETHING YOU CAN'T AVOID SEEING.
BUT IT'S *HORRIBLE!*
THIS IS A CLEANSING, AND WE HAVE THE HONOR OF CARRYING OUT THE CREATOR'S WILL. YOU SHOULD REJOICE, CHILD!
WHY DO WE HAVE TO HATE CHILDREN, AND BABES IN ARMS?
IT'S A RIGHTEOUS HATRED. THESE PEOPLE ALLIED THEMSELVES TO THE FILTHY, UNGODLY CREATURES THAT INFEST THIS LAND. THAT ALONE IS ENOUGH TO CONDEMN THEM IN THE EYES OF OUR LORD.
AND DO I HAVE TO REMIND YOU, MERCY, OF THE FATE THAT BEFELL YOUR MOTHER AT THE HANDS OF THOSE VERMIN?
NO, FATHER.
THE DAY WILL COME WHEN I LAY DOWN MY MANTLE. MY FERVENT WISH IS THAT YOU'LL BE THERE TO CARRY ON MY WORK. WHICH IS TO SAY, THE LORD'S WORK.
DO YOU UNDERSTAND, MERCY?
NOW GO! BUT I EXPECT YOU TO BE MORE OPEN-MINED NEXT TIME.

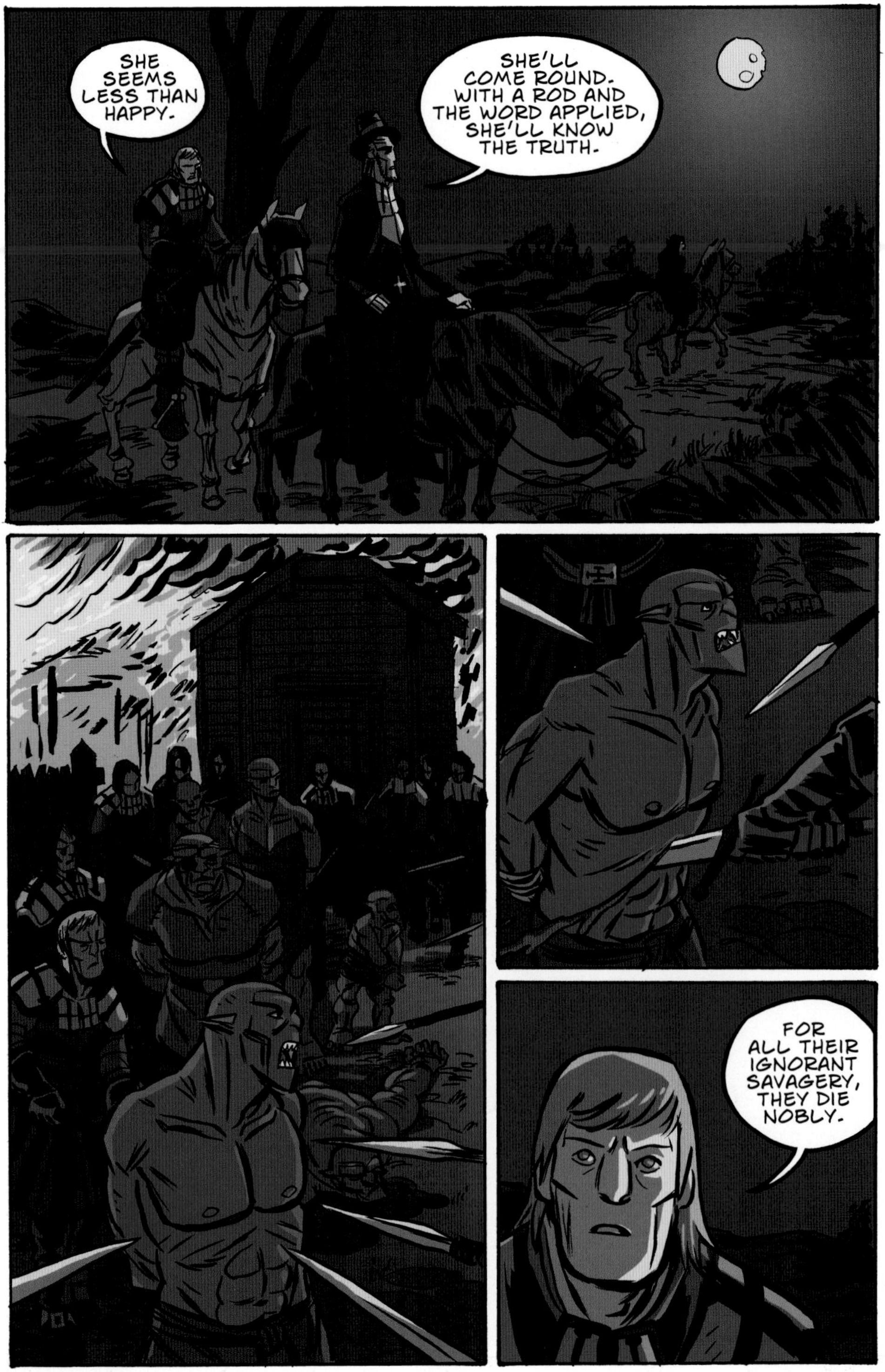
SHE SEEMS LESS THAN HAPPY.
SHE'LL COME ROUND. WITH A ROD AND THE WORD APPLIED, SHE'LL KNOW THE TRUTH.
FOR ALL THEIR IGNORANT SAVAGERY, THEY DIE NOBLY.

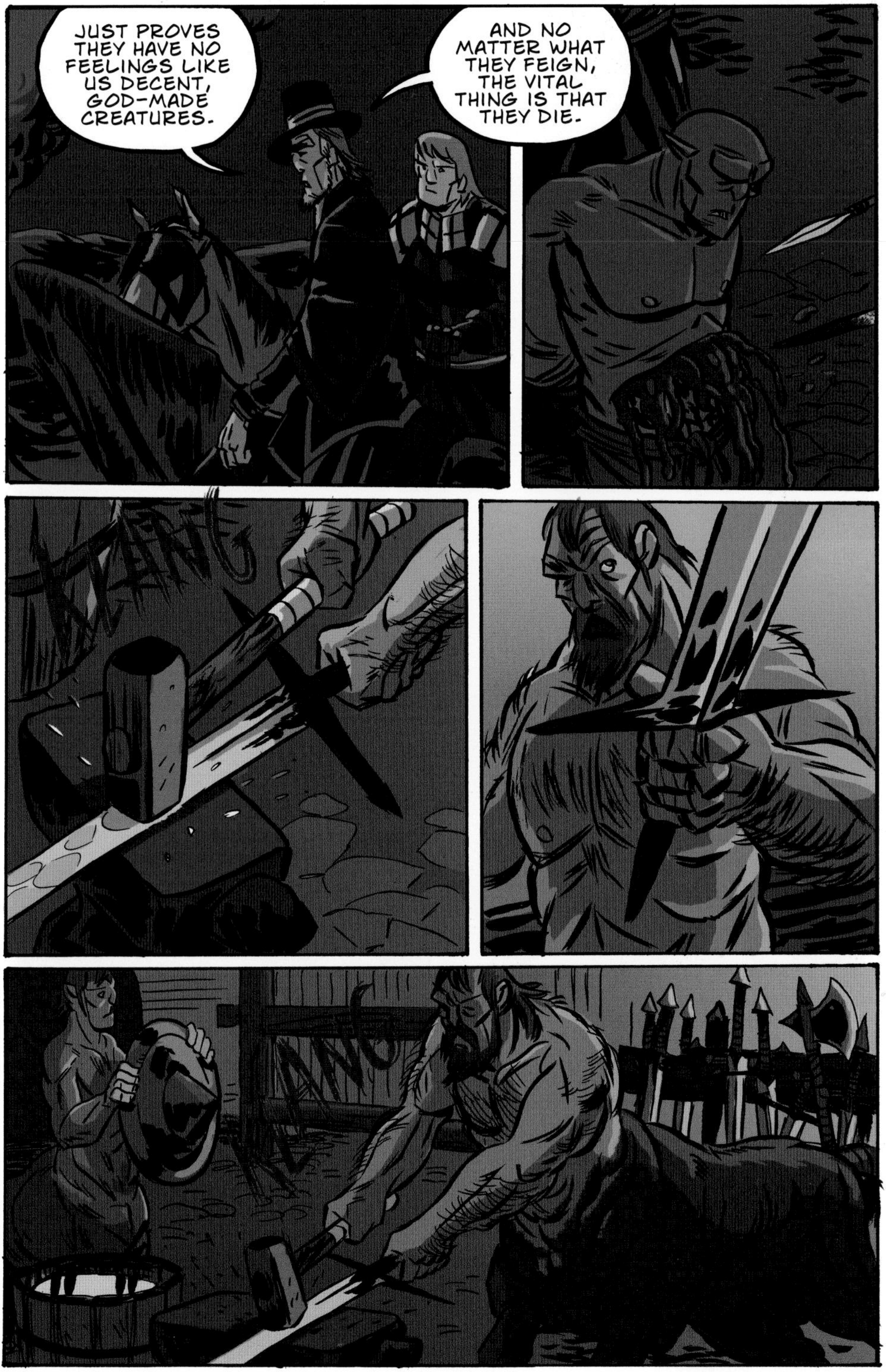
JUST PROVES THEY HAVE NO FEELINGS LIKE US DECENT, GOD-MADE CREATURES.
AND NO MATTER WHAT THEY FEIGN, THE VITAL THING IS THAT THEY DIE.

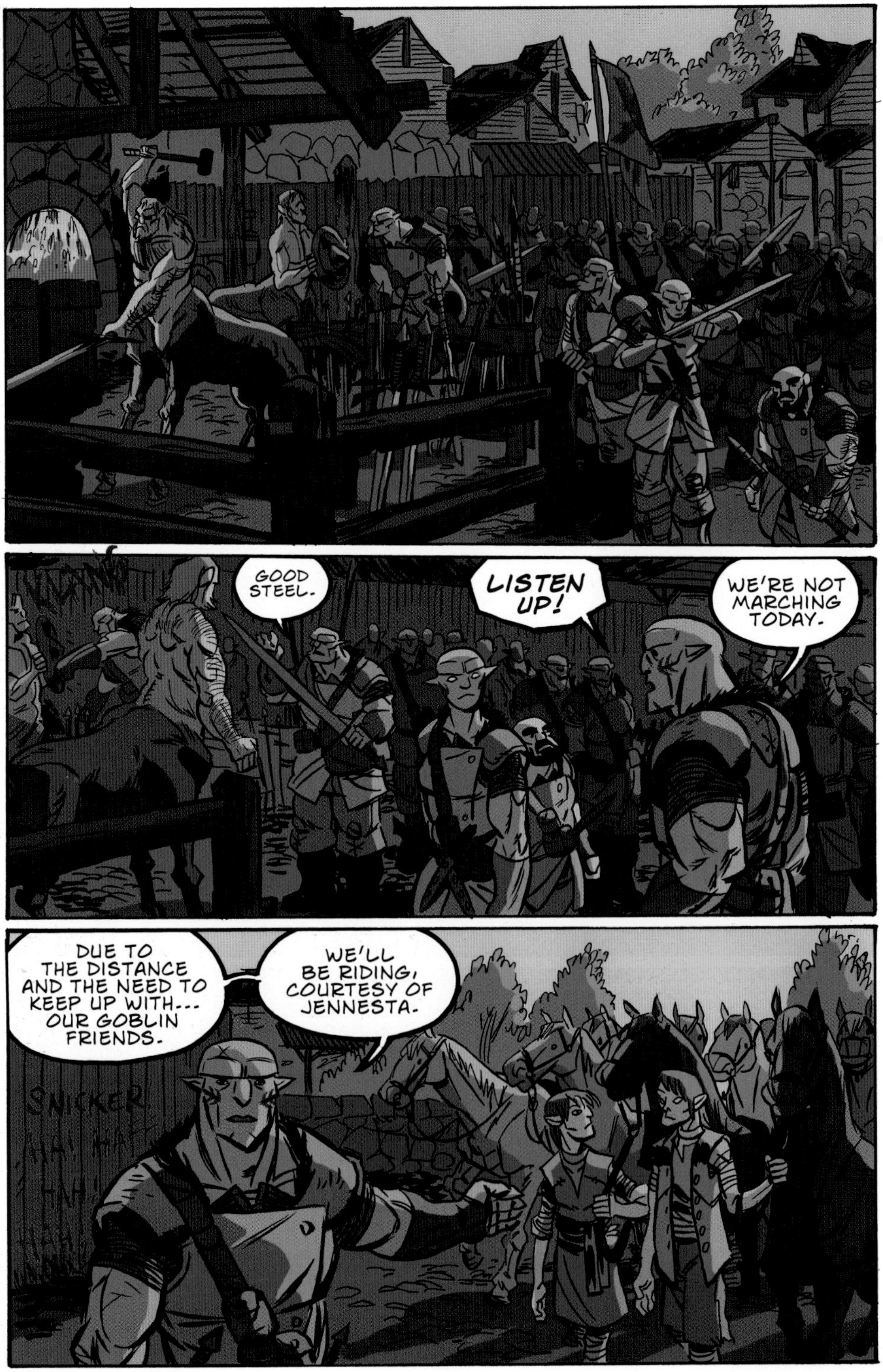
GOOD STEEL.
LISTEN UP!
WE'RE NOT MARCHING TODAY.
DUE TO THE DISTANCE AND THE NEED TO KEEP UP WITH... OUR GOBLIN FRIENDS.
WE'LL BE RIDING, COURTESY OF JENNESTA.
SNICKER

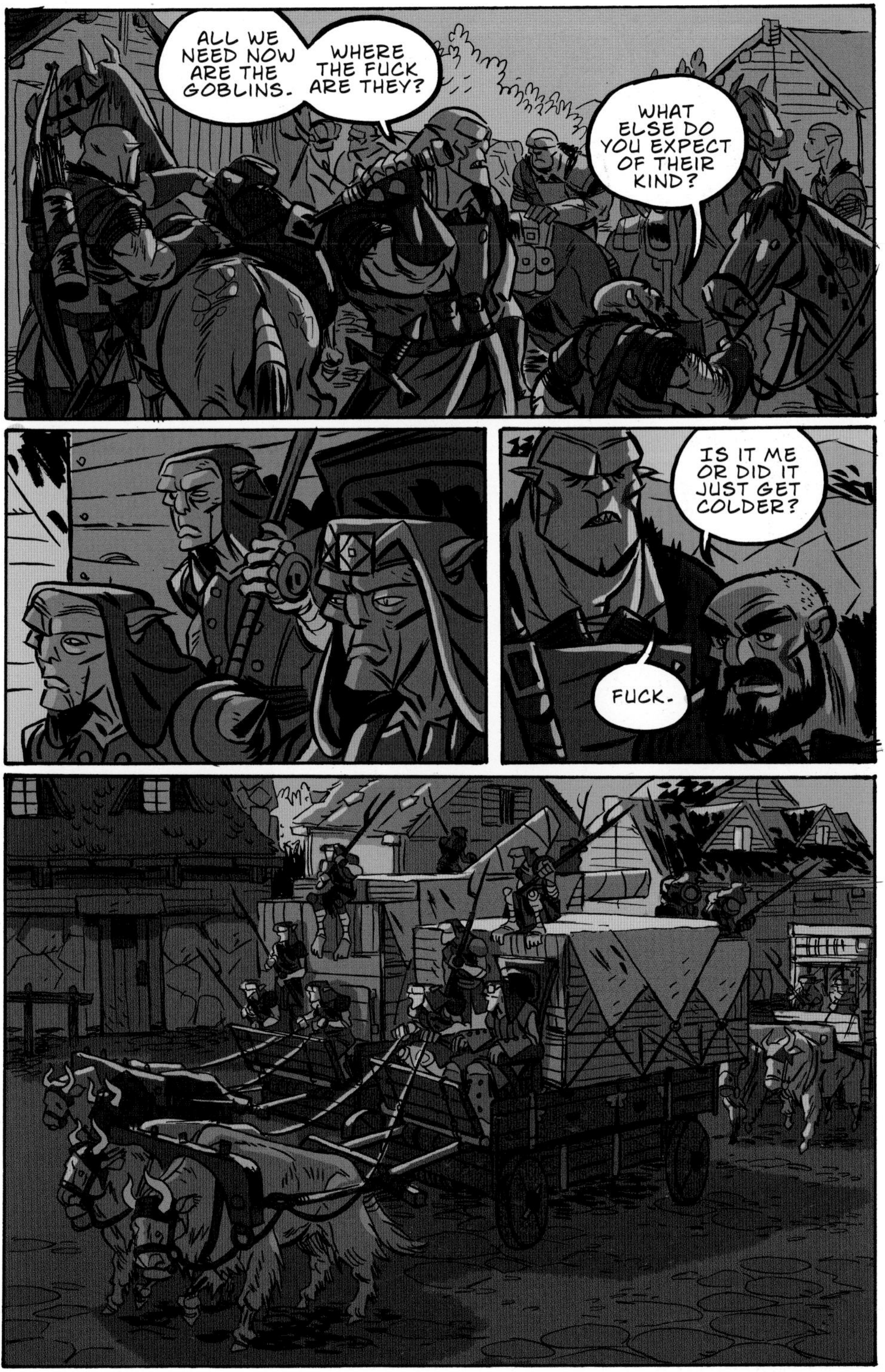
ALL WE NEED NOW ARE THE GOBLINS.
WHERE THE FUCK ARE THEY?
WHAT ELSE DO YOU EXPECT OF THEIR KIND?
IS IT ME OR DID IT JUST GET COLDER?
FUCK.

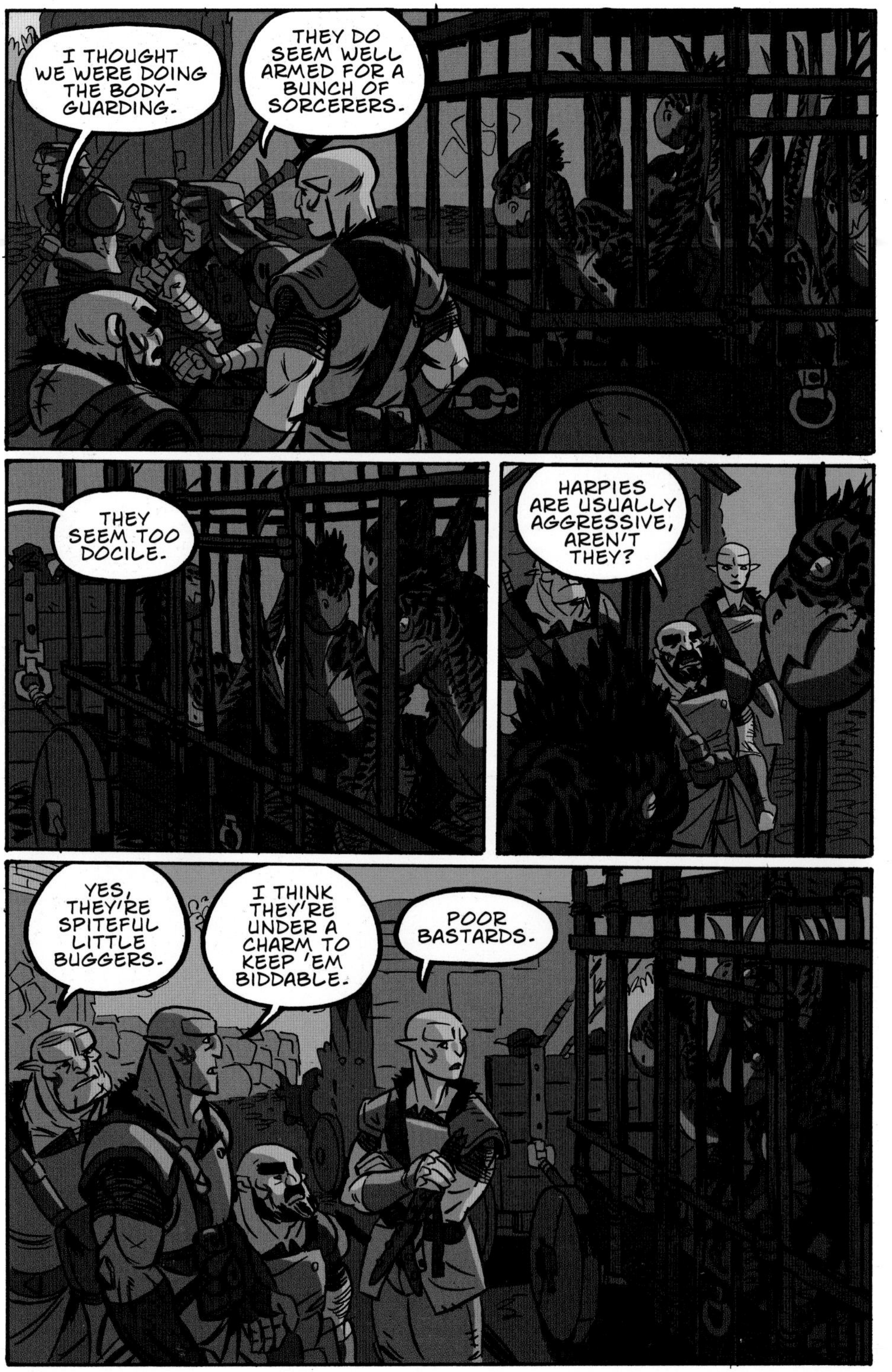
I THOUGHT WE WERE DOING THE BODY-GUARDING.
THEY DO SEEM WELL ARMED FOR A BUNCH OF SORCERERS.
THEY SEEM TOO DOCILE.
HARPIES ARE USUALLY AGGRESSIVE, AREN'T THEY?
YES, THEY'RE SPITEFUL LITTLE BUGGERS.
I THINK THEY'RE UNDER A CHARM TO KEEP 'EM BIDDABLE.
POOR BASTARDS.

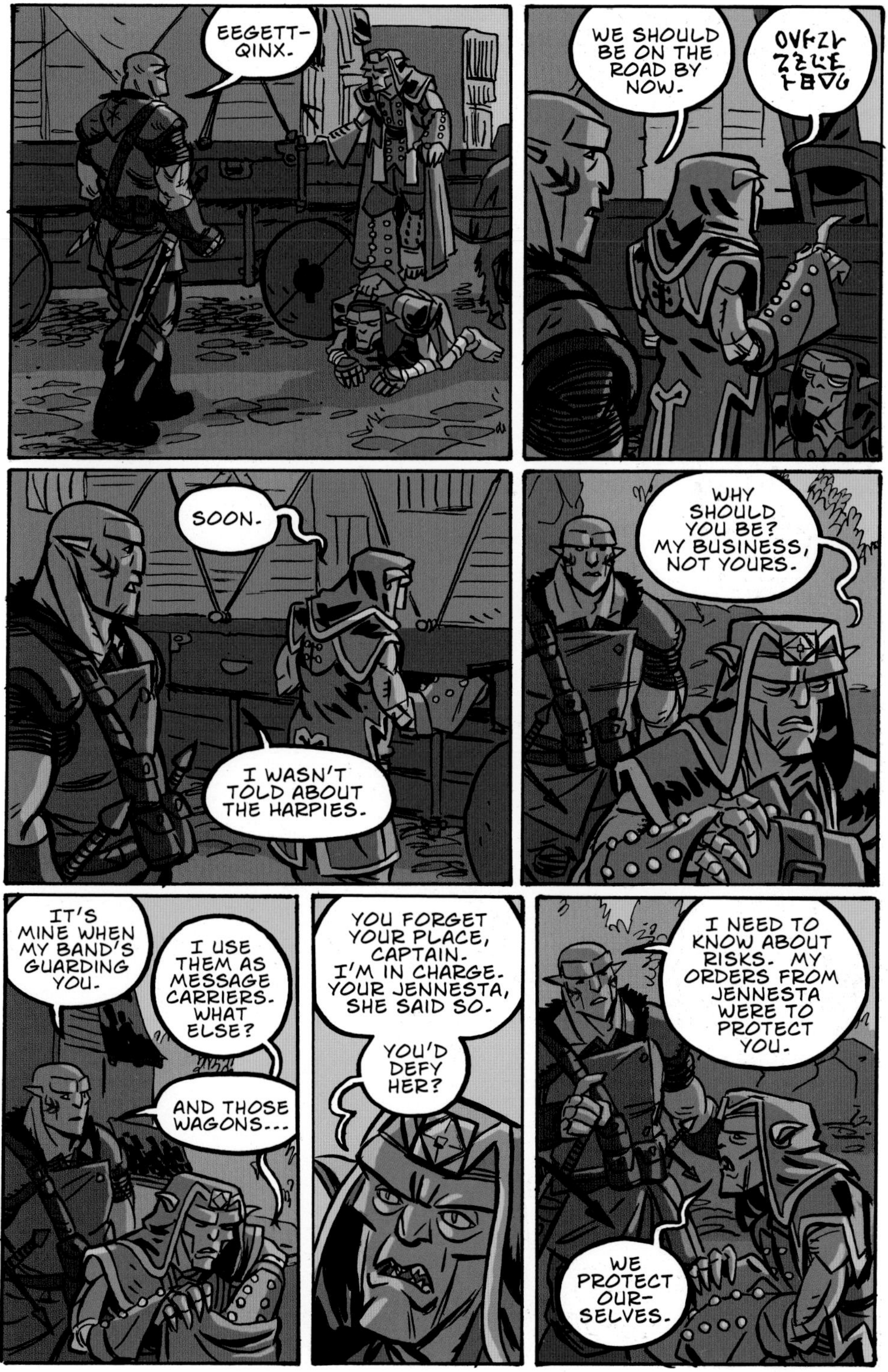
EEGETT-QINX.
WE SHOULD BE ON THE ROAD BY NOW.
SOON.
I WASN'T TOLD ABOUT THE HARPIES.
WHY SHOULD YOU BE? MY BUSINESS, NOT YOURS.
IT'S MINE WHEN MY BAND'S GUARDING YOU.
I USE THEM AS MESSAGE CARRIERS. WHAT ELSE?
AND THOSE WAGONS...
YOU FORGET YOUR PLACE, CAPTAIN. I'M IN CHARGE. YOUR JENNESTA, SHE SAID SO.
YOU'D DEFY HER?
I NEED TO KNOW ABOUT RISKS. MY ORDERS FROM JENNESTA WERE TO PROTECT YOU.
WE PROTECT OUR-SELVES.

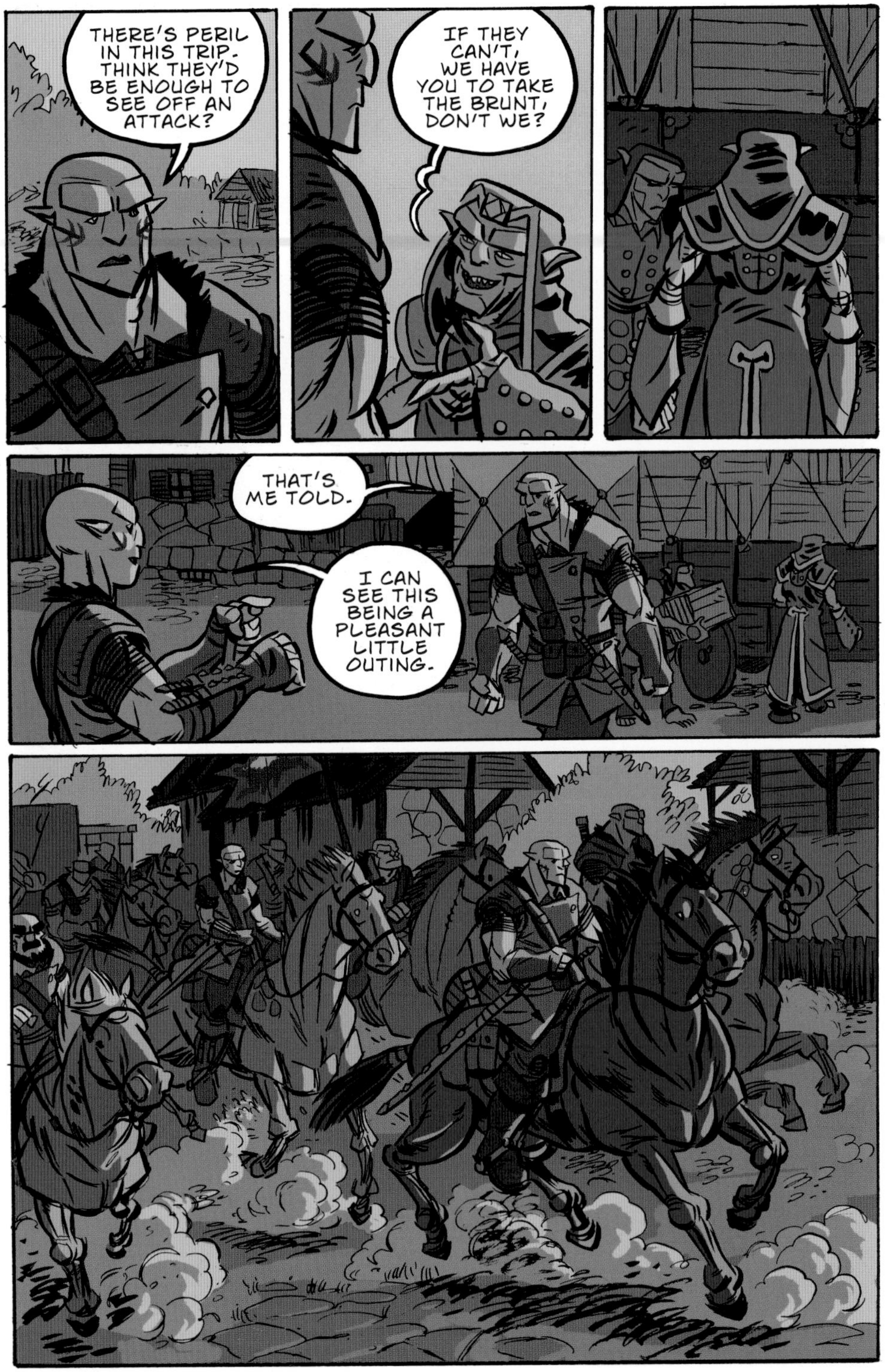
THERE'S PERIL IN THIS TRIP. THINK THEY'D BE ENOUGH TO SEE OFF AN ATTACK?
IF THEY CAN'T, WE HAVE YOU TO TAKE THE BRUNT, DON'T WE?
THAT'S ME TOLD.
I CAN SEE THIS BEING A PLEASANT LITTLE OUTING.

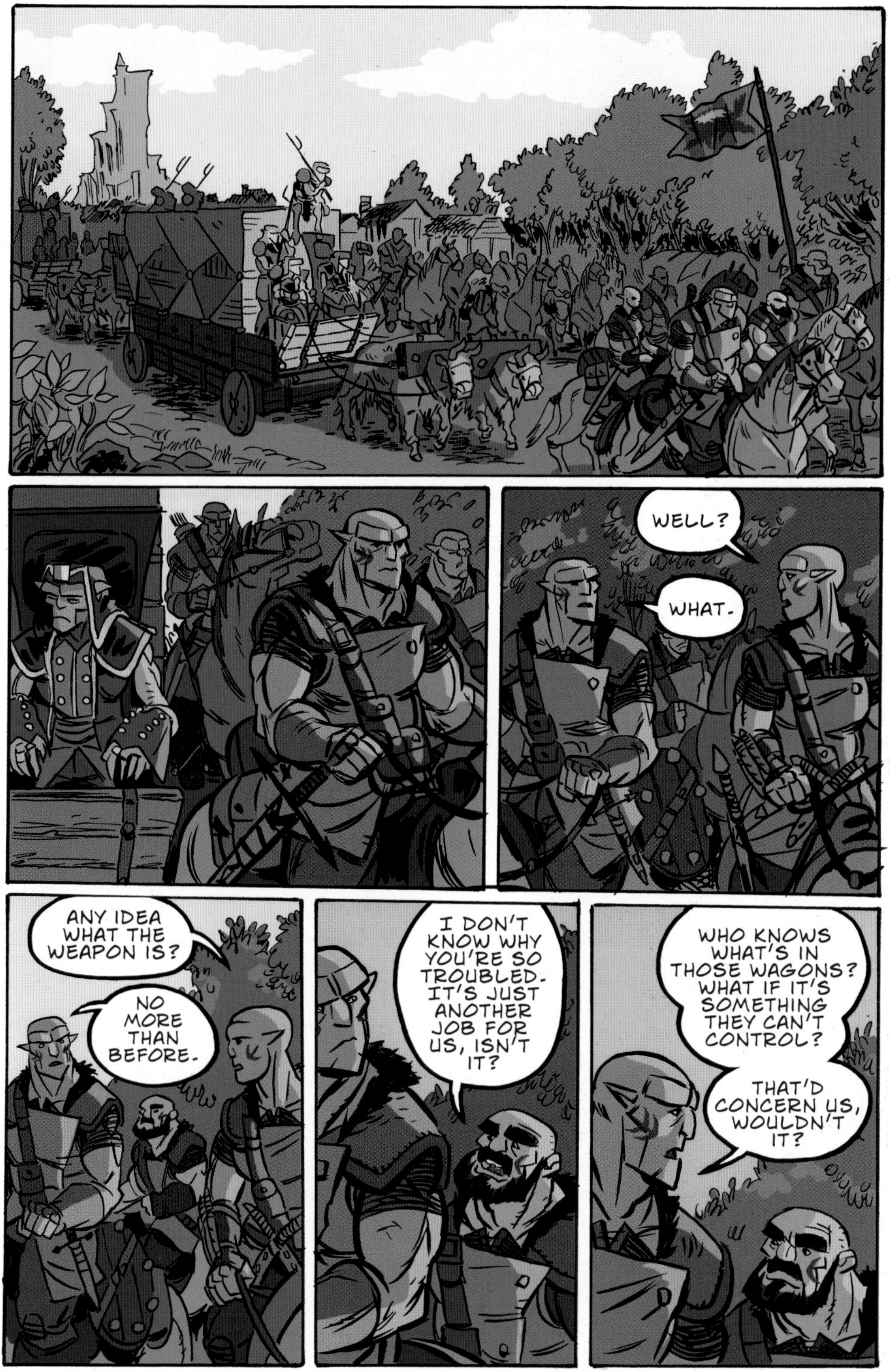
WELL?
WHAT.
ANY IDEA WHAT THE WEAPON IS?
NO MORE THAN BEFORE.
I DON'T KNOW WHY YOU'RE SO TROUBLED. IT'S JUST ANOTHER JOB FOR US, ISN'T IT?
WHO KNOWS WHAT'S IN THOSE WAGONS? WHAT IF IT'S SOMETHING THEY CAN'T CONTROL?
THAT'D CONCERN US, WOULDN'T IT?

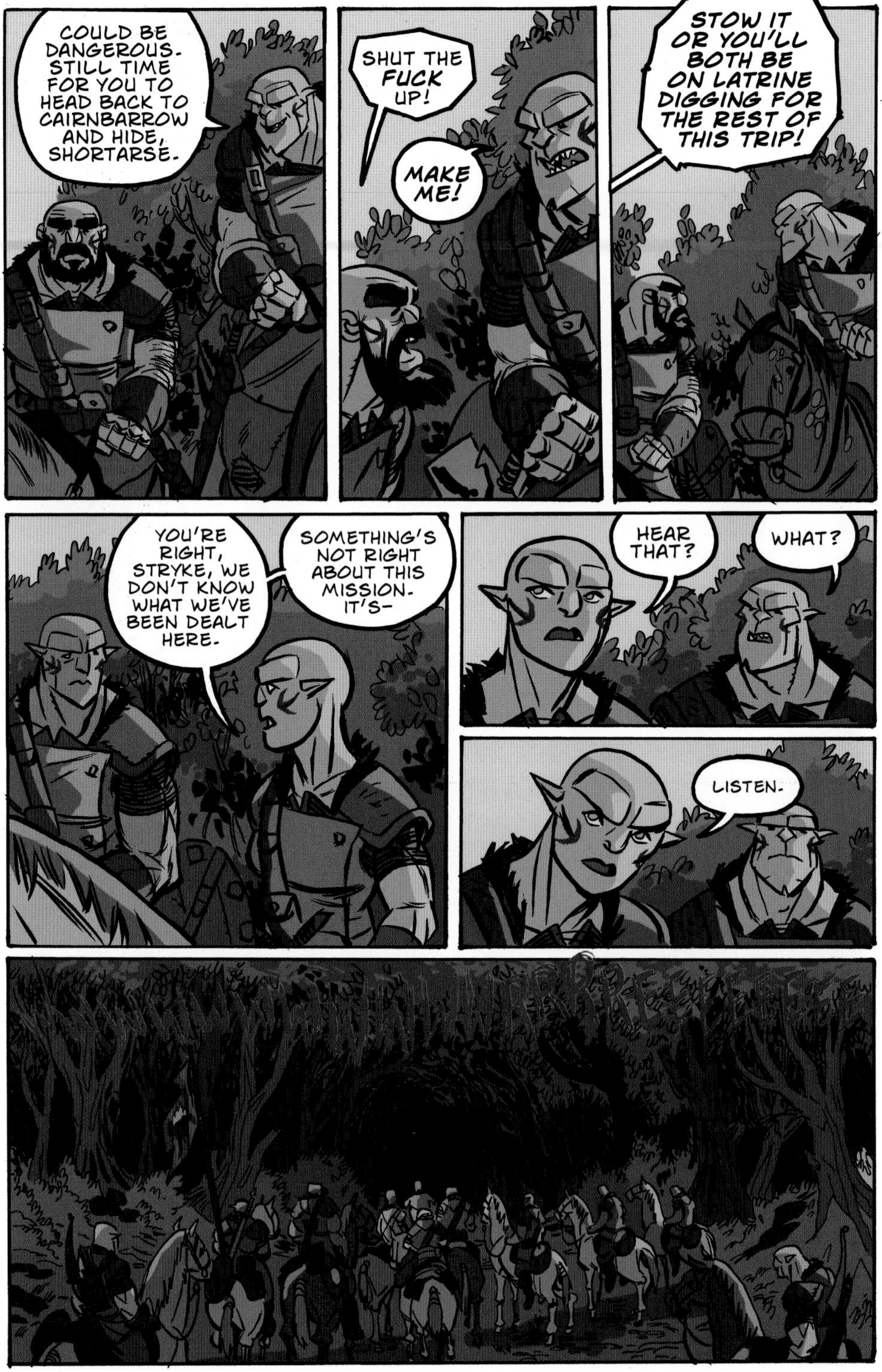
COULD BE DANGEROUS. STILL TIME FOR YOU TO HEAD BACK TO CAIRNBARROW AND HIDE, SHORTARSE.
SHUT THE FUCK UP!
MAKE ME!
STOW IT OR YOU'LL BOTH BE ON LATRINE DIGGING FOR THE REST OF THIS TRIP!
SOMETHING'S NOT RIGHT ABOUT THIS MISSION. IT'S-
YOU'RE RIGHT, STRYKE, WE DON'T KNOW WHAT WE'VE BEEN DEALT HERE.
HEAR THAT?
WHAT?
LISTEN.

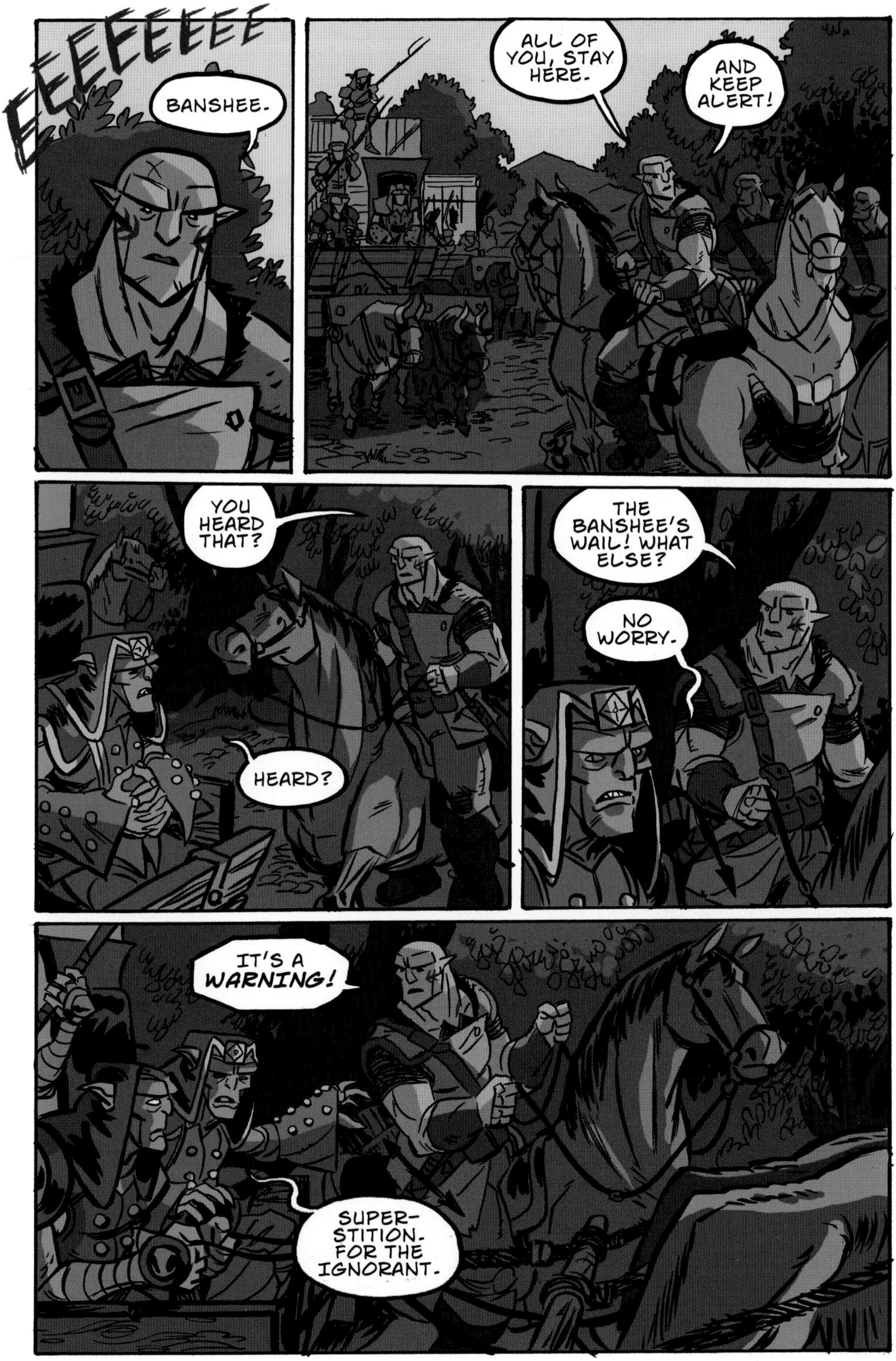
EEEEEEEE
BANSHEE.
ALL OF YOU, STAY HERE.
AND KEEP ALERT!
YOU HEARD THAT?
HEARD?
THE BANSHEE'S WAIL! WHAT ELSE?
NO WORRY.
IT'S A WARNING!
SUPER-STITION. FOR THE IGNORANT.

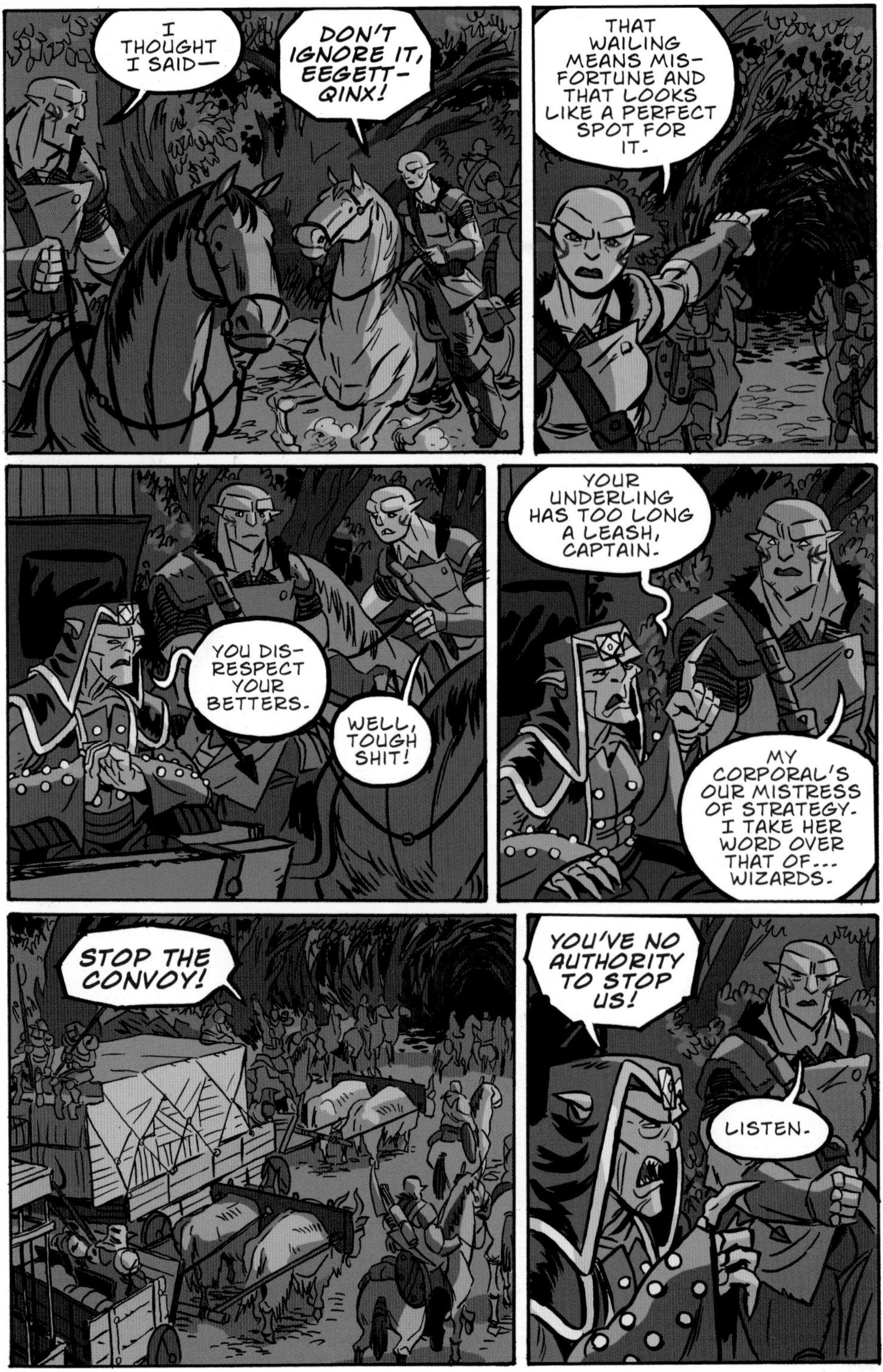
I THOUGHT I SAID—
DON'T IGNORE IT, EEGETT-QINX!
THAT WAILING MEANS MIS-FORTUNE AND THAT LOOKS LIKE A PERFECT SPOT FOR IT.
YOU DIS-RESPECT YOUR BETTERS.
WELL, TOUGH SHIT!
YOUR UNDERLING HAS TOO LONG A LEASH, CAPTAIN.
MY CORPORAL'S OUR MISTRESS OF STRATEGY. I TAKE HER WORD OVER THAT OF... WIZARDS.
STOP THE CONVOY!
YOU'VE NO AUTHORITY TO STOP US!
LISTEN.

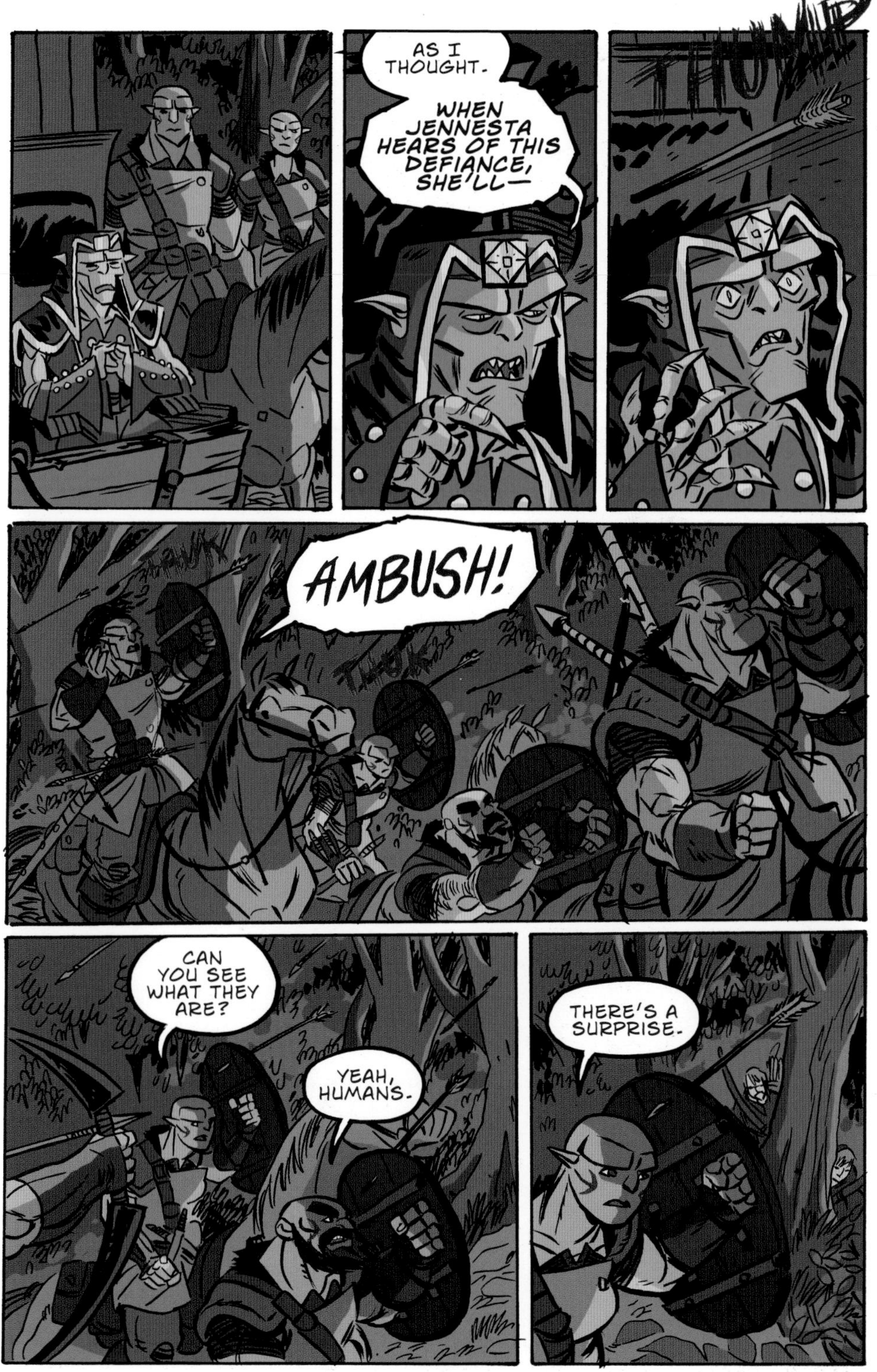

AS I THOUGHT.
WHEN JENNESTA HEARS OF THIS DEFIANCE, SHE'LL—
THUMP
AMBUSH!
CAN YOU SEE WHAT THEY ARE?
YEAH, HUMANS.
THERE'S A SURPRISE.

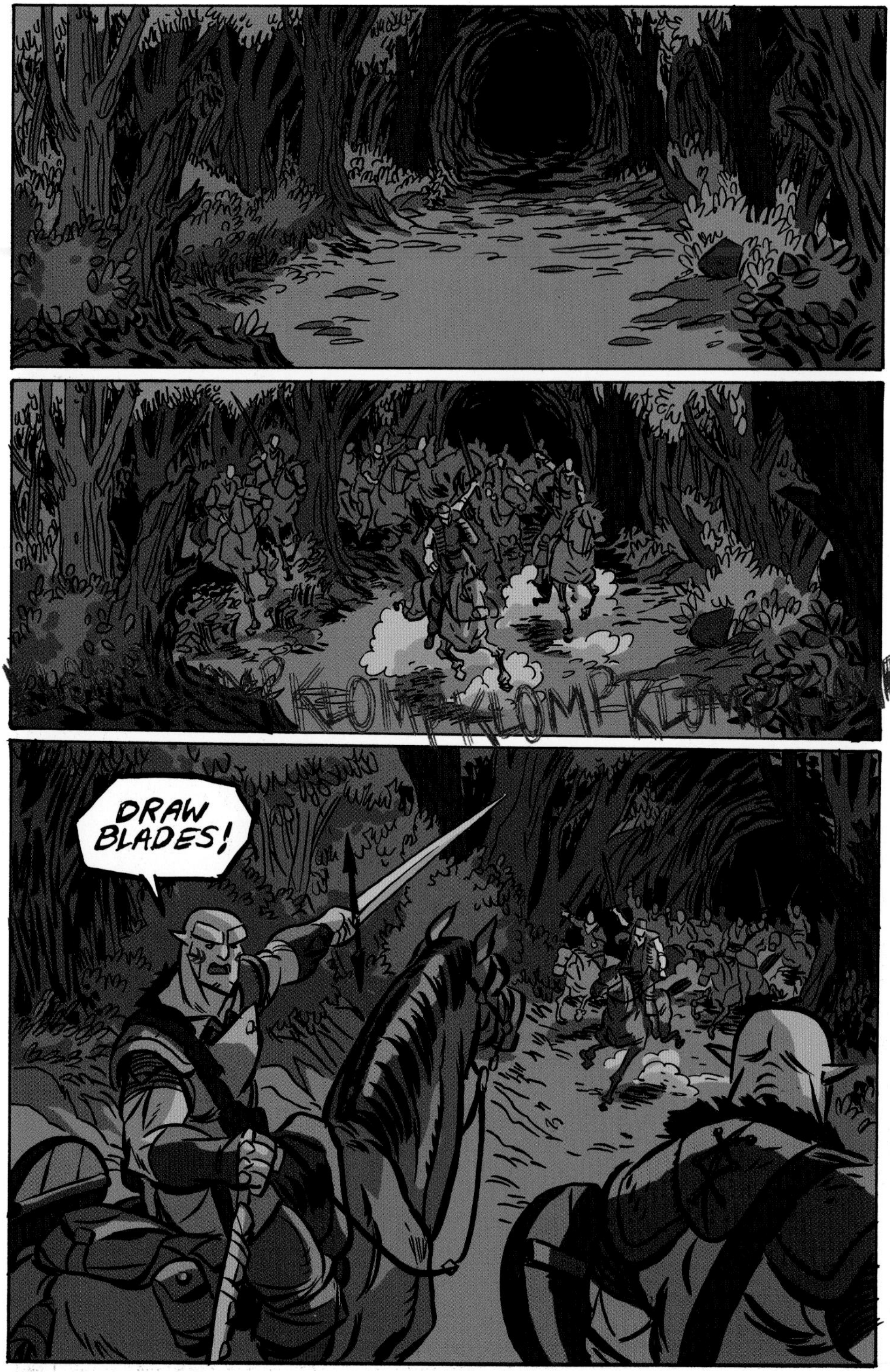
KLOMP KLOMP
DRAW BLADES!

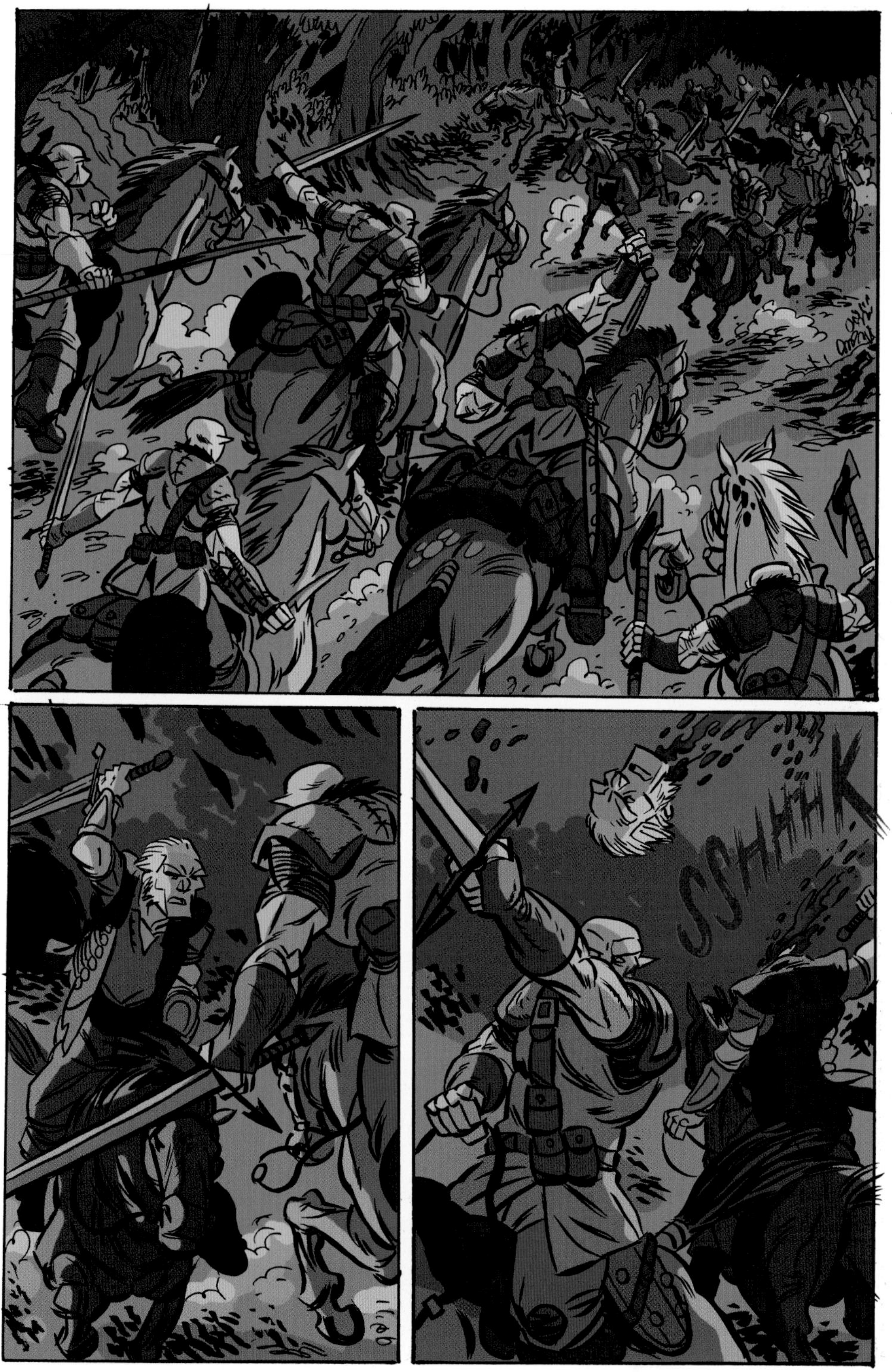
SSHHHK

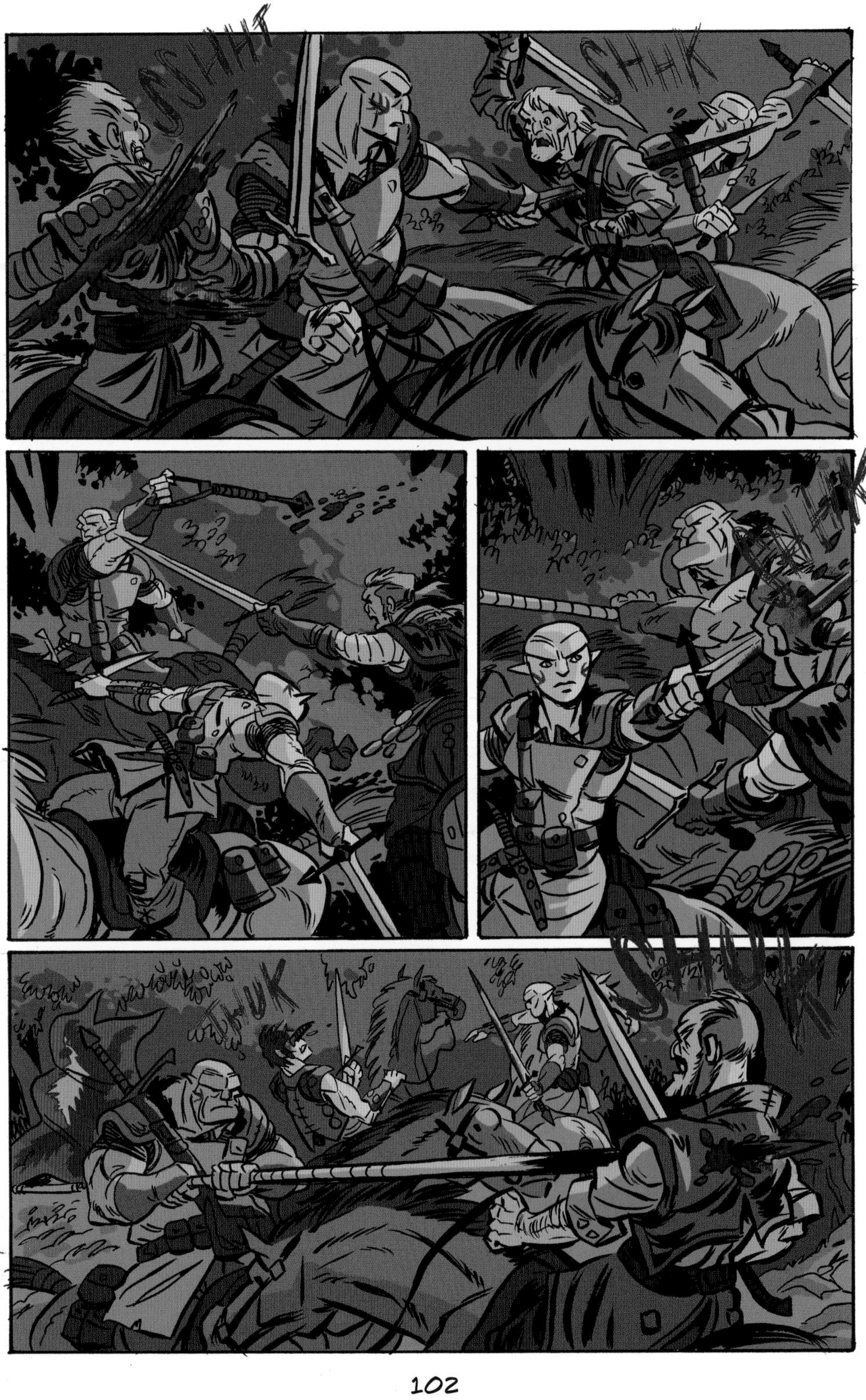
SHHT
SHHK
THUK
SHUK

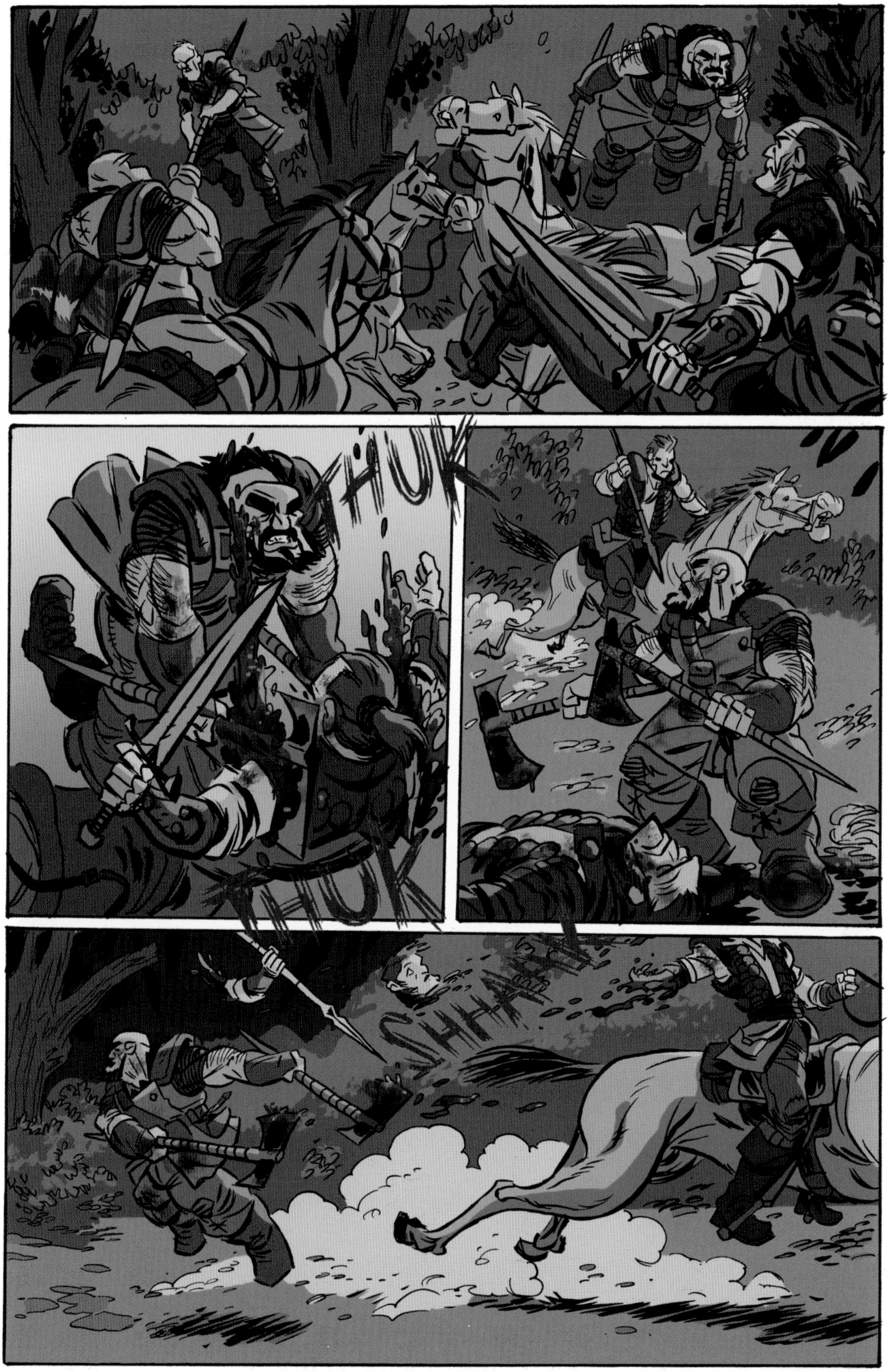
THUK
THUK

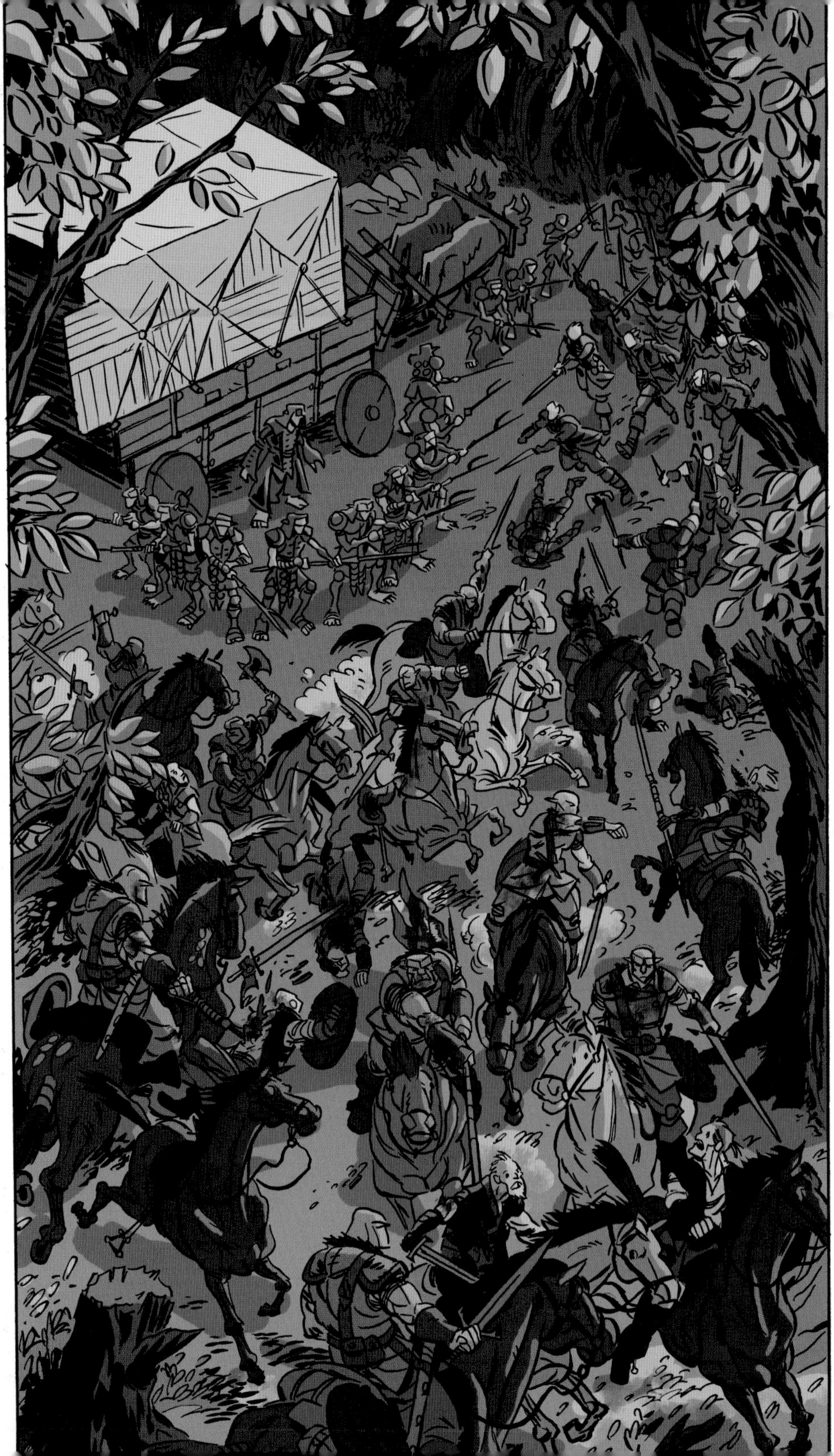

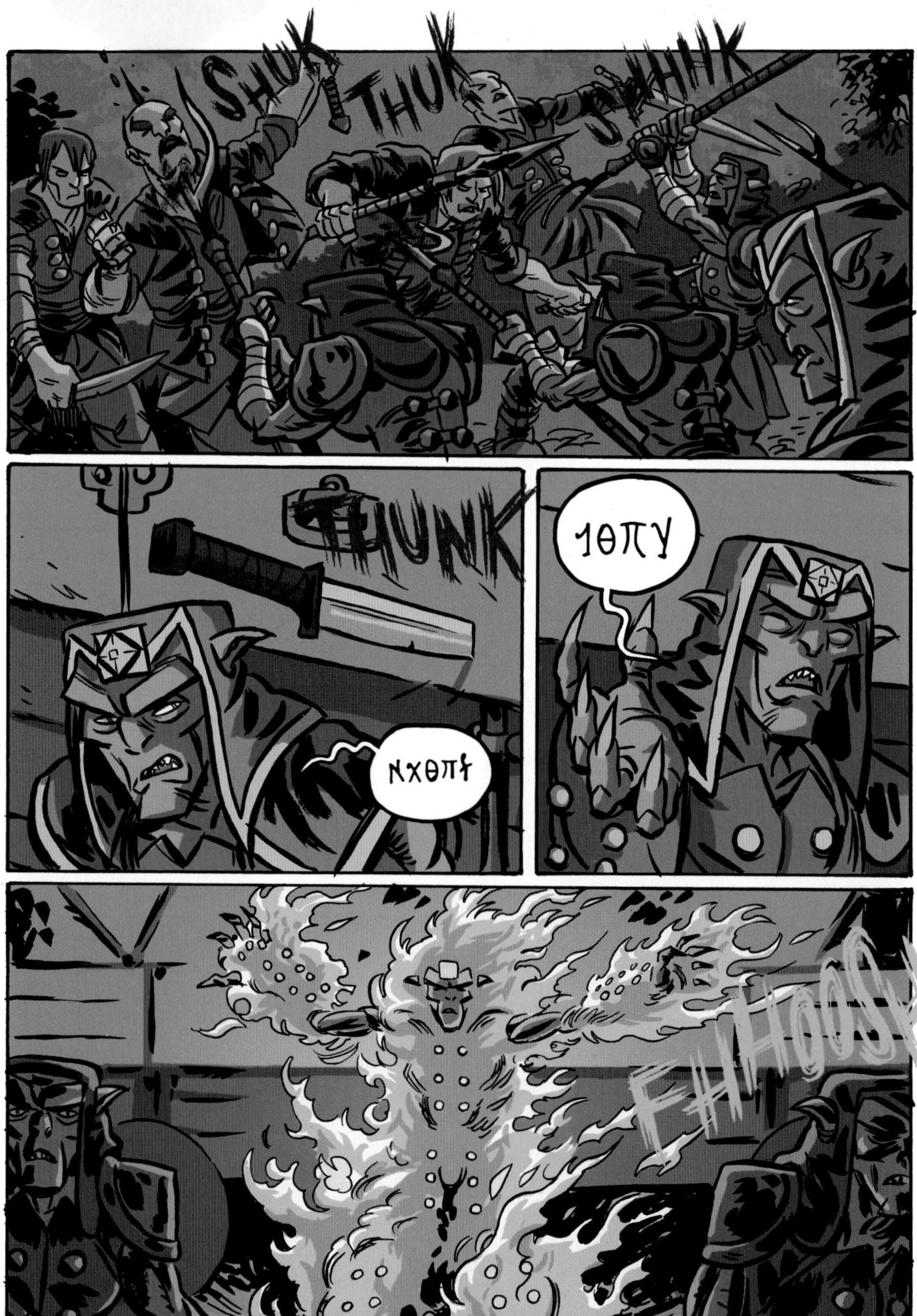
SHUK
THUK
THUNK
FHHOOSH

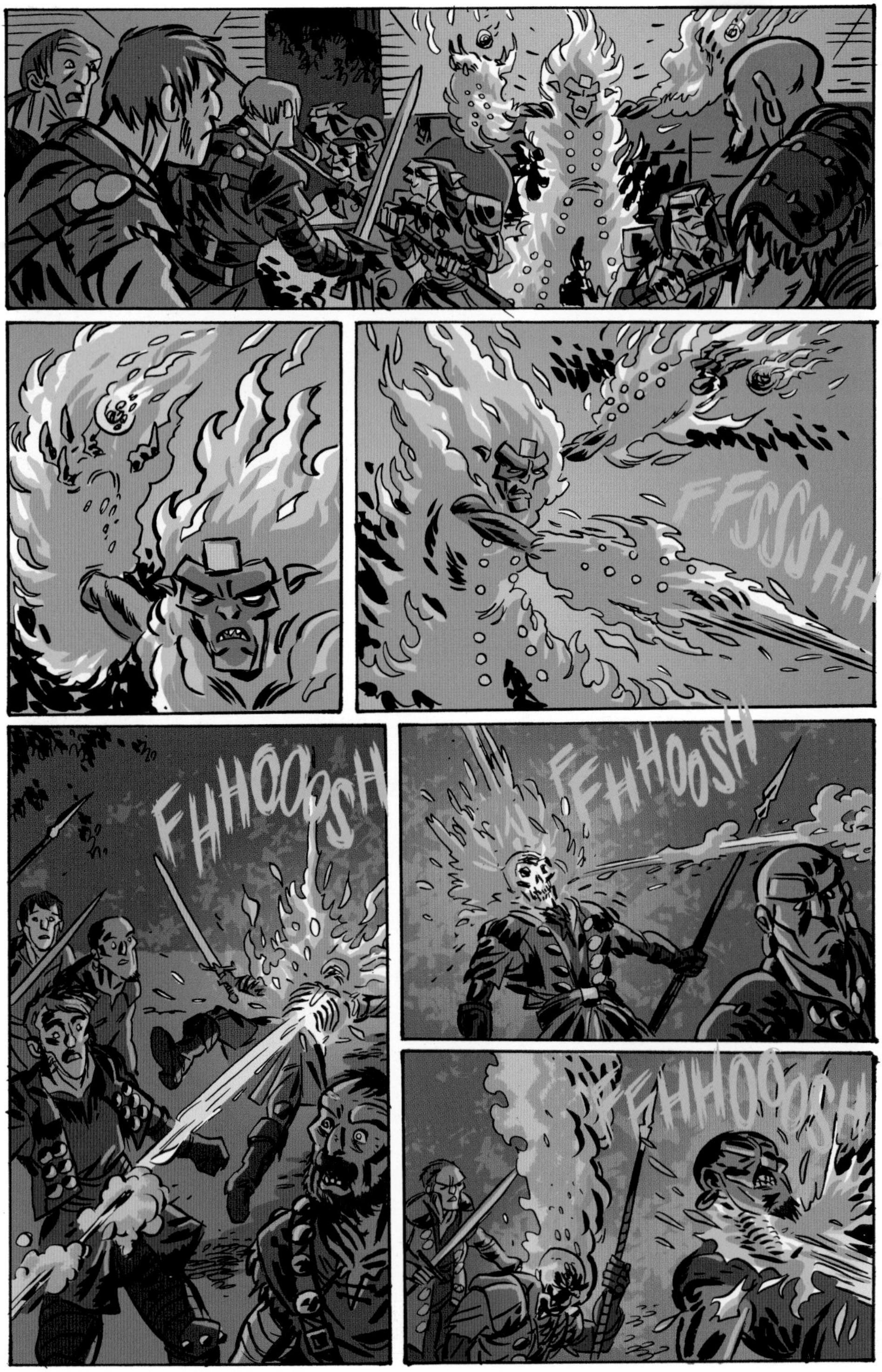
FFSSSHH
FHHOOSH
FHHOOSH
FHHOOOSH

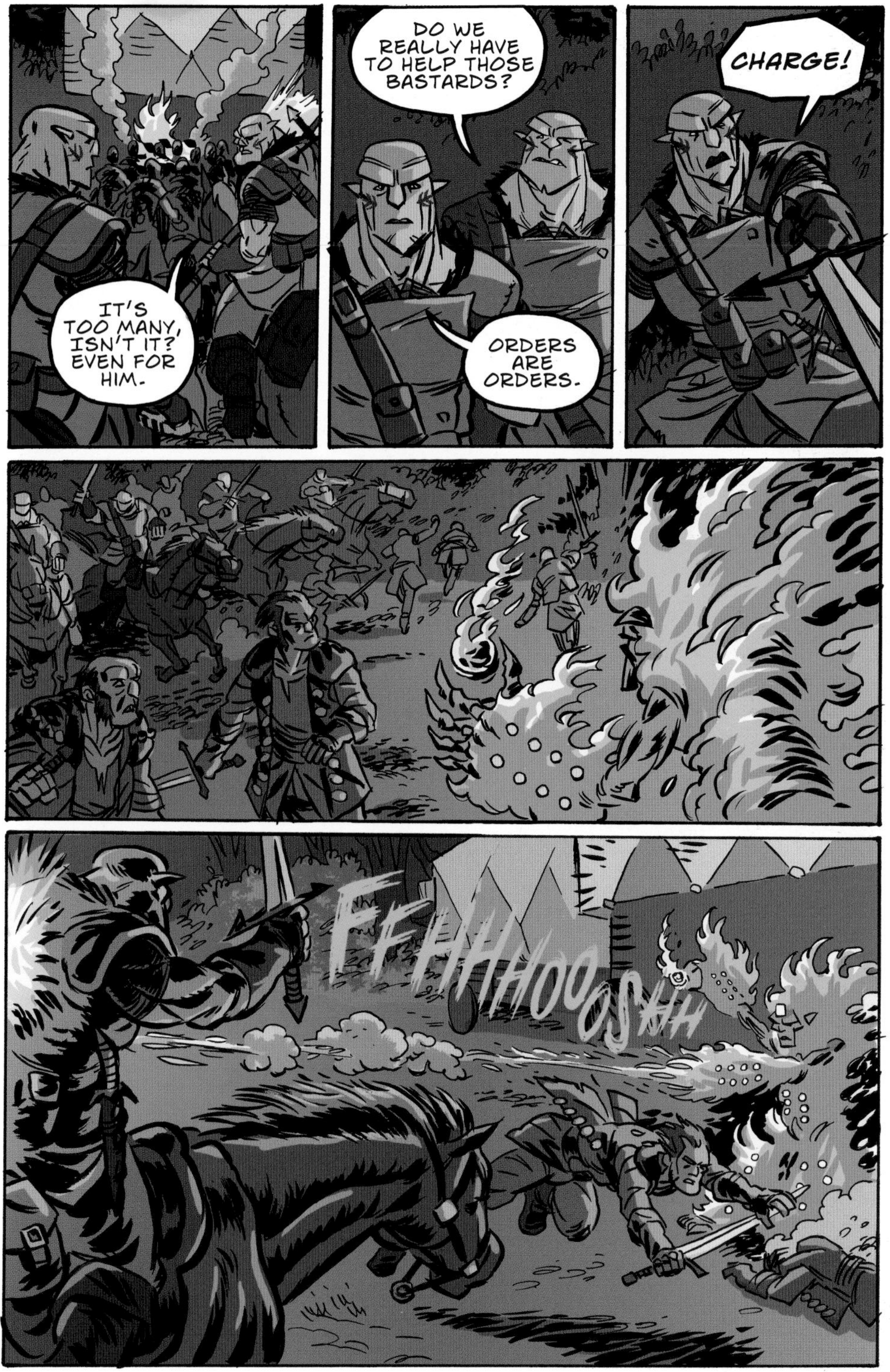
IT'S TOO MANY, ISN'T IT? EVEN FOR HIM.
DO WE REALLY HAVE TO HELP THOSE BASTARDS?
ORDERS ARE ORDERS.
CHARGE!
FFFHHHOOOSHH

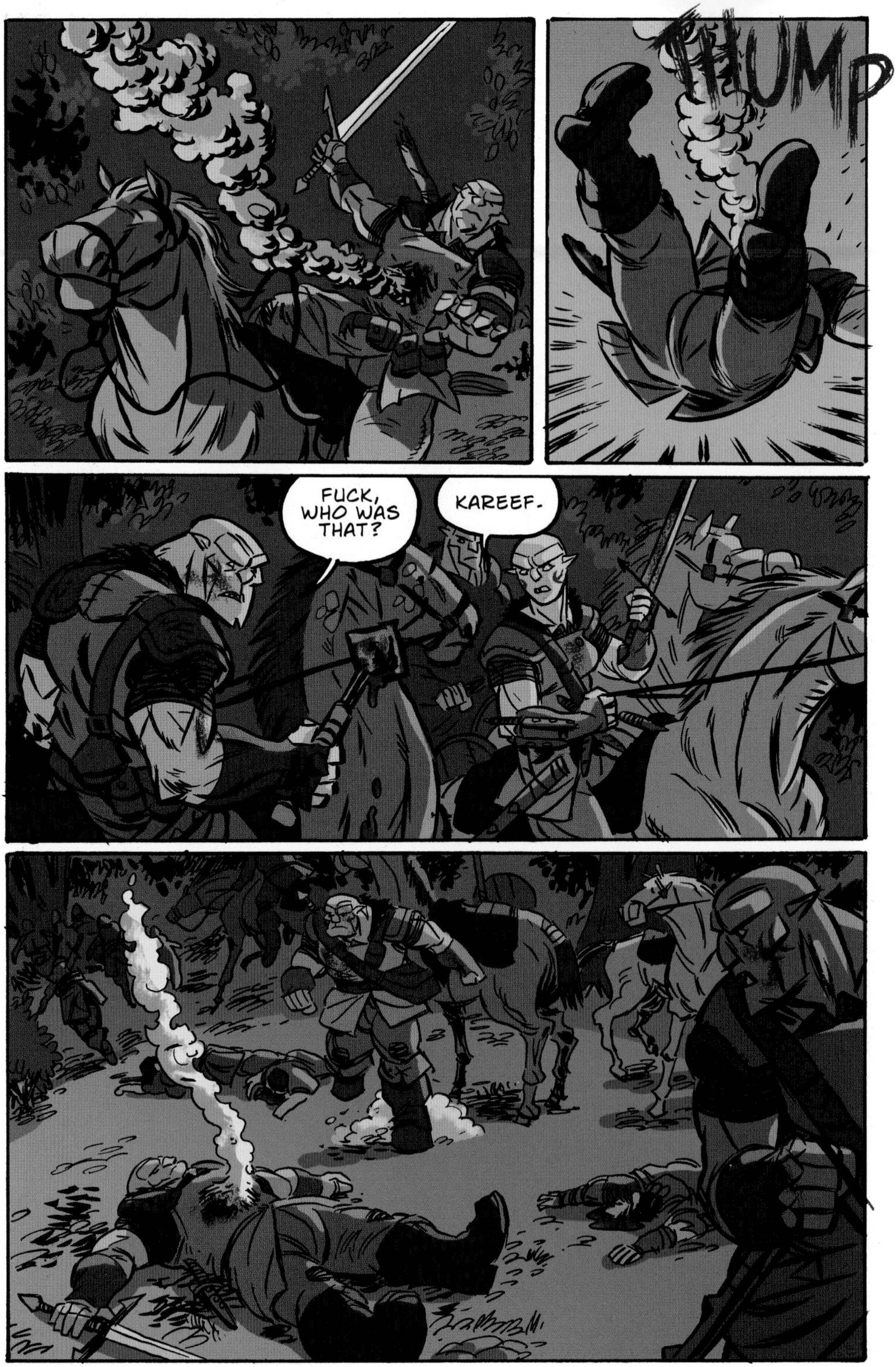
THUMP
FUCK, WHO WAS THAT?
KAREEF.

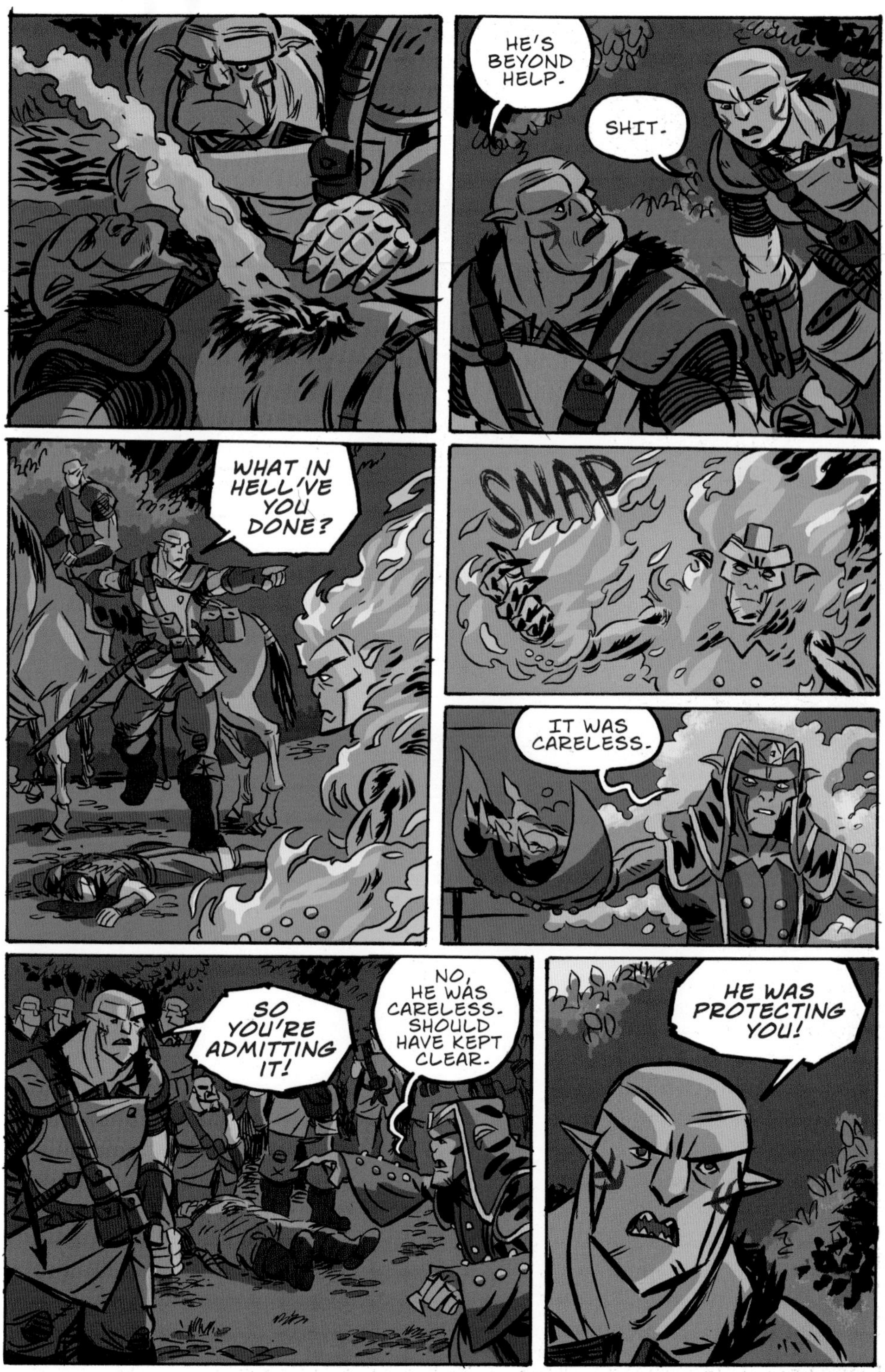
HE'S BEYOND HELP.
SHIT.
WHAT IN HELL'VE YOU DONE?
SNAP
IT WAS CARELESS.
SO YOU'RE ADMITTING IT!
NO, HE WAS CARELESS. SHOULD HAVE KEPT CLEAR.
HE WAS PROTECTING YOU!

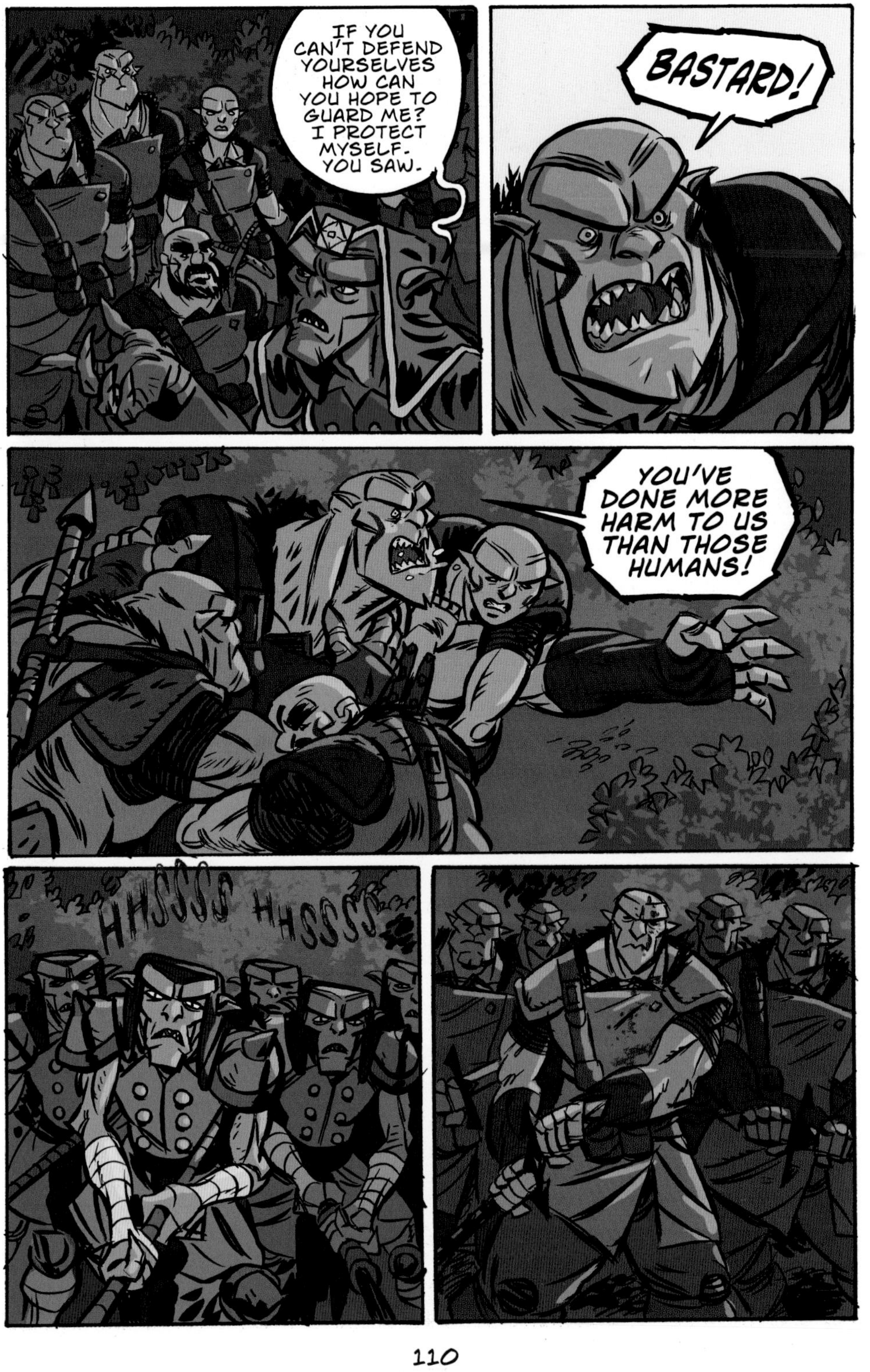
IF YOU CAN'T DEFEND YOURSELVES HOW CAN YOU HOPE TO GUARD ME? I PROTECT MYSELF. YOU SAW.
BASTARD!
YOU'VE DONE MORE HARM TO US THAN THOSE HUMANS!
HHSSSS HHSSSS

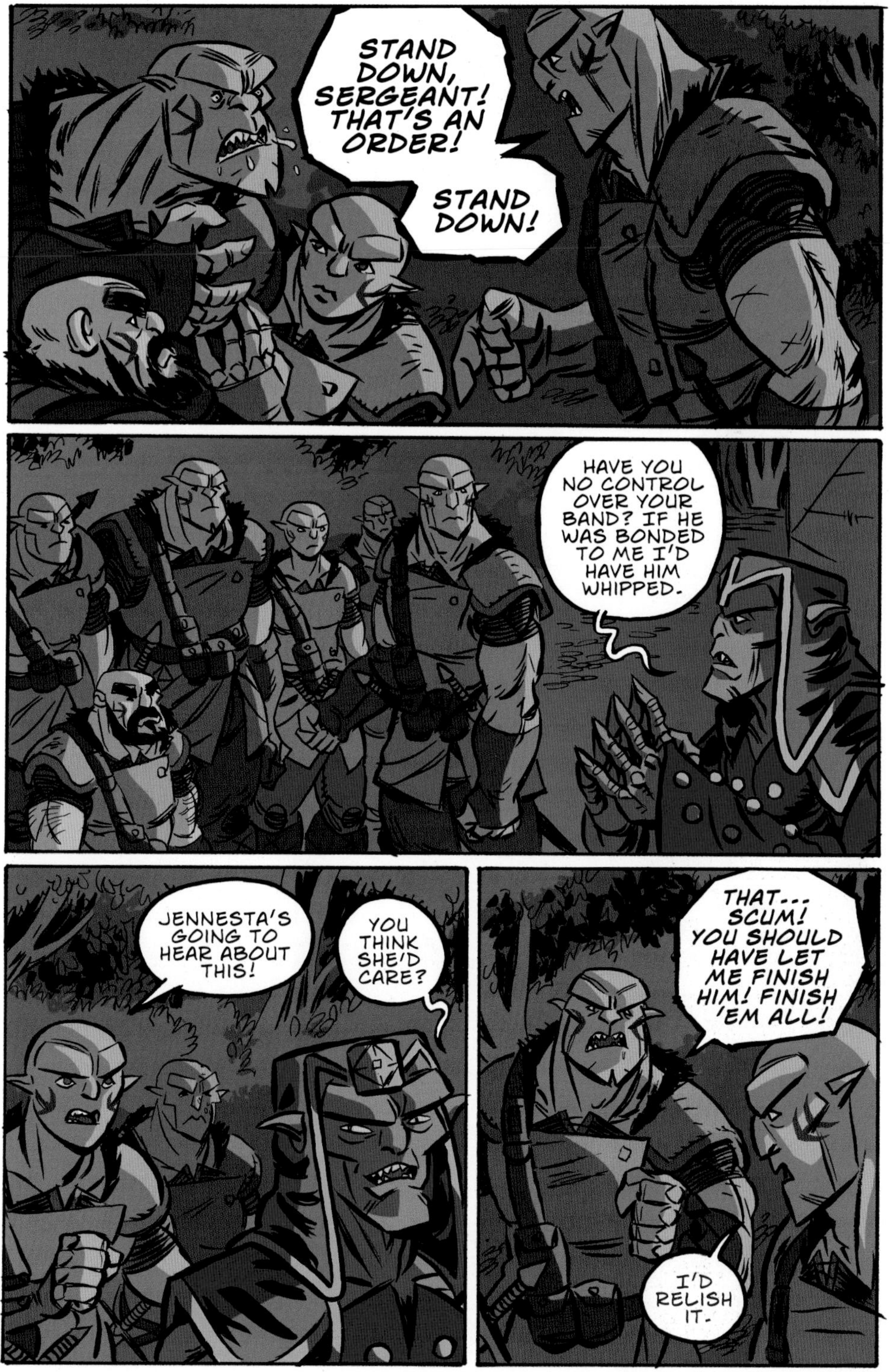
STAND DOWN, SERGEANT! THAT'S AN ORDER!
STAND DOWN!
HAVE YOU NO CONTROL OVER YOUR BAND? IF HE WAS BONDED TO ME I'D HAVE HIM WHIPPED.
JENNESTA'S GOING TO HEAR ABOUT THIS!
YOU THINK SHE'D CARE?
THAT... SCUM! YOU SHOULD HAVE LET ME FINISH HIM! FINISH 'EM ALL!
I'D RELISH IT.

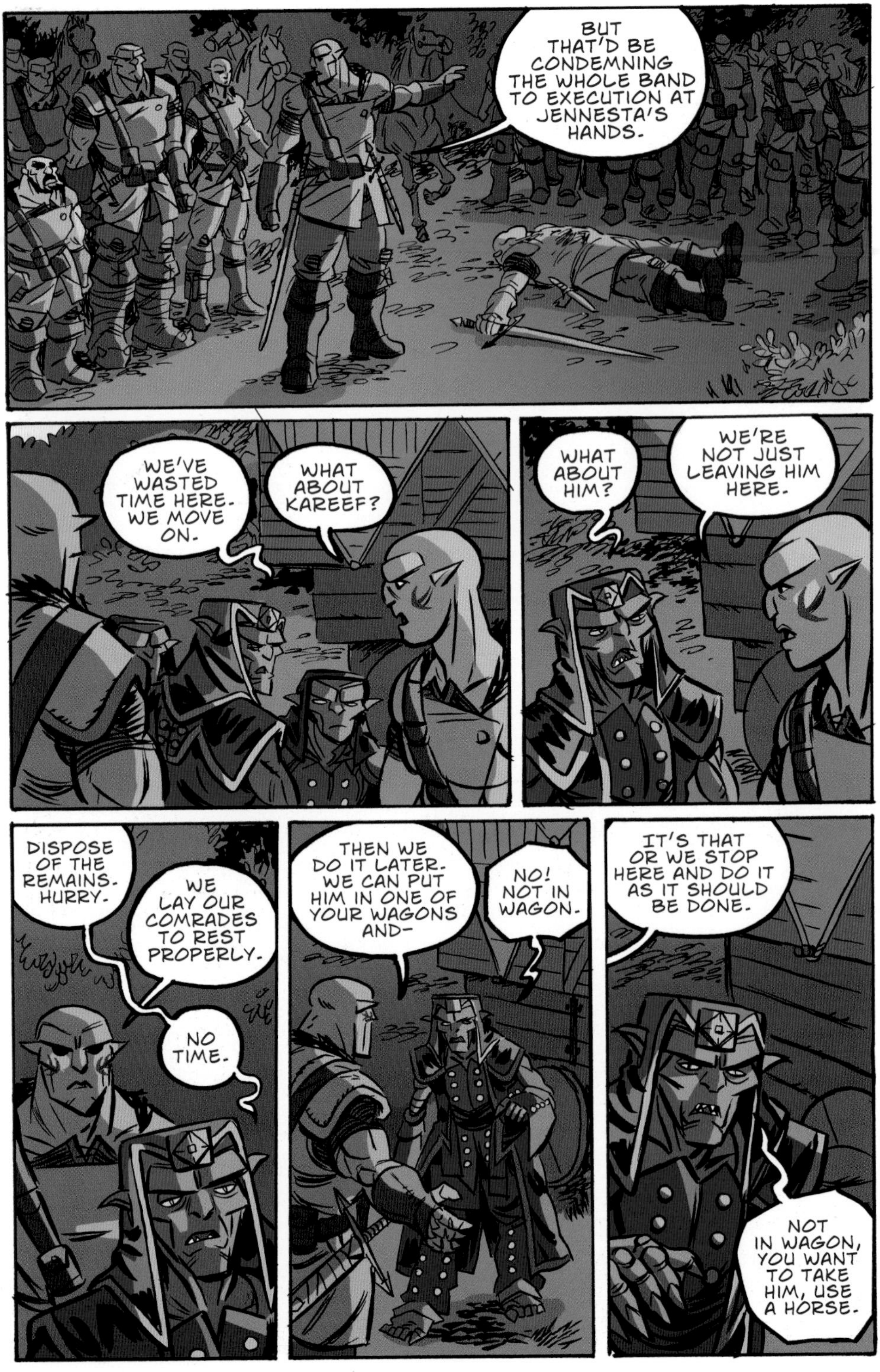
BUT THAT'D BE CONDEMNING THE WHOLE BAND TO EXECUTION AT JENNESTA'S HANDS.
WE'VE WASTED TIME HERE. WE MOVE ON.
WHAT ABOUT KAREEF?
WHAT ABOUT HIM?
WE'RE NOT JUST LEAVING HIM HERE.
DISPOSE OF THE REMAINS. HURRY.
WE LAY OUR COMRADES TO REST PROPERLY.
NO TIME.
THEN WE DO IT LATER. WE CAN PUT HIM IN ONE OF YOUR WAGONS AND-
NO! NOT IN WAGON.
IT'S THAT OR WE STOP HERE AND DO IT AS IT SHOULD BE DONE.
NOT IN WAGON, YOU WANT TO TAKE HIM, USE A HORSE.

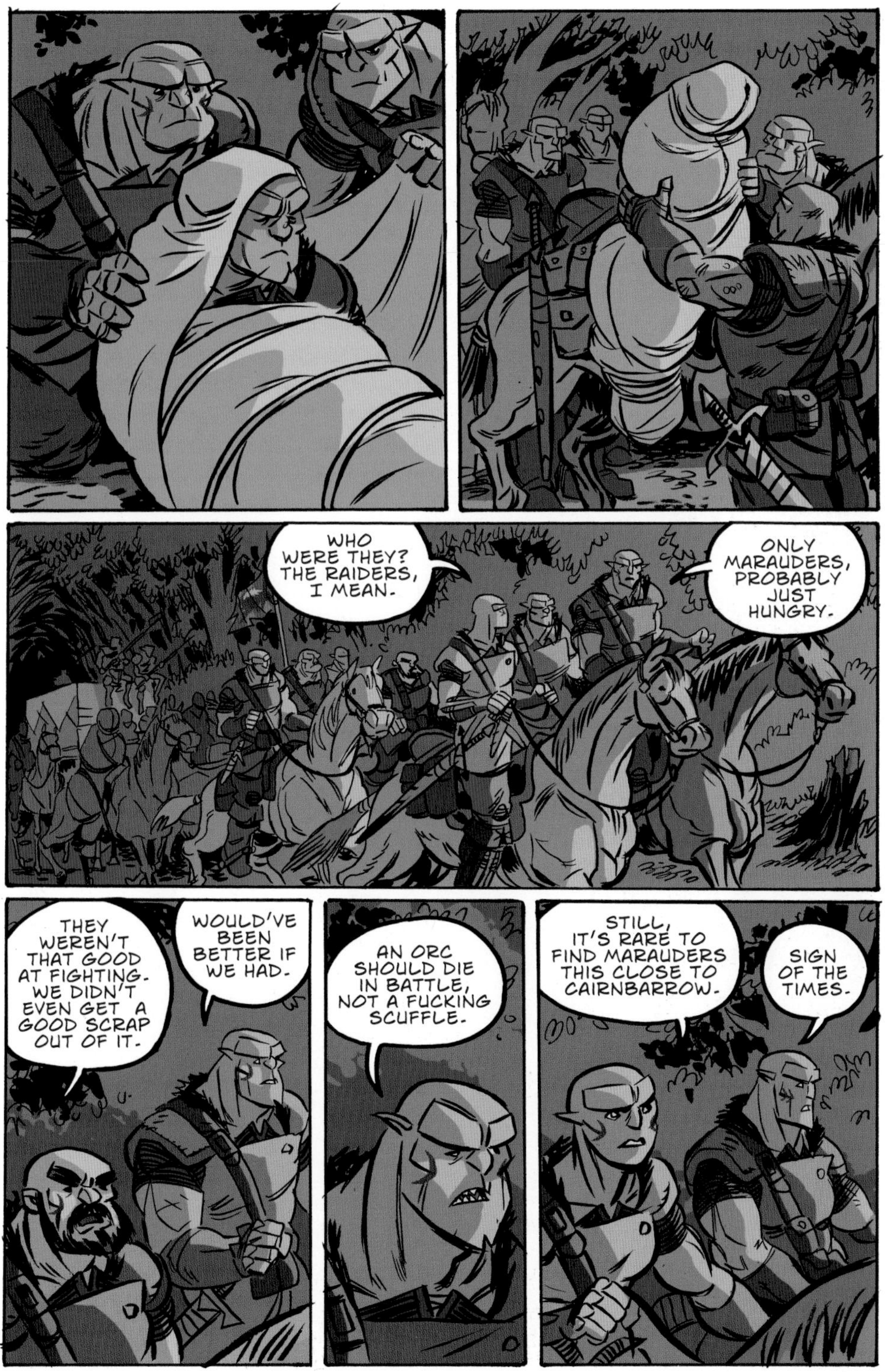
WHO WERE THEY? THE RAIDERS, I MEAN.
ONLY MARAUDERS, PROBABLY JUST HUNGRY.
THEY WEREN'T THAT GOOD AT FIGHTING. WE DIDN'T EVEN GET A GOOD SCRAP OUT OF IT.
WOULD'VE BEEN BETTER IF WE HAD.
AN ORC SHOULD DIE IN BATTLE, NOT A FUCKING SCUFFLE.
STILL, IT'S RARE TO FIND MARAUDERS THIS CLOSE TO CAIRNBARROW.
SIGN OF THE TIMES.

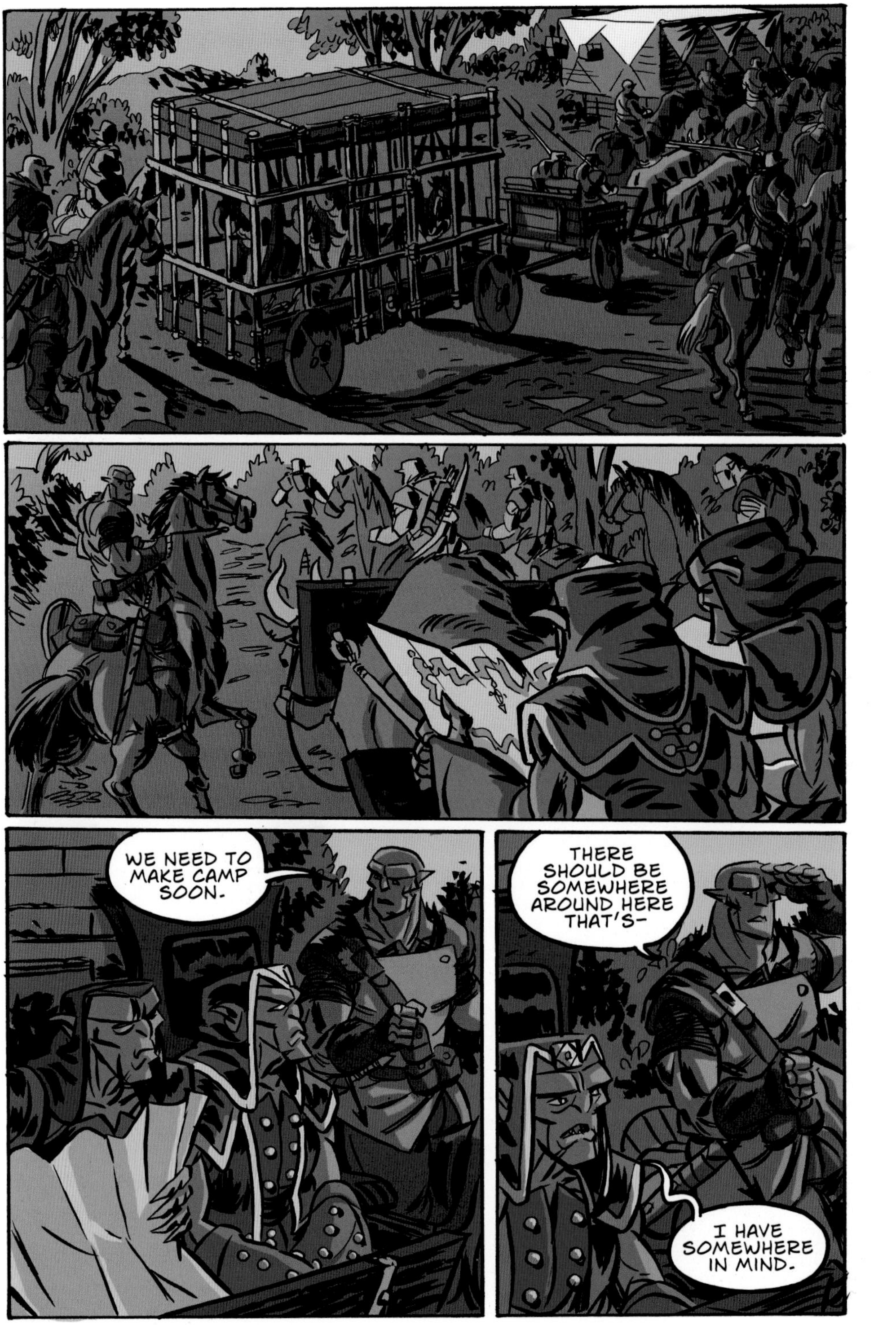
WE NEED TO MAKE CAMP SOON.
THERE SHOULD BE SOMEWHERE AROUND HERE THAT'S-
I HAVE SOMEWHERE IN MIND.

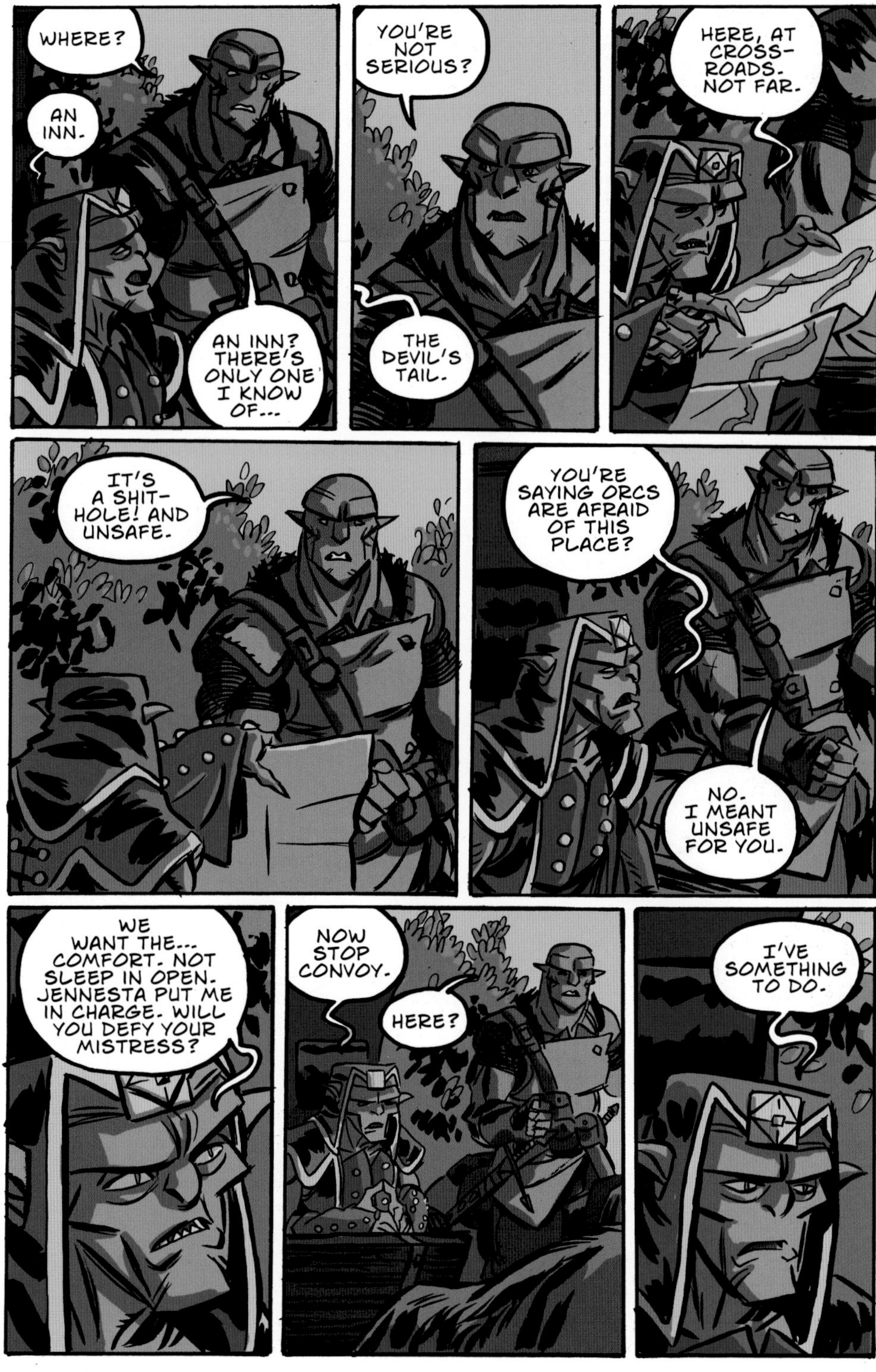
WHERE?
AN INN.
AN INN? THERE'S ONLY ONE I KNOW OF...
YOU'RE NOT SERIOUS?
THE DEVIL'S TAIL.
HERE, AT CROSS-ROADS. NOT FAR.
IT'S A SHIT-HOLE! AND UNSAFE.
YOU'RE SAYING ORCS ARE AFRAID OF THIS PLACE?
NO. I MEANT UNSAFE FOR YOU.
WE WANT THE... COMFORT. NOT SLEEP IN OPEN. JENNESTA PUT ME IN CHARGE. WILL YOU DEFY YOUR MISTRESS?
NOW STOP CONVOY.
HERE?
I'VE SOMETHING TO DO.

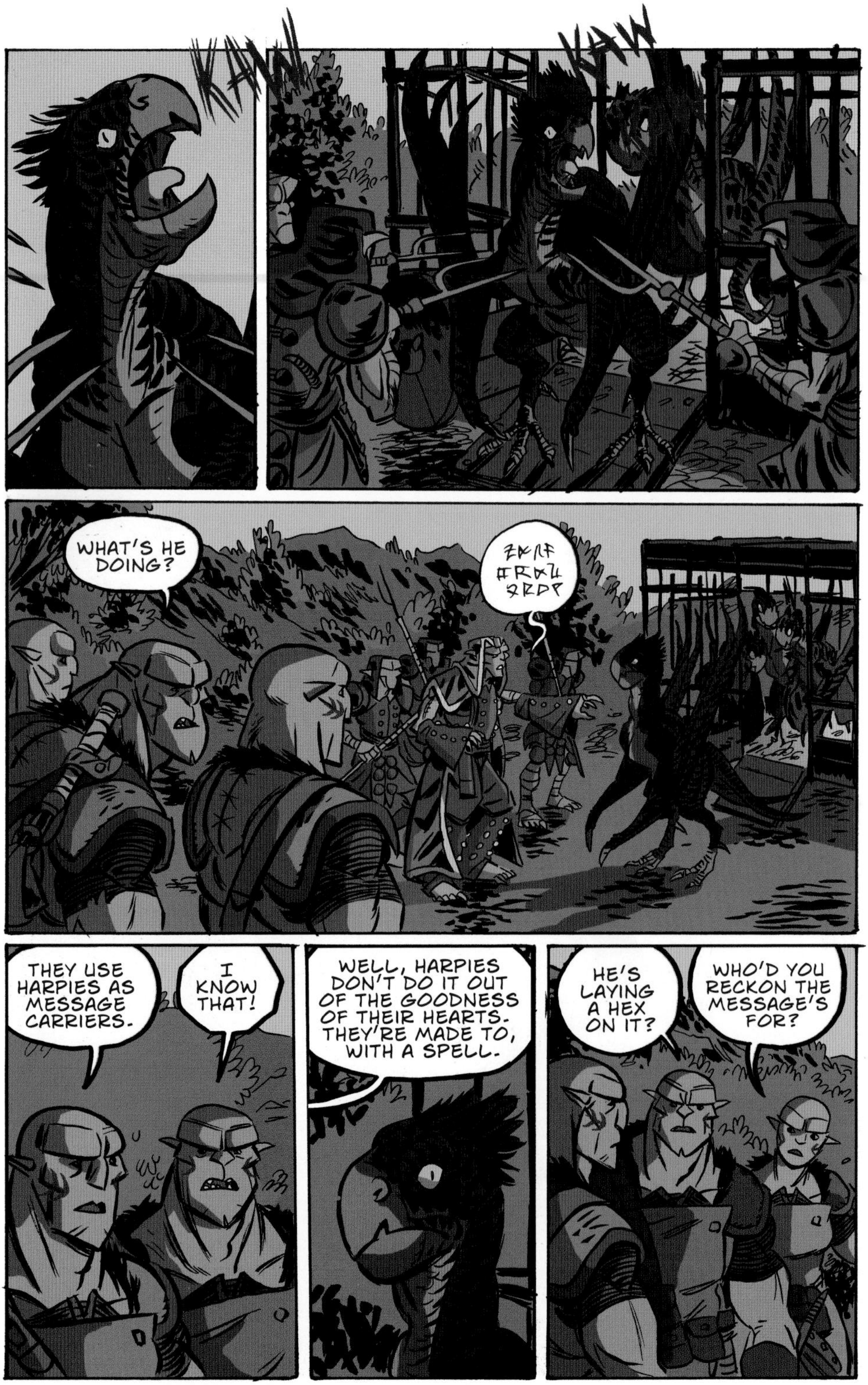
KAW
KAW
WHAT'S HE DOING?
THEY USE HARPIES AS MESSAGE CARRIERS.
I KNOW THAT!
WELL, HARPIES DON'T DO IT OUT OF THE GOODNESS OF THEIR HEARTS. THEY'RE MADE TO, WITH A SPELL.
HE'S LAYING A HEX ON IT?
WHO'D YOU RECKON THE MESSAGE'S FOR?

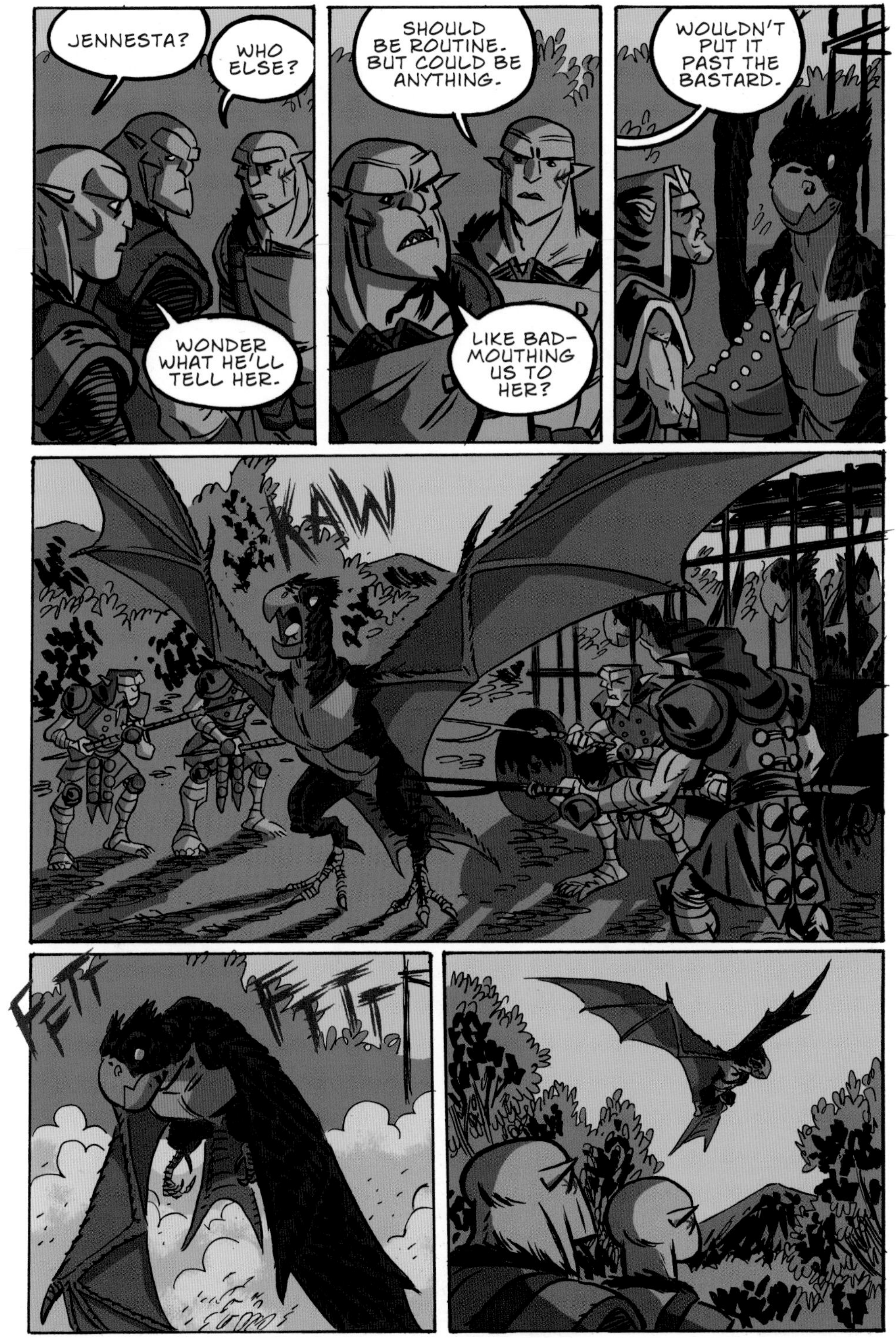
JENNESTA?
WHO ELSE?
WONDER WHAT HE'LL TELL HER.
SHOULD BE ROUTINE. BUT COULD BE ANYTHING.
LIKE BAD-MOUTHING US TO HER?
WOULDN'T PUT IT PAST THE BASTARD.
KAW

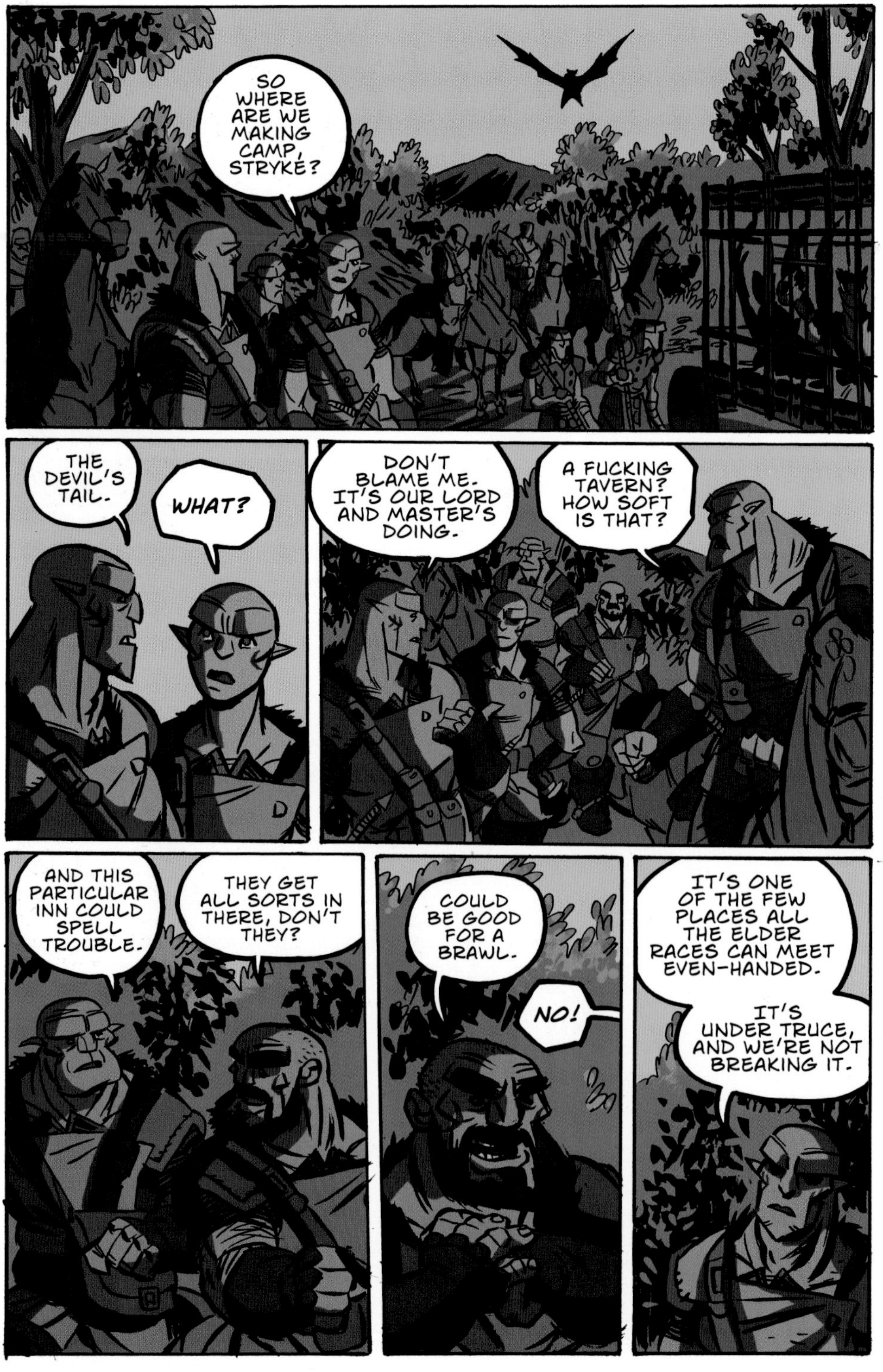

SO WHERE ARE WE MAKING CAMP, STRYKE?
THE DEVIL'S TAIL.
WHAT?
DON'T BLAME ME. IT'S OUR LORD AND MASTER'S DOING.
A FUCKING TAVERN? HOW SOFT IS THAT?
AND THIS PARTICULAR INN COULD SPELL TROUBLE.
THEY GET ALL SORTS IN THERE, DON'T THEY?
COULD BE GOOD FOR A BRAWL.
NO!
IT'S ONE OF THE FEW PLACES ALL THE ELDER RACES CAN MEET EVEN-HANDED.
IT'S UNDER TRUCE, AND WE'RE NOT BREAKING IT.

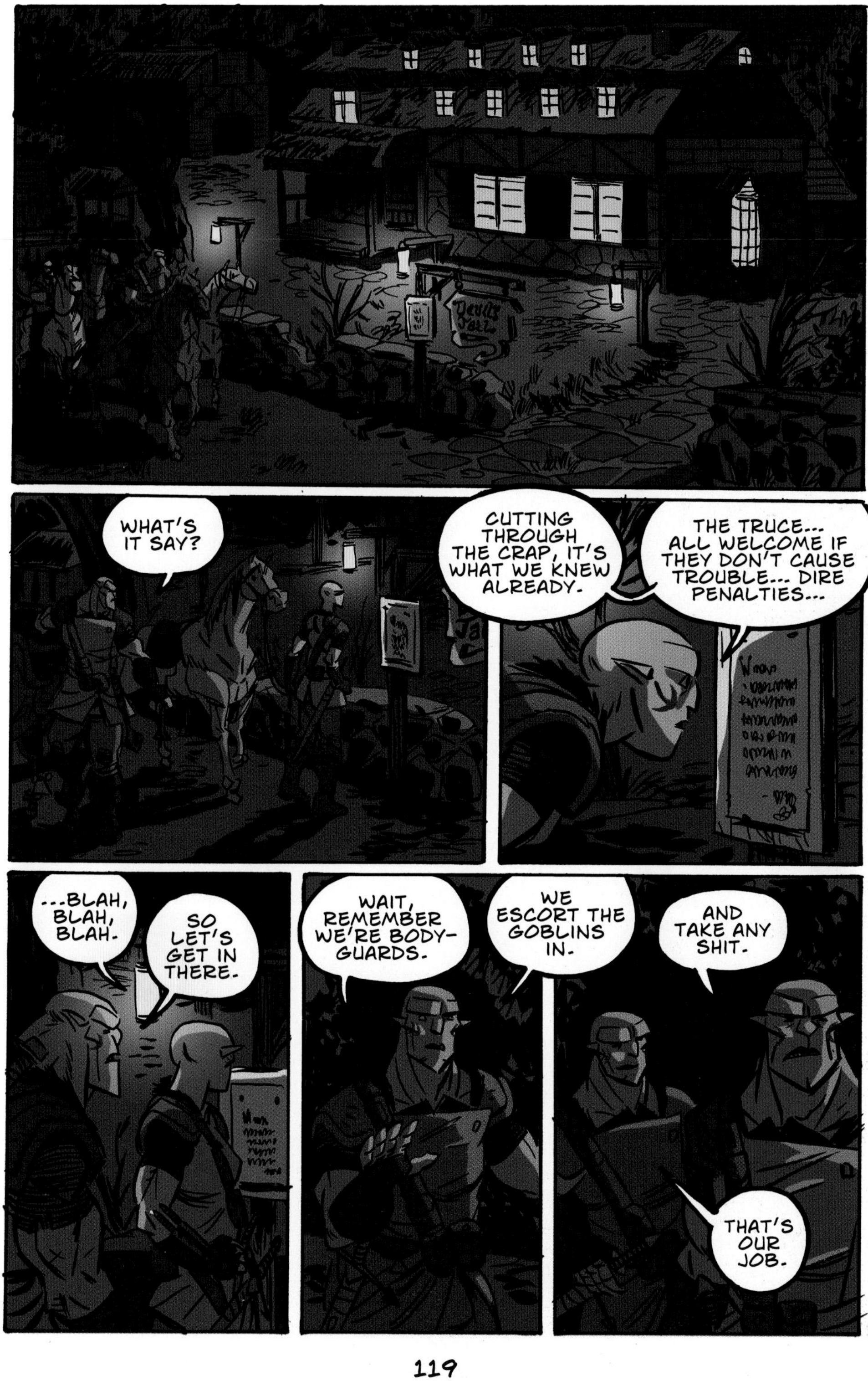
WHAT'S IT SAY?
CUTTING THROUGH THE CRAP, IT'S WHAT WE KNEW ALREADY.
THE TRUCE... ALL WELCOME IF THEY DON'T CAUSE TROUBLE... DIRE PENALTIES...
...BLAH, BLAH, BLAH.
SO LET'S GET IN THERE.
WAIT, REMEMBER WE'RE BODY-GUARDS.
WE ESCORT THE GOBLINS IN.
AND TAKE ANY SHIT.
THAT'S OUR JOB.

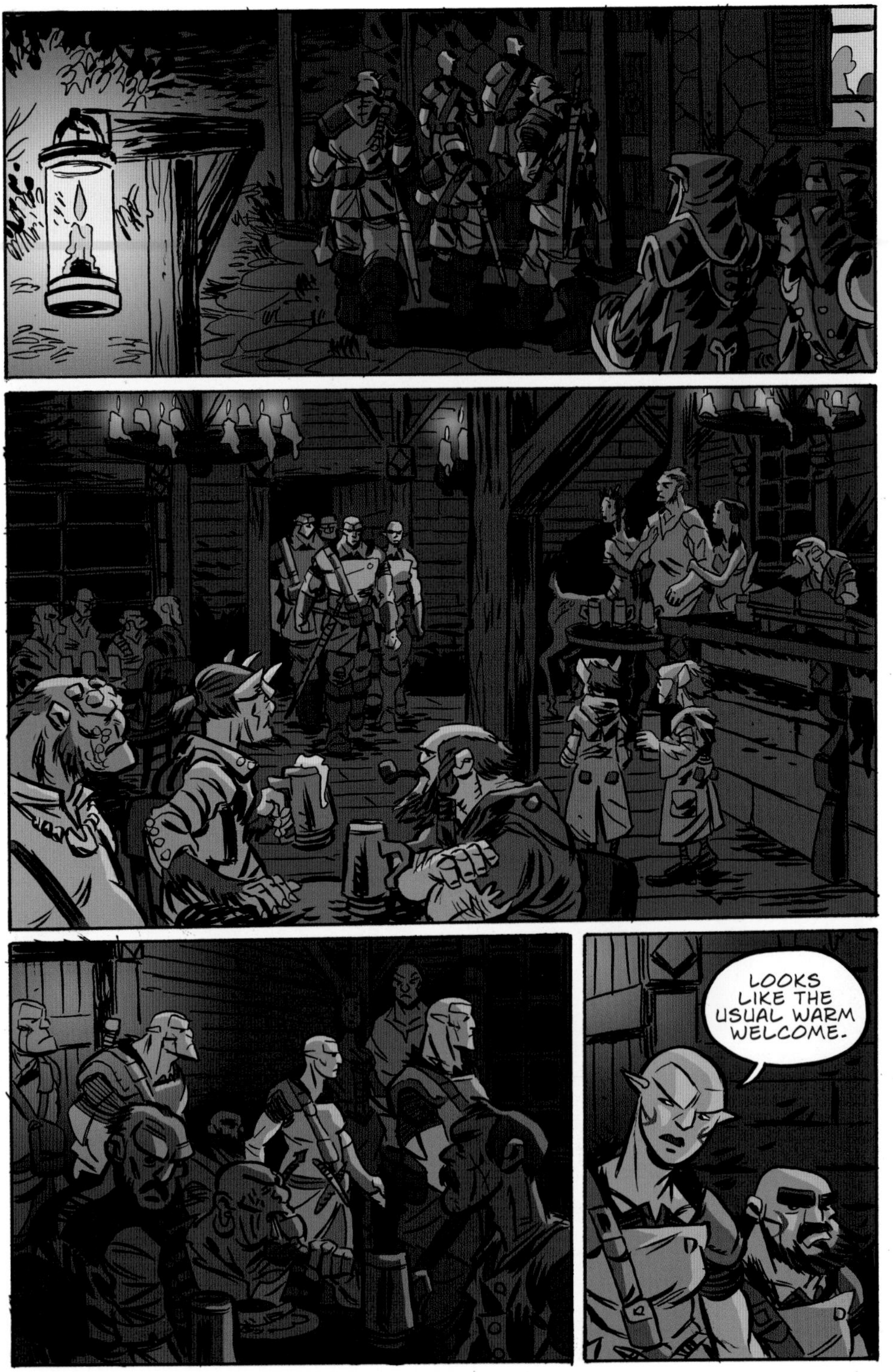
LOOKS LIKE THE USUAL WARM WELCOME.

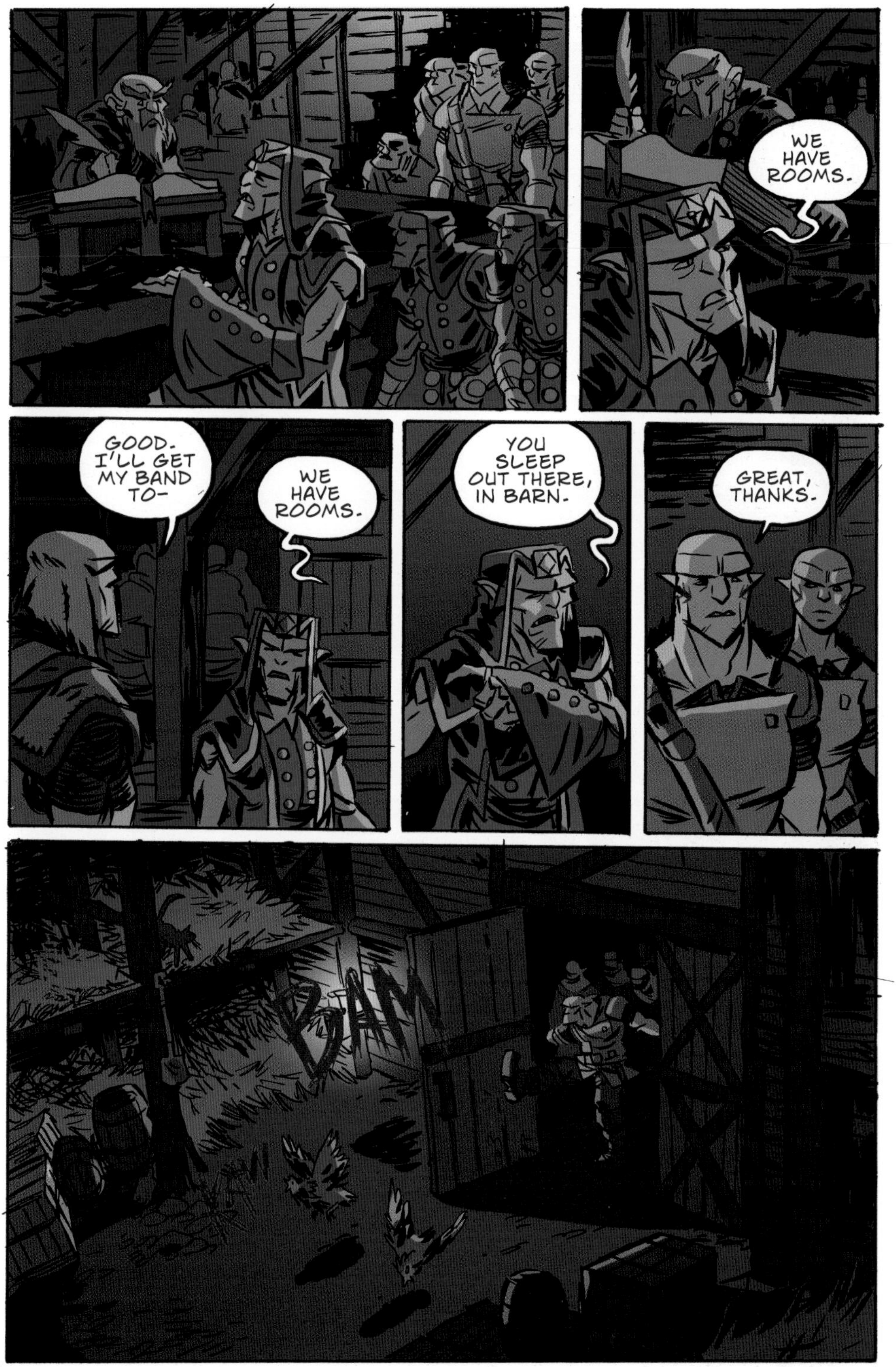
WE HAVE ROOMS.
GOOD. I'LL GET MY BAND TO-
WE HAVE ROOMS.
YOU SLEEP OUT THERE, IN BARN.
GREAT, THANKS.
BAM

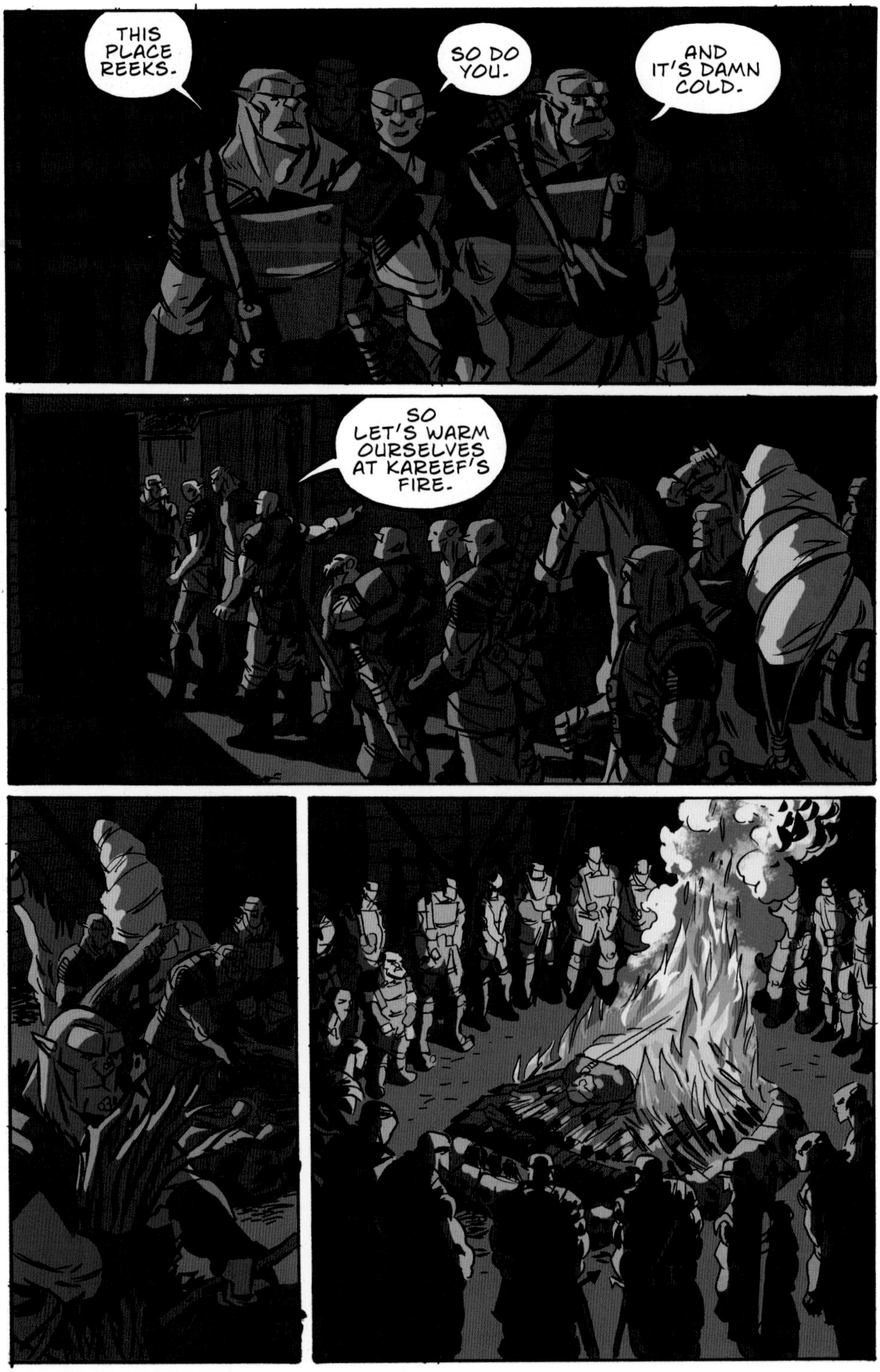
THIS PLACE REEKS.
SO DO YOU.
AND IT'S DAMN COLD.
SO LET'S WARM OURSELVES AT KAREEF'S FIRE.

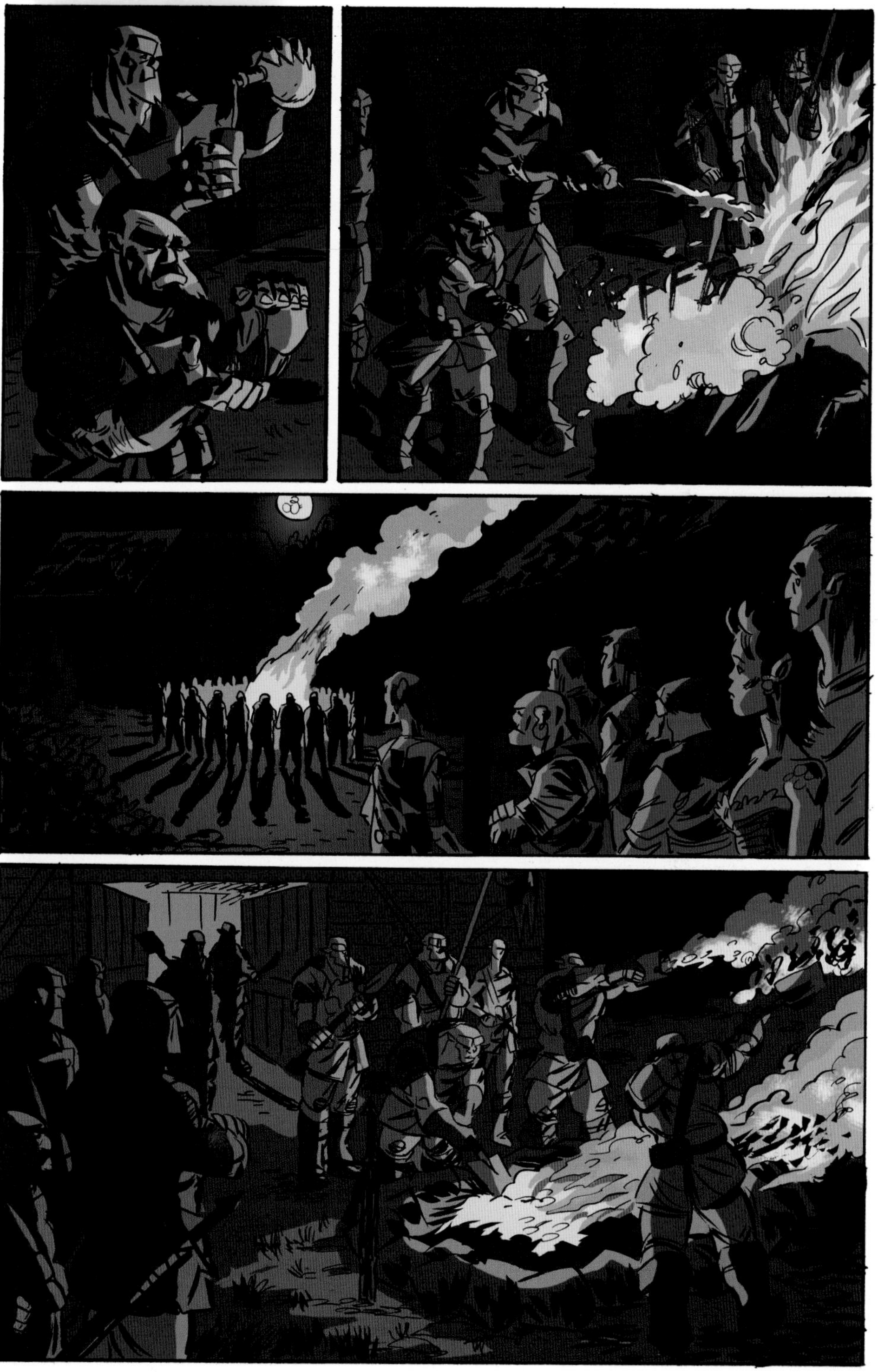

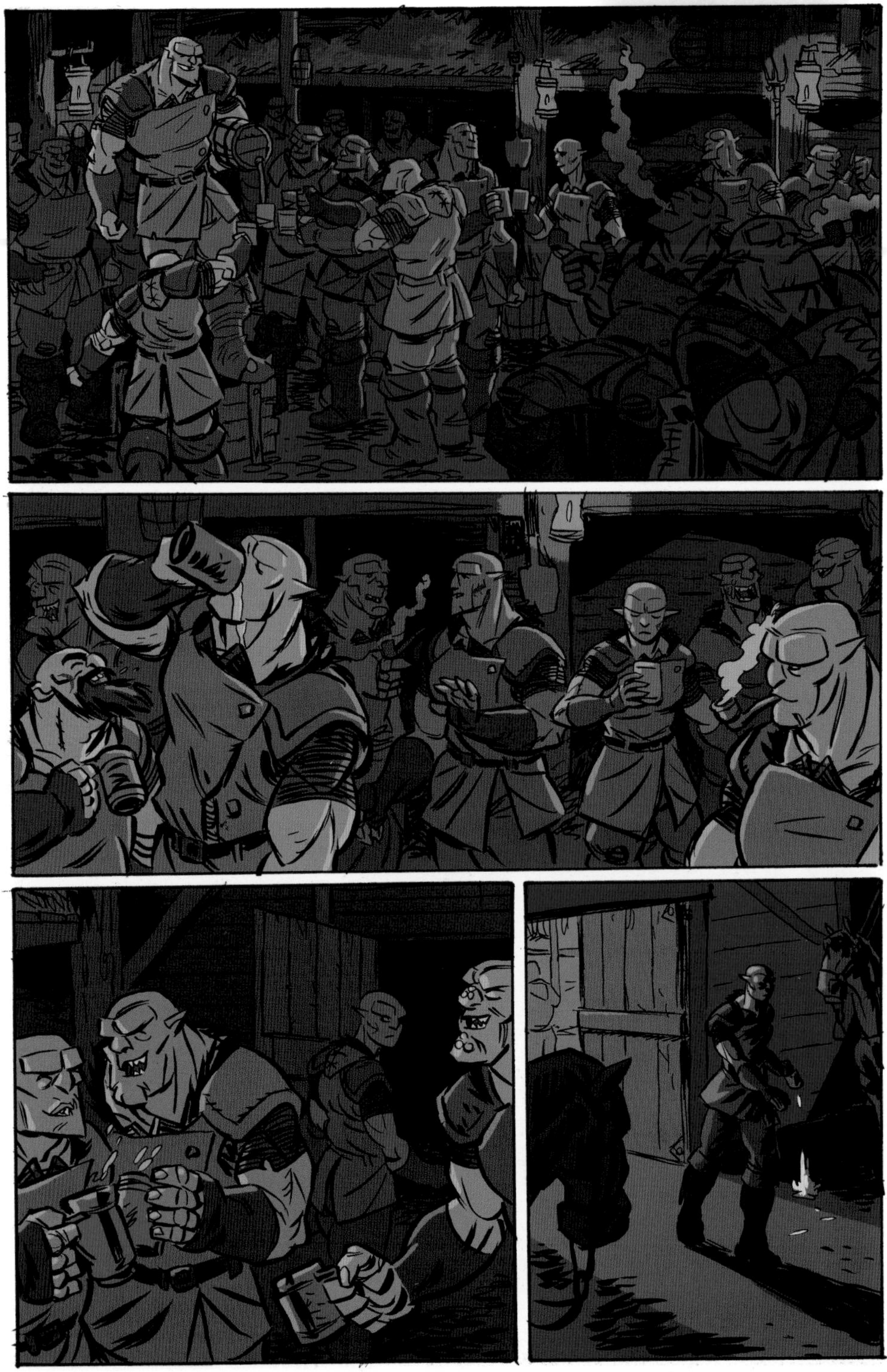

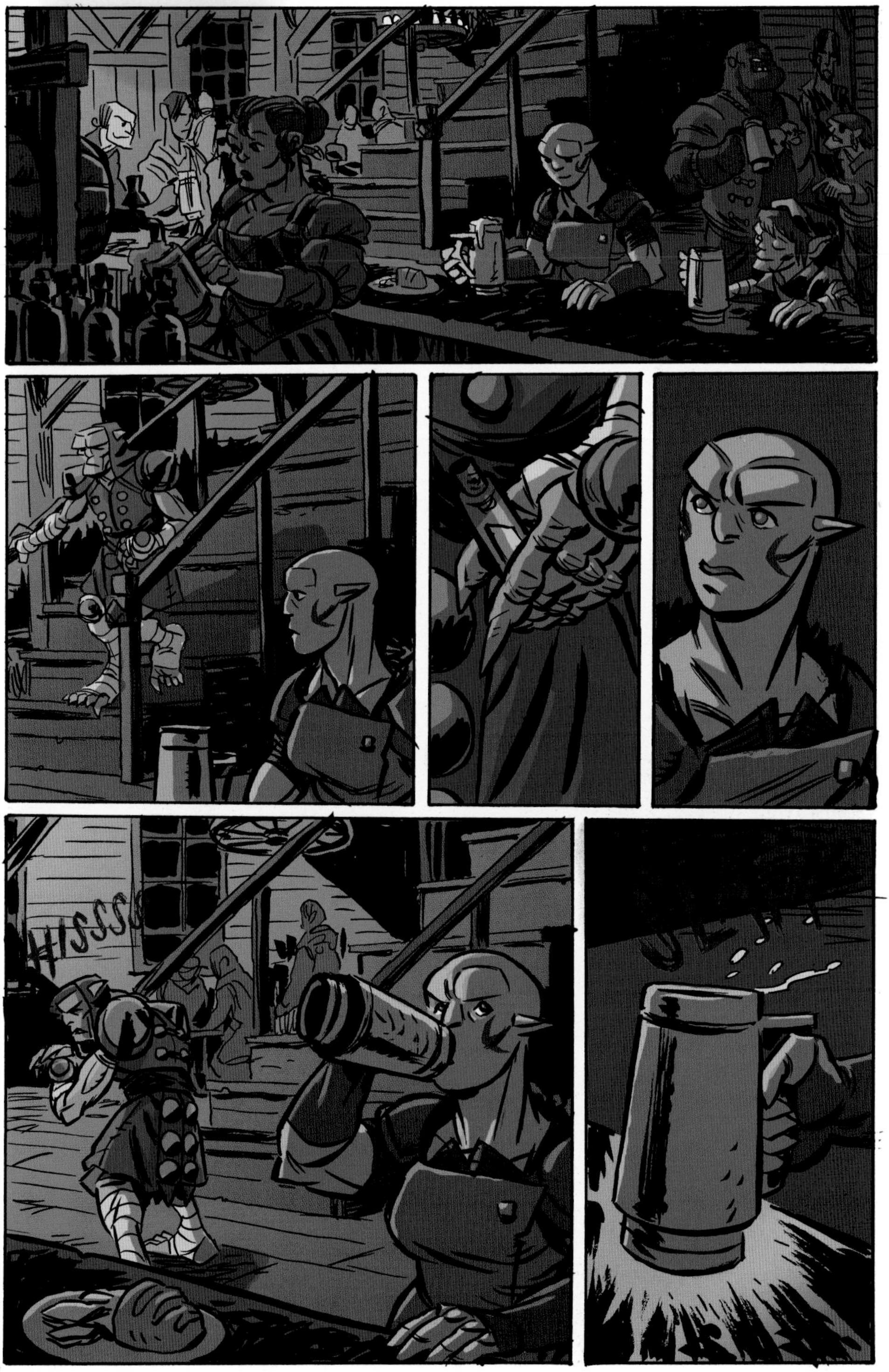
HISSSS
SLAM

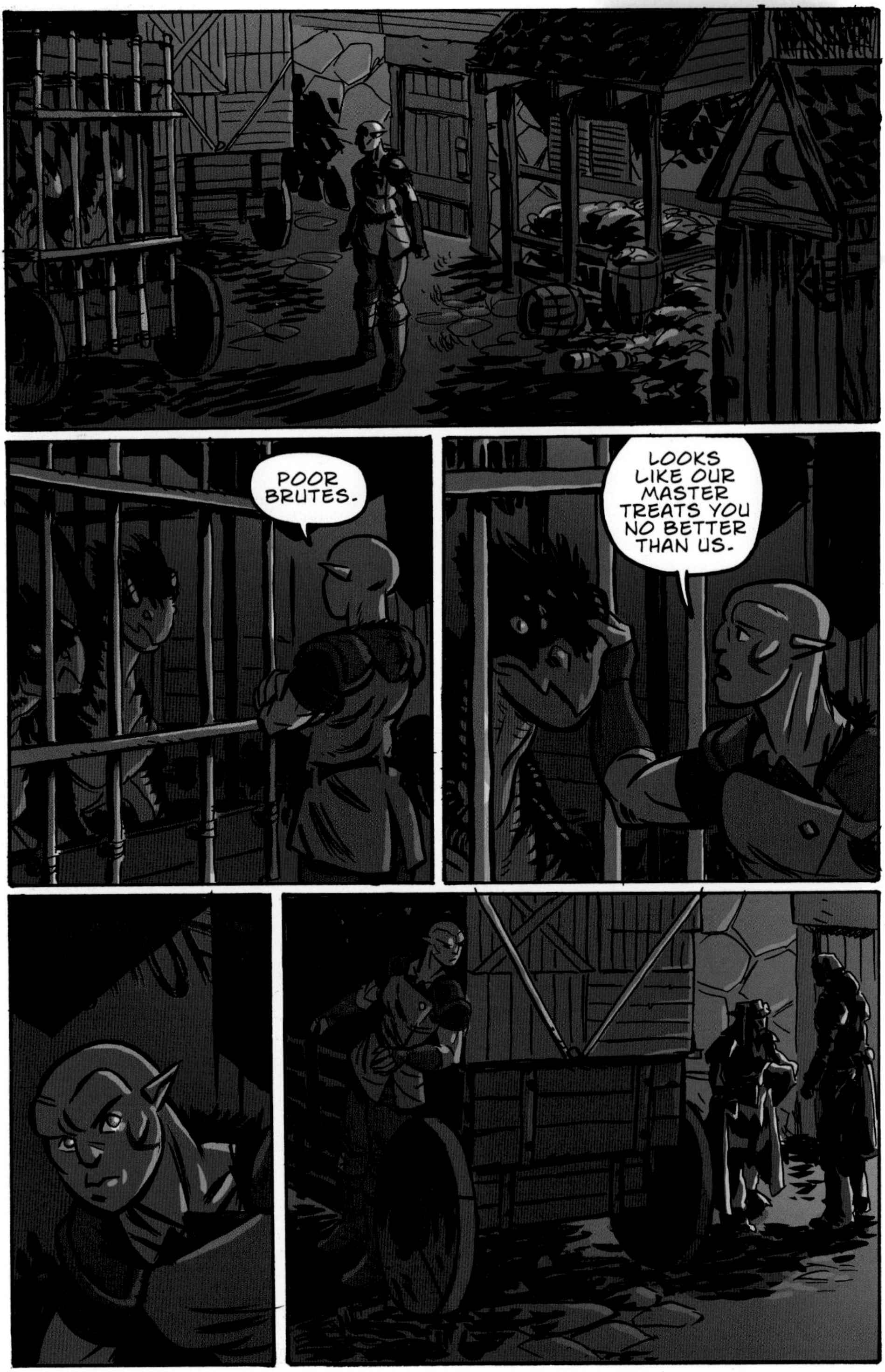
POOR BRUTES.
LOOKS LIKE OUR MASTER TREATS YOU NO BETTER THAN US.

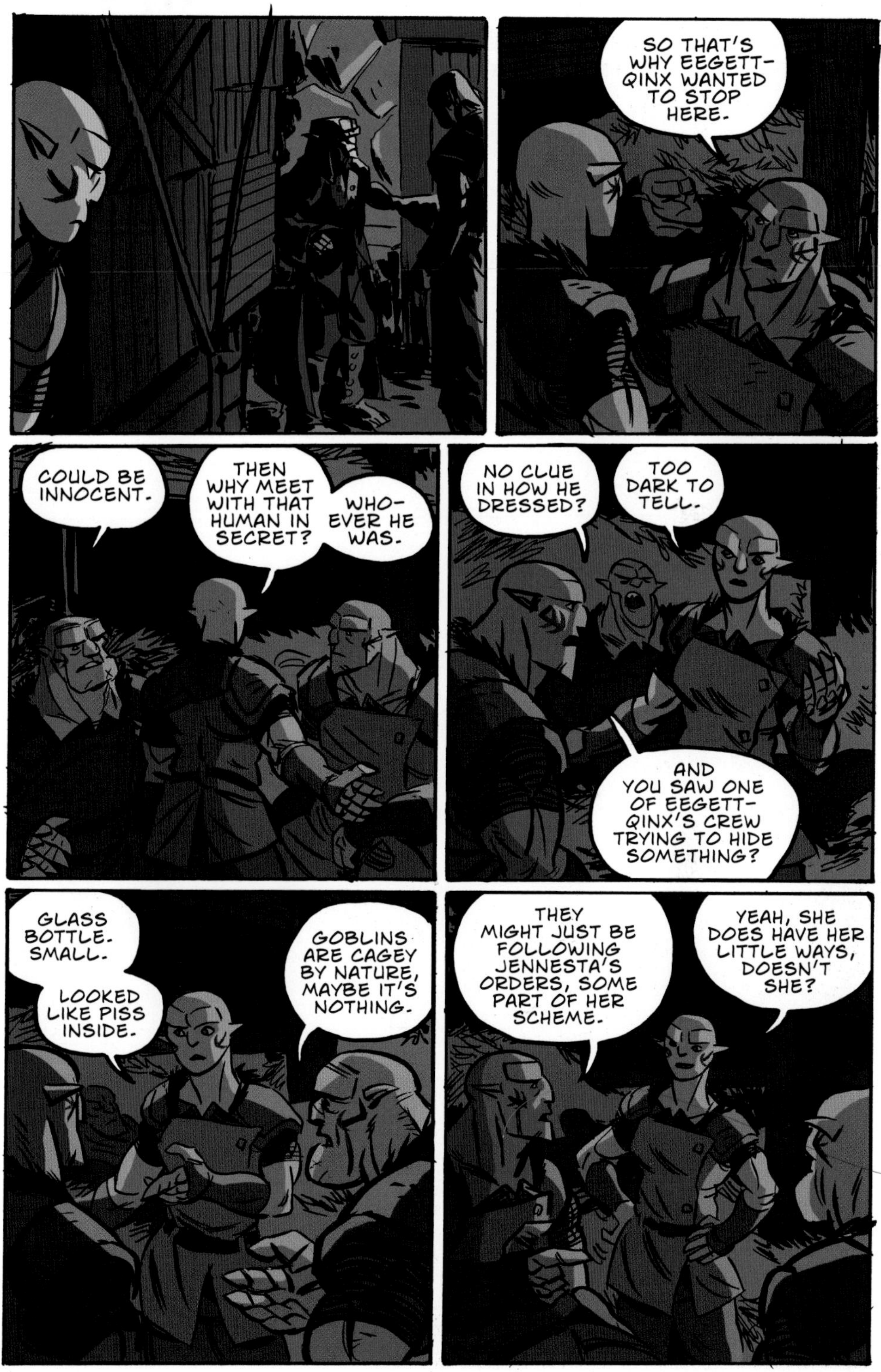

SO THAT'S WHY EEGETT-QINX WANTED TO STOP HERE.
COULD BE INNOCENT.
THEN WHY MEET WITH THAT HUMAN IN SECRET?
WHO-EVER HE WAS.
NO CLUE IN HOW HE DRESSED?
TOO DARK TO TELL.
AND YOU SAW ONE OF EEGETT-QINX'S CREW TRYING TO HIDE SOMETHING?
GLASS BOTTLE. SMALL.
LOOKED LIKE PISS INSIDE.
GOBLINS ARE CAGEY BY NATURE, MAYBE IT'S NOTHING.
THEY MIGHT JUST BE FOLLOWING JENNESTA'S ORDERS, SOME PART OF HER SCHEME.
YEAH, SHE DOES HAVE HER LITTLE WAYS, DOESN'T SHE?

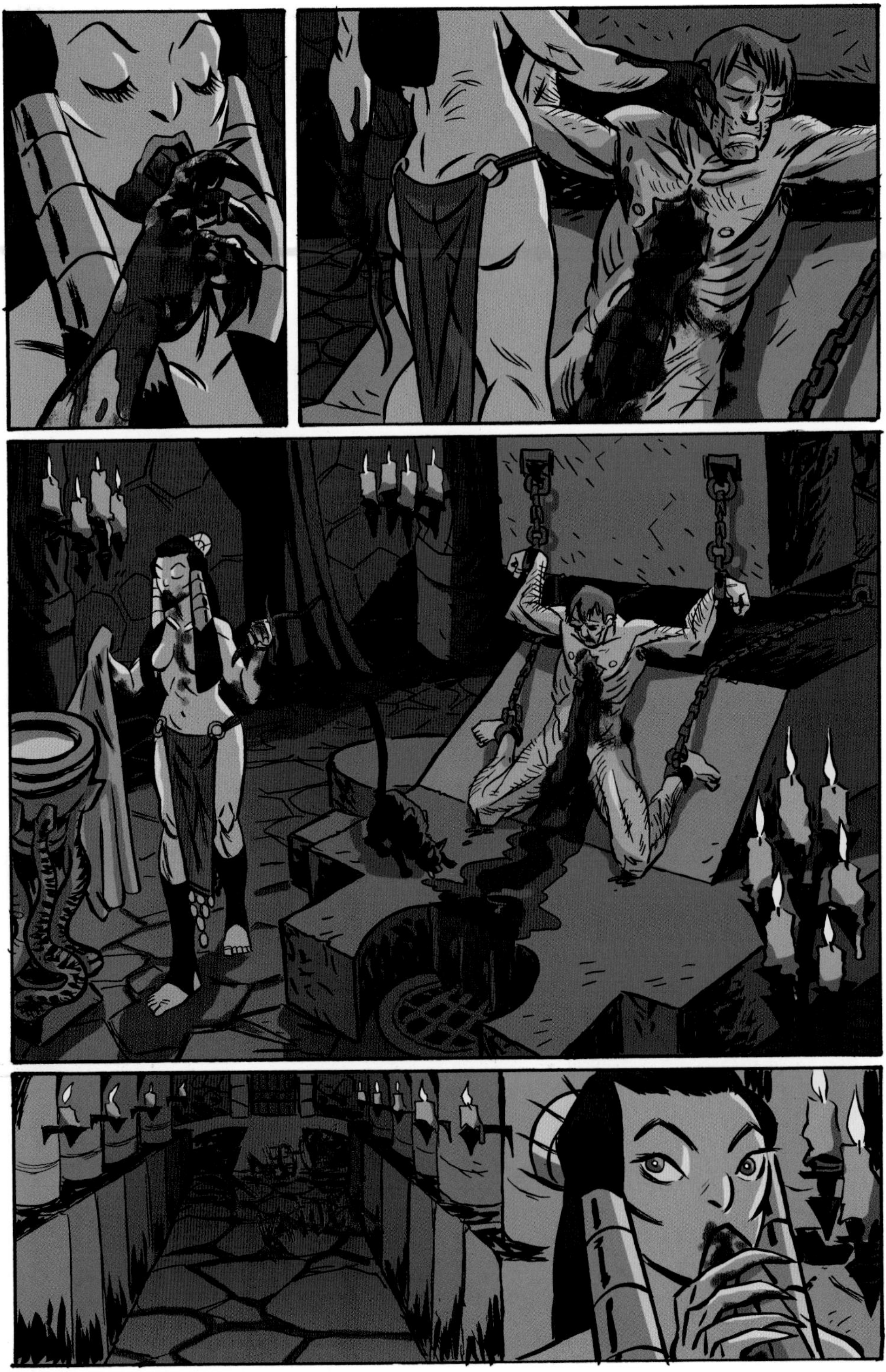

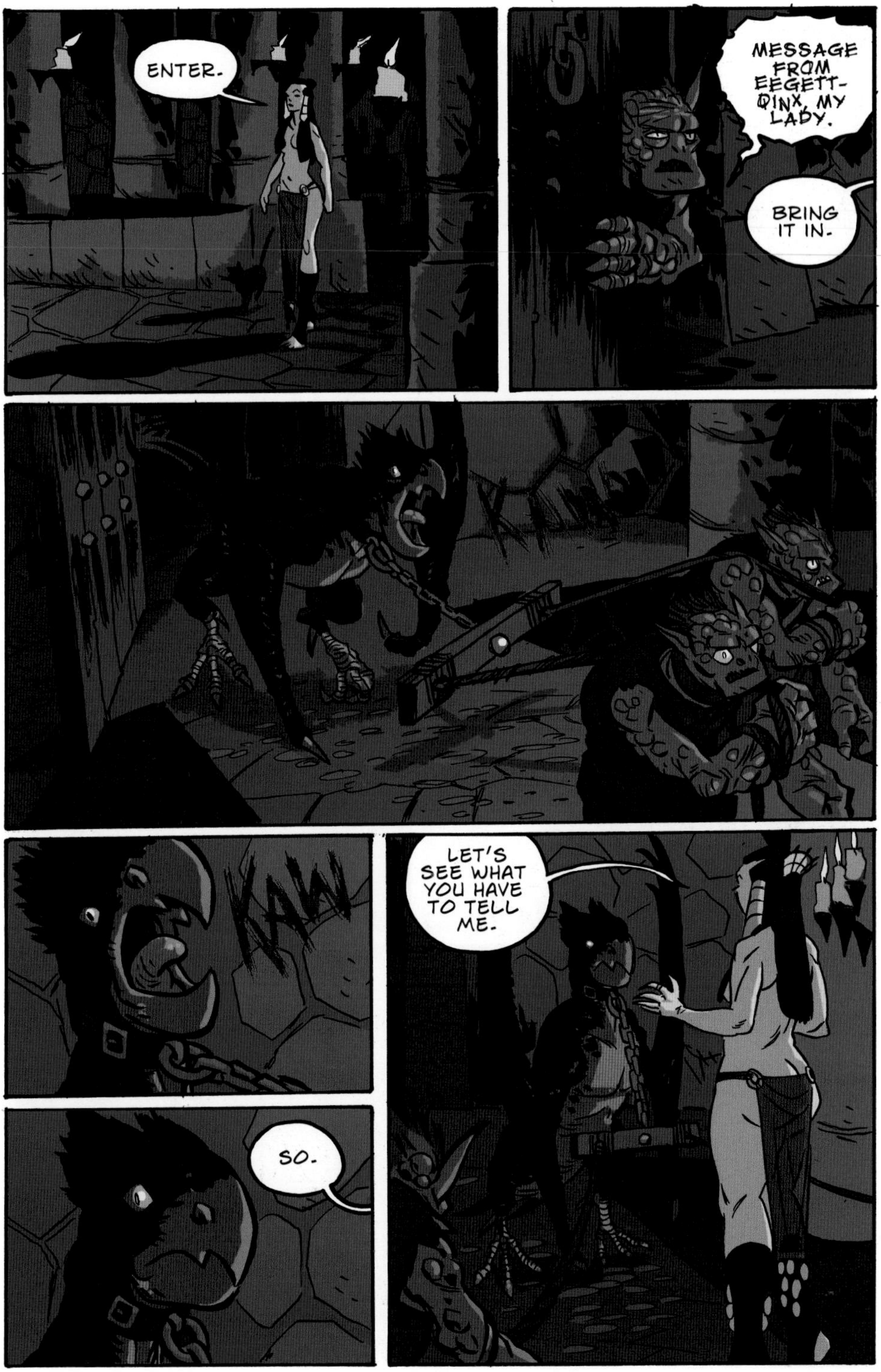
ENTER.
MESSAGE FROM EEGETT-QINX, MY LADY.
BRING IT IN.
KAW
KAW
LET'S SEE WHAT YOU HAVE TO TELL ME.
SO.

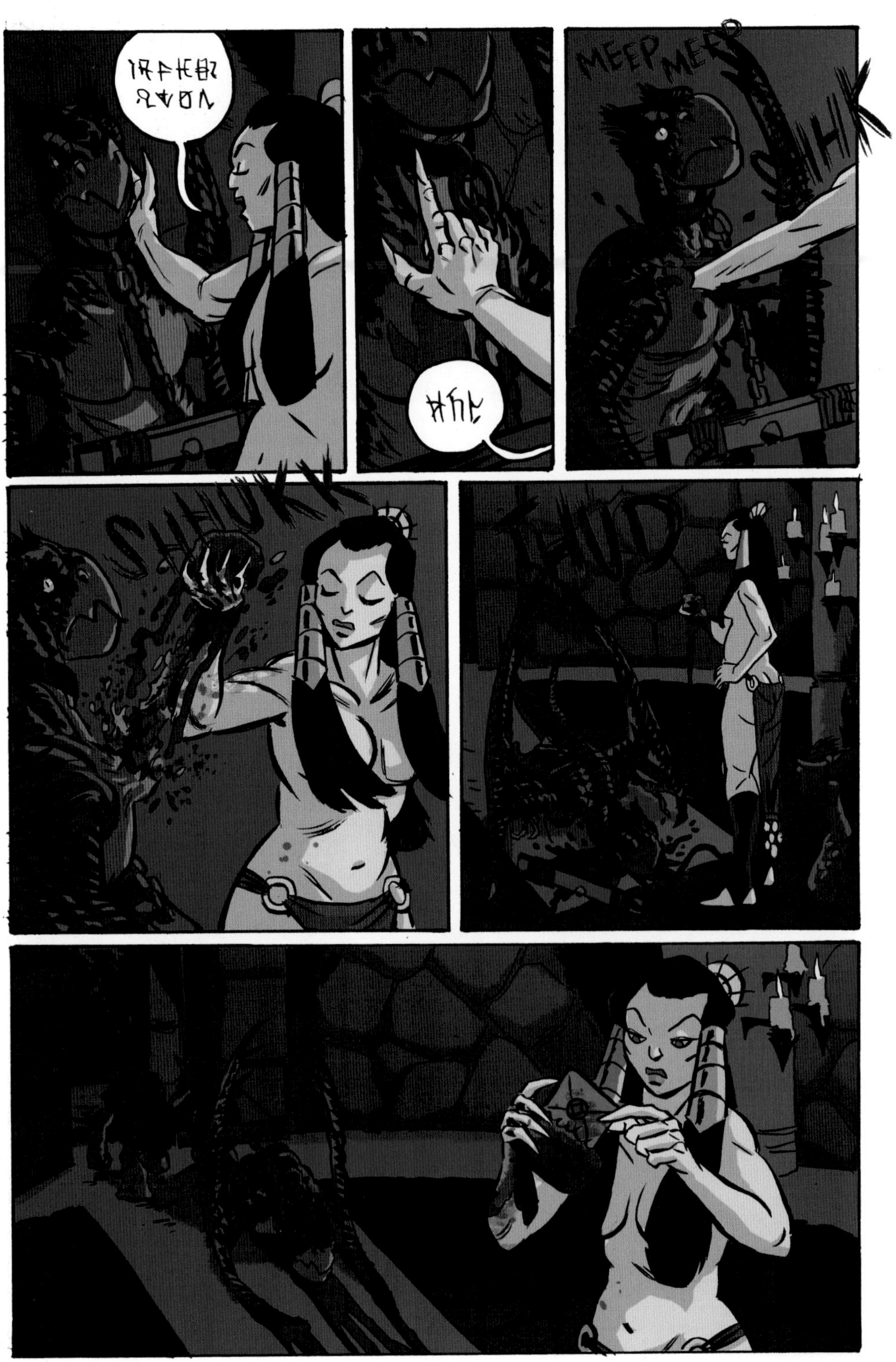
MEEP MEEP
THUD

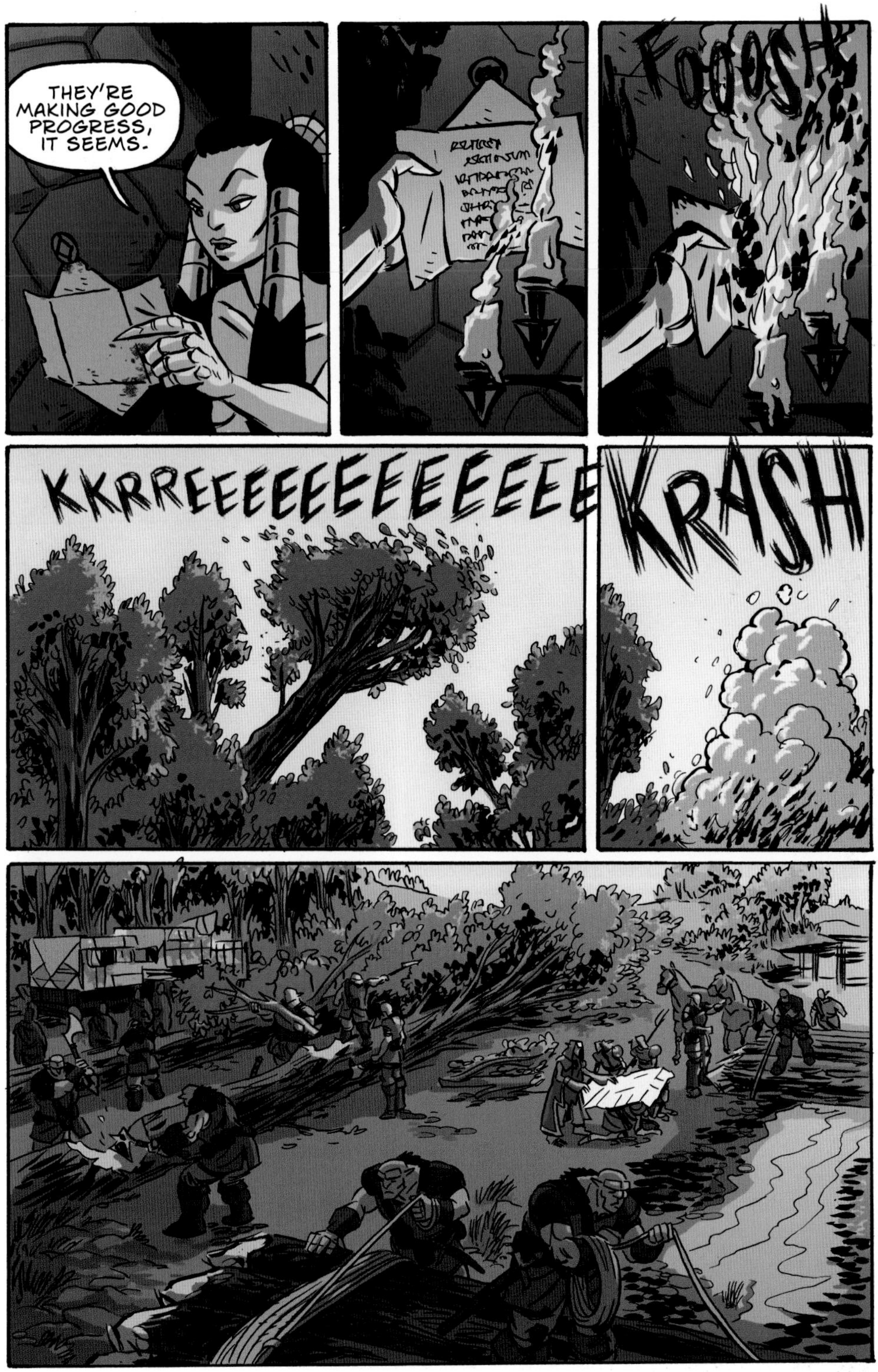
THEY'RE MAKING GOOD PROGRESS, IT SEEMS.
FOOOSH
KKRREEEEEEEEEEEEE
KRASH

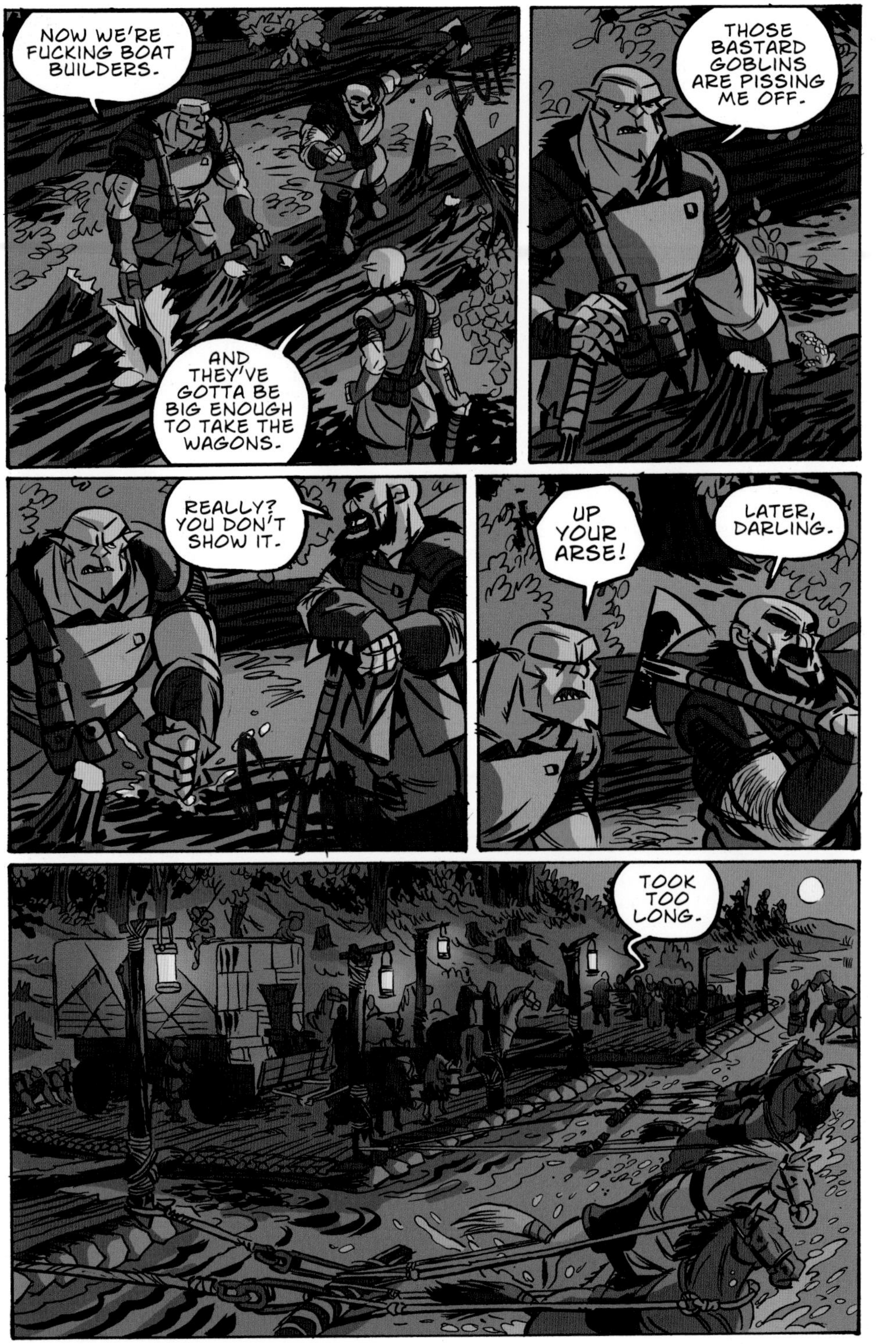
NOW WE'RE FUCKING BOAT BUILDERS.
AND THEY'VE GOTTA BE BIG ENOUGH TO TAKE THE WAGONS.
THOSE BASTARD GOBLINS ARE PISSING ME OFF.
REALLY? YOU DON'T SHOW IT.
UP YOUR ARSE!
LATER, DARLING.
TOOK TOO LONG.

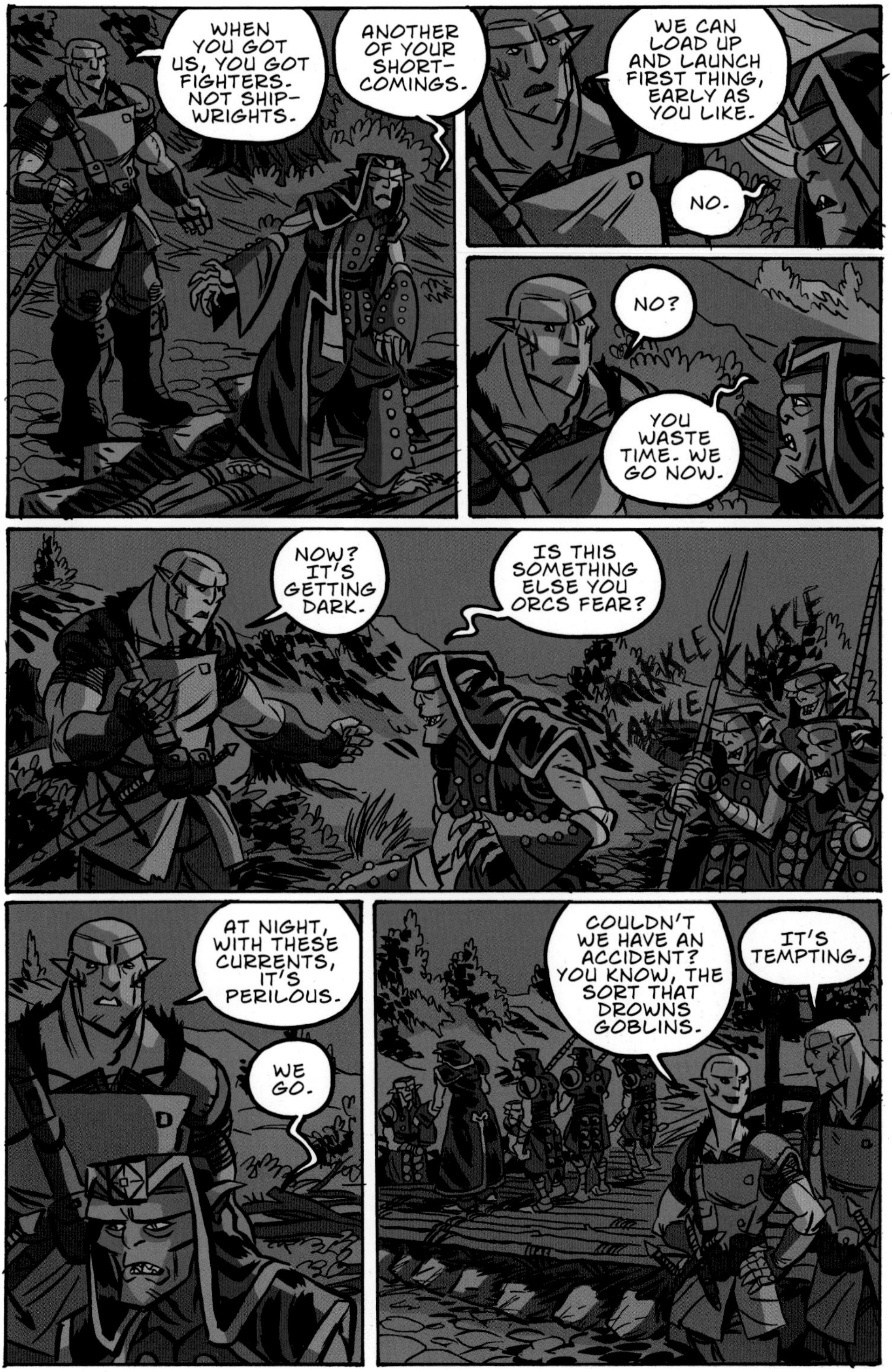
WHEN YOU GOT US, YOU GOT FIGHTERS. NOT SHIP-WRIGHTS.
ANOTHER OF YOUR SHORT-COMINGS.
WE CAN LOAD UP AND LAUNCH FIRST THING, EARLY AS YOU LIKE.
NO.
NO?
YOU WASTE TIME. WE GO NOW.
NOW? IT'S GETTING DARK.
IS THIS SOMETHING ELSE YOU ORCS FEAR?
AT NIGHT, WITH THESE CURRENTS, IT'S PERILOUS.
WE GO.
COULDN'T WE HAVE AN ACCIDENT? YOU KNOW, THE SORT THAT DROWNS GOBLINS.
IT'S TEMPTING.

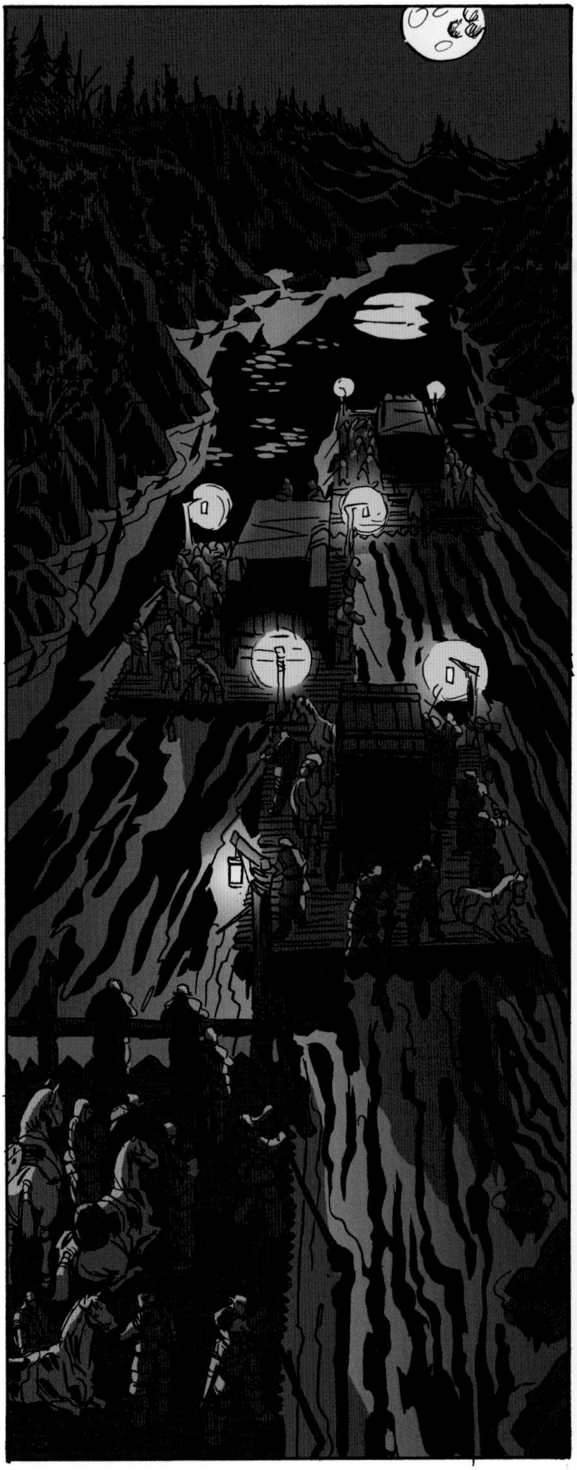

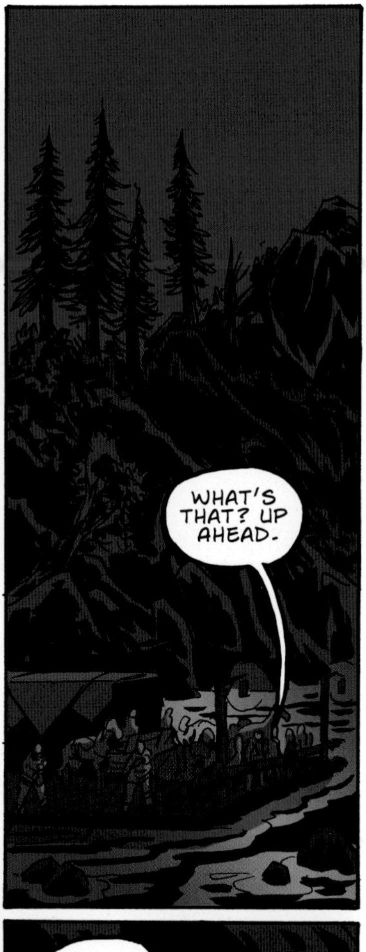
WHAT'S THAT? UP AHEAD.

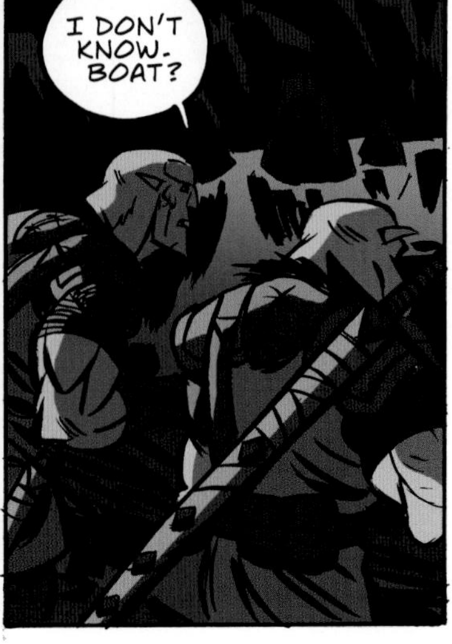
I DON'T KNOW. BOAT?

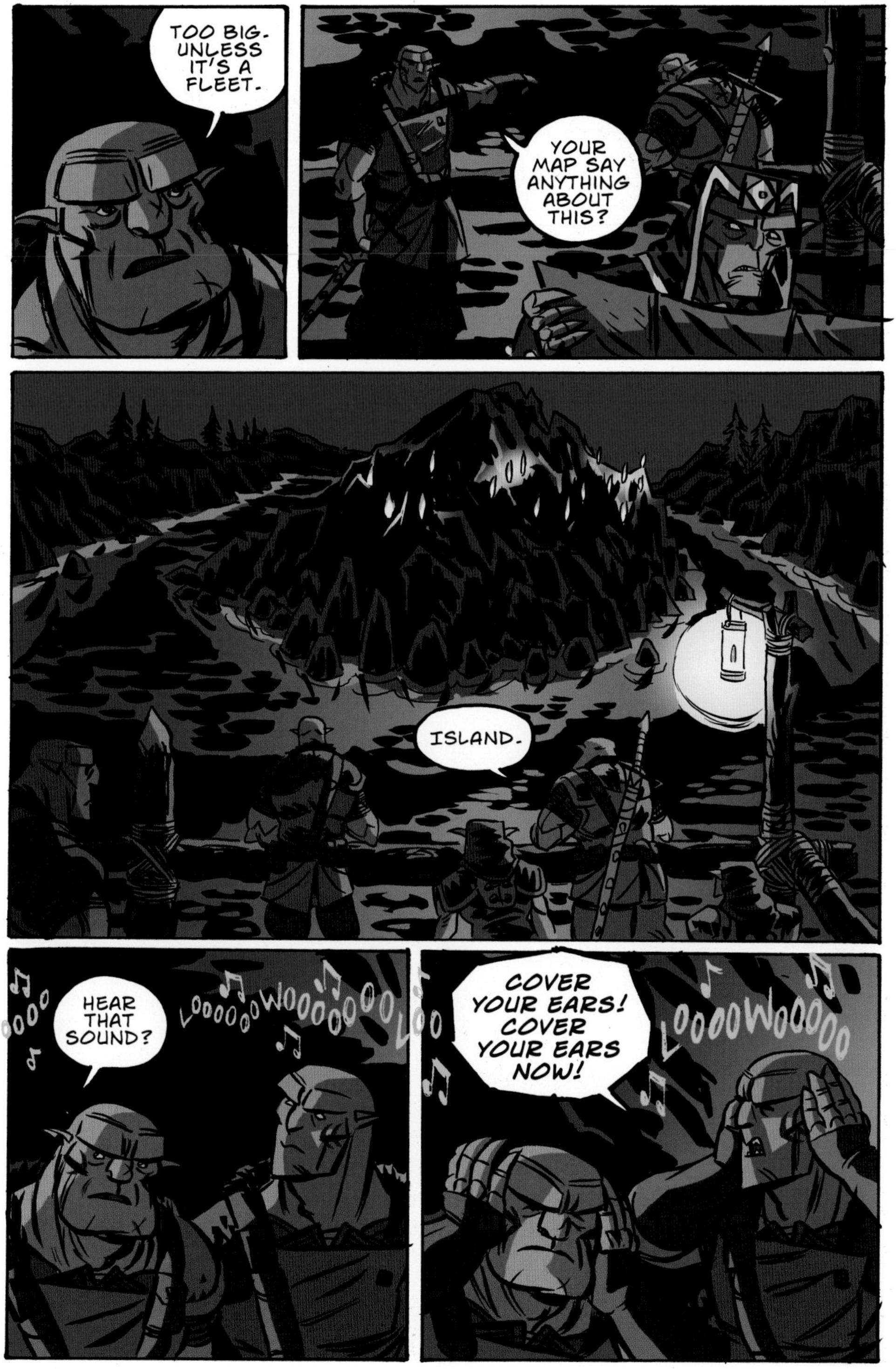
TOO BIG. UNLESS IT'S A FLEET.
YOUR MAP SAY ANYTHING ABOUT THIS?
ISLAND.
HEAR THAT SOUND?
LOOOOOOWOOOOOOOOLOO
COVER YOUR EARS! COVER YOUR EARS NOW!
LOOOOWOOOOO

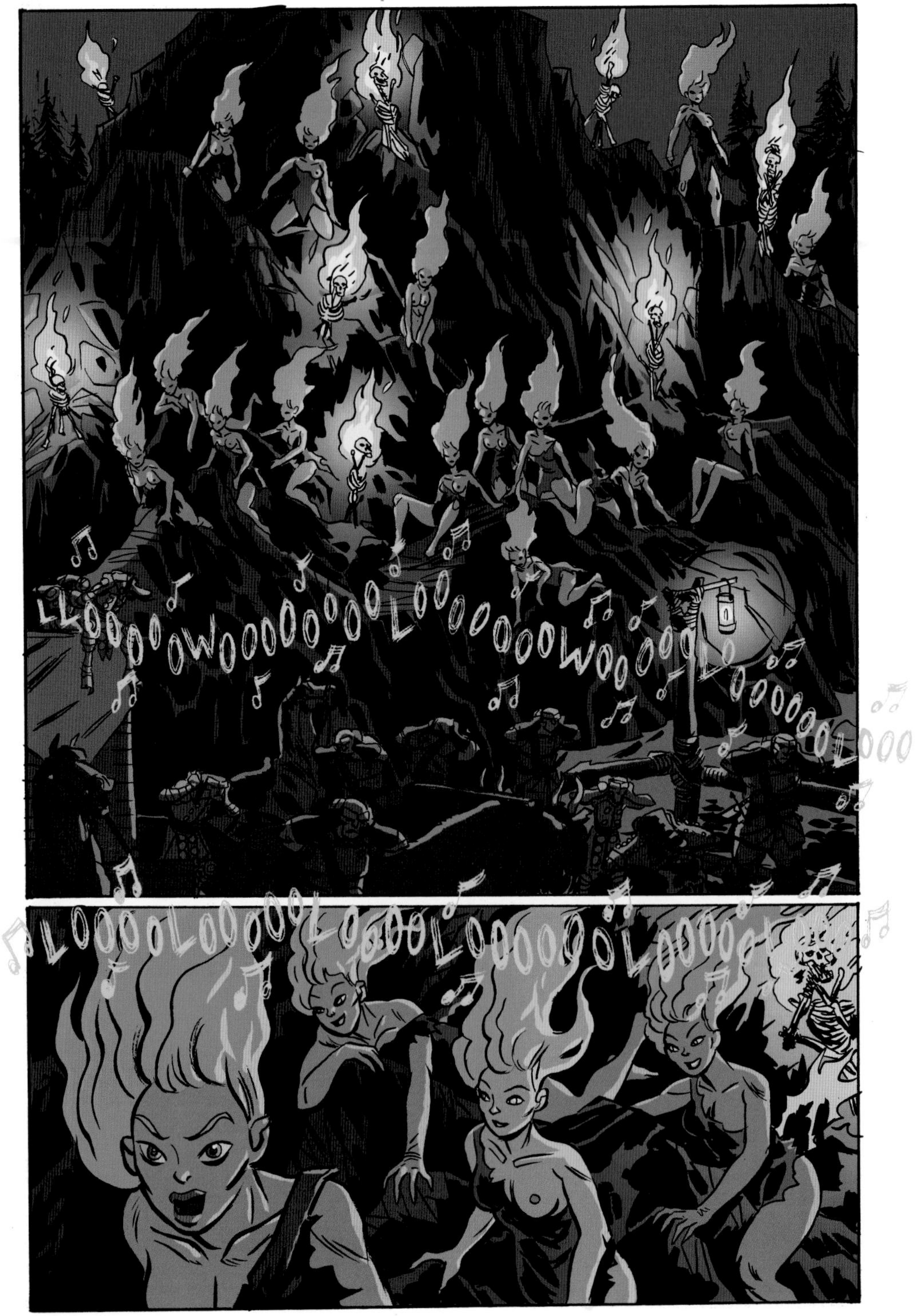
LLOOOOOWOOOOOOOOOLOOOOOOOOWOOOOO-LOOOOOOOOLOOO
LOOOOLOOOOOOLOOOOOLOOOOOOOLOOOO

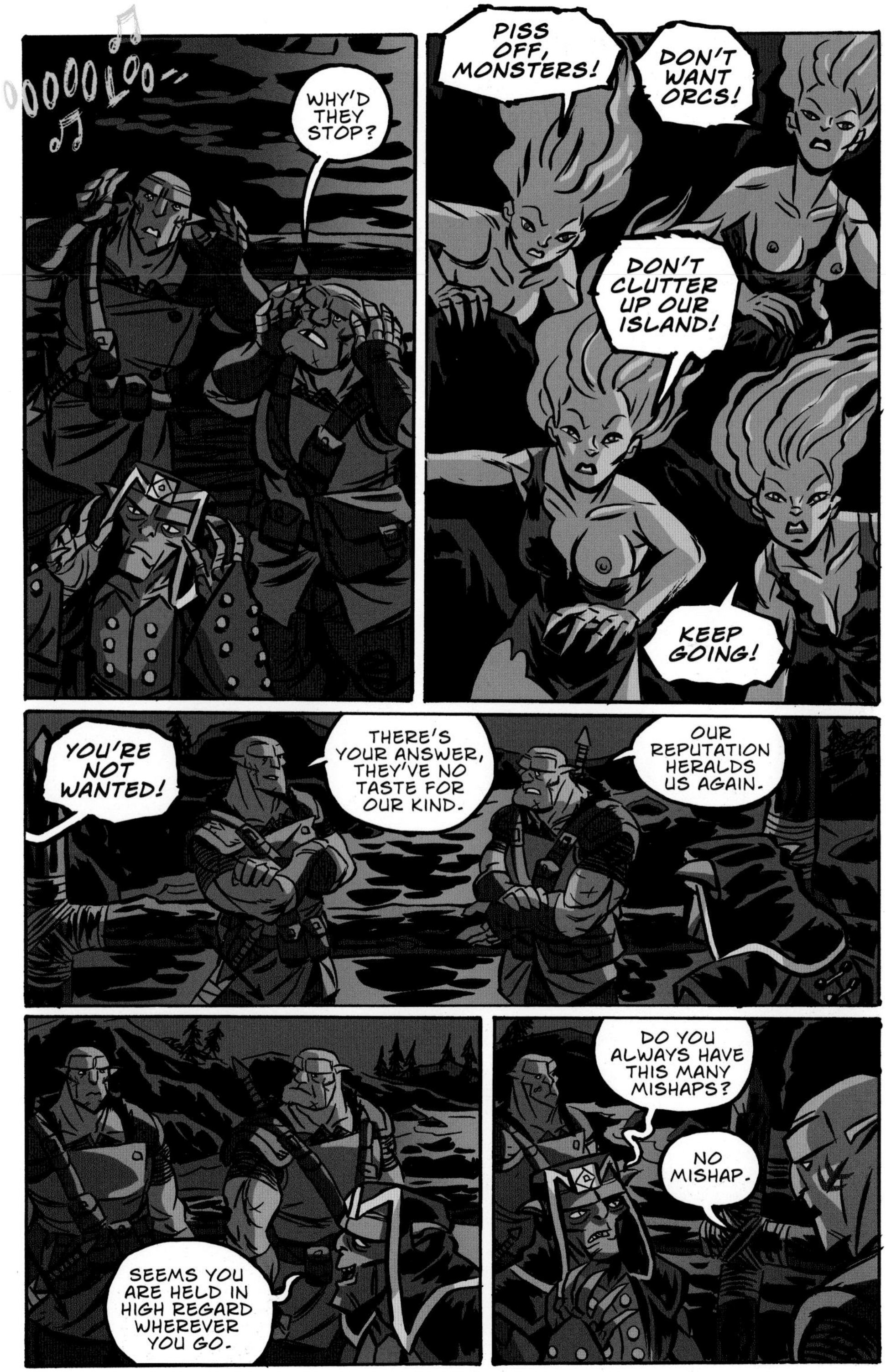

OOOOOLOO--
WHY'D THEY STOP?
PISS OFF, MONSTERS!
DON'T WANT ORCS!
DON'T CLUTTER UP OUR ISLAND!
KEEP GOING!
YOU'RE NOT WANTED!
THERE'S YOUR ANSWER, THEY'VE NO TASTE FOR OUR KIND.
OUR REPUTATION HERALDS US AGAIN.
SEEMS YOU ARE HELD IN HIGH REGARD WHEREVER YOU GO.
DO YOU ALWAYS HAVE THIS MANY MISHAPS?
NO MISHAP.

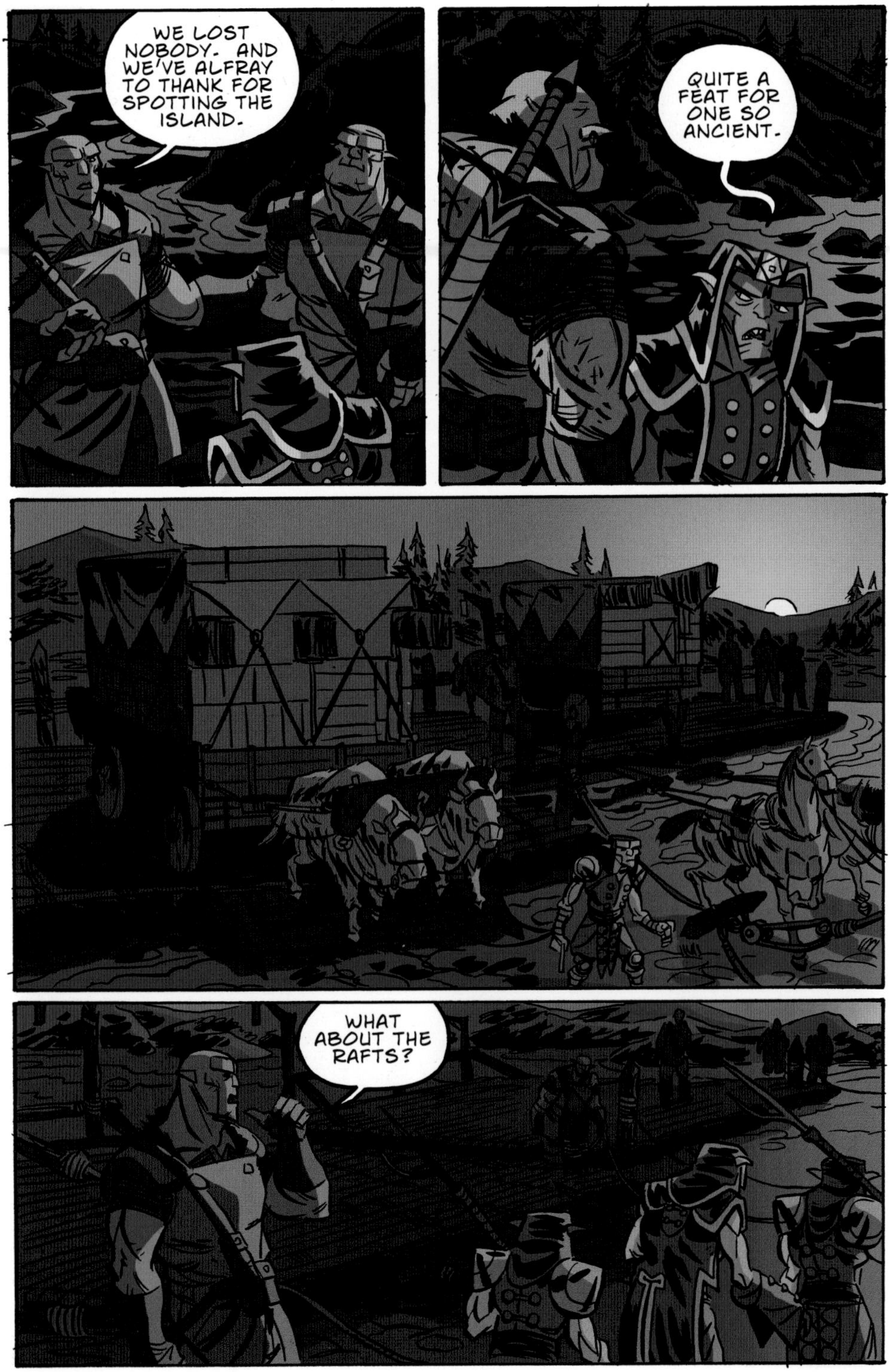
WE LOST NOBODY. AND WE'VE ALFRAY TO THANK FOR SPOTTING THE ISLAND.
QUITE A FEAT FOR ONE SO ANCIENT.
WHAT ABOUT THE RAFTS?

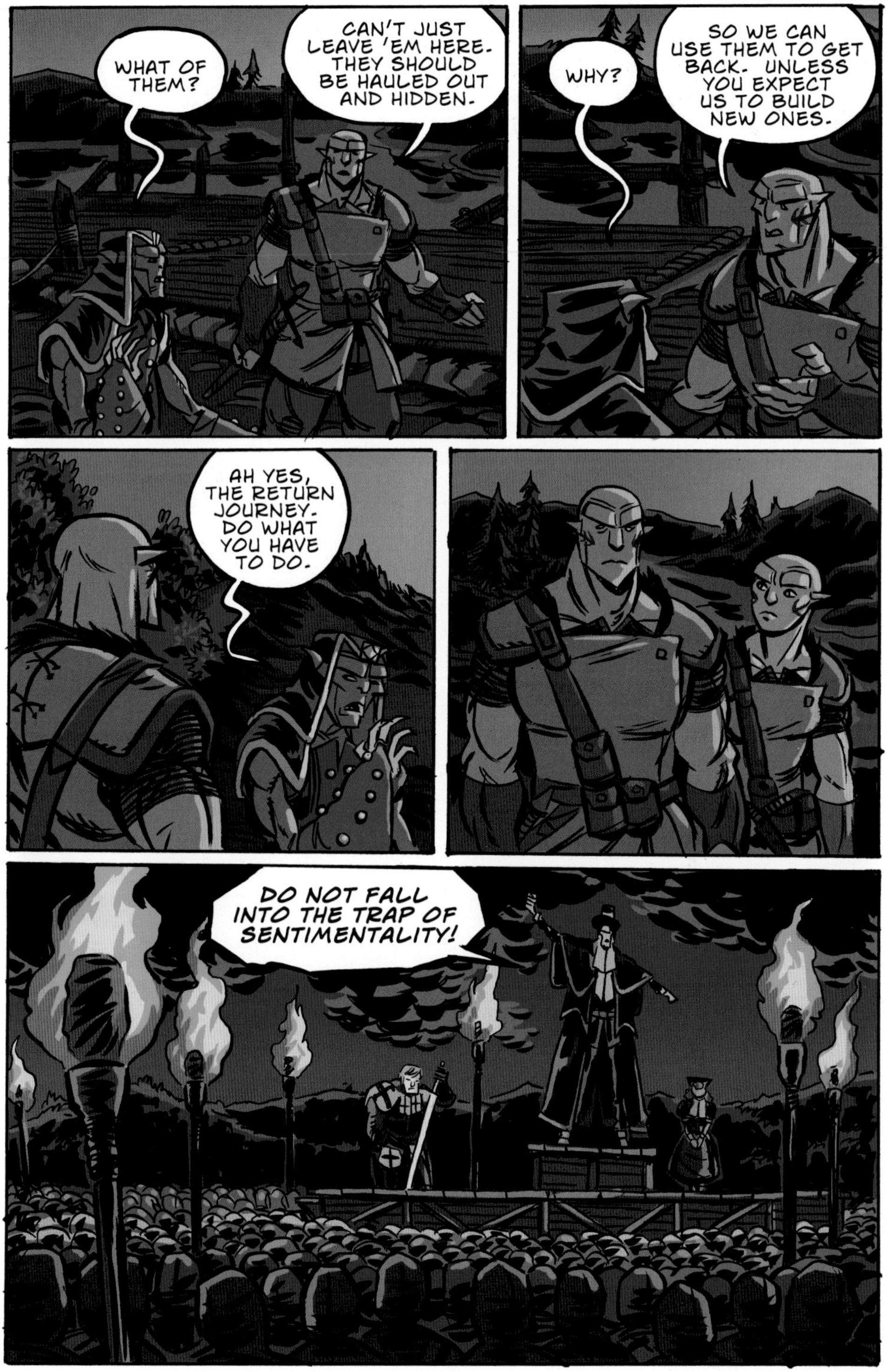
WHAT OF THEM?
CAN'T JUST LEAVE 'EM HERE. THEY SHOULD BE HAULED OUT AND HIDDEN.
WHY?
SO WE CAN USE THEM TO GET BACK. UNLESS YOU EXPECT US TO BUILD NEW ONES.
AH YES, THE RETURN JOURNEY. DO WHAT YOU HAVE TO DO.
DO NOT FALL INTO THE TRAP OF SENTIMENTALITY!

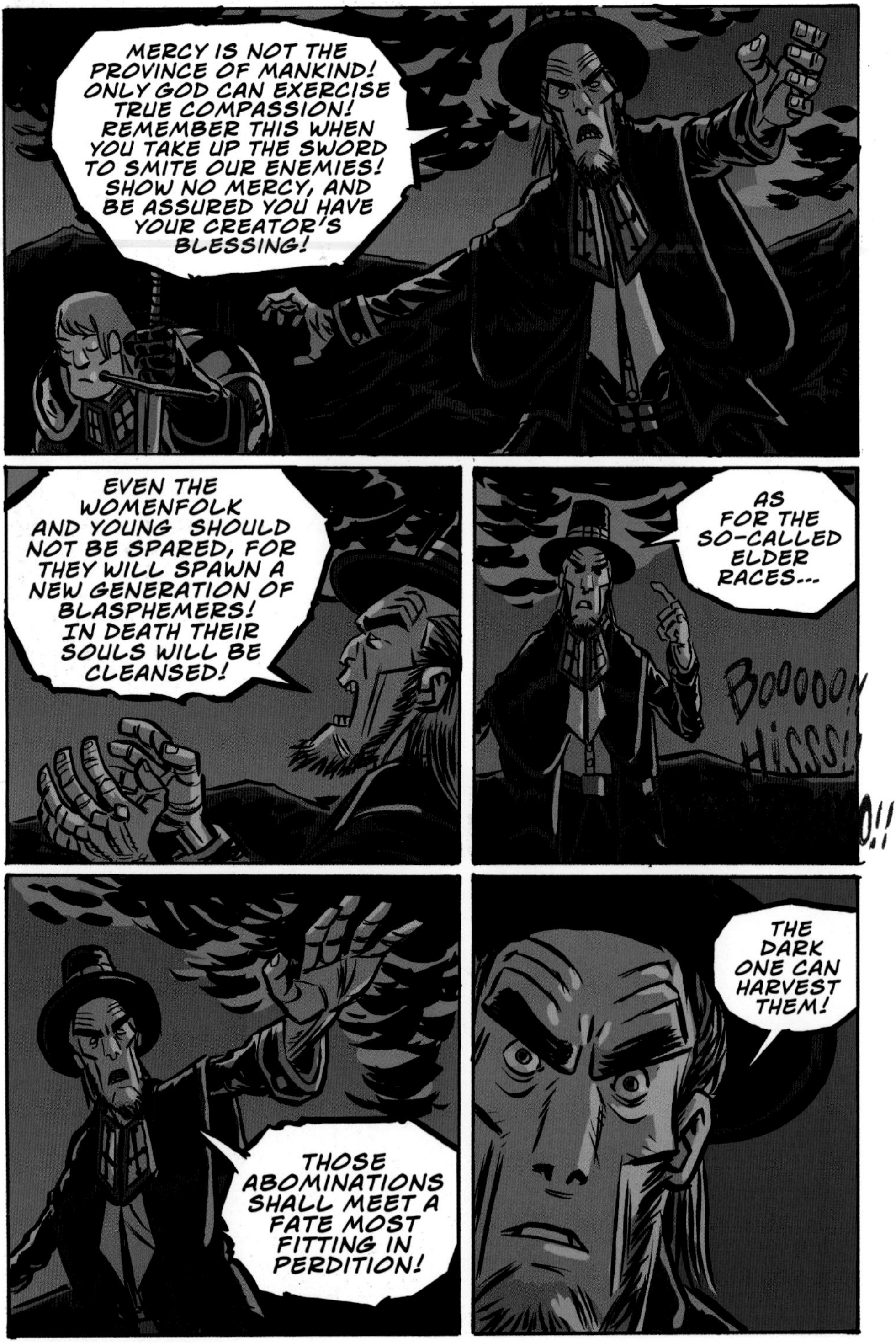
MERCY IS NOT THE PROVINCE OF MANKIND! ONLY GOD CAN EXERCISE TRUE COMPASSION! REMEMBER THIS WHEN YOU TAKE UP THE SWORD TO SMITE OUR ENEMIES! SHOW NO MERCY, AND BE ASSURED YOU HAVE YOUR CREATOR'S BLESSING!
EVEN THE WOMENFOLK AND YOUNG SHOULD NOT BE SPARED, FOR THEY WILL SPAWN A NEW GENERATION OF BLASPHEMERS! IN DEATH THEIR SOULS WILL BE CLEANSED!
AS FOR THE SO-CALLED ELDER RACES...
BOOOOO!!
HISSS!!
THOSE ABOMINATIONS SHALL MEET A FATE MOST FITTING IN PERDITION!
THE DARK ONE CAN HARVEST THEM!

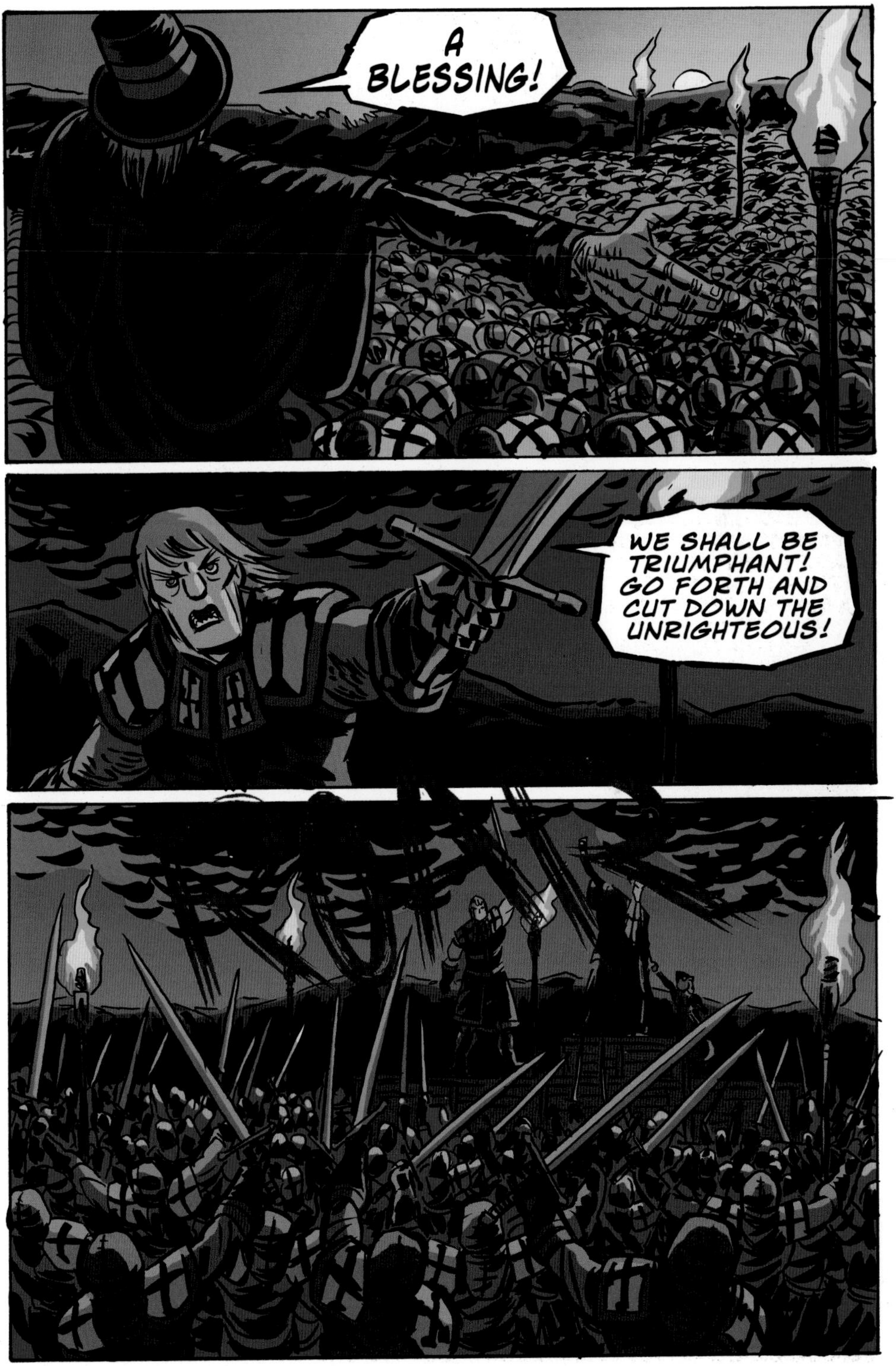
A BLESSING!
WE SHALL BE TRIUMPHANT! GO FORTH AND CUT DOWN THE UNRIGHTEOUS!

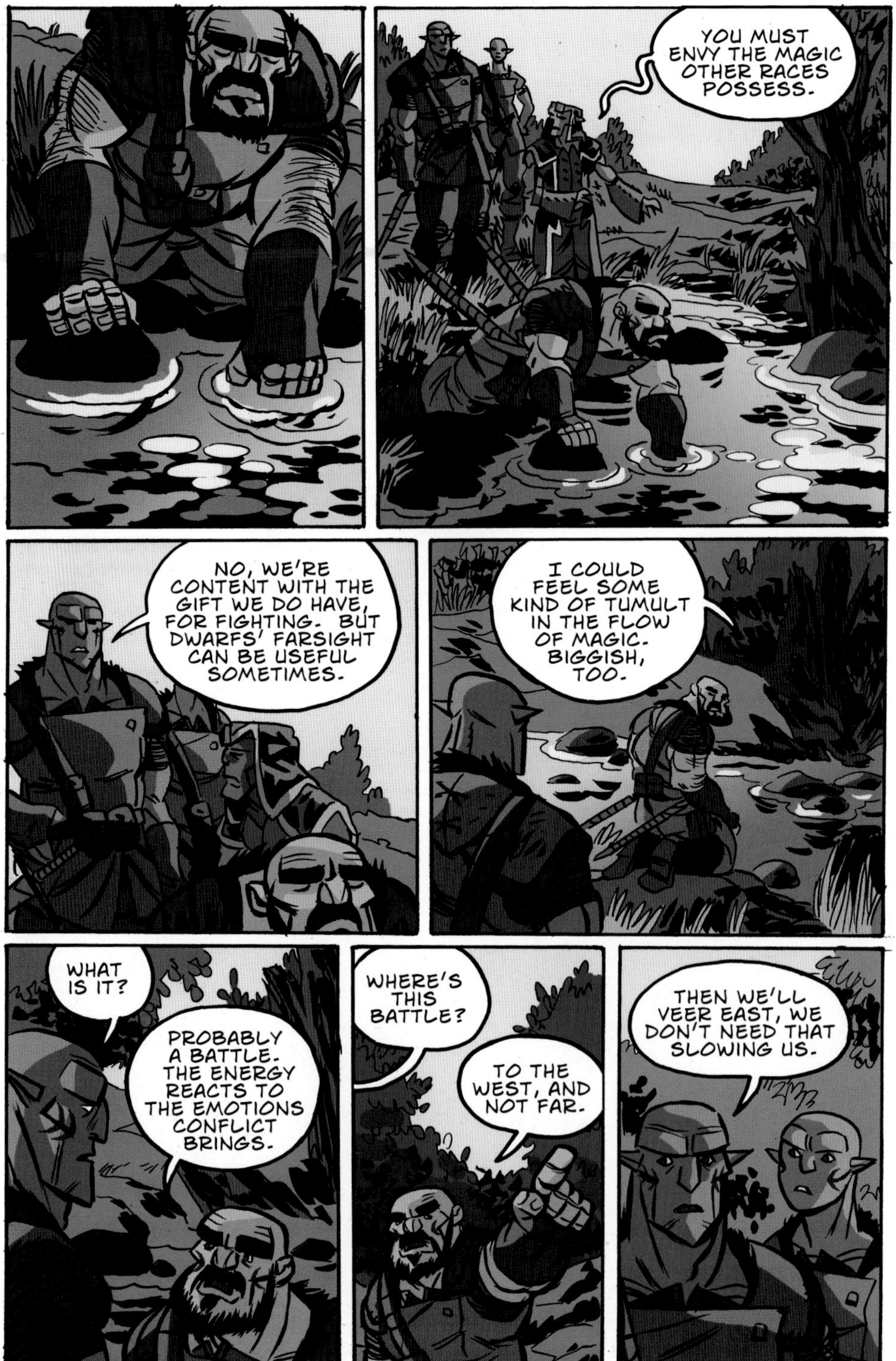
YOU MUST ENVY THE MAGIC OTHER RACES POSSESS.
NO, WE'RE CONTENT WITH THE GIFT WE DO HAVE, FOR FIGHTING. BUT DWARFS' FARSIGHT CAN BE USEFUL SOMETIMES.
I COULD FEEL SOME KIND OF TUMULT IN THE FLOW OF MAGIC. BIGGISH, TOO.
WHAT IS IT?
PROBABLY A BATTLE. THE ENERGY REACTS TO THE EMOTIONS CONFLICT BRINGS.
WHERE'S THIS BATTLE?
TO THE WEST, AND NOT FAR.
THEN WE'LL VEER EAST, WE DON'T NEED THAT SLOWING US.

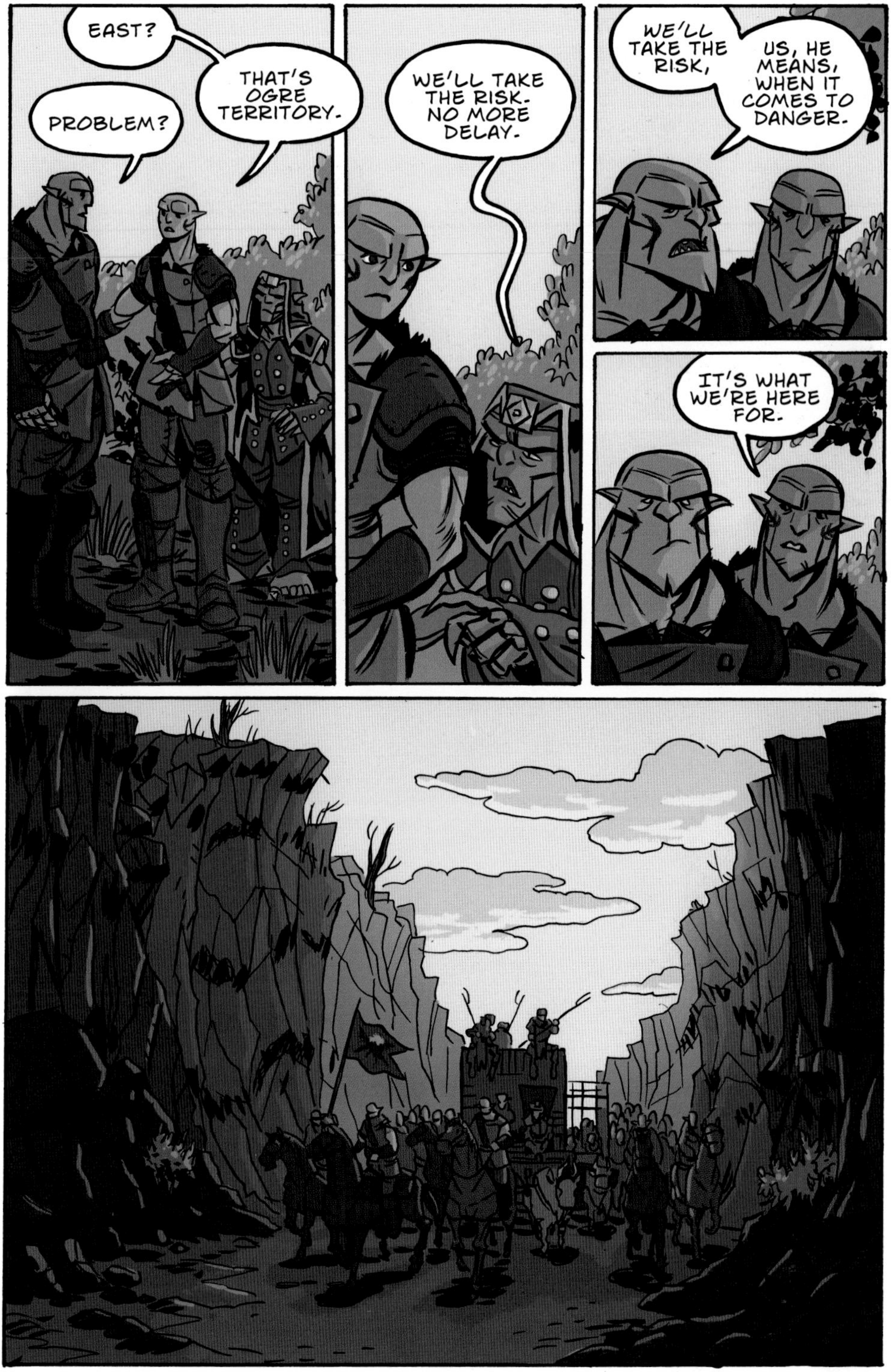
EAST?
THAT'S OGRE TERRITORY.
PROBLEM?
WE'LL TAKE THE RISK. NO MORE DELAY.
WE'LL TAKE THE RISK,
US, HE MEANS, WHEN IT COMES TO DANGER.
IT'S WHAT WE'RE HERE FOR.

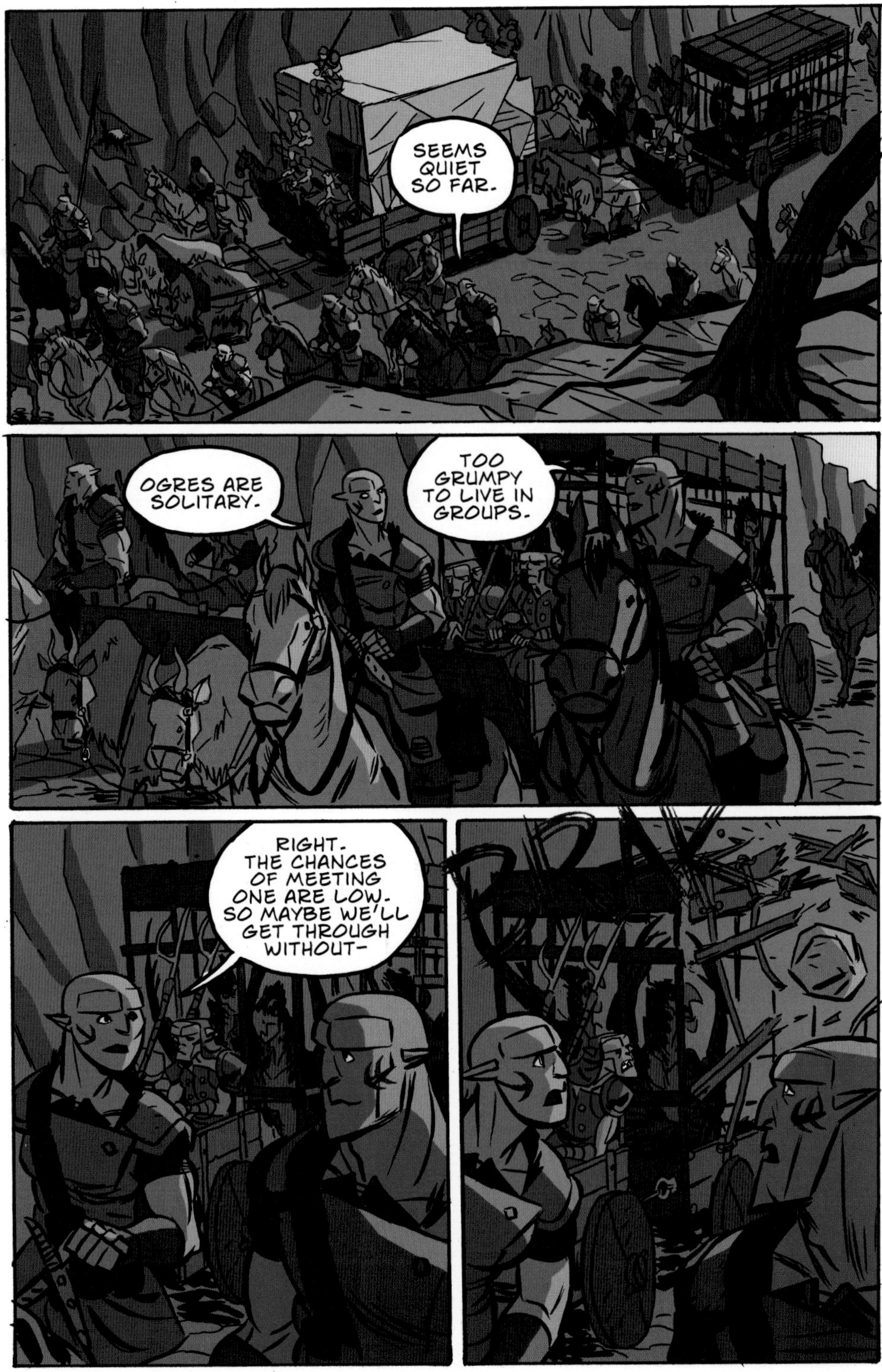
SEEMS QUIET SO FAR.
OGRES ARE SOLITARY.
TOO GRUMPY TO LIVE IN GROUPS.
RIGHT. THE CHANCES OF MEETING ONE ARE LOW. SO MAYBE WE'LL GET THROUGH WITHOUT-

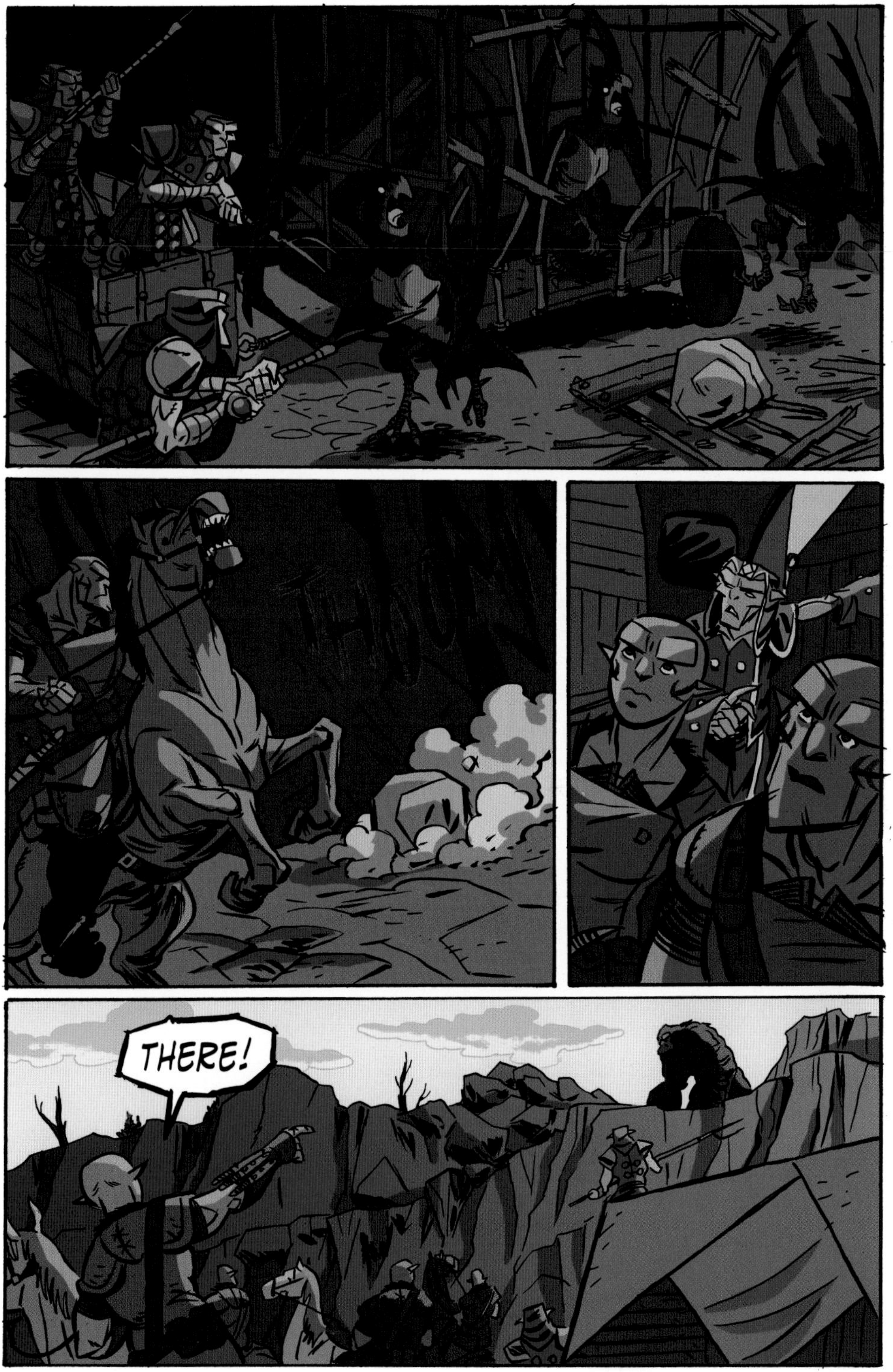
THOOM
THERE!

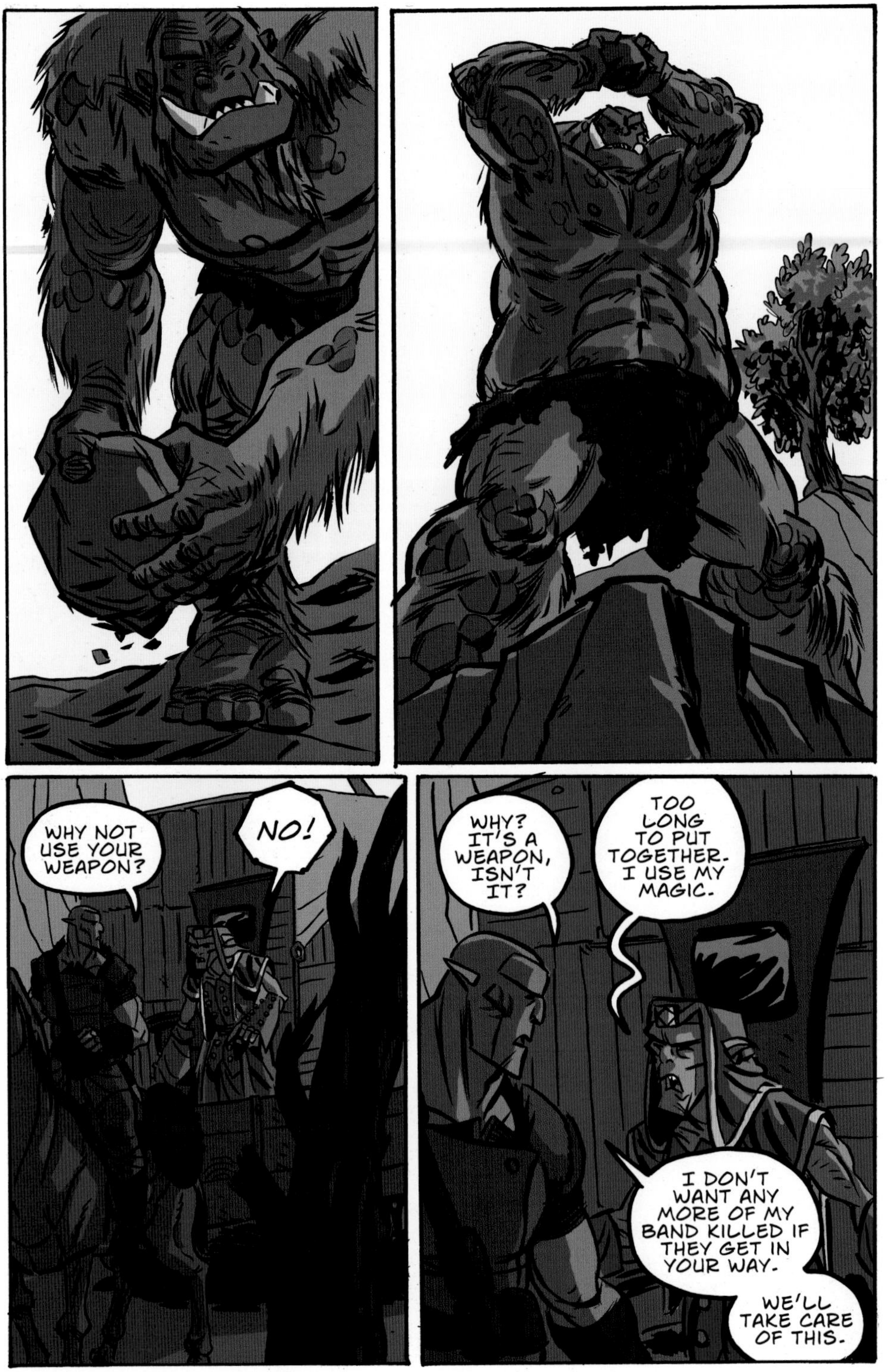
WHY NOT USE YOUR WEAPON?
NO!
WHY? IT'S A WEAPON, ISN'T IT?
TOO LONG TO PUT TOGETHER. I USE MY MAGIC.
I DON'T WANT ANY MORE OF MY BAND KILLED IF THEY GET IN YOUR WAY.
WE'LL TAKE CARE OF THIS.

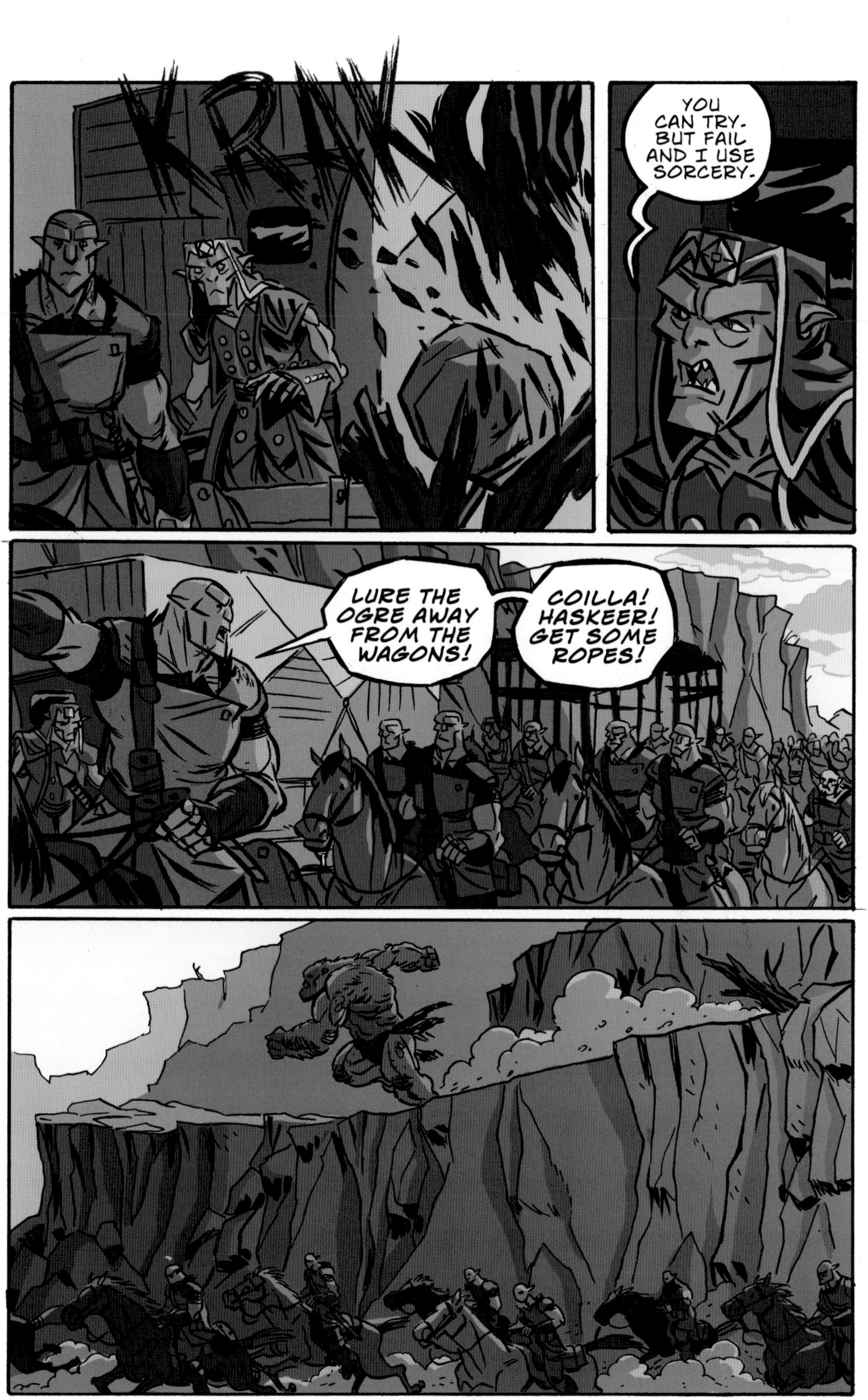
KRAK
YOU CAN TRY. BUT FAIL AND I USE SORCERY.
LURE THE OGRE AWAY FROM THE WAGONS!
COILLA! HASKEER! GET SOME ROPES!

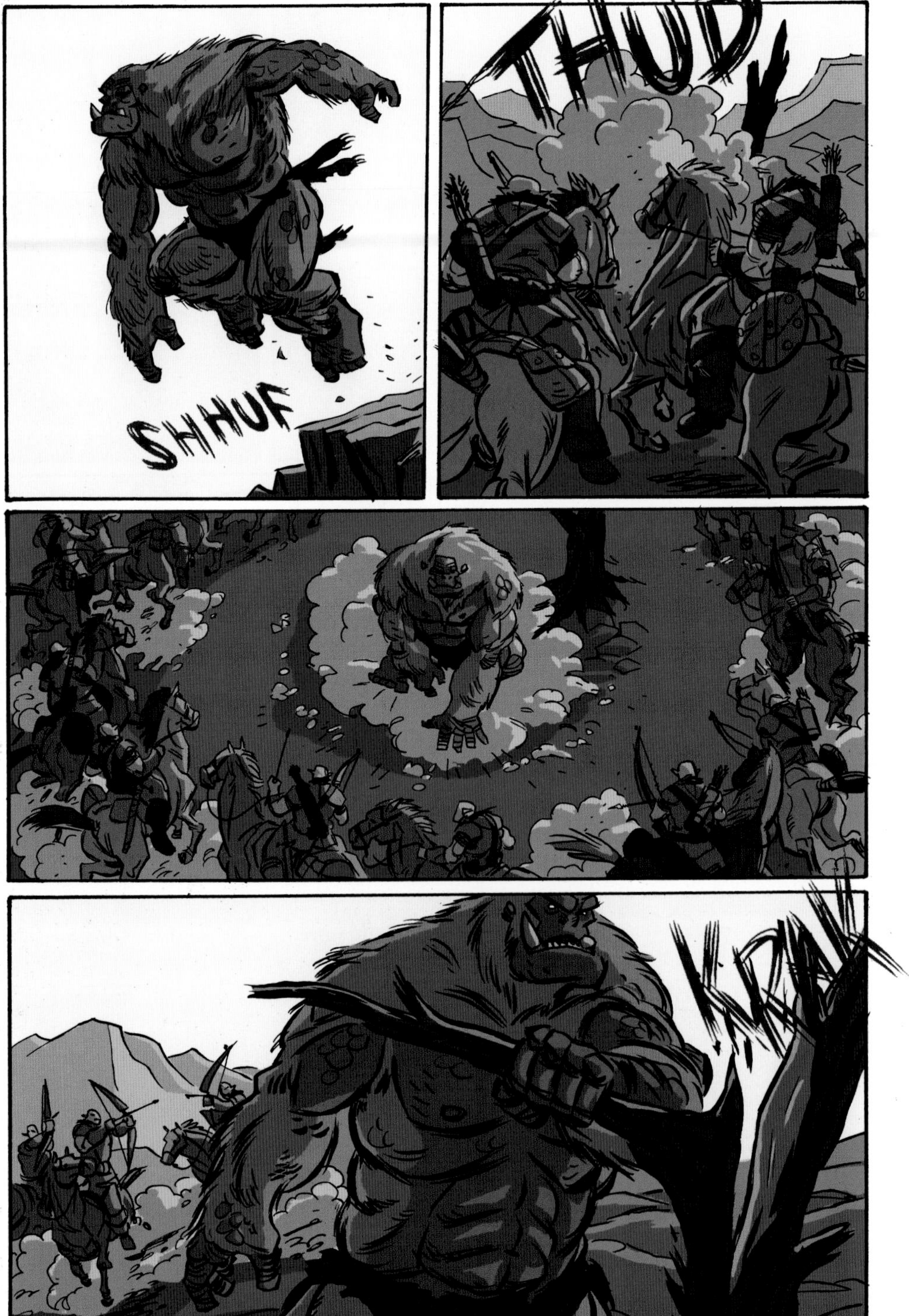
SHHUF
THUD

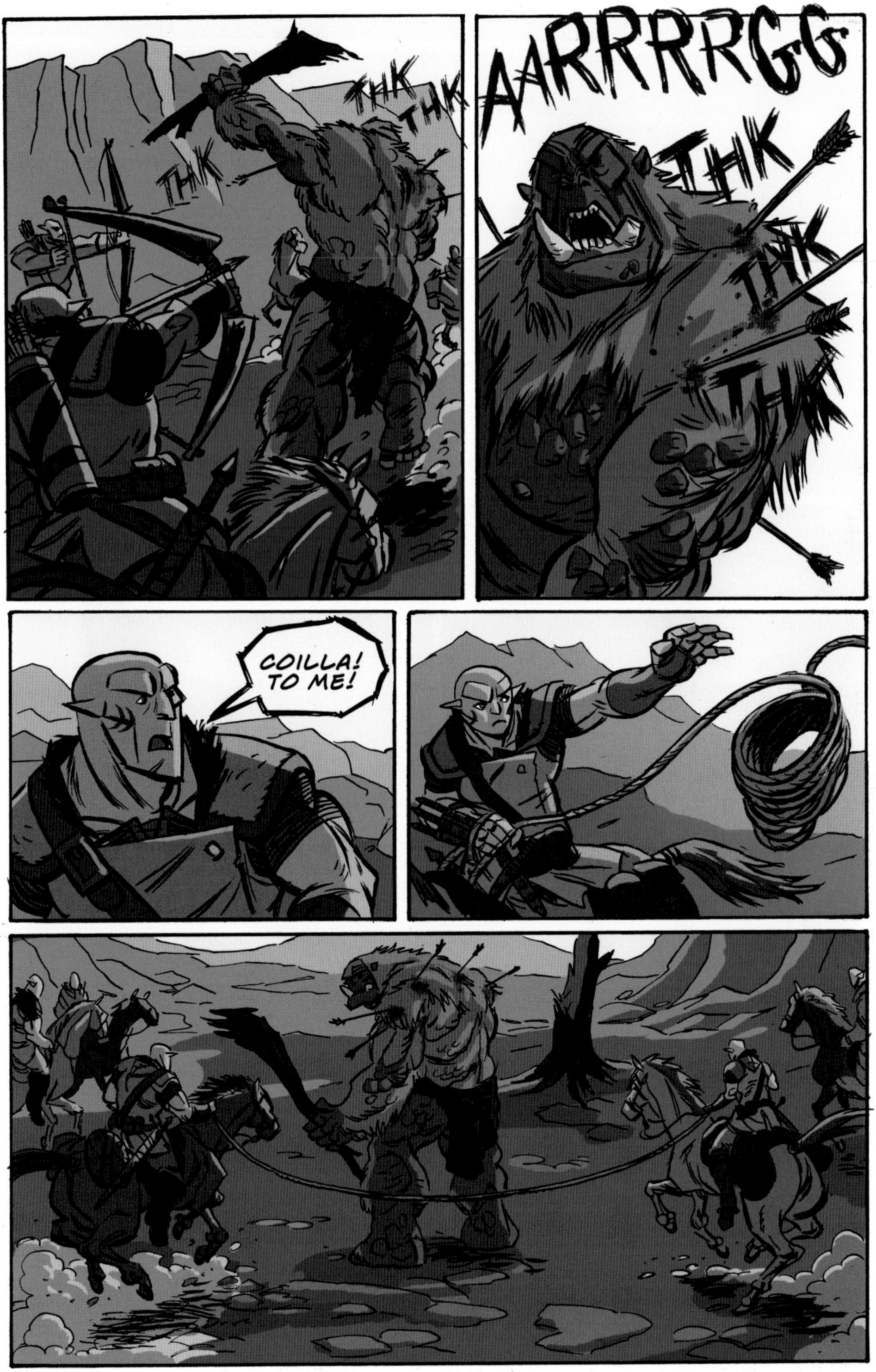
THK
THK
THK
AARRRRGG
THK
THK
THK
COILLA! TO ME!

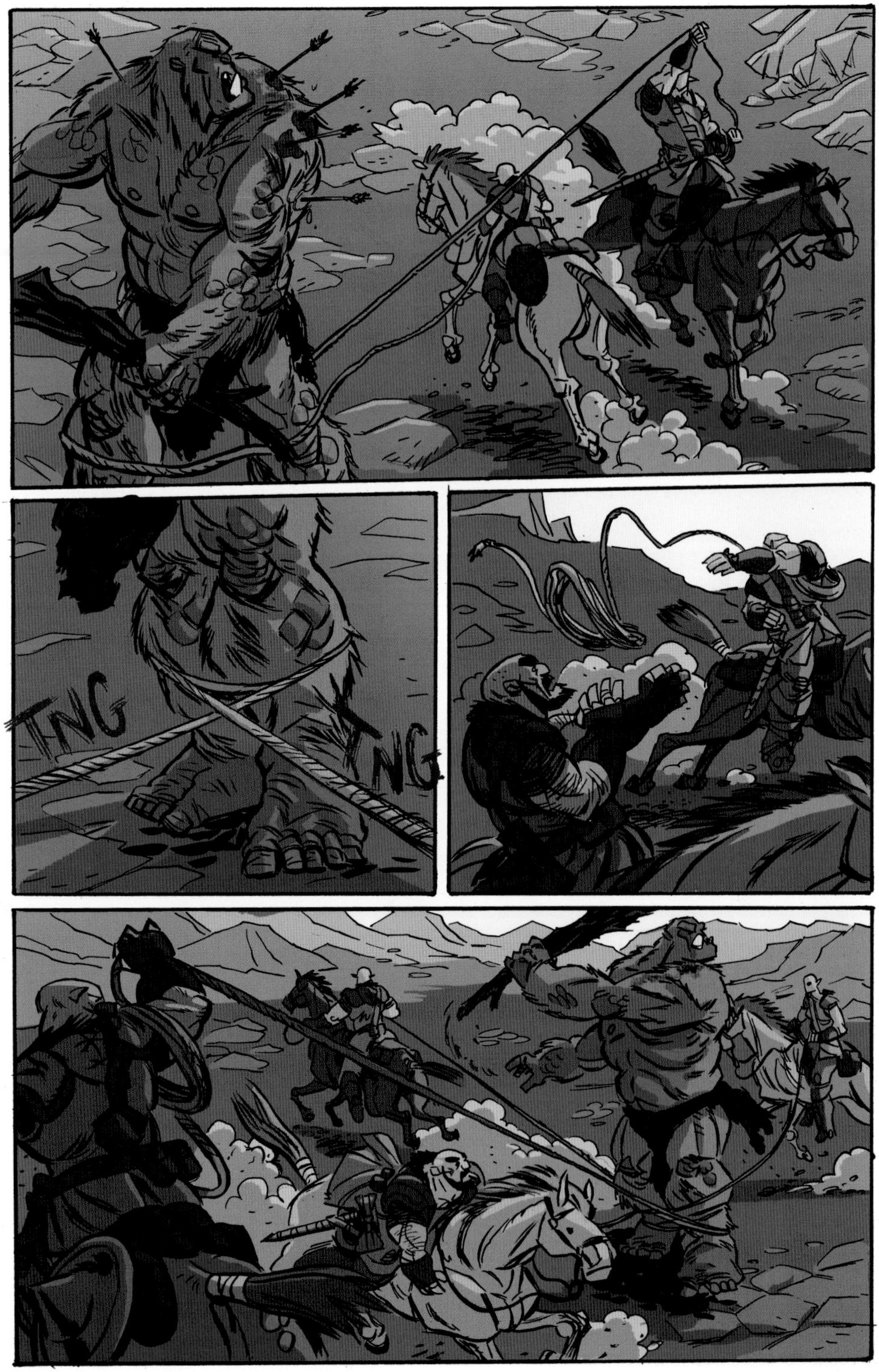
TNG
TNG

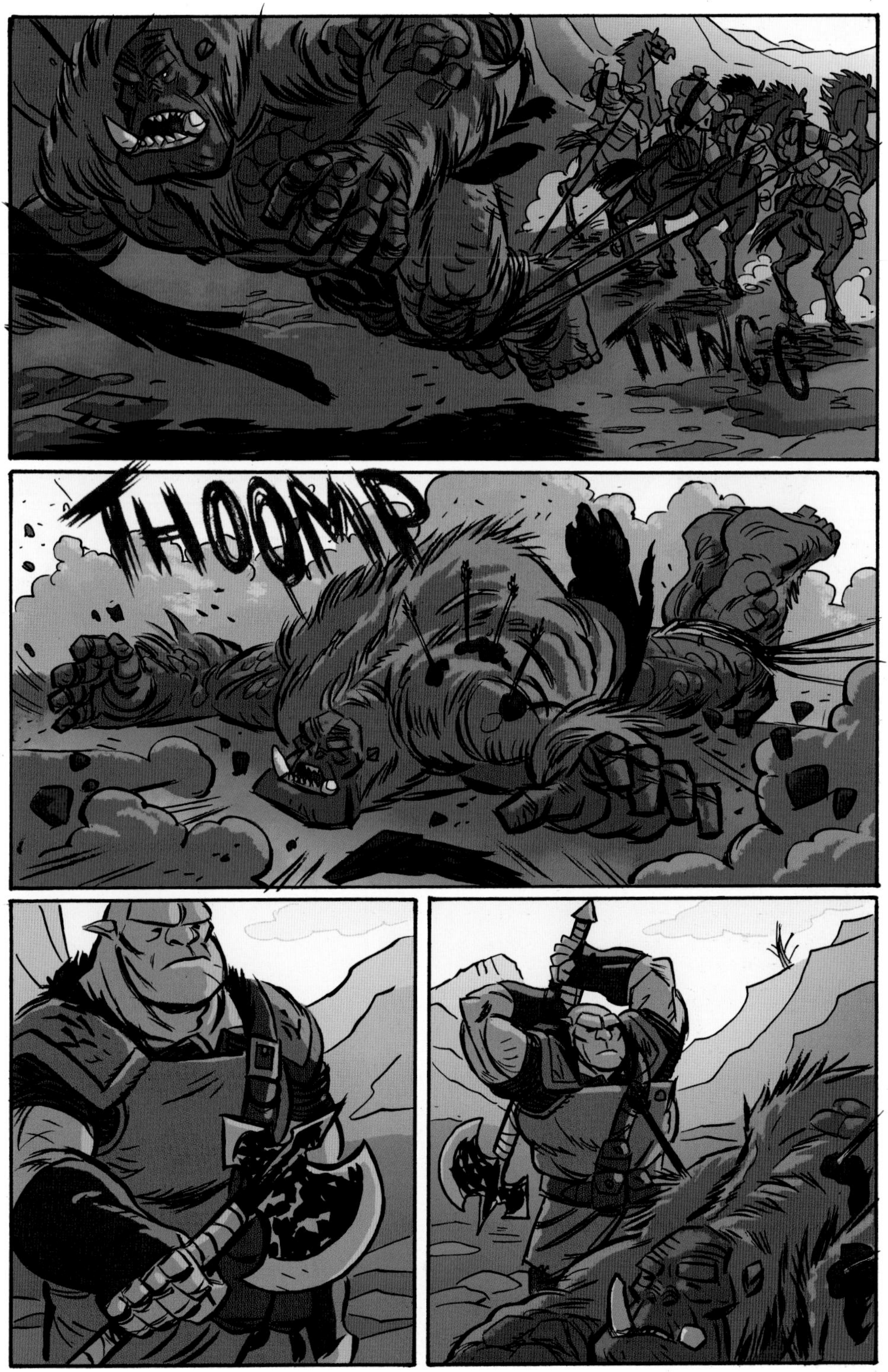
TWANGG
THOOMP

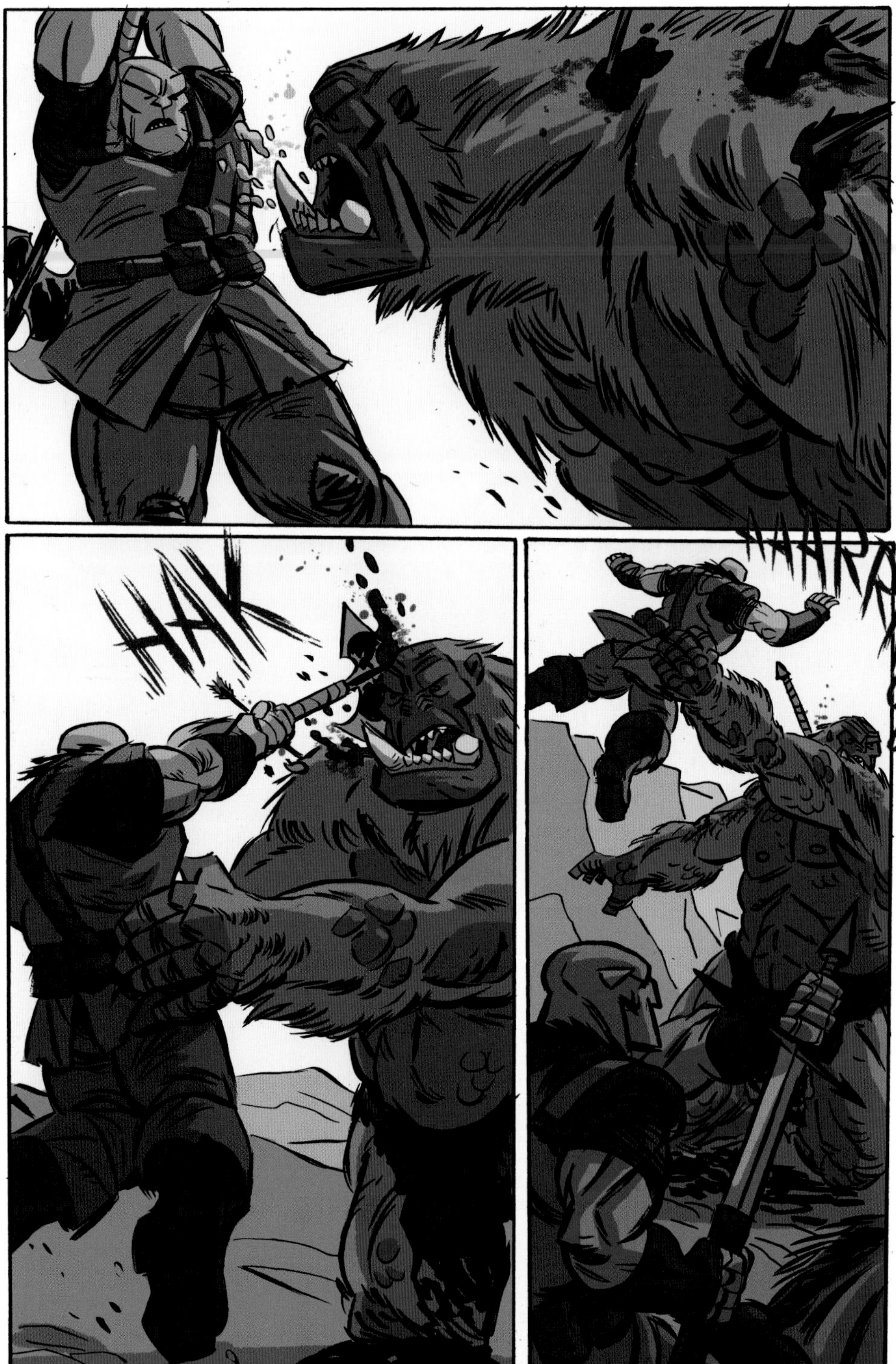
HAK
AAHRRRGG

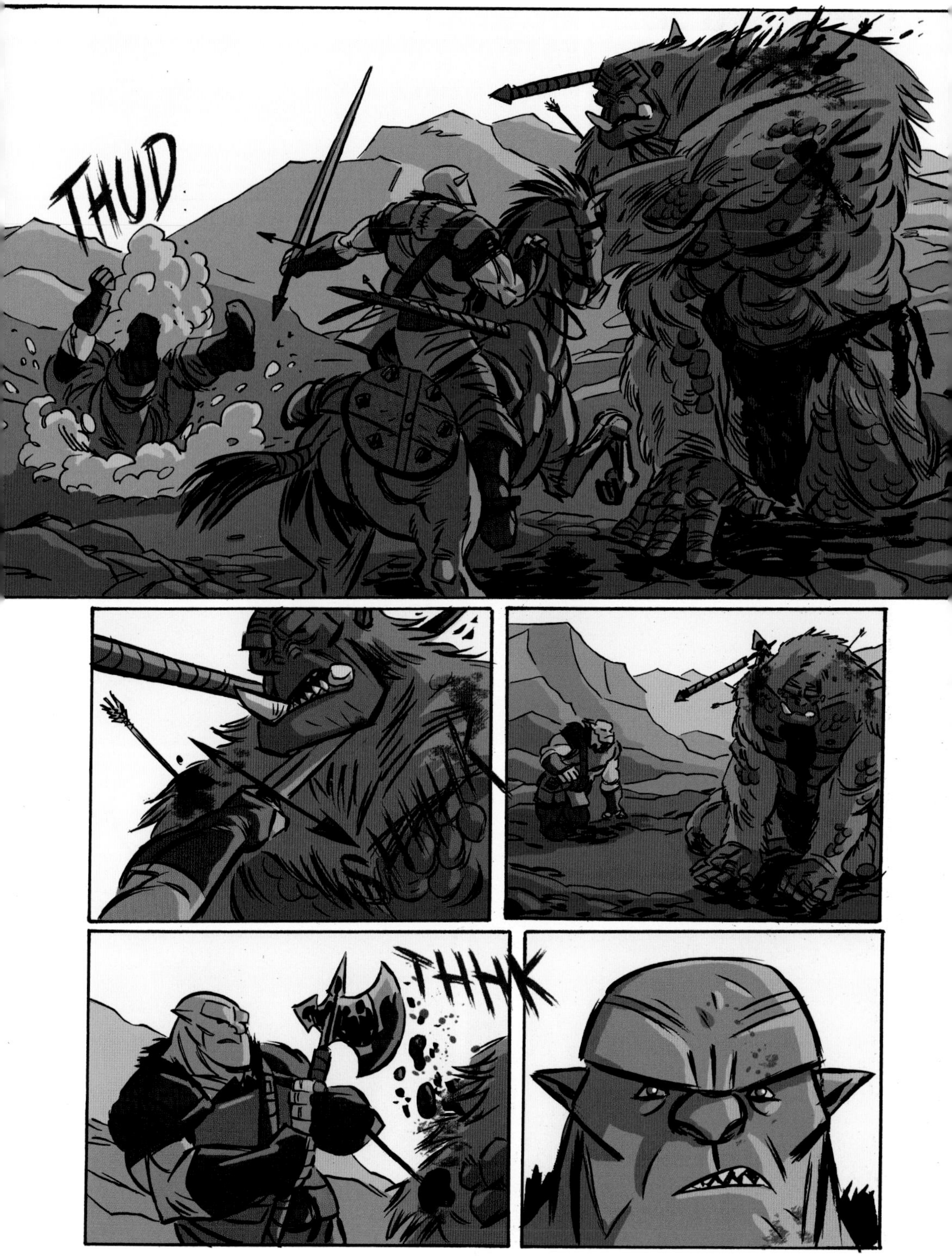
THUD
THHK

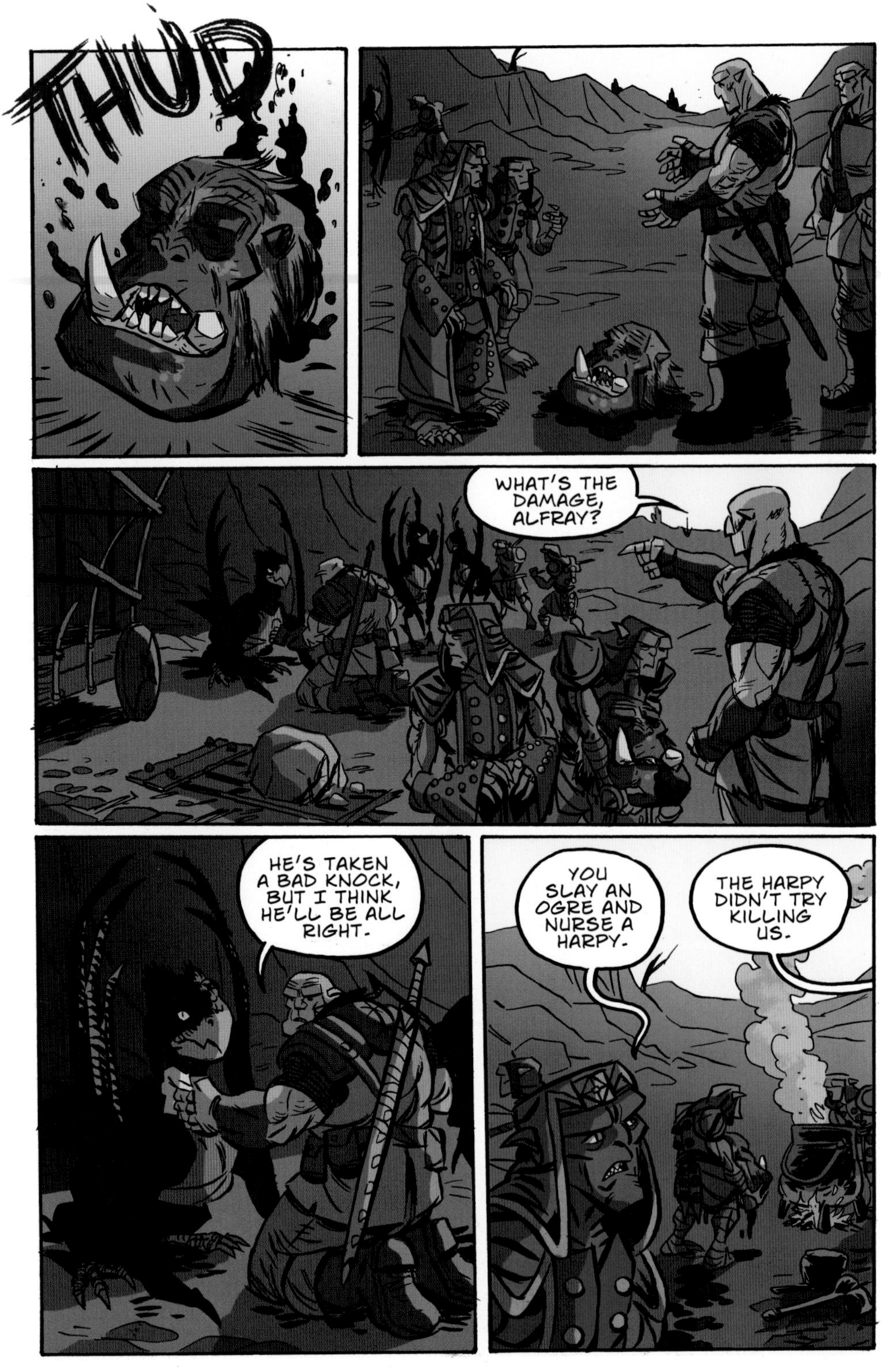
THUD
WHAT'S THE DAMAGE, ALFRAY?
HE'S TAKEN A BAD KNOCK, BUT I THINK HE'LL BE ALL RIGHT.
YOU SLAY AN OGRE AND NURSE A HARPY.
THE HARPY DIDN'T TRY KILLING US.

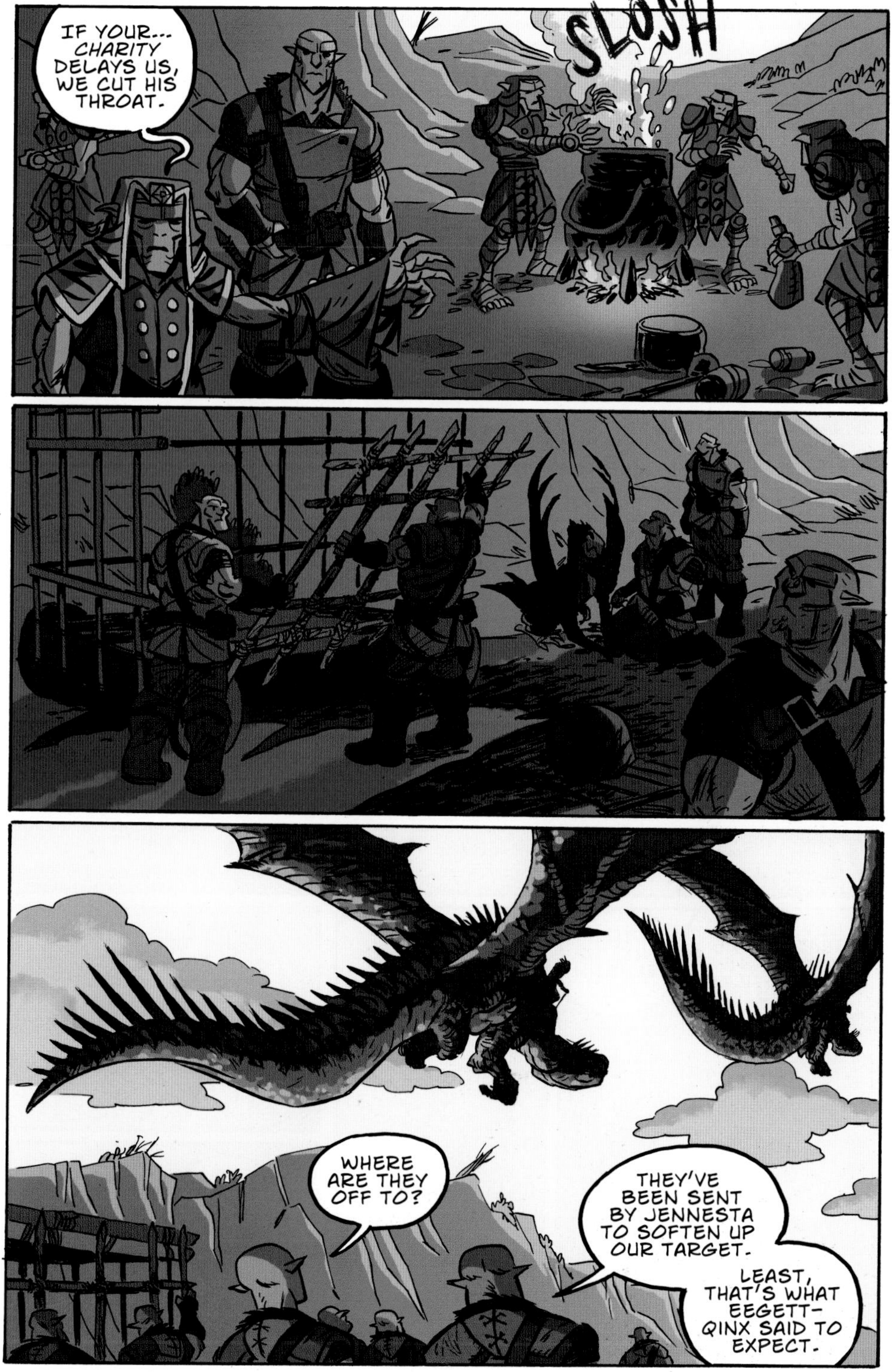

IF YOUR... CHARITY DELAYS US, WE CUT HIS THROAT.
SLOSH
WHERE ARE THEY OFF TO?
THEY'VE BEEN SENT BY JENNESTA TO SOFTEN UP OUR TARGET.
LEAST, THAT'S WHAT EEGETT-QINX SAID TO EXPECT.

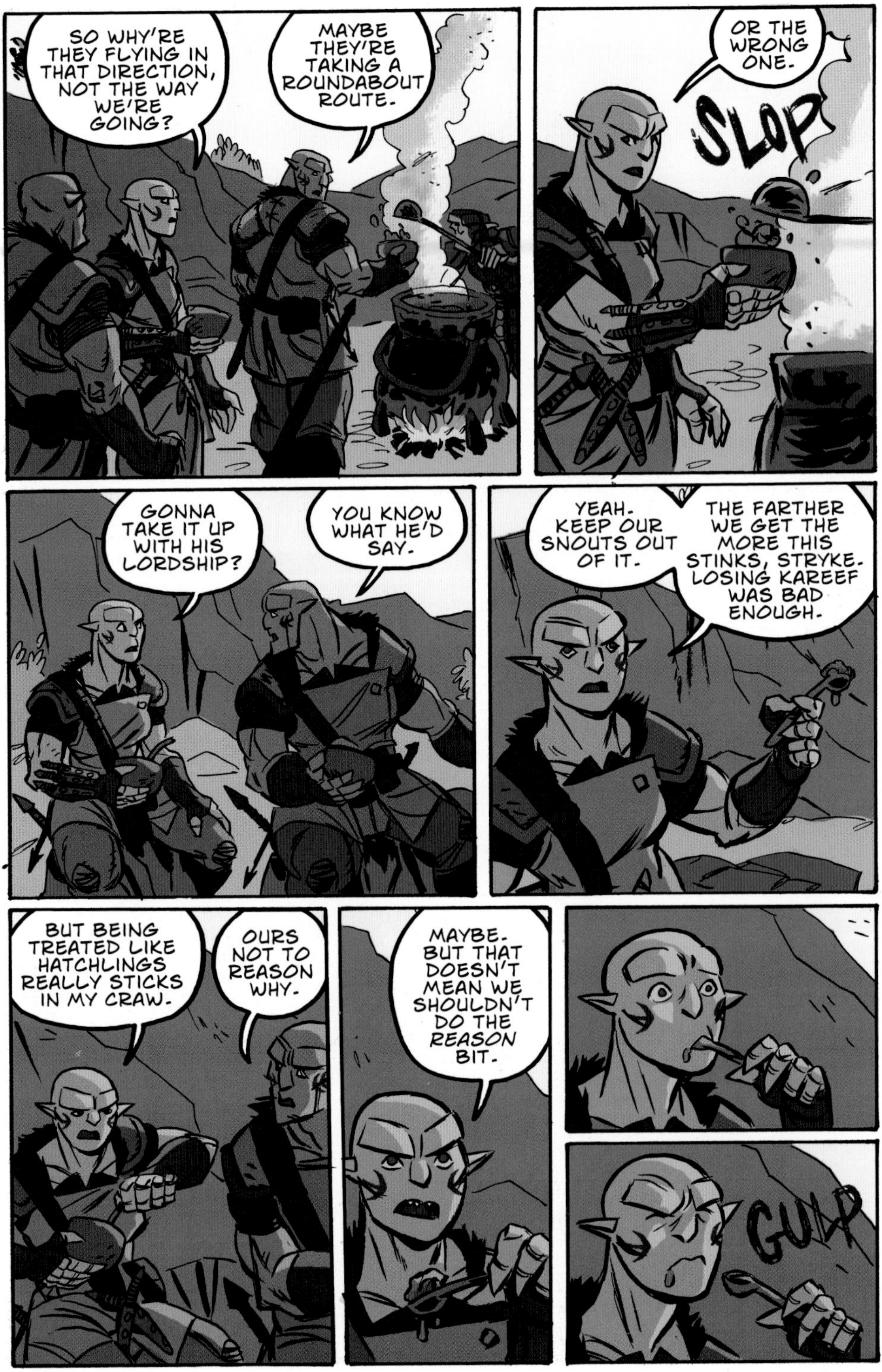
SO WHY'RE THEY FLYING IN THAT DIRECTION, NOT THE WAY WE'RE GOING?
MAYBE THEY'RE TAKING A ROUNDABOUT ROUTE.
OR THE WRONG ONE.
SLOP
GONNA TAKE IT UP WITH HIS LORDSHIP?
YOU KNOW WHAT HE'D SAY.
YEAH. KEEP OUR SNOUTS OUT OF IT.
THE FARTHER WE GET THE MORE THIS STINKS, STRYKE. LOSING KAREEF WAS BAD ENOUGH.
BUT BEING TREATED LIKE HATCHLINGS REALLY STICKS IN MY CRAW.
OURS NOT TO REASON WHY.
MAYBE. BUT THAT DOESN'T MEAN WE SHOULDN'T DO THE REASON BIT.
GULP

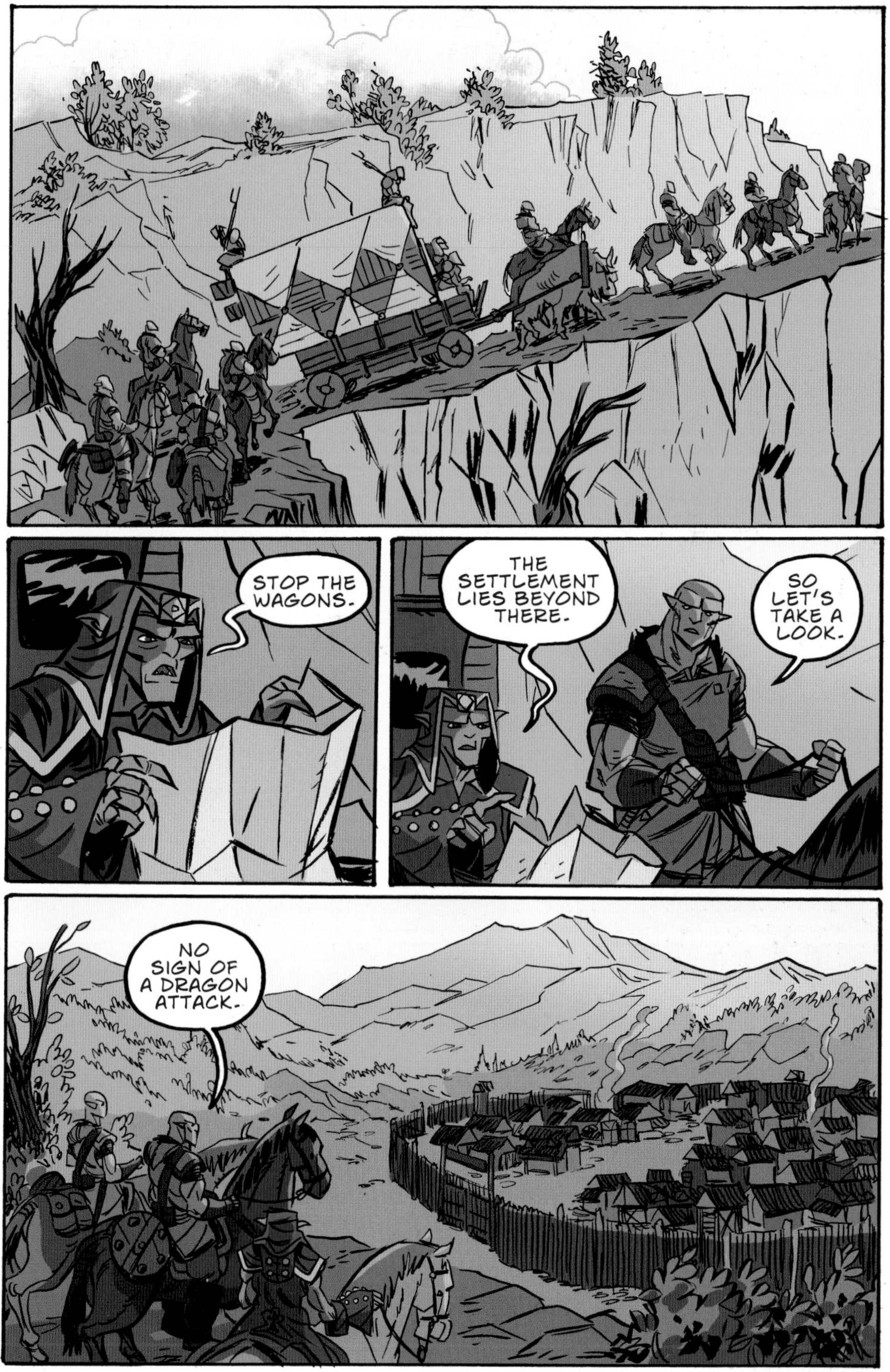
STOP THE WAGONS.
THE SETTLEMENT LIES BEYOND THERE.
SO LET'S TAKE A LOOK.
NO SIGN OF A DRAGON ATTACK.

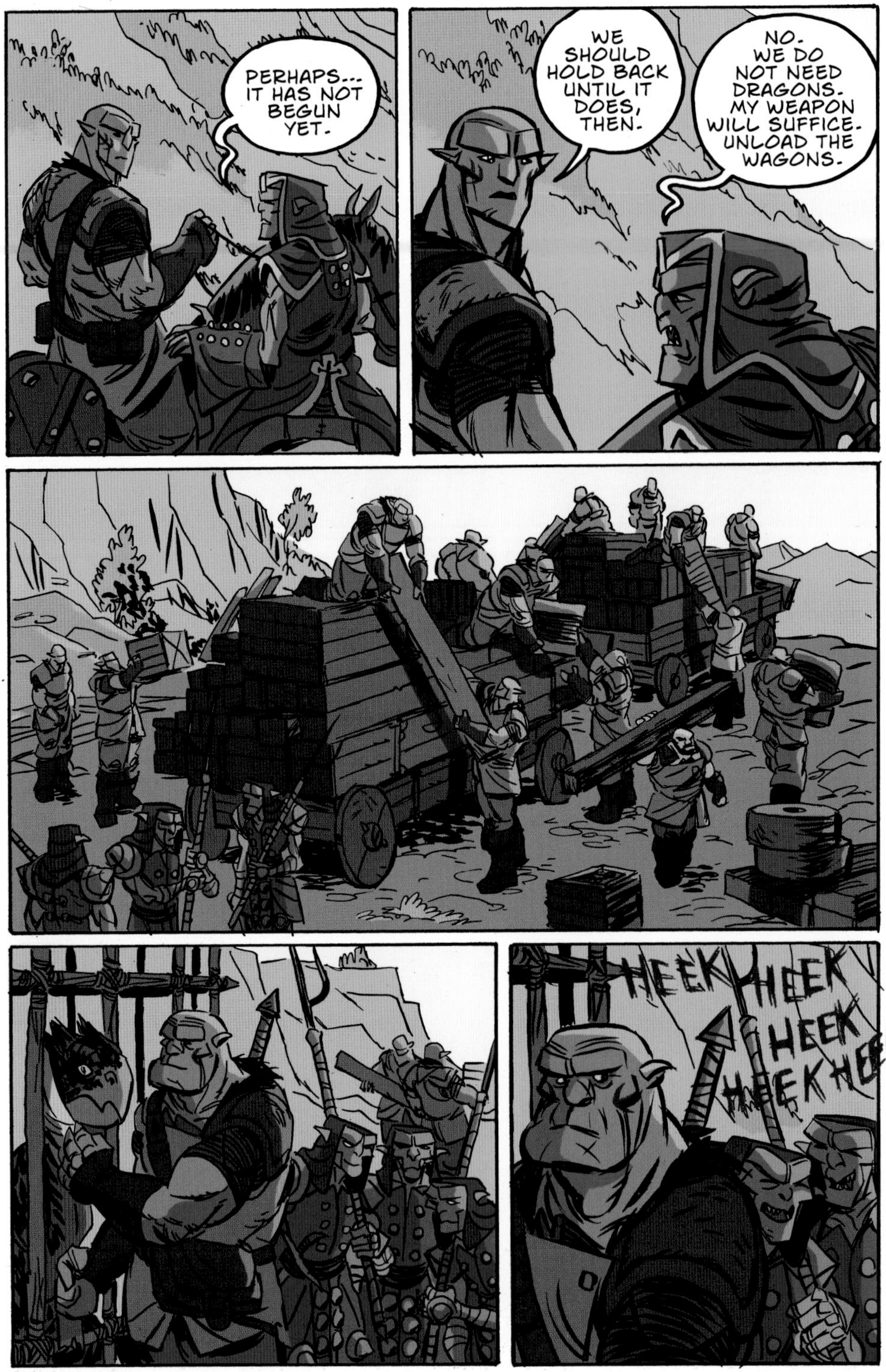
PERHAPS... IT HAS NOT BEGUN YET.
WE SHOULD HOLD BACK UNTIL IT DOES, THEN.
NO. WE DO NOT NEED DRAGONS. MY WEAPON WILL SUFFICE. UNLOAD THE WAGONS.
HEEK HEEK HEEK HEEK HEEK

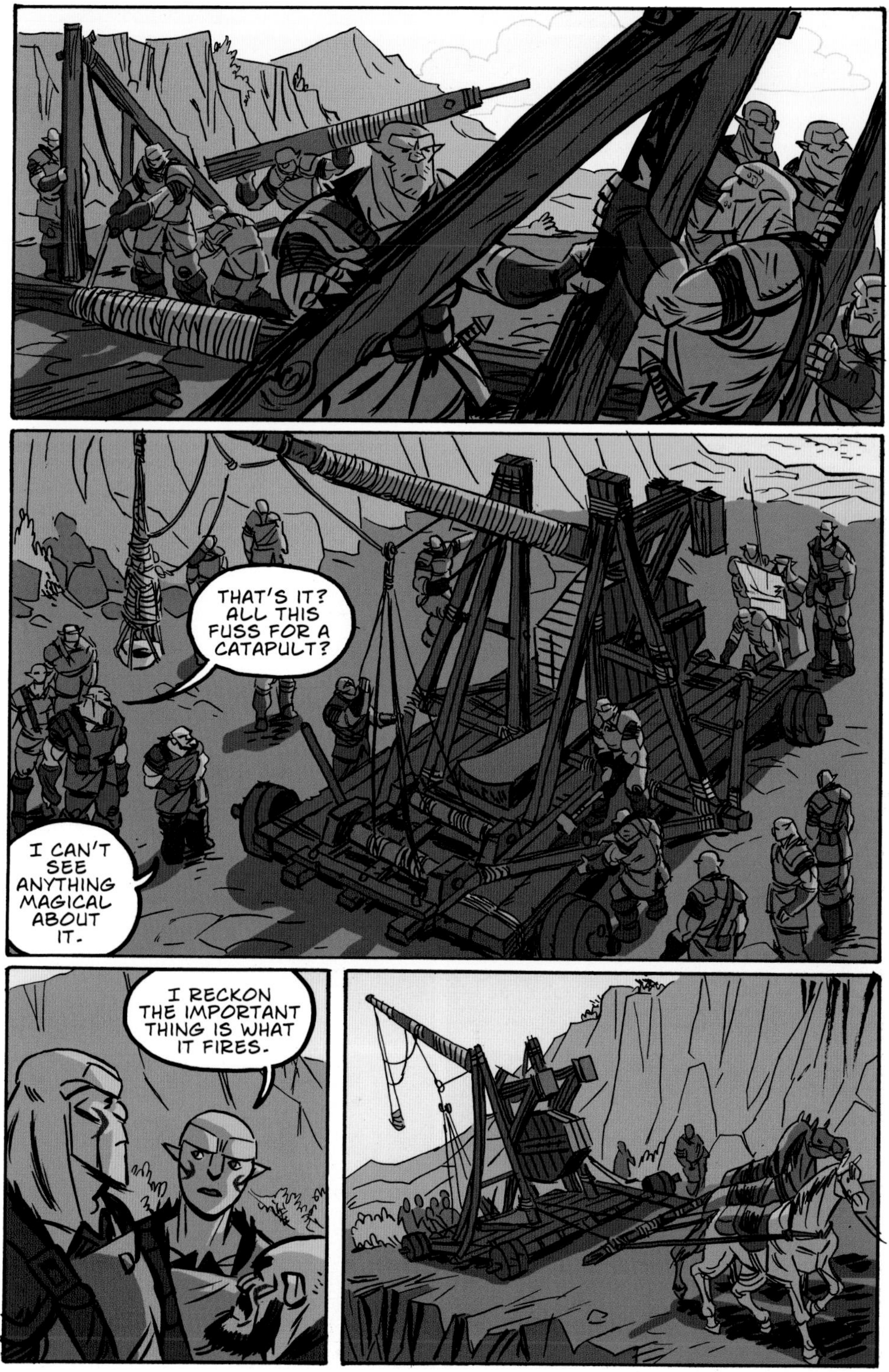
THAT'S IT? ALL THIS FUSS FOR A CATAPULT?
I CAN'T SEE ANYTHING MAGICAL ABOUT IT.
I RECKON THE IMPORTANT THING IS WHAT IT FIRES.

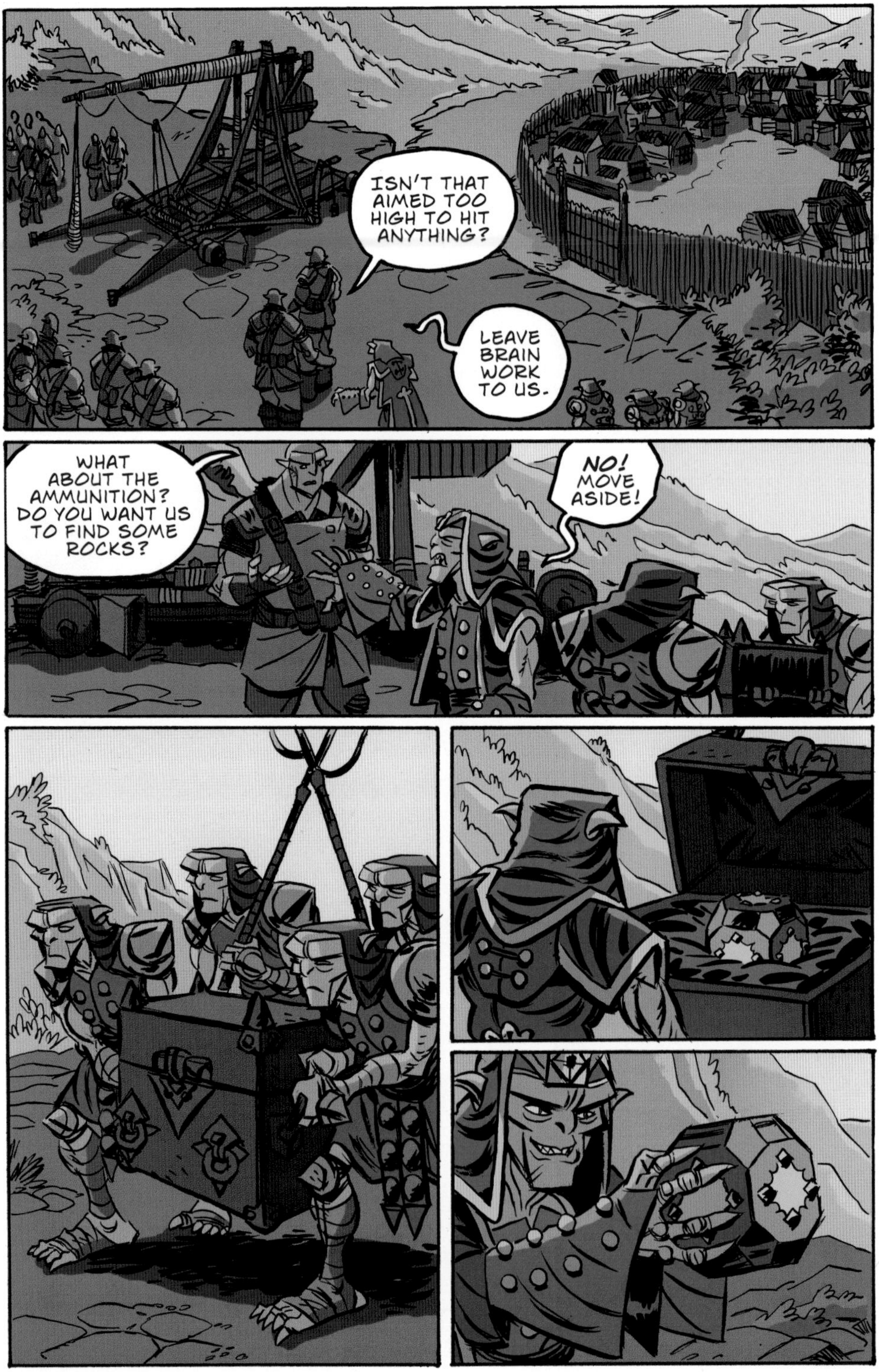
ISN'T THAT AIMED TOO HIGH TO HIT ANYTHING?
LEAVE BRAIN WORK TO US.
WHAT ABOUT THE AMMUNITION? DO YOU WANT US TO FIND SOME ROCKS?
NO! MOVE ASIDE!

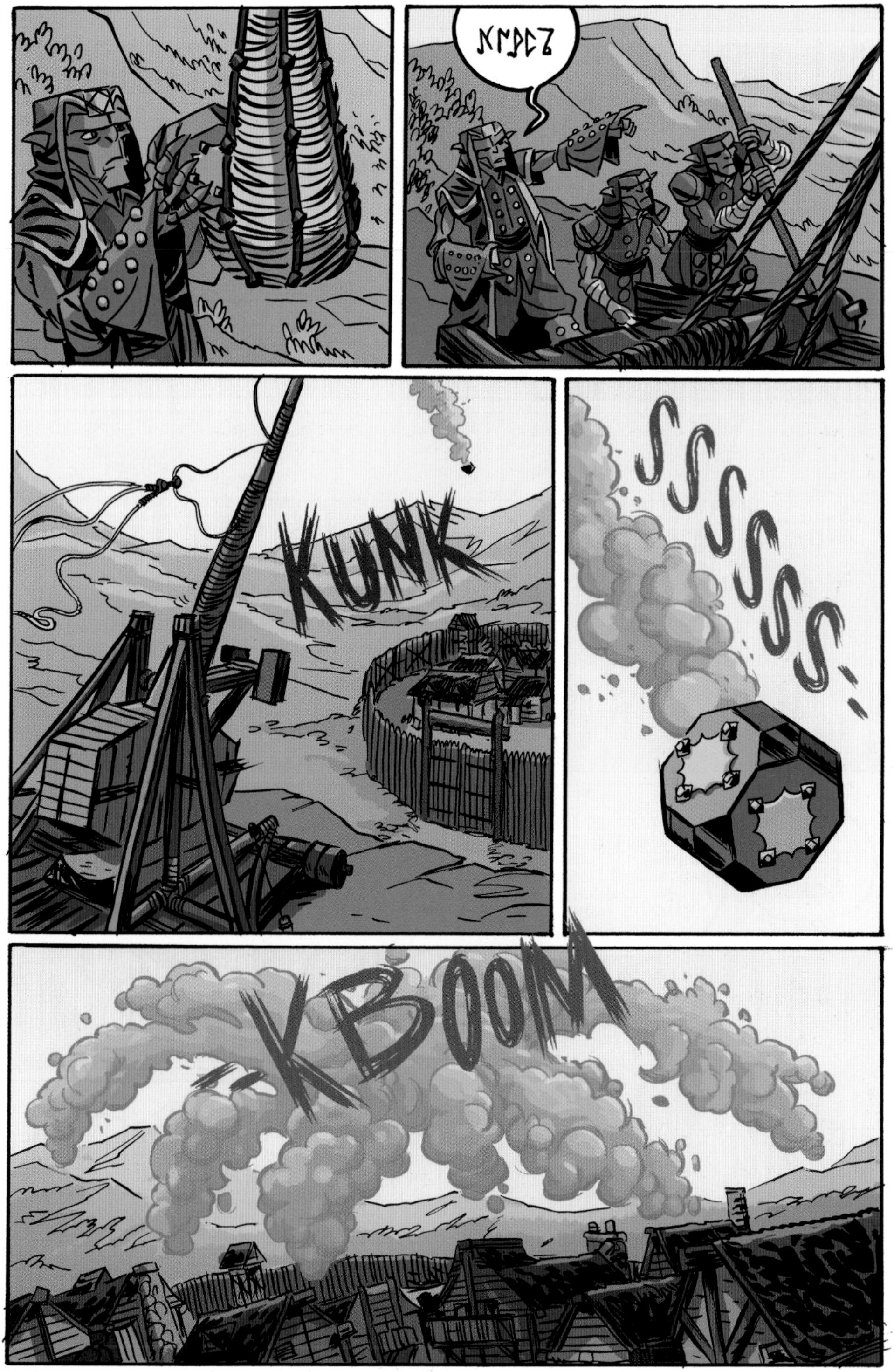
KUNK
SSSSSS
KBOOM

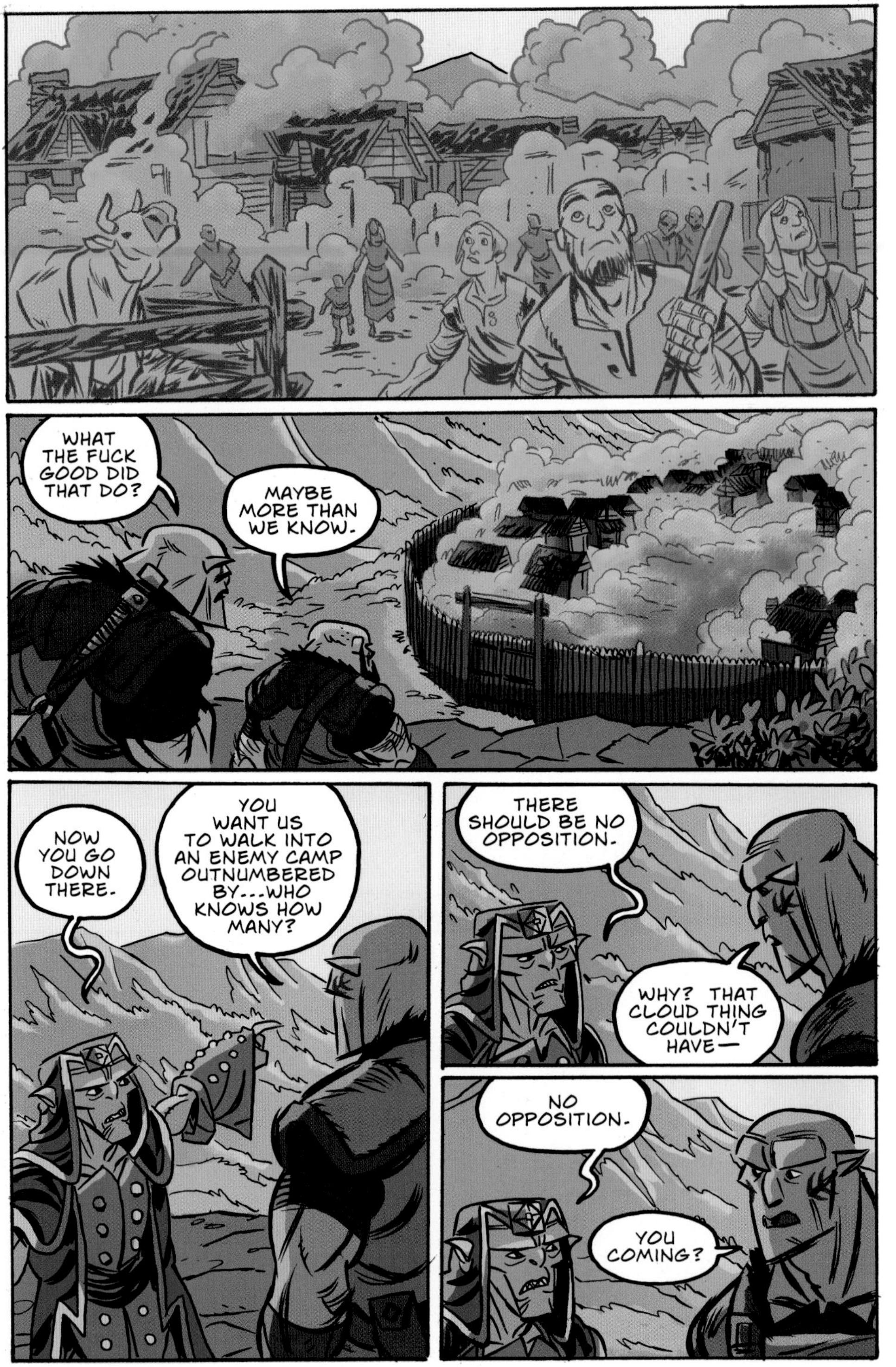
WHAT THE FUCK GOOD DID THAT DO?
MAYBE MORE THAN WE KNOW.
NOW YOU GO DOWN THERE.
YOU WANT US TO WALK INTO AN ENEMY CAMP OUTNUMBERED BY...WHO KNOWS HOW MANY?
THERE SHOULD BE NO OPPOSITION.
WHY? THAT CLOUD THING COULDN'T HAVE—
NO OPPOSITION.
YOU COMING?

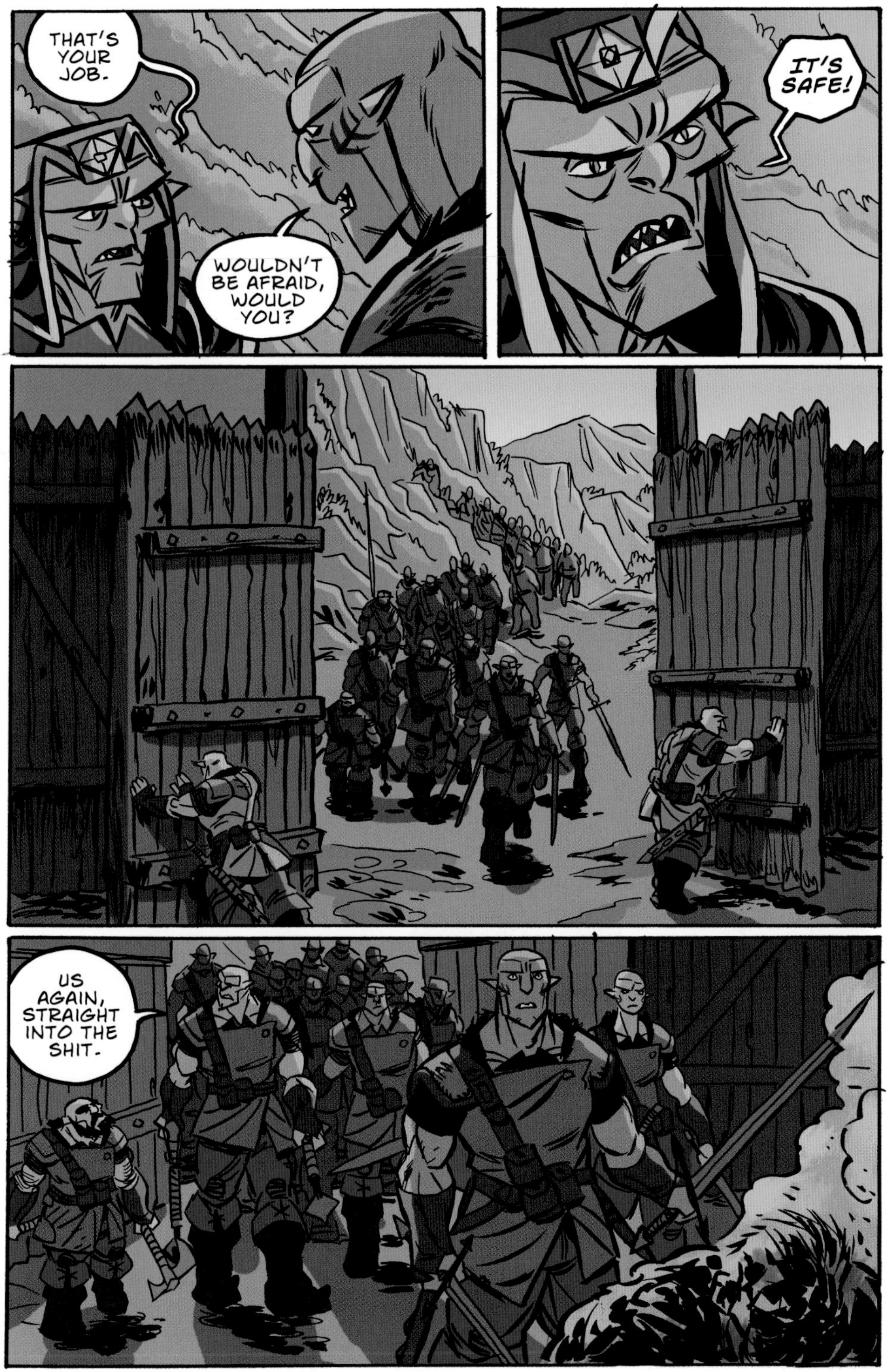
THAT'S YOUR JOB.
WOULDN'T BE AFRAID, WOULD YOU?
IT'S SAFE!
US AGAIN, STRAIGHT INTO THE SHIT.

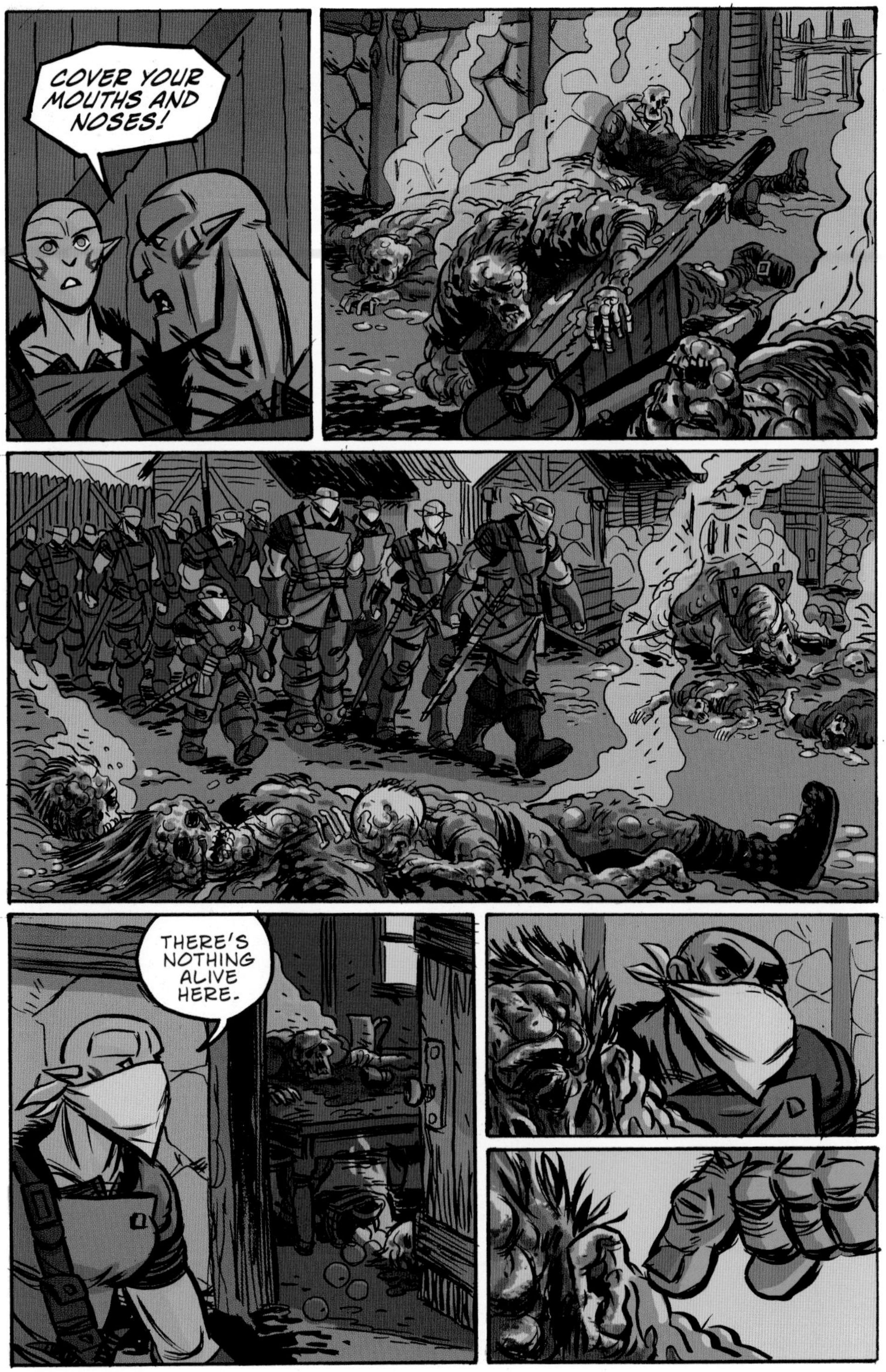
COVER YOUR MOUTHS AND NOSES!
THERE'S NOTHING ALIVE HERE.

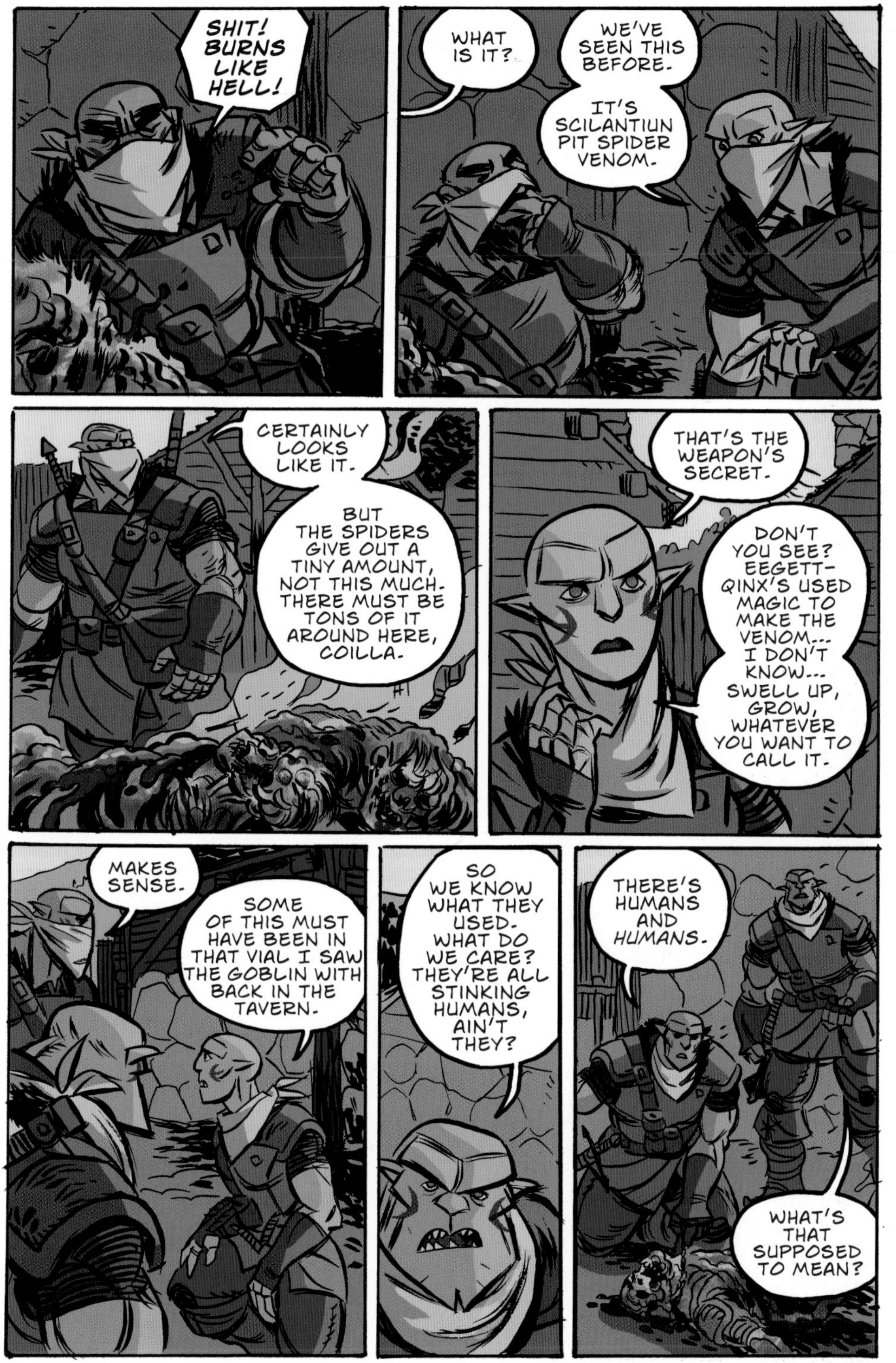

SHIT! BURNS LIKE HELL!
WHAT IS IT?
WE'VE SEEN THIS BEFORE.
IT'S SCILANTIUN PIT SPIDER VENOM.
CERTAINLY LOOKS LIKE IT.
BUT THE SPIDERS GIVE OUT A TINY AMOUNT, NOT THIS MUCH. THERE MUST BE TONS OF IT AROUND HERE, COILLA.
THAT'S THE WEAPON'S SECRET.
DON'T YOU SEE? EEGETT-QINX'S USED MAGIC TO MAKE THE VENOM... I DON'T KNOW... SWELL UP, GROW, WHATEVER YOU WANT TO CALL IT.
MAKES SENSE.
SOME OF THIS MUST HAVE BEEN IN THAT VIAL I SAW THE GOBLIN WITH BACK IN THE TAVERN.
SO WE KNOW WHAT THEY USED. WHAT DO WE CARE? THEY'RE ALL STINKING HUMANS, AIN'T THEY?
THERE'S HUMANS AND *HUMANS*.
WHAT'S THAT SUPPOSED TO MEAN?

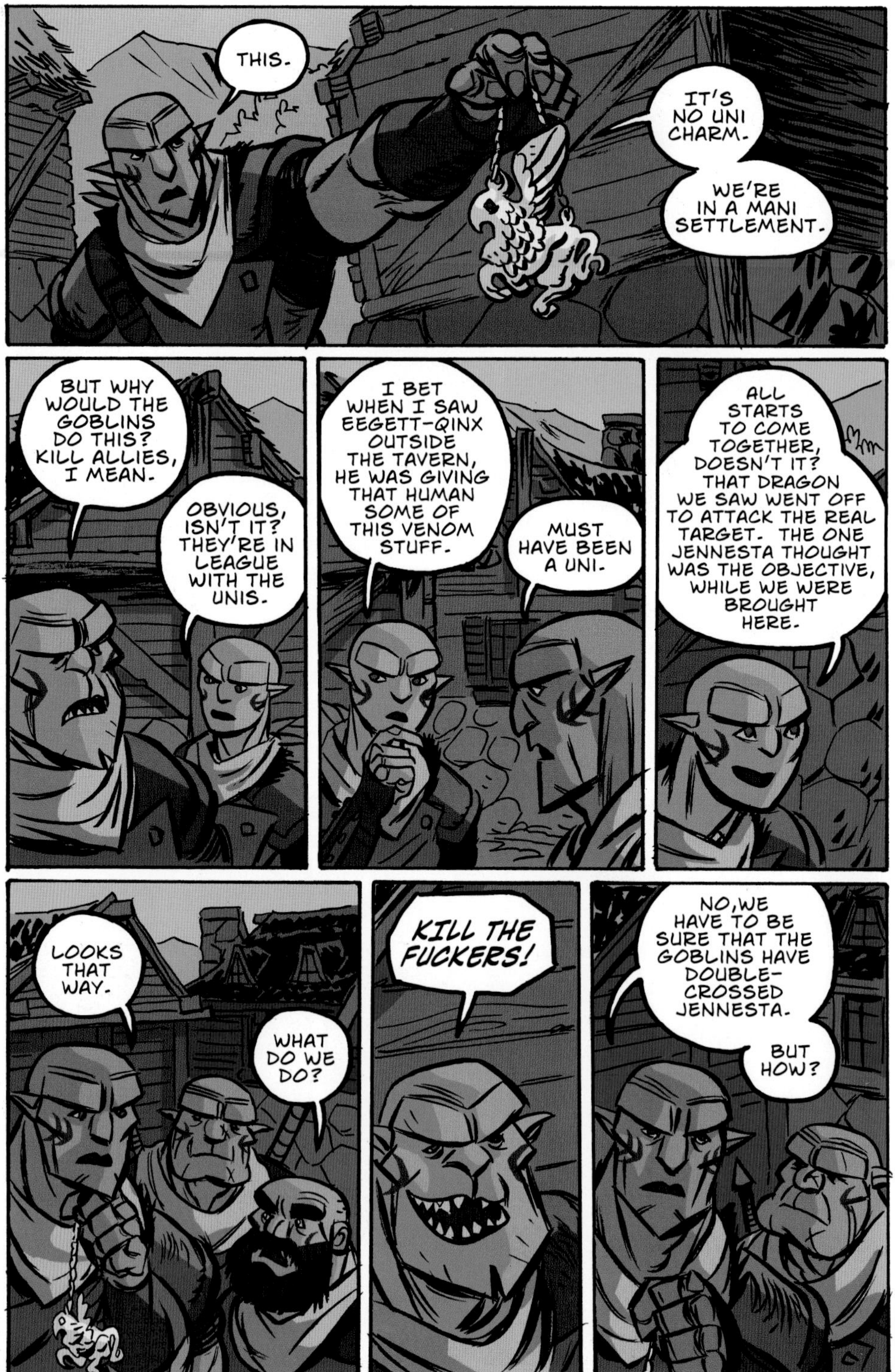
THIS.
IT'S NO UNI CHARM.
WE'RE IN A MANI SETTLEMENT.
BUT WHY WOULD THE GOBLINS DO THIS? KILL ALLIES, I MEAN.
OBVIOUS, ISN'T IT? THEY'RE IN LEAGUE WITH THE UNIS.
I BET WHEN I SAW EEGETT-QINX OUTSIDE THE TAVERN, HE WAS GIVING THAT HUMAN SOME OF THIS VENOM STUFF.
MUST HAVE BEEN A UNI.
ALL STARTS TO COME TOGETHER, DOESN'T IT? THAT DRAGON WE SAW WENT OFF TO ATTACK THE REAL TARGET. THE ONE JENNESTA THOUGHT WAS THE OBJECTIVE, WHILE WE WERE BROUGHT HERE.
LOOKS THAT WAY.
WHAT DO WE DO?
KILL THE FUCKERS!
NO, WE HAVE TO BE SURE THAT THE GOBLINS HAVE DOUBLE-CROSSED JENNESTA.
BUT HOW?

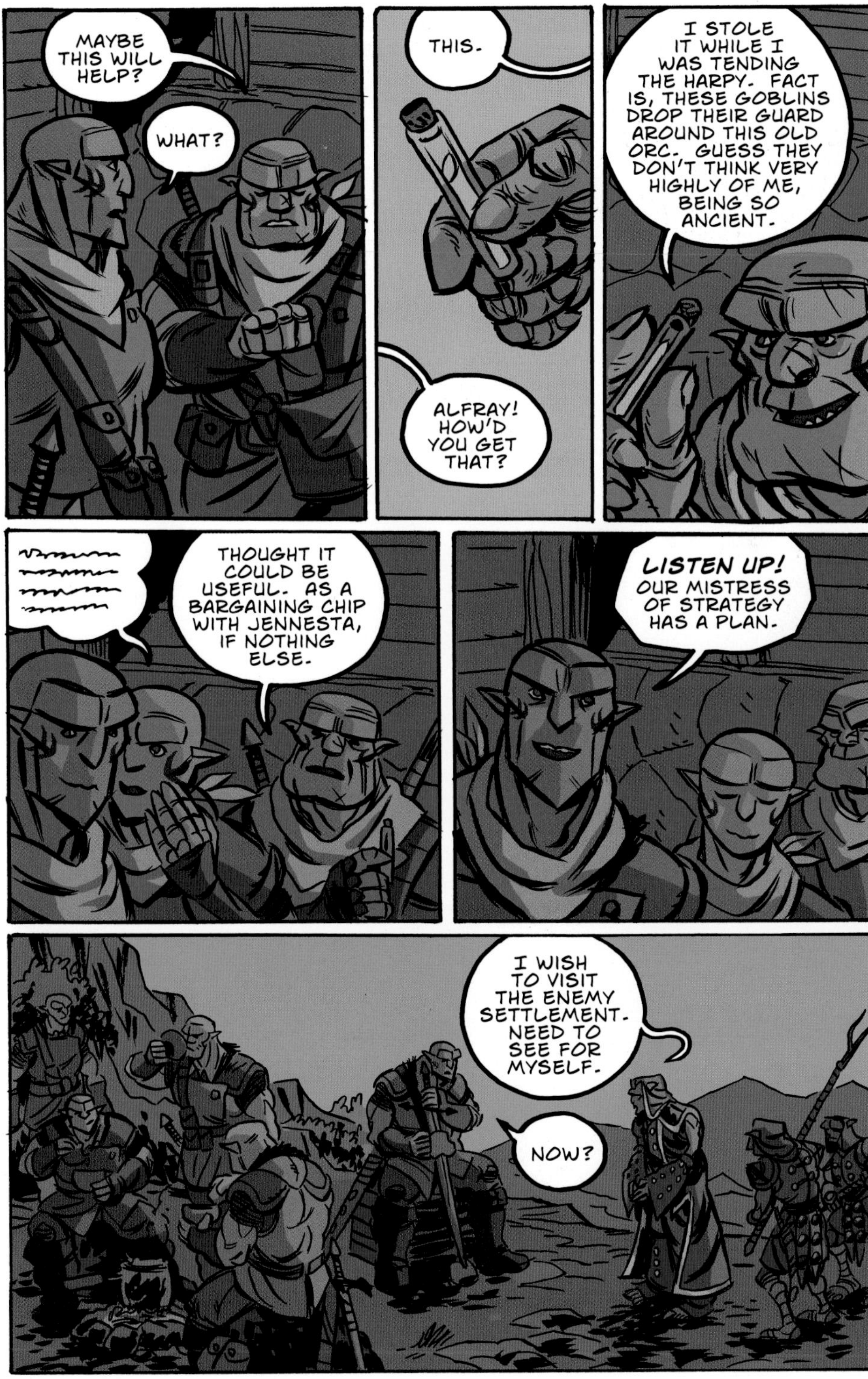
MAYBE THIS WILL HELP?
WHAT?
THIS.
ALFRAY! HOW'D YOU GET THAT?
I STOLE IT WHILE I WAS TENDING THE HARPY. FACT IS, THESE GOBLINS DROP THEIR GUARD AROUND THIS OLD ORC. GUESS THEY DON'T THINK VERY HIGHLY OF ME, BEING SO ANCIENT.
THOUGHT IT COULD BE USEFUL. AS A BARGAINING CHIP WITH JENNESTA, IF NOTHING ELSE.
LISTEN UP! OUR MISTRESS OF STRATEGY HAS A PLAN.
I WISH TO VISIT THE ENEMY SETTLEMENT. NEED TO SEE FOR MYSELF.
NOW?

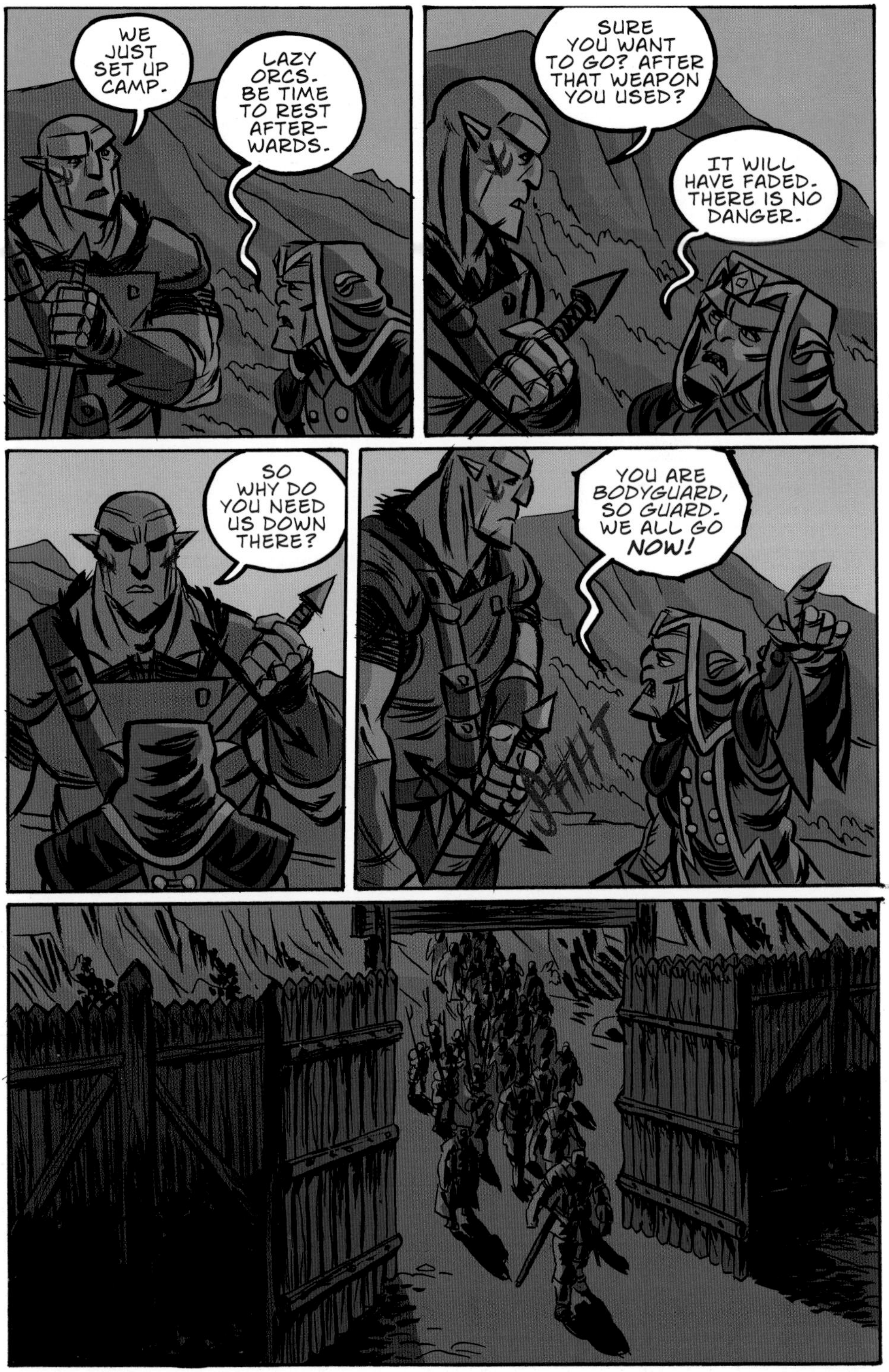
WE JUST SET UP CAMP.
LAZY ORCS. BE TIME TO REST AFTER-WARDS.
SURE YOU WANT TO GO? AFTER THAT WEAPON YOU USED?
IT WILL HAVE FADED. THERE IS NO DANGER.
SO WHY DO YOU NEED US DOWN THERE?
YOU ARE BODYGUARD, SO GUARD. WE ALL GO NOW!
SHHT

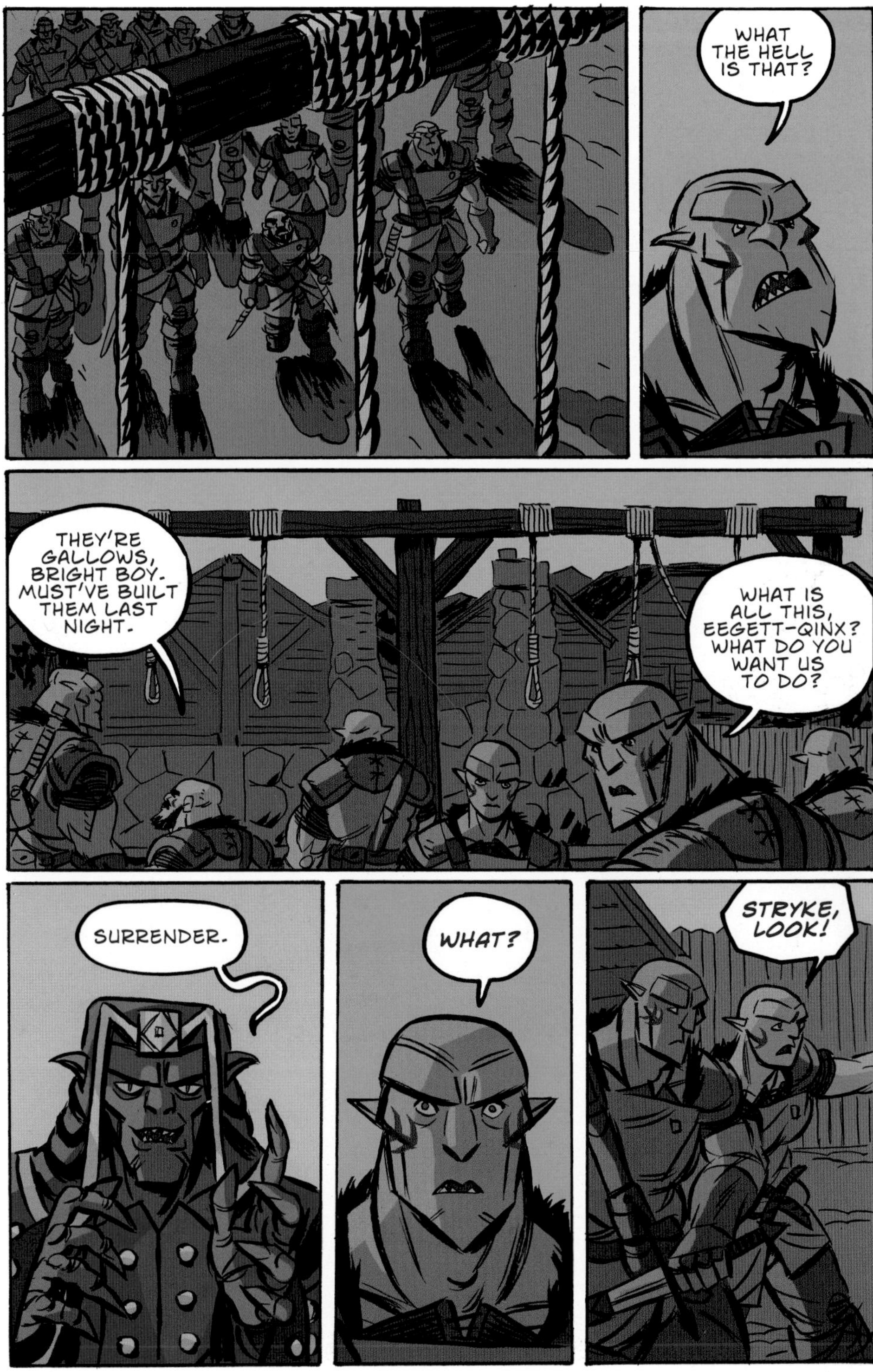
WHAT THE HELL IS THAT?
THEY'RE GALLOWS, BRIGHT BOY. MUST'VE BUILT THEM LAST NIGHT.
WHAT IS ALL THIS, EEGETT-QINX? WHAT DO YOU WANT US TO DO?
SURRENDER.
WHAT?
STRYKE, LOOK!

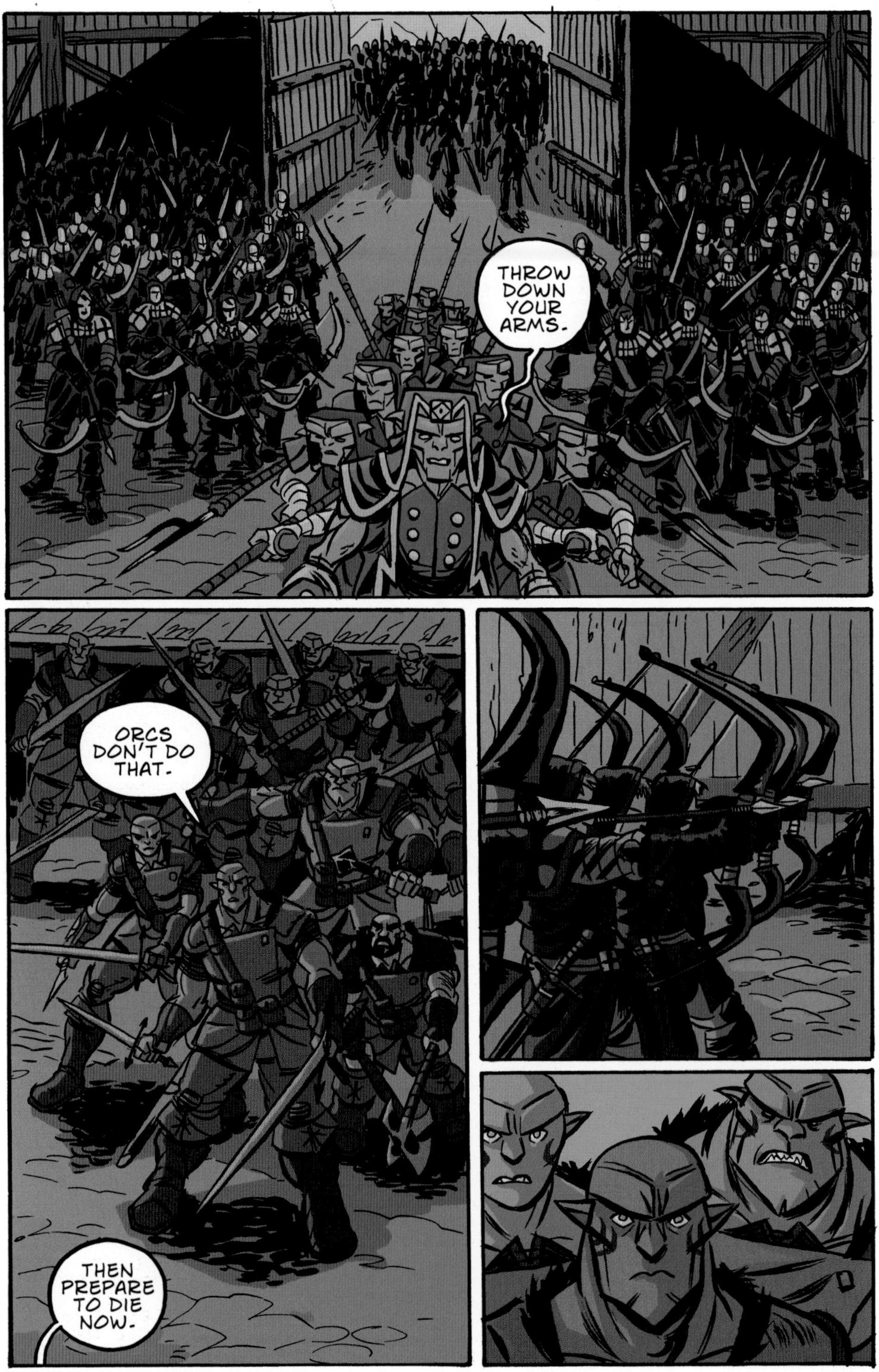
THROW DOWN YOUR ARMS.
ORCS DON'T DO THAT.
THEN PREPARE TO DIE NOW.

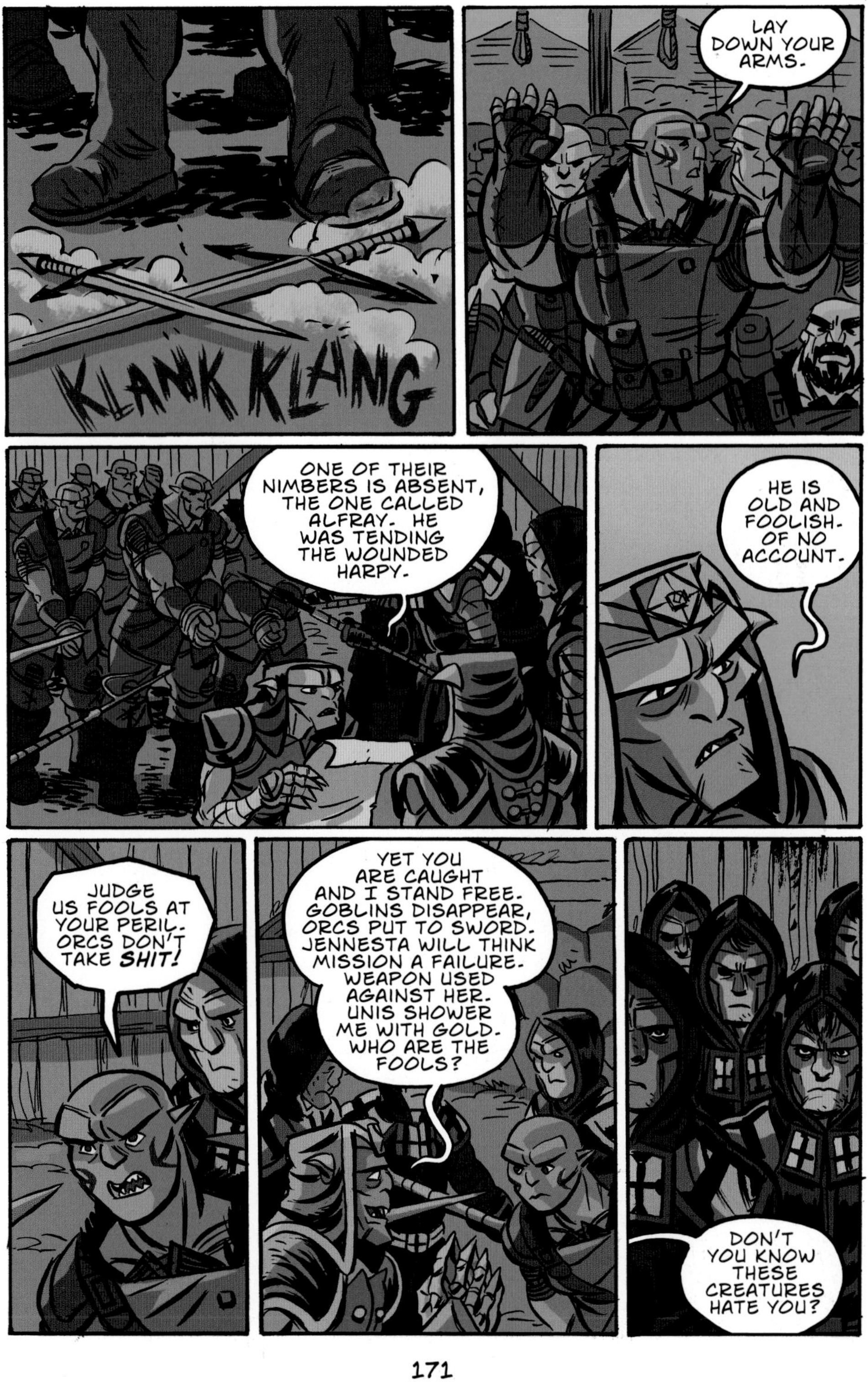
KLANK KLANG
LAY DOWN YOUR ARMS.
ONE OF THEIR NIMBERS IS ABSENT, THE ONE CALLED ALFRAY. HE WAS TENDING THE WOUNDED HARPY.
HE IS OLD AND FOOLISH- OF NO ACCOUNT.
JUDGE US FOOLS AT YOUR PERIL. ORCS DON'T TAKE **SHIT!**
YET YOU ARE CAUGHT AND I STAND FREE. GOBLINS DISAPPEAR, ORCS PUT TO SWORD. JENNESTA WILL THINK MISSION A FAILURE. WEAPON USED AGAINST HER. UNIS SHOWER ME WITH GOLD. WHO ARE THE FOOLS?
DON'T YOU KNOW THESE CREATURES HATE YOU?

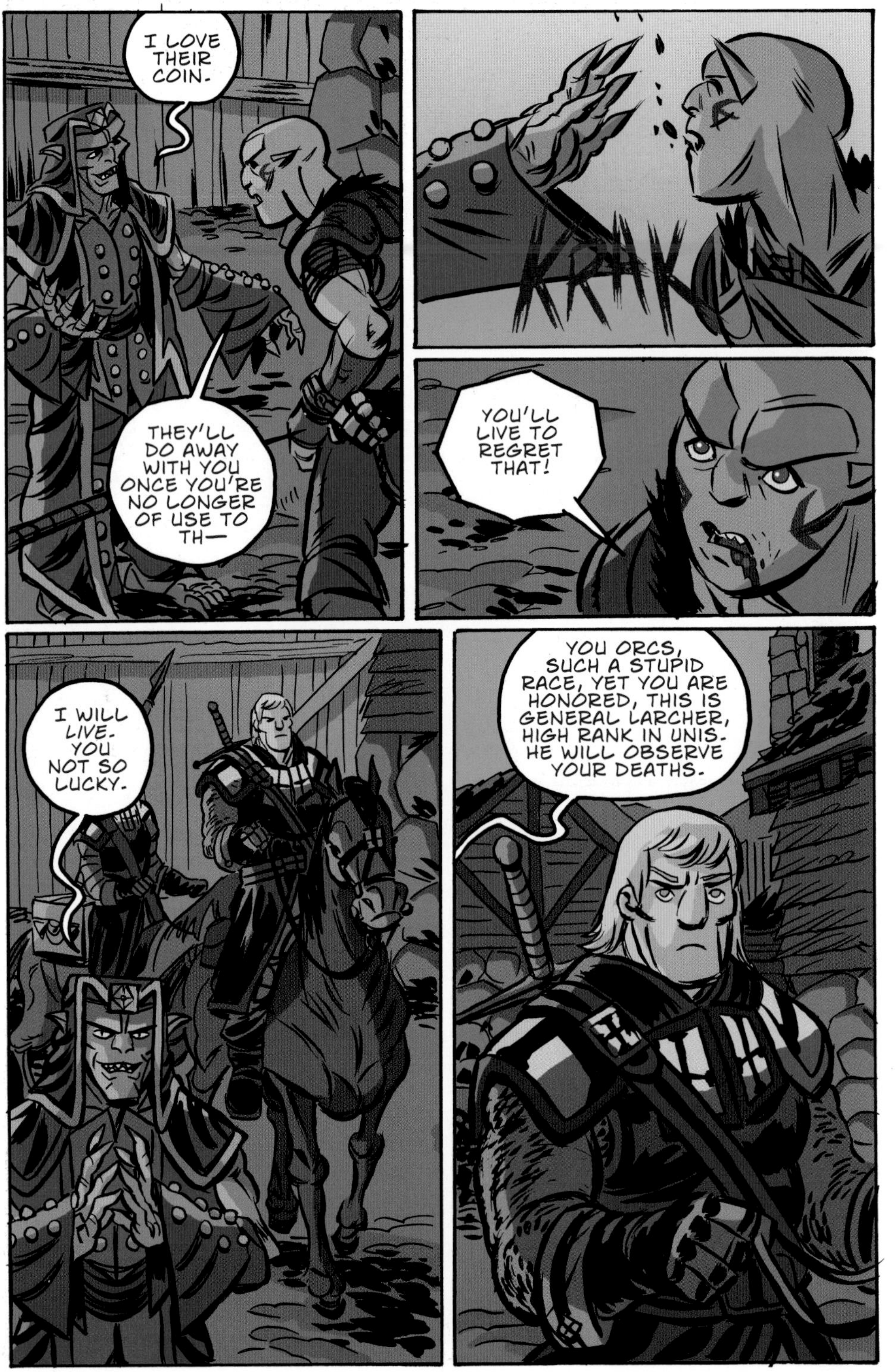
I LOVE THEIR COIN.
THEY'LL DO AWAY WITH YOU ONCE YOU'RE NO LONGER OF USE TO TH—
KRAK
YOU'LL LIVE TO REGRET THAT!
I WILL LIVE. YOU NOT SO LUCKY.
YOU ORCS, SUCH A STUPID RACE, YET YOU ARE HONORED, THIS IS GENERAL LARCHER, HIGH RANK IN UNIS. HE WILL OBSERVE YOUR DEATHS.

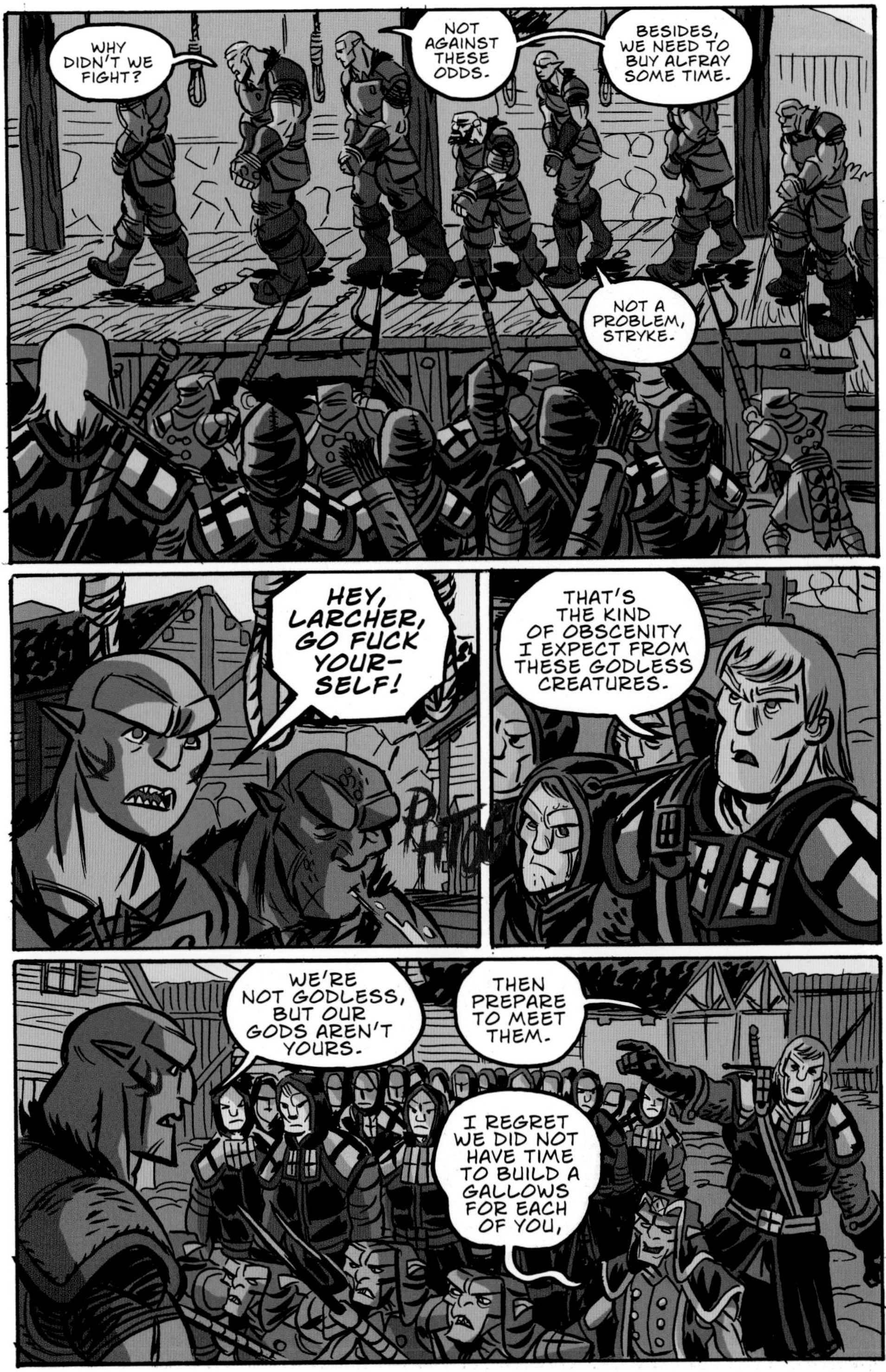
WHY DIDN'T WE FIGHT?
NOT AGAINST THESE ODDS.
BESIDES, WE NEED TO BUY ALFRAY SOME TIME.
NOT A PROBLEM, STRYKE.
HEY, LARCHER, GO FUCK YOURSELF!
THAT'S THE KIND OF OBSCENITY I EXPECT FROM THESE GODLESS CREATURES.
WE'RE NOT GODLESS, BUT OUR GODS AREN'T YOURS.
THEN PREPARE TO MEET THEM.
I REGRET WE DID NOT HAVE TIME TO BUILD A GALLOWS FOR EACH OF YOU,

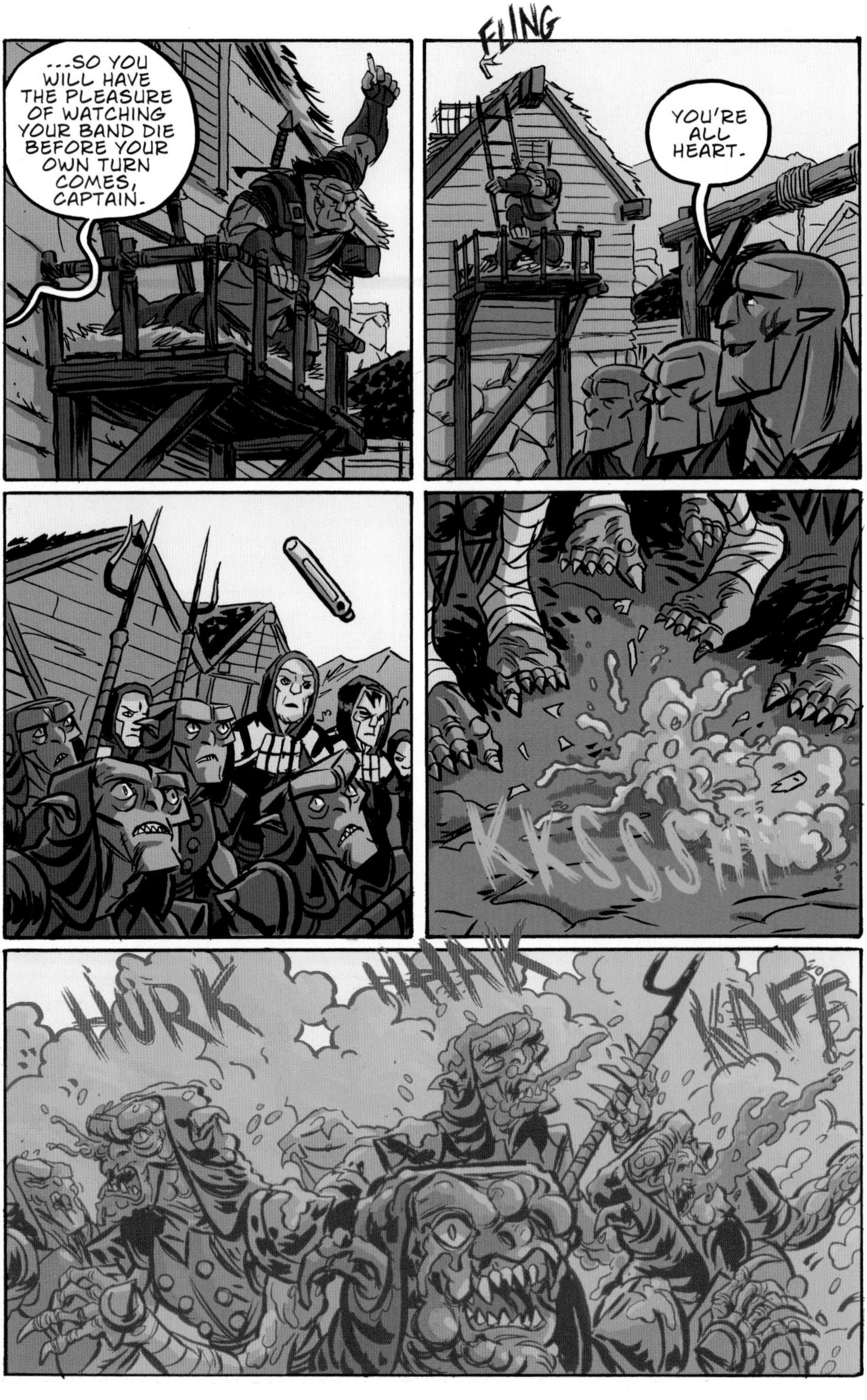
...SO YOU WILL HAVE THE PLEASURE OF WATCHING YOUR BAND DIE BEFORE YOUR OWN TURN COMES, CAPTAIN.
FLING
YOU'RE ALL HEART.
KKSSSSH
HURK
KAFF

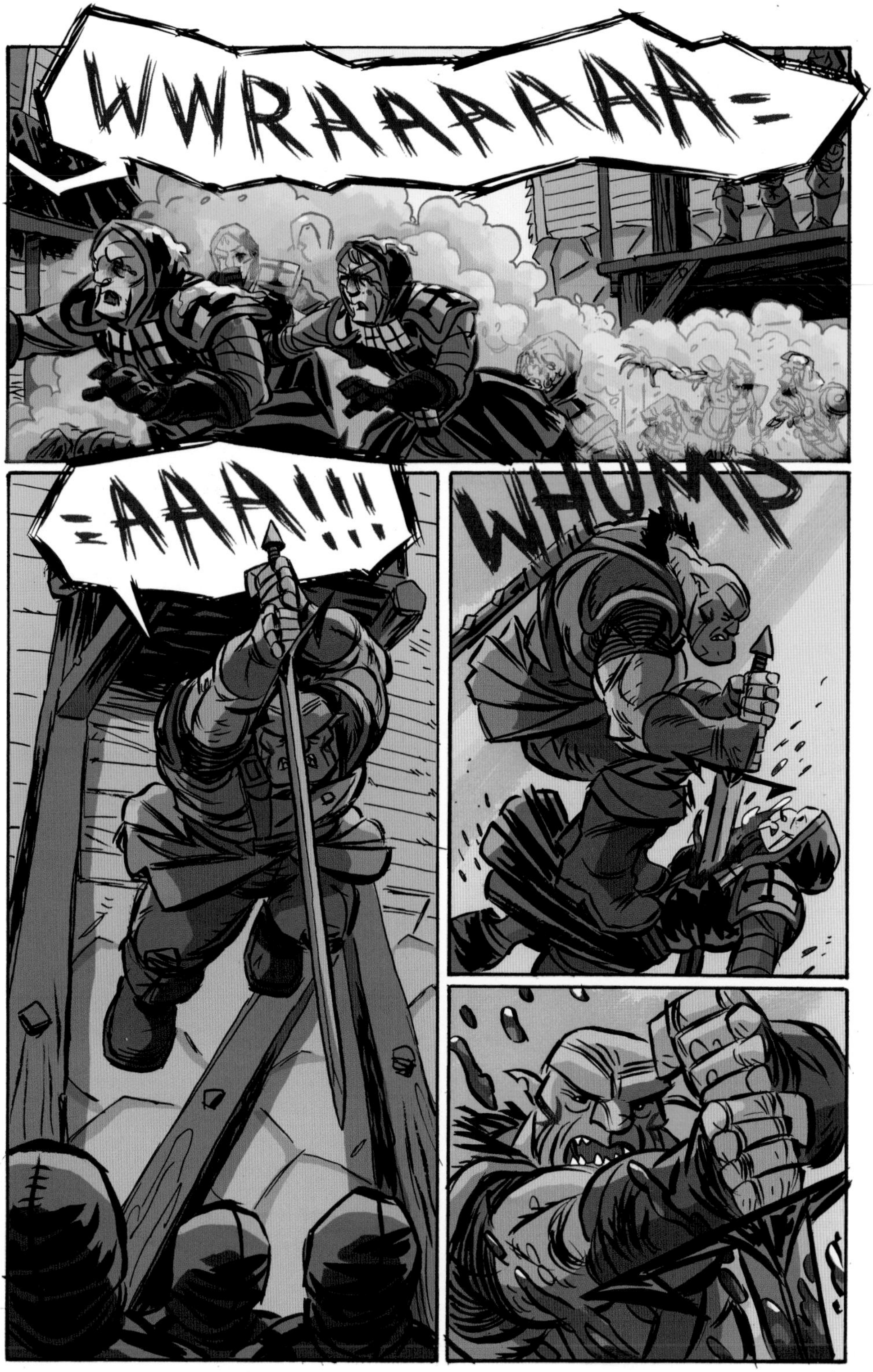
WWRAAAAAAA=
=AAA!!!
WHUMP

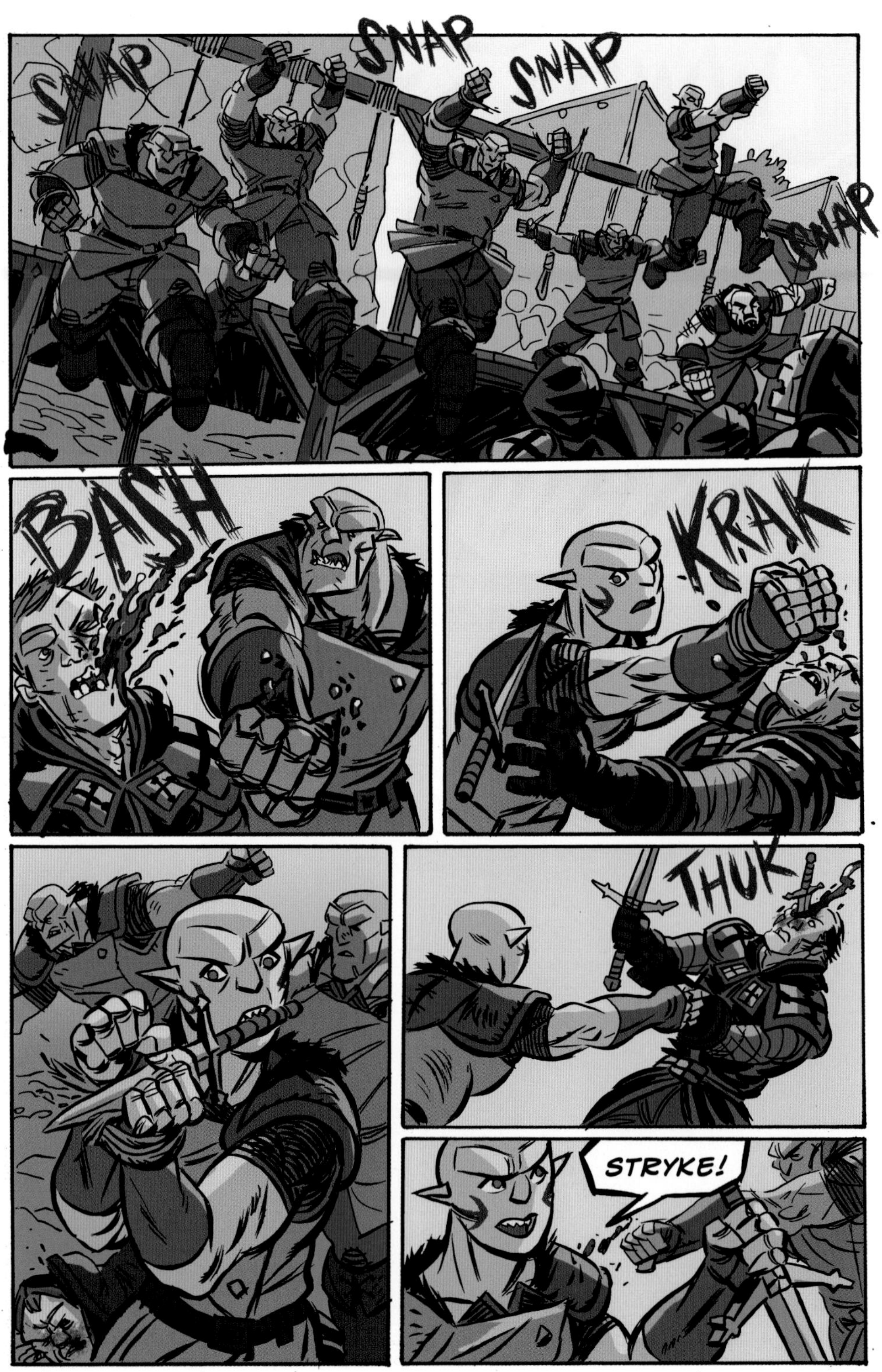
SNAP
SNAP
SNAP
SNAP
BASH
KRAK
THUK
STRYKE!

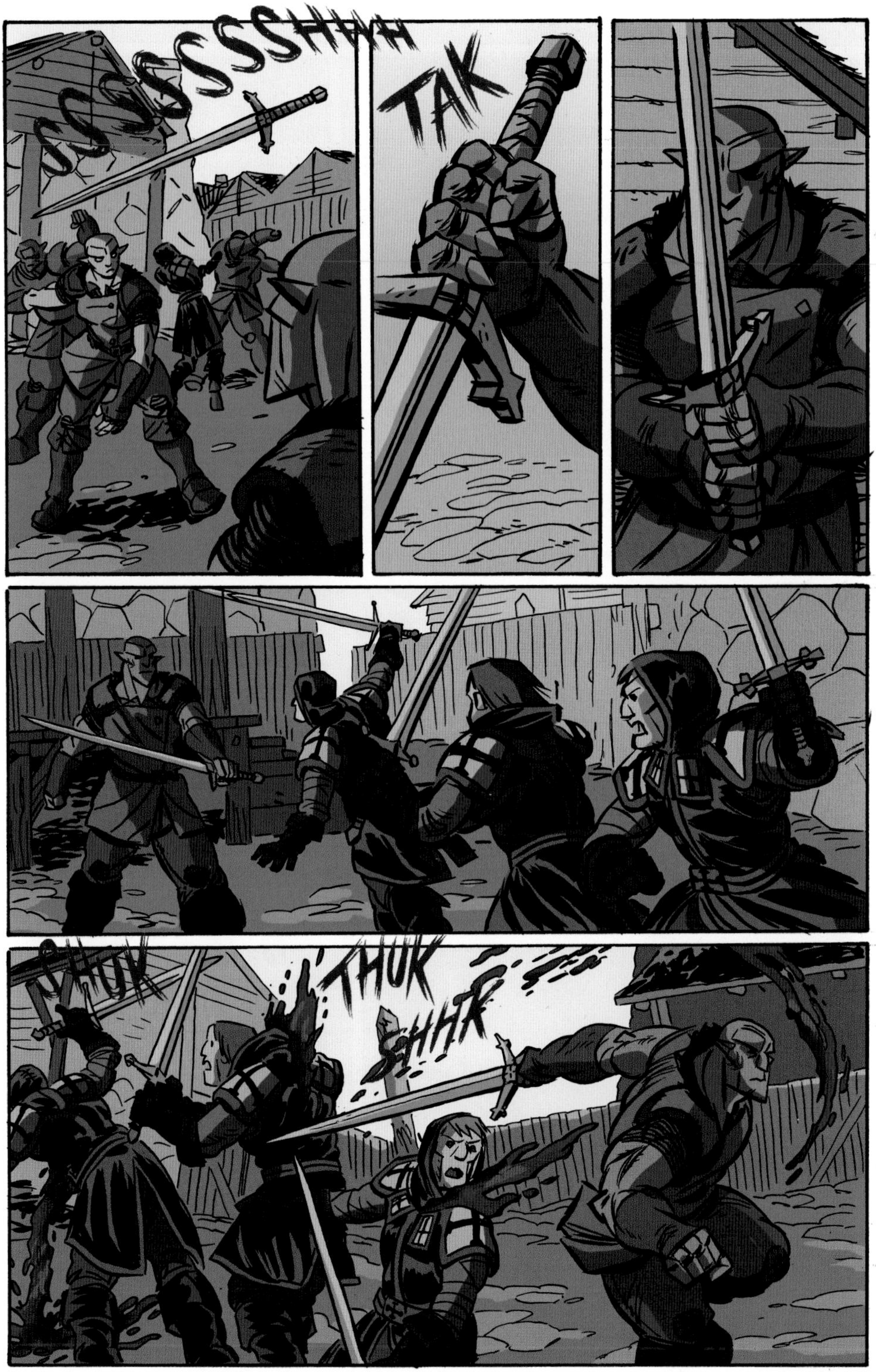
SSSSSSSHHHH
TAK
SHUK
THUK
SHHR

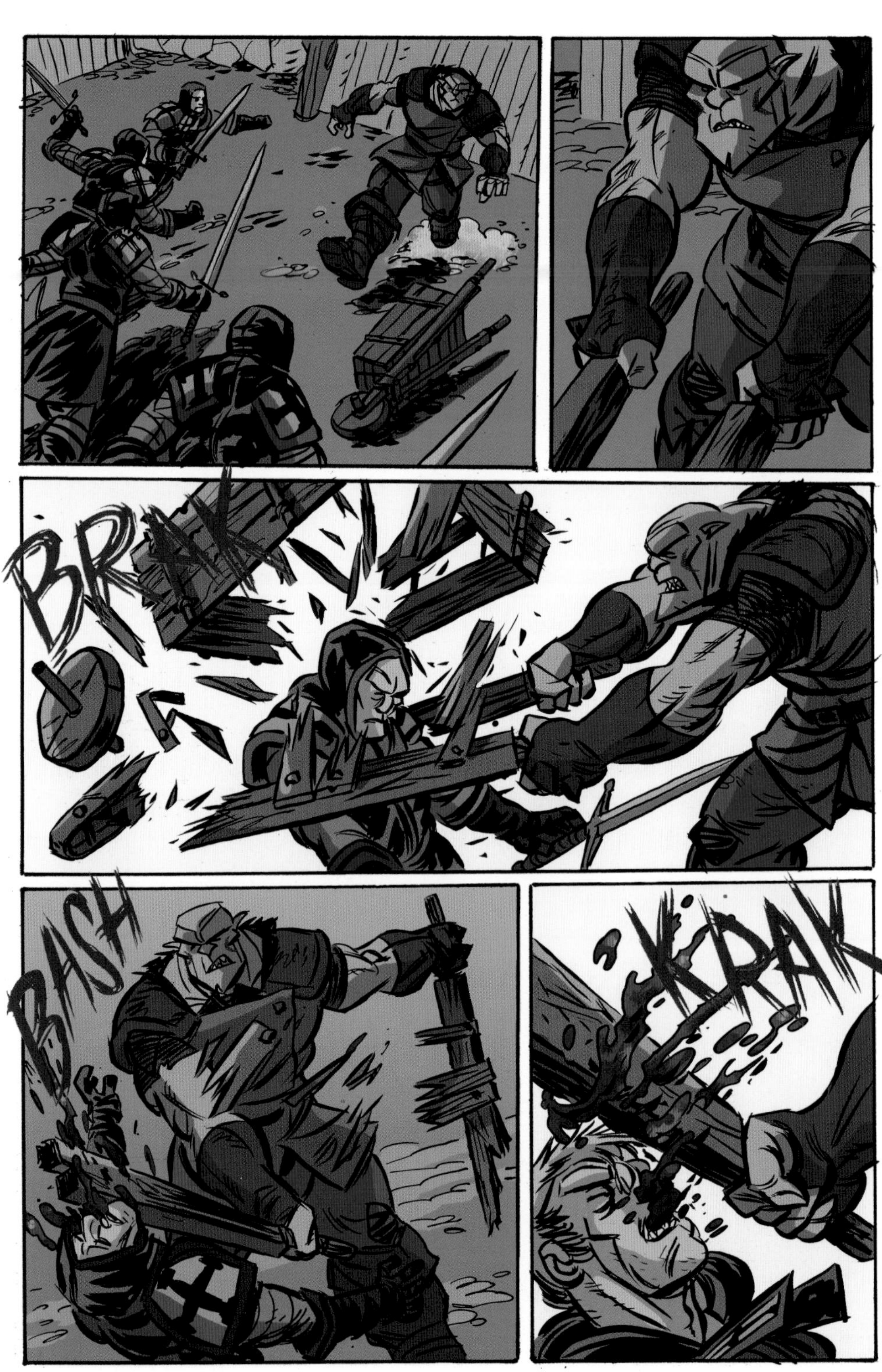
BRAK
BASH
KRAK

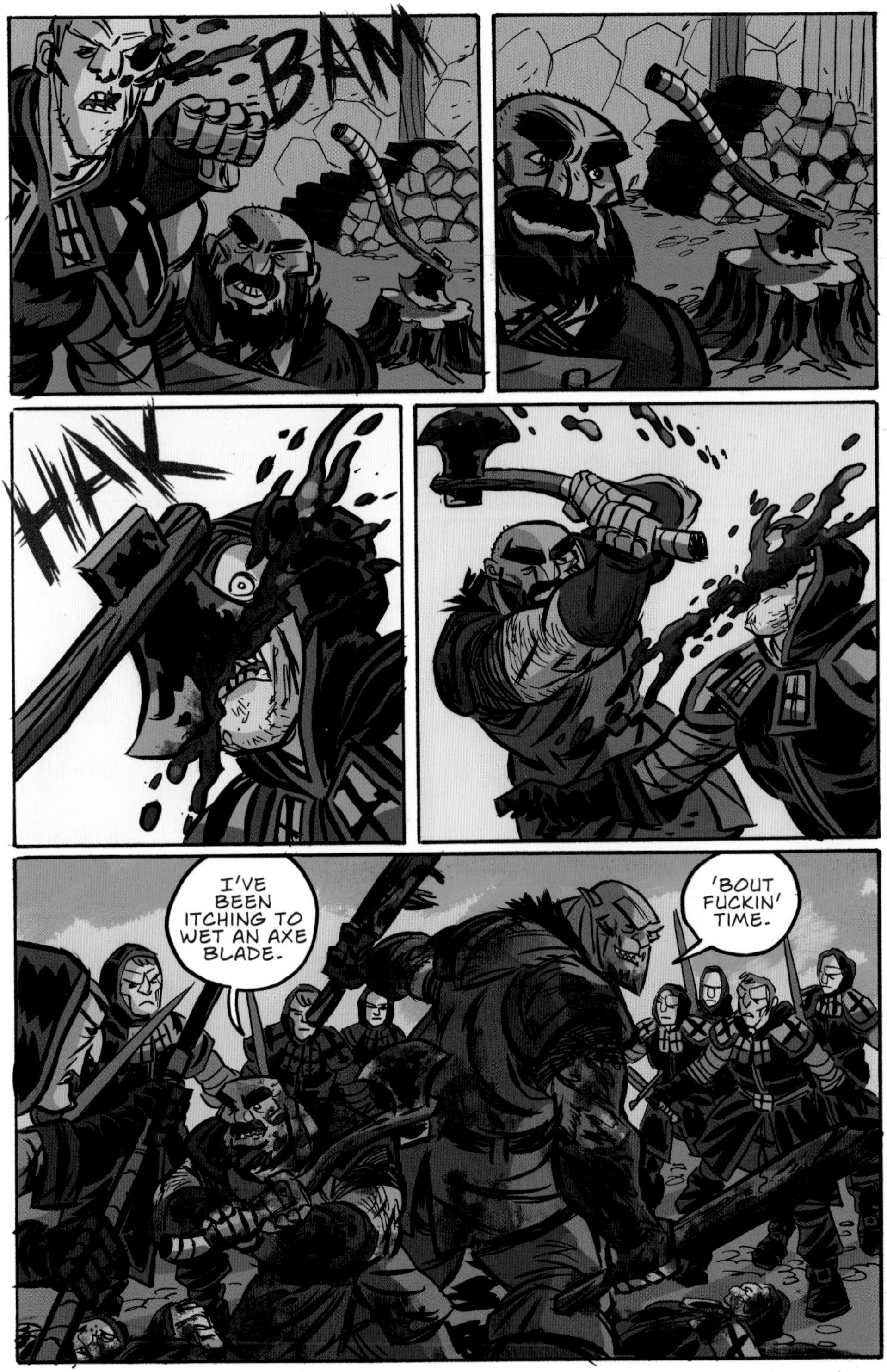
BAM
HAK
I'VE BEEN ITCHING TO WET AN AXE BLADE.
'BOUT FUCKIN' TIME.

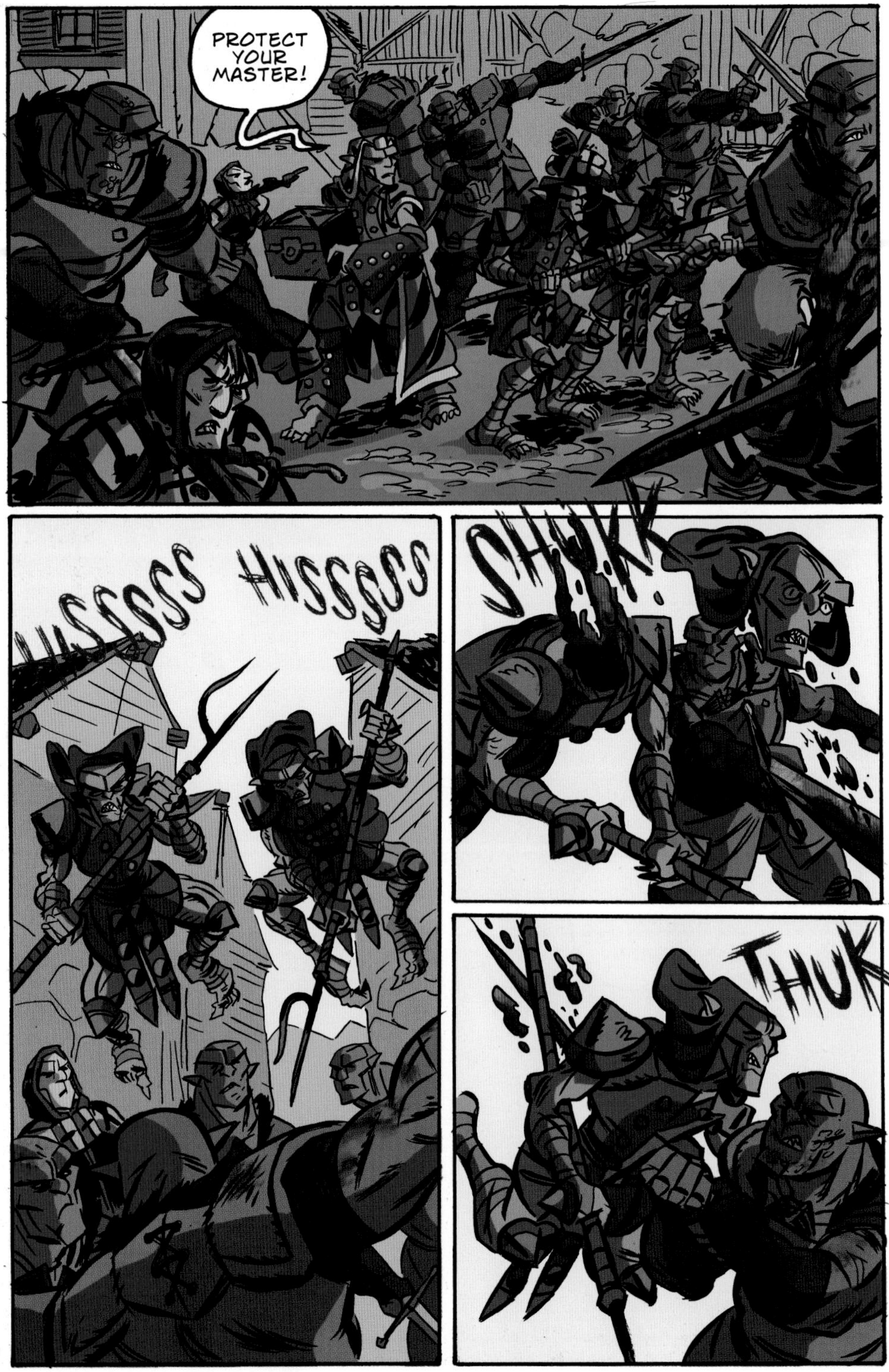
PROTECT YOUR MASTER!
HISSSSS HISSSSS
SHUKK
THUK

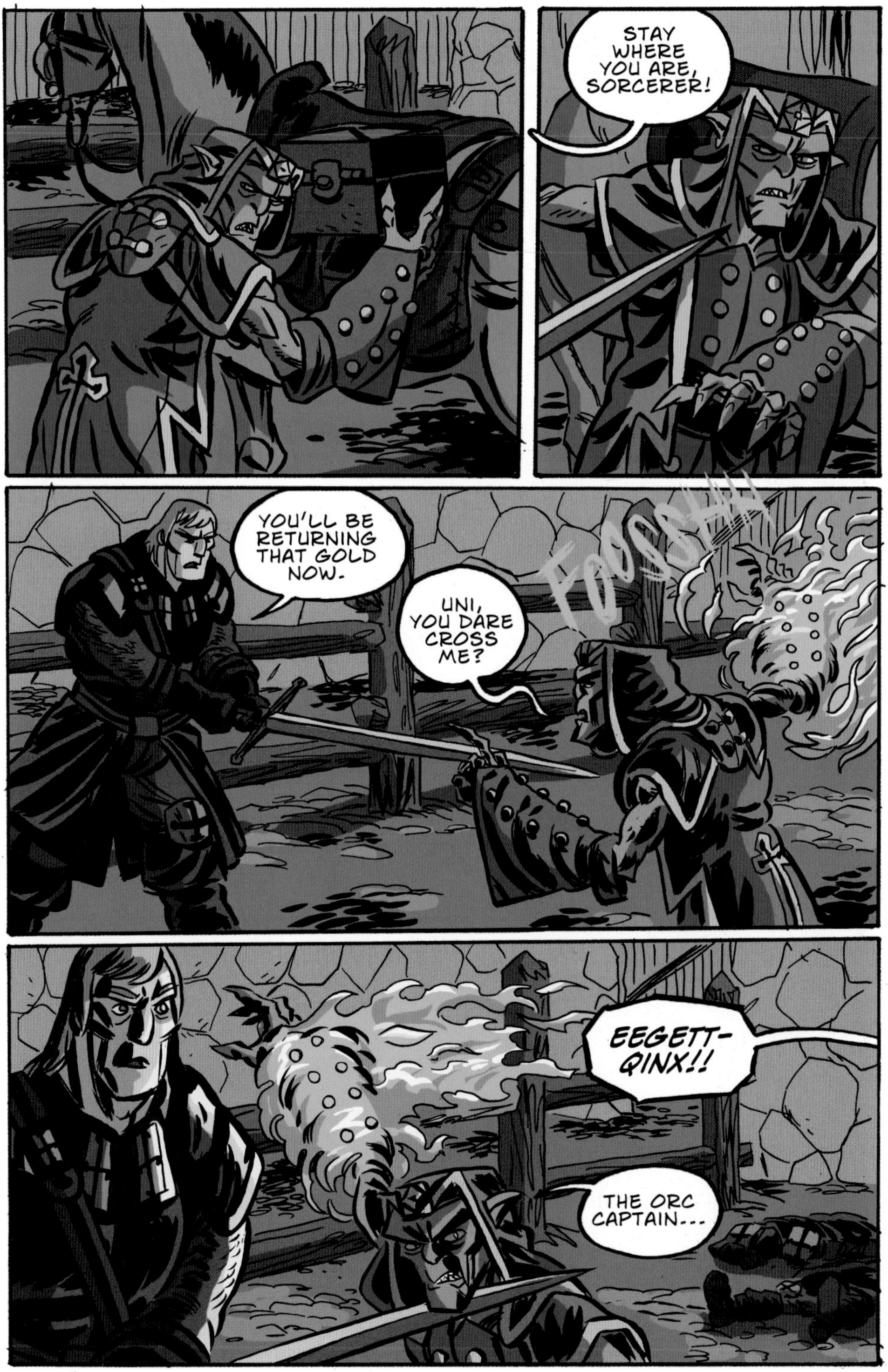

STAY WHERE YOU ARE, SORCERER!
YOU'LL BE RETURNING THAT GOLD NOW.
UNI, YOU DARE CROSS ME?
EEGETT-QINX!!
THE ORC CAPTAIN...

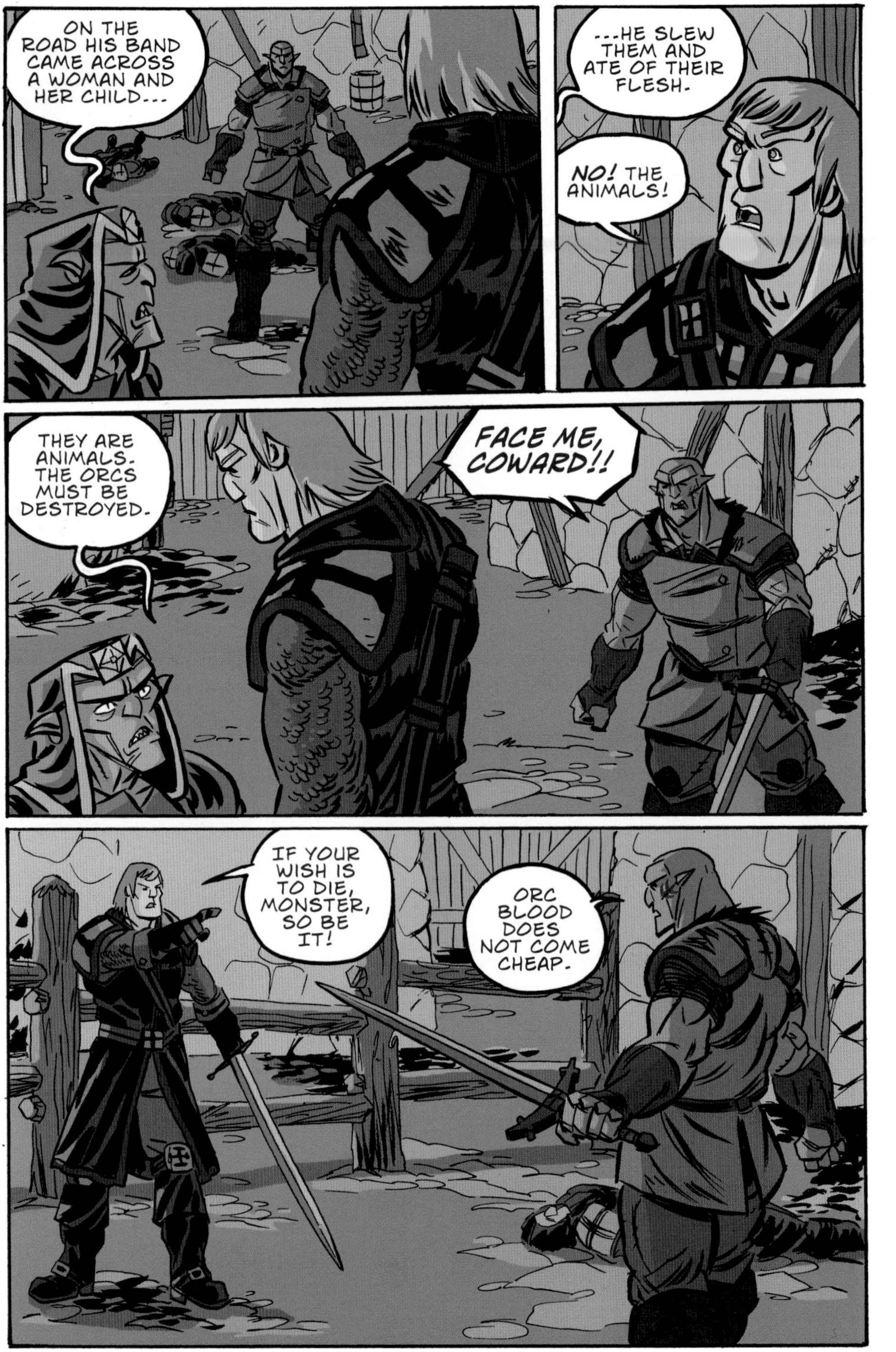
ON THE ROAD HIS BAND CAME ACROSS A WOMAN AND HER CHILD...
...HE SLEW THEM AND ATE OF THEIR FLESH.
NO! THE ANIMALS!
THEY ARE ANIMALS. THE ORCS MUST BE DESTROYED.
FACE ME, COWARD!!
IF YOUR WISH IS TO DIE, MONSTER, SO BE IT!
ORC BLOOD DOES NOT COME CHEAP.

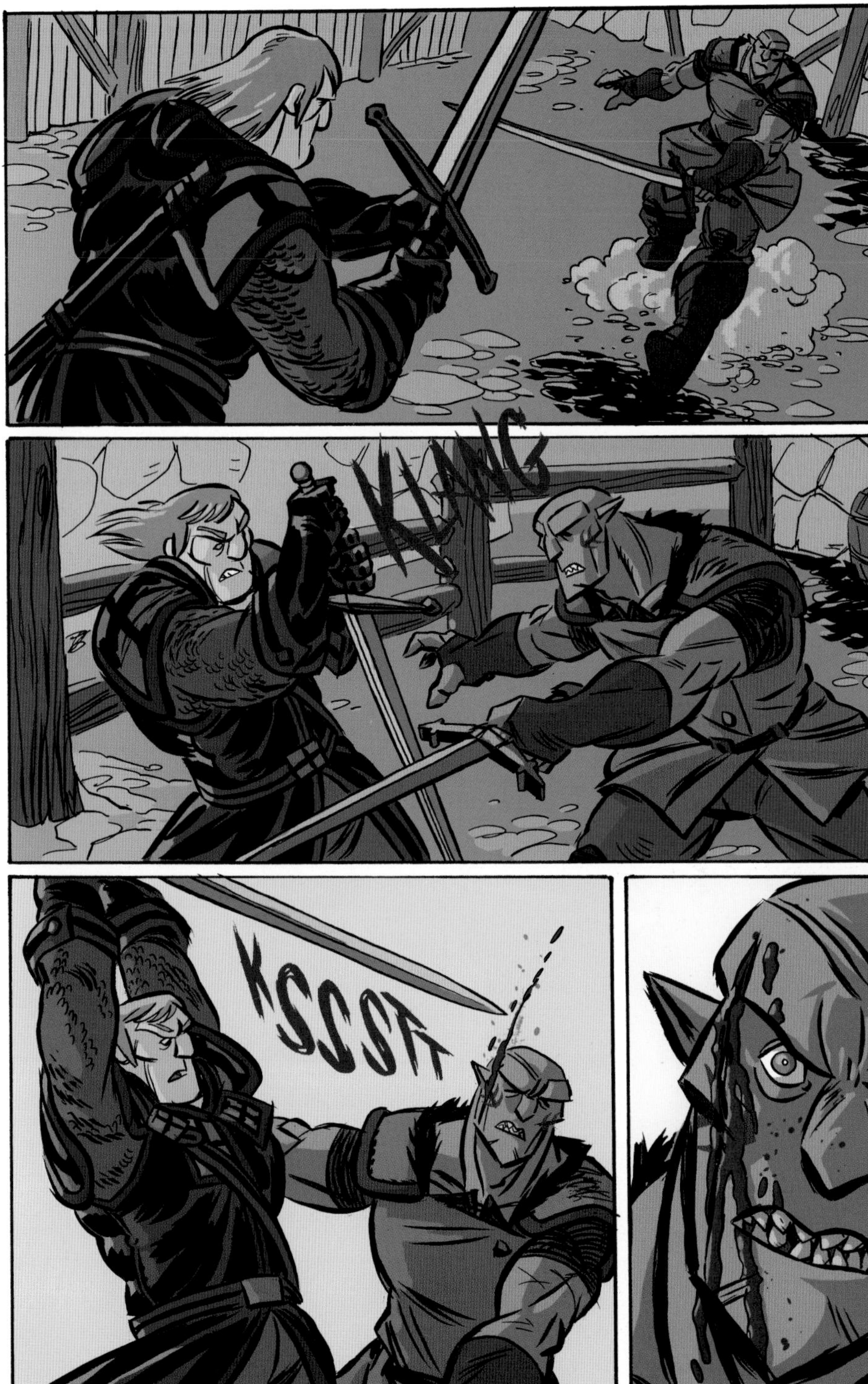
KLANG
KSSSFT

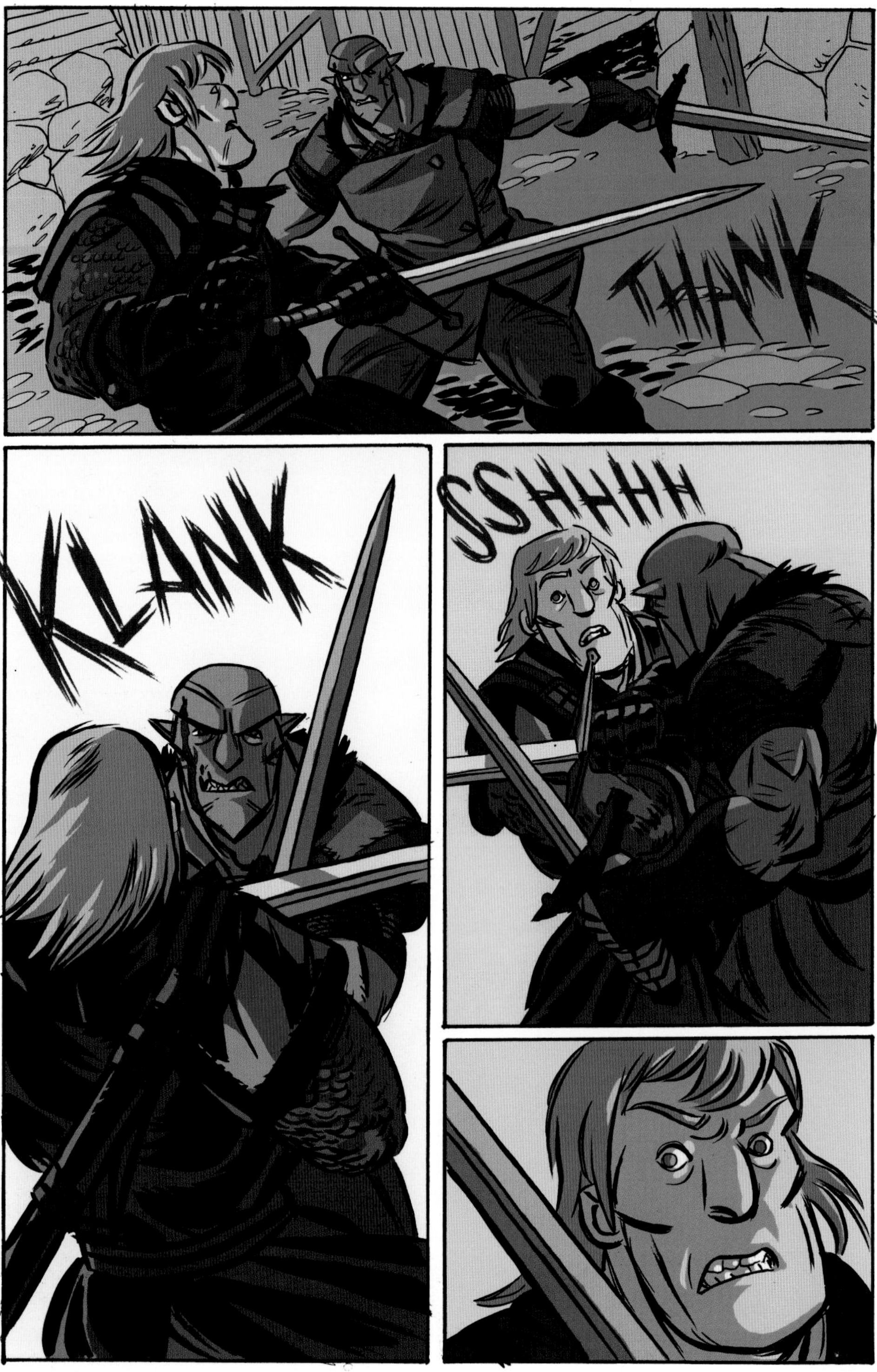
THANK
KLANK
SSHHHH

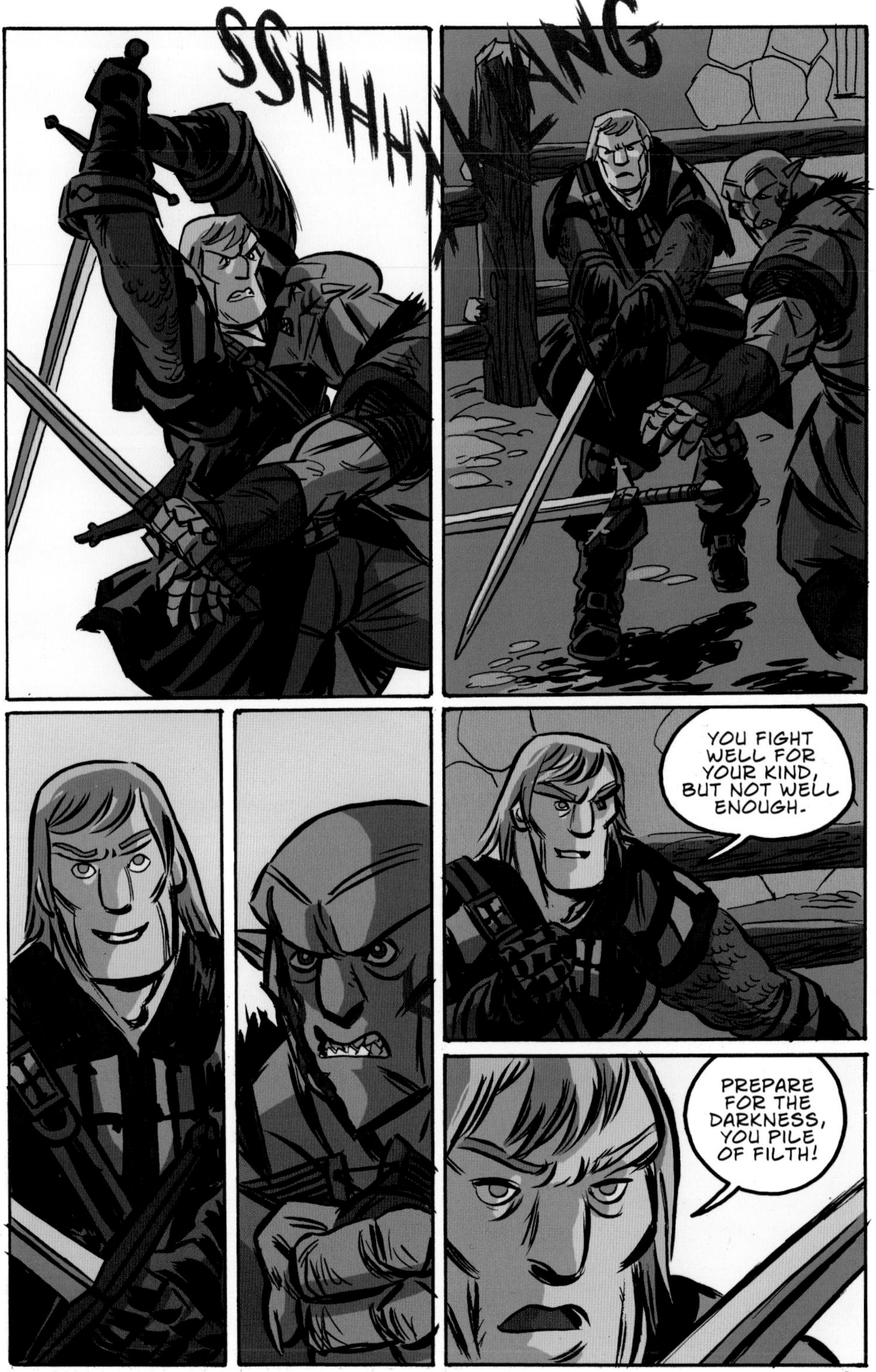
SSHHHWANG
YOU FIGHT WELL FOR YOUR KIND, BUT NOT WELL ENOUGH.
PREPARE FOR THE DARKNESS, YOU PILE OF FILTH!

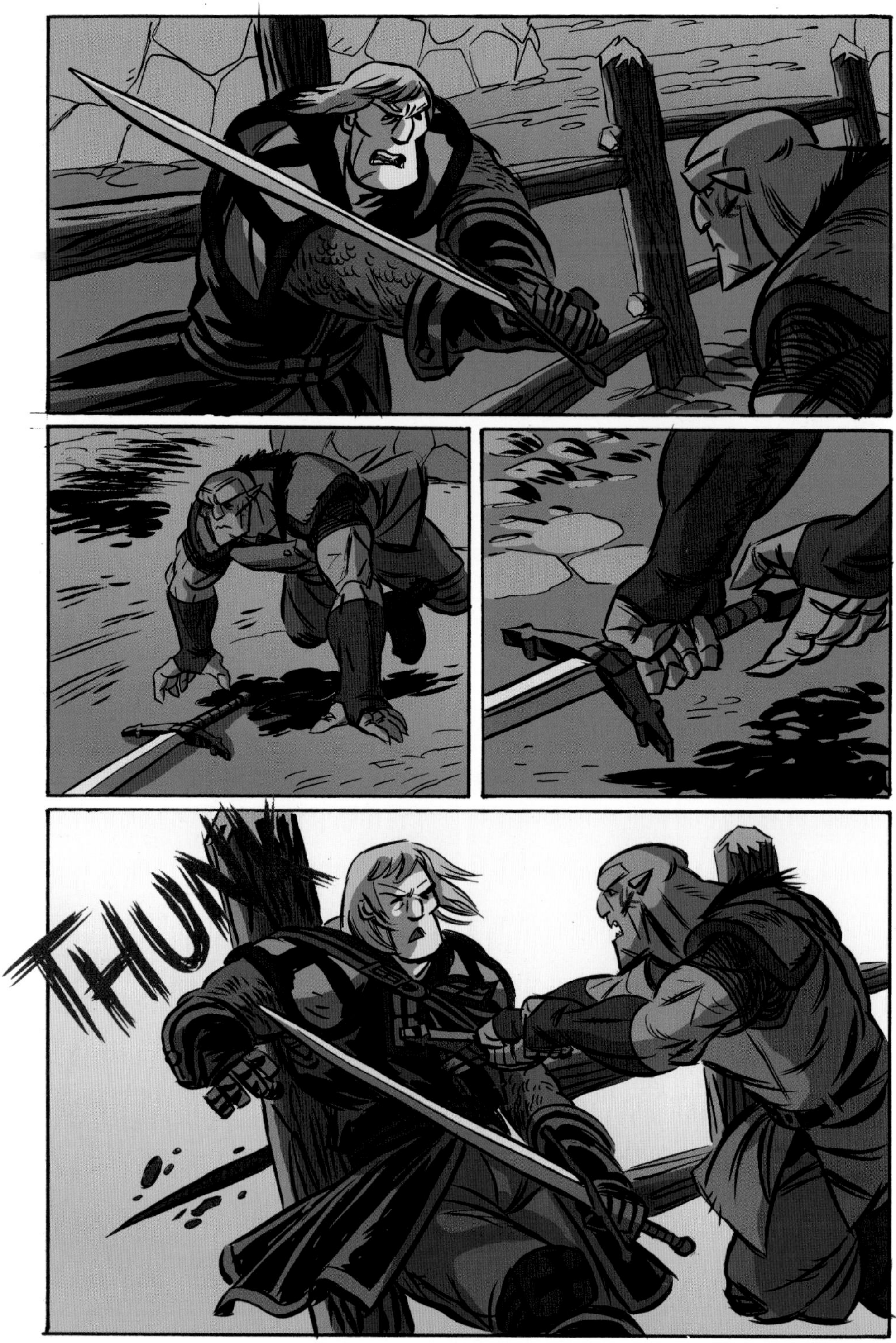
THUN

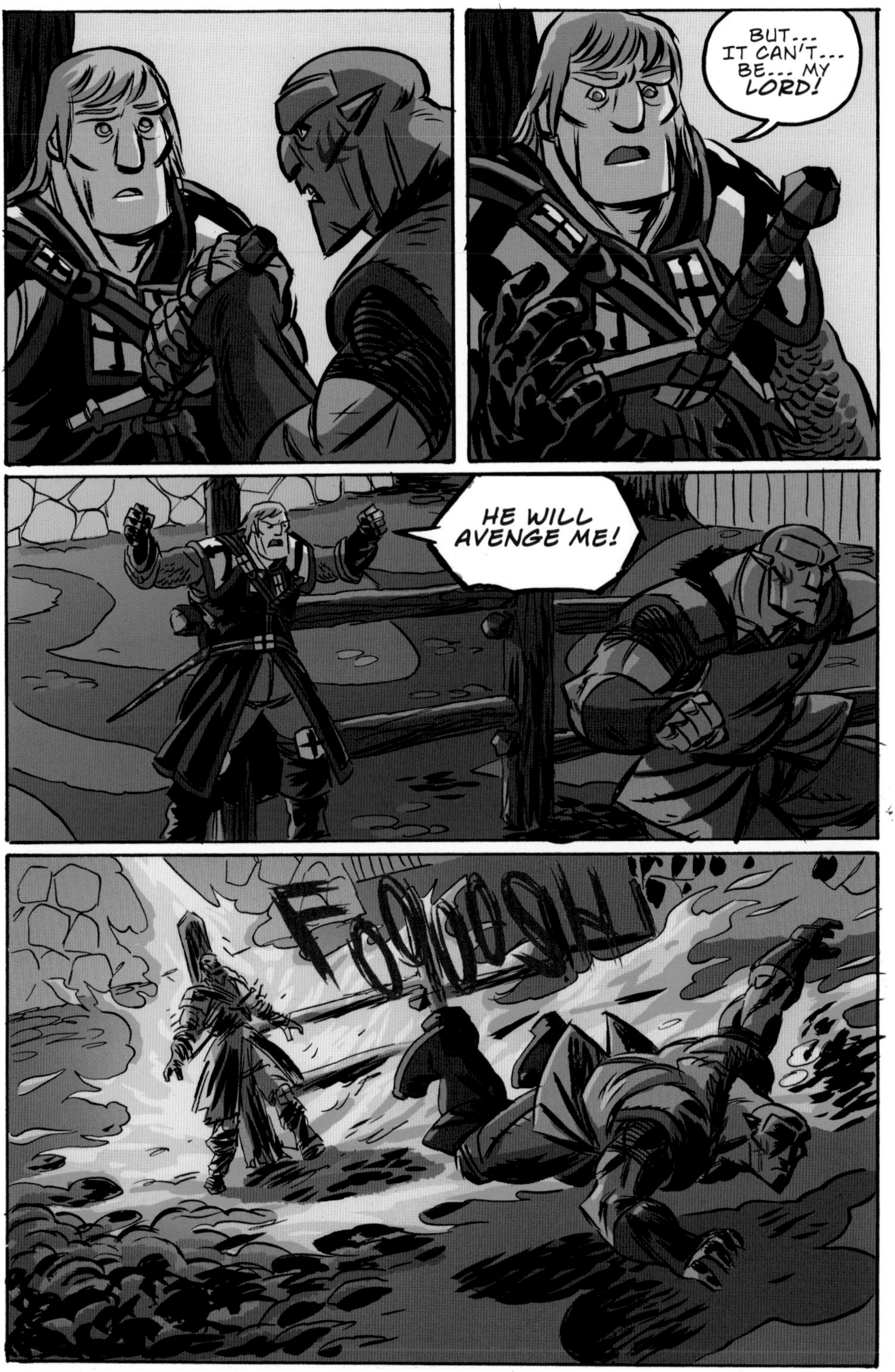
BUT... IT CAN'T... BE... MY LORD!
HE WILL AVENGE ME!
FOOOOSH!

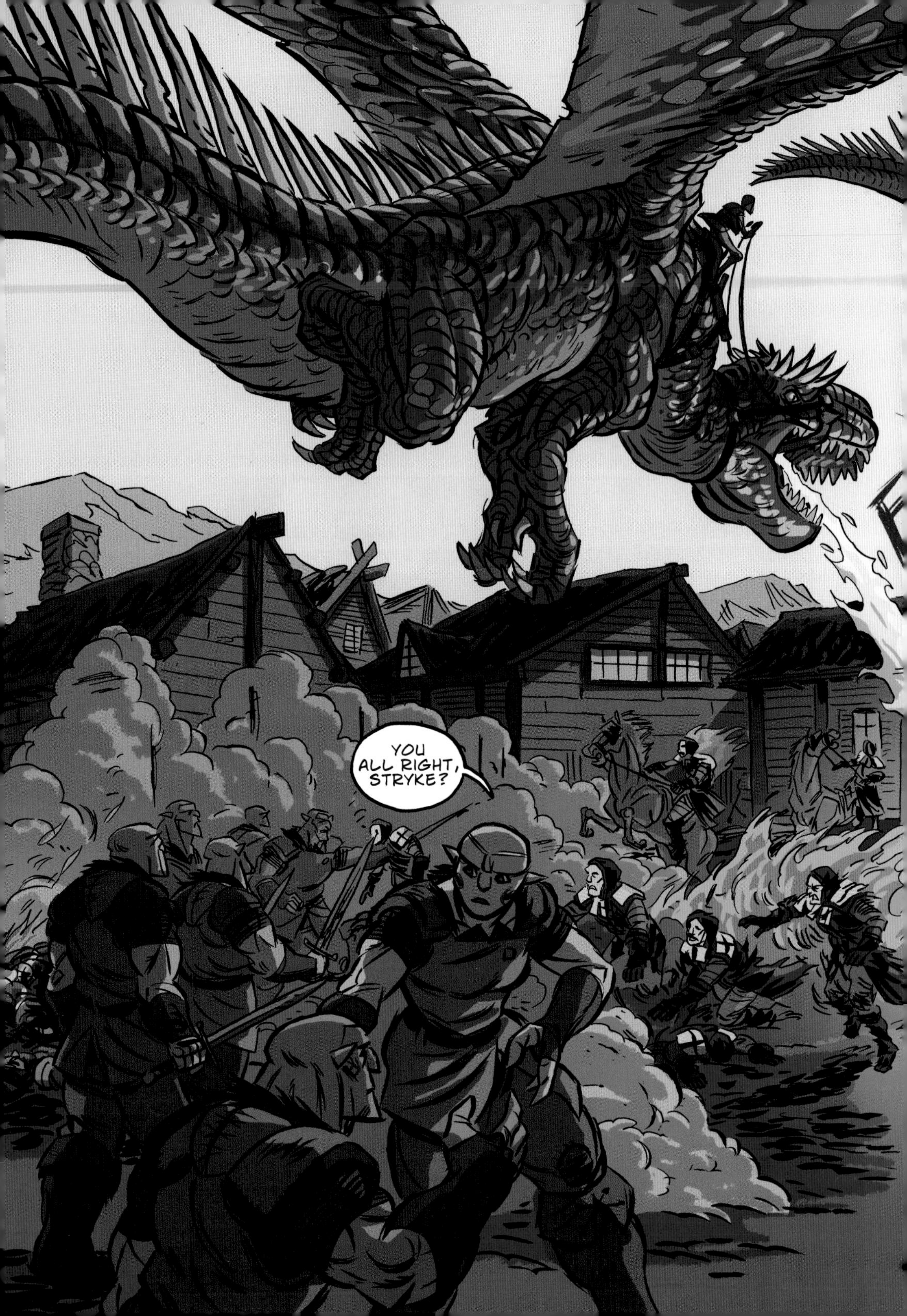
YOU ALL RIGHT, STRYKE?

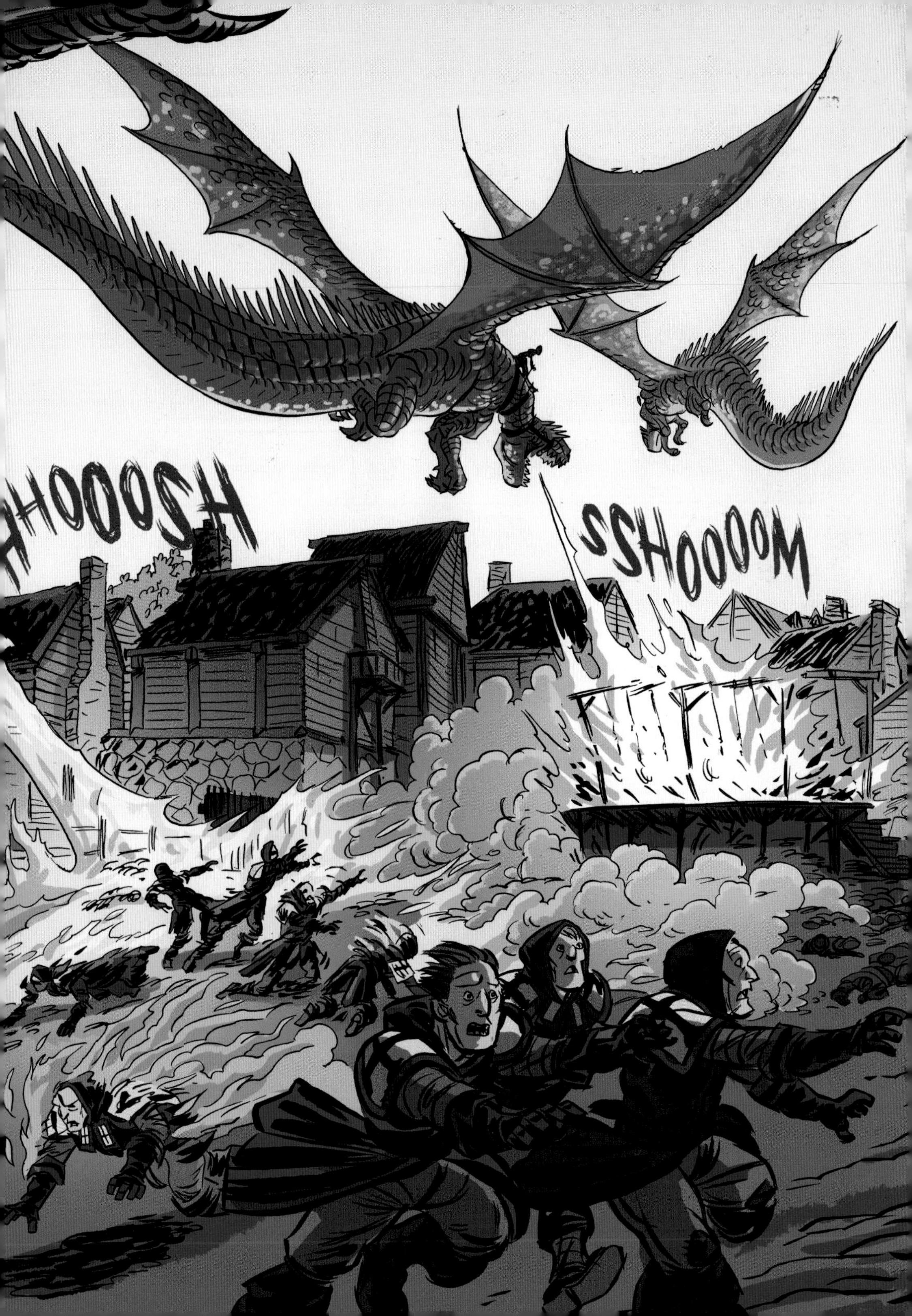

HOOOSH
SSHOOOM

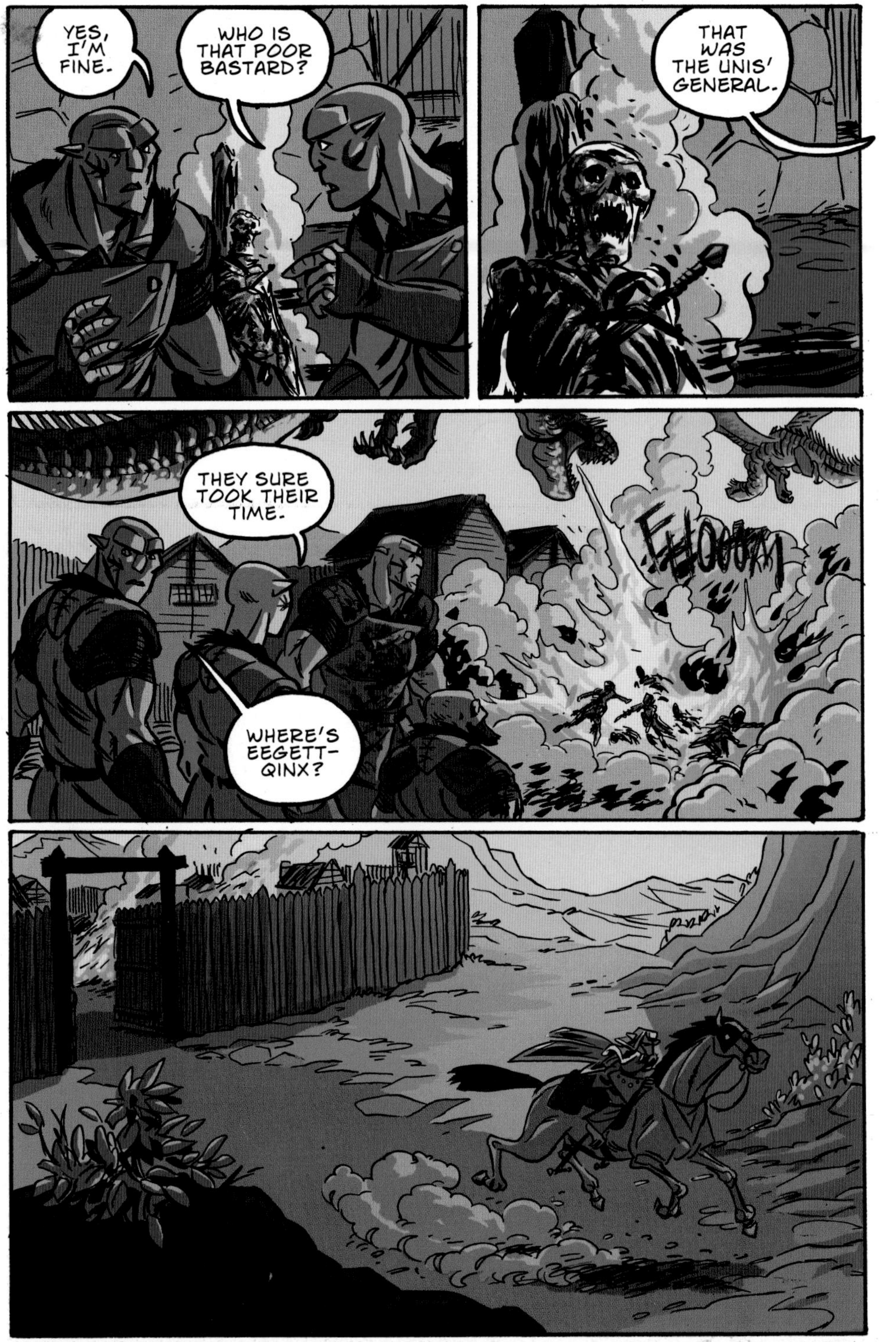
YES, I'M FINE.
WHO IS THAT POOR BASTARD?
THAT WAS THE UNIS' GENERAL.
THEY SURE TOOK THEIR TIME.
FWOOM
WHERE'S EEGETT-QINX?

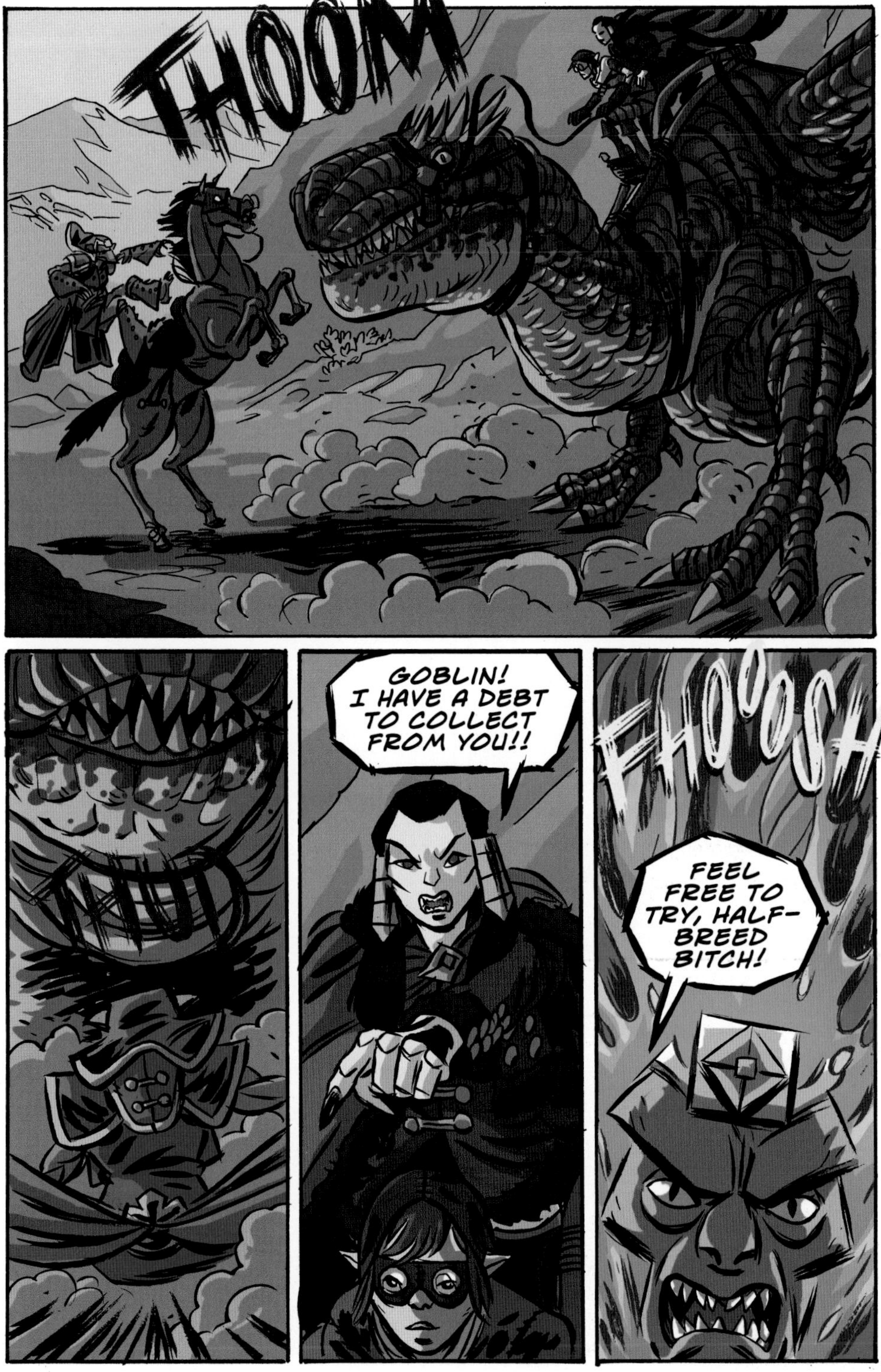
THOOM
GOBLIN! I HAVE A DEBT TO COLLECT FROM YOU!!
FHOOOSH
FEEL FREE TO TRY, HALF-BREED BITCH!

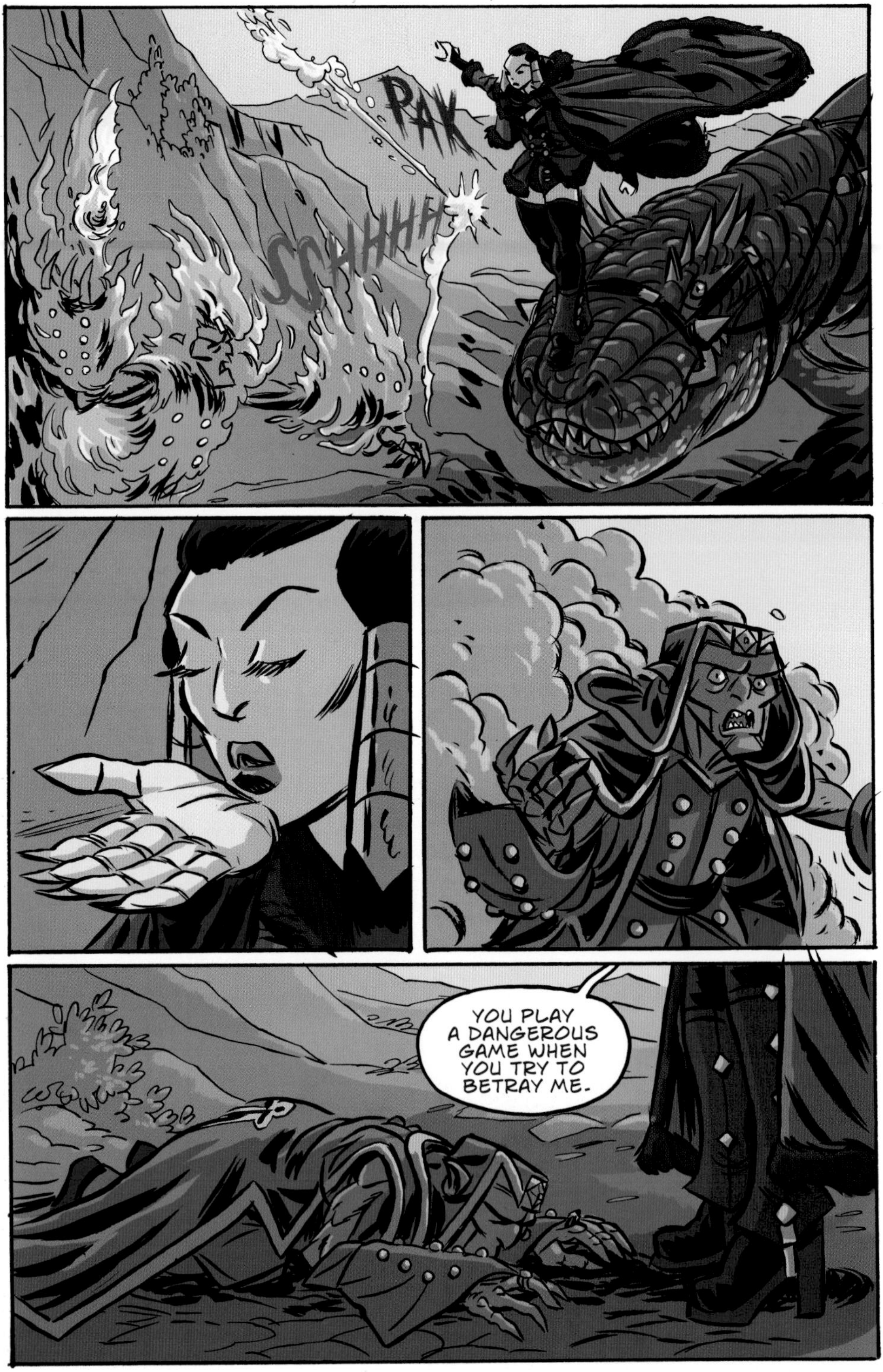
PAK
SCHHHH
YOU PLAY A DANGEROUS GAME WHEN YOU TRY TO BETRAY ME.

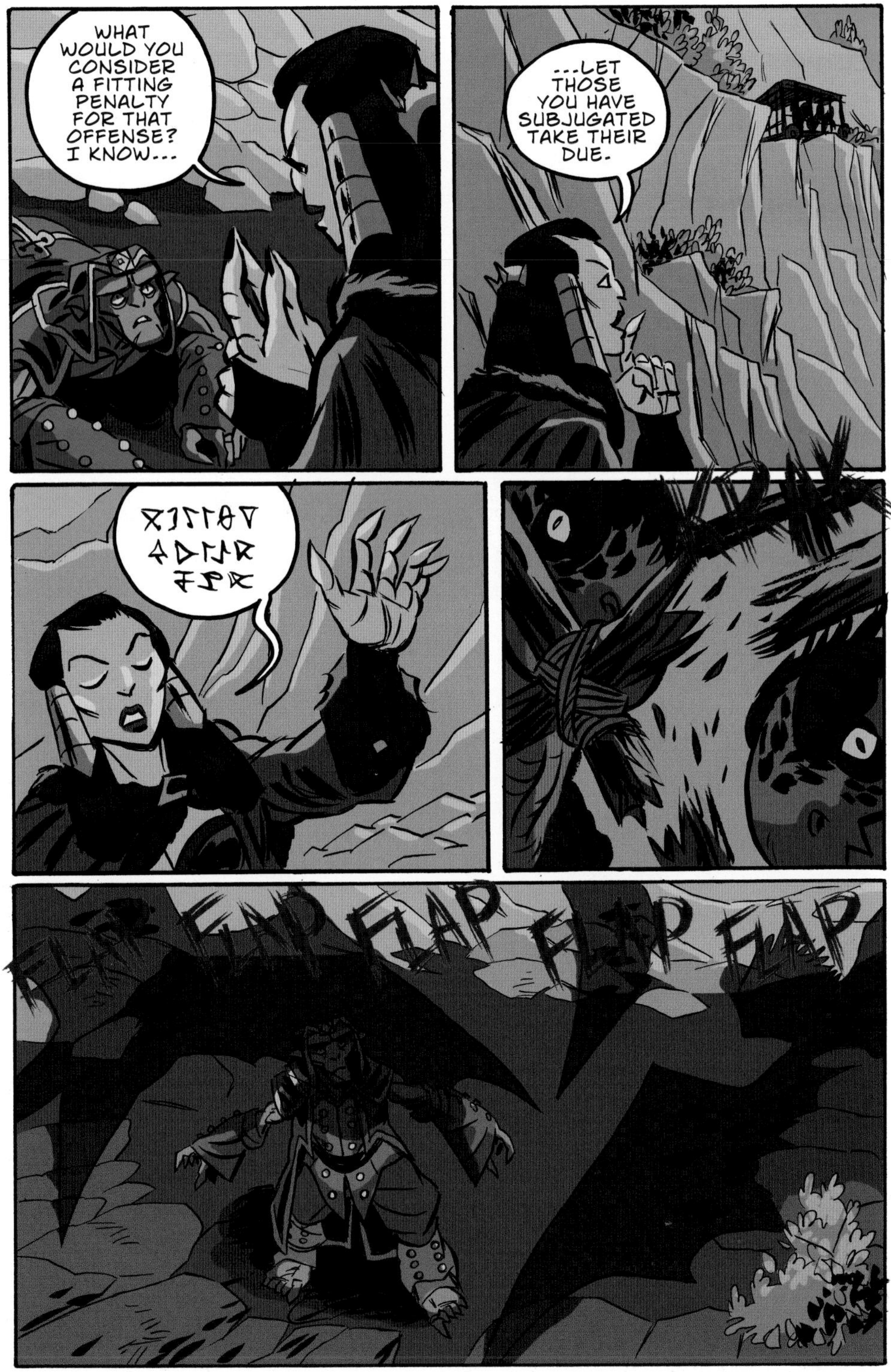
WHAT WOULD YOU CONSIDER A FITTING PENALTY FOR THAT OFFENSE? I KNOW...
...LET THOSE YOU HAVE SUBJUGATED TAKE THEIR DUE.
FLAP FLAP FLAP FLAP FLAP

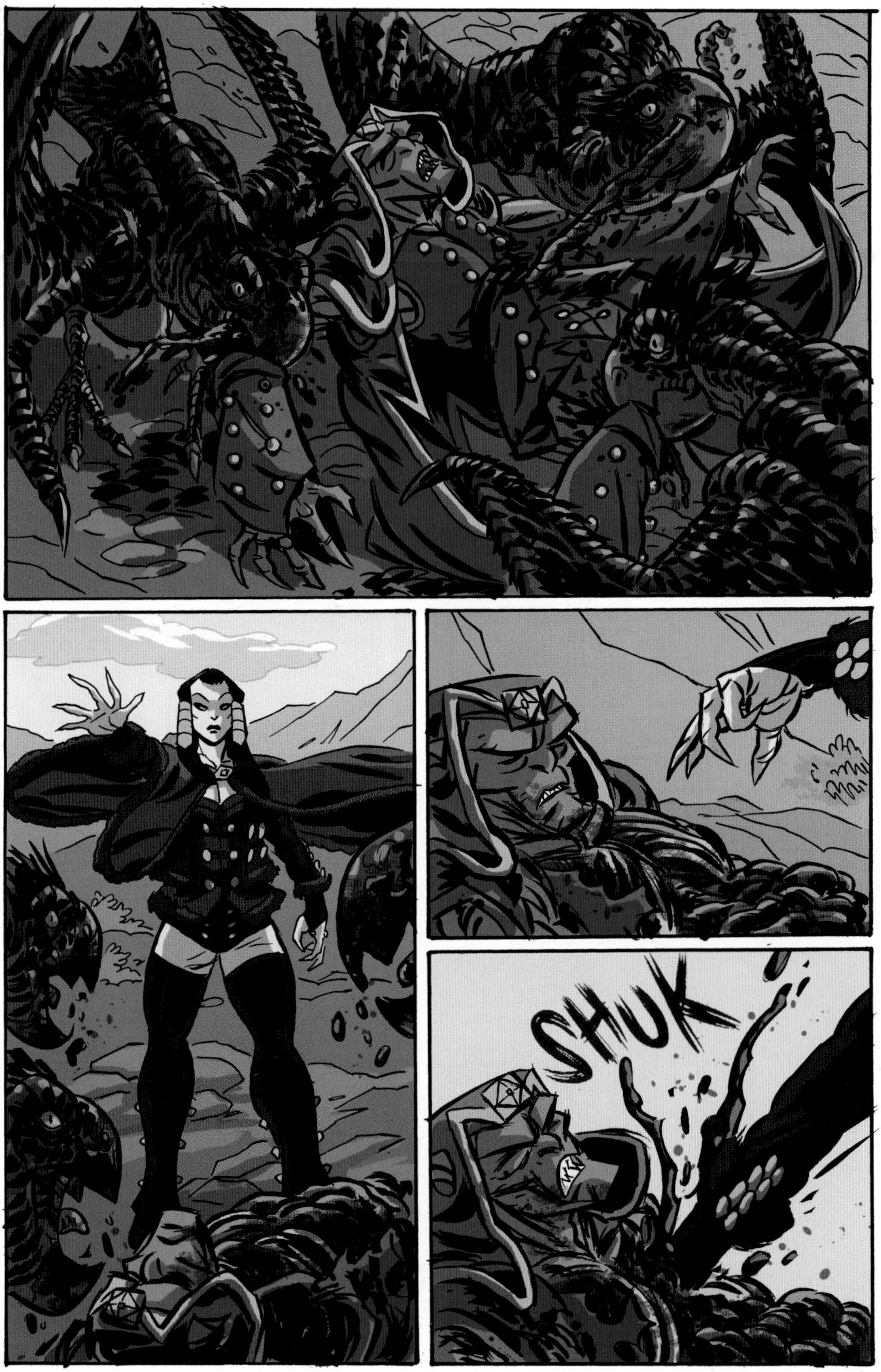
SHUK

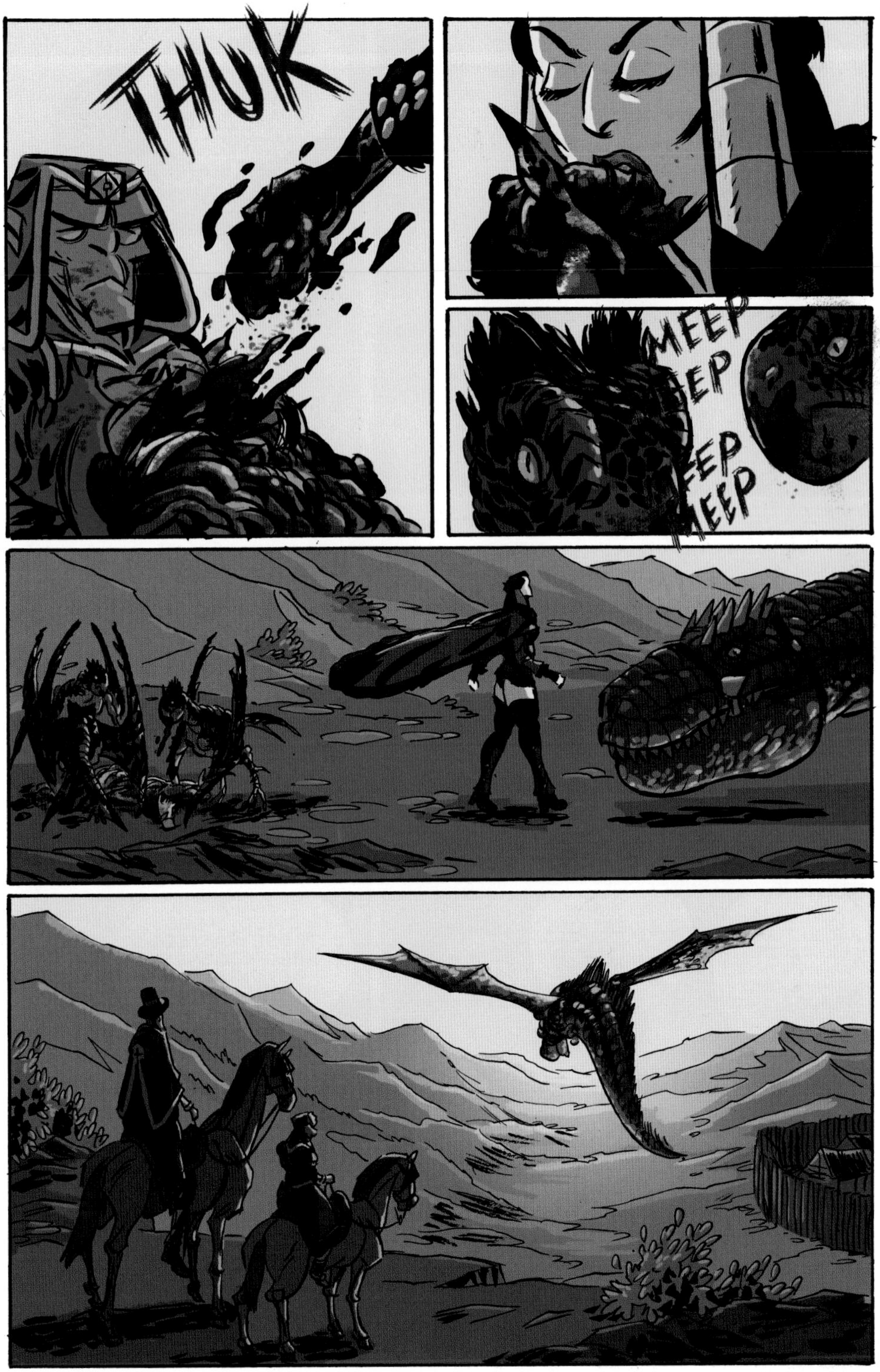
THUK
MEEP
MEEP

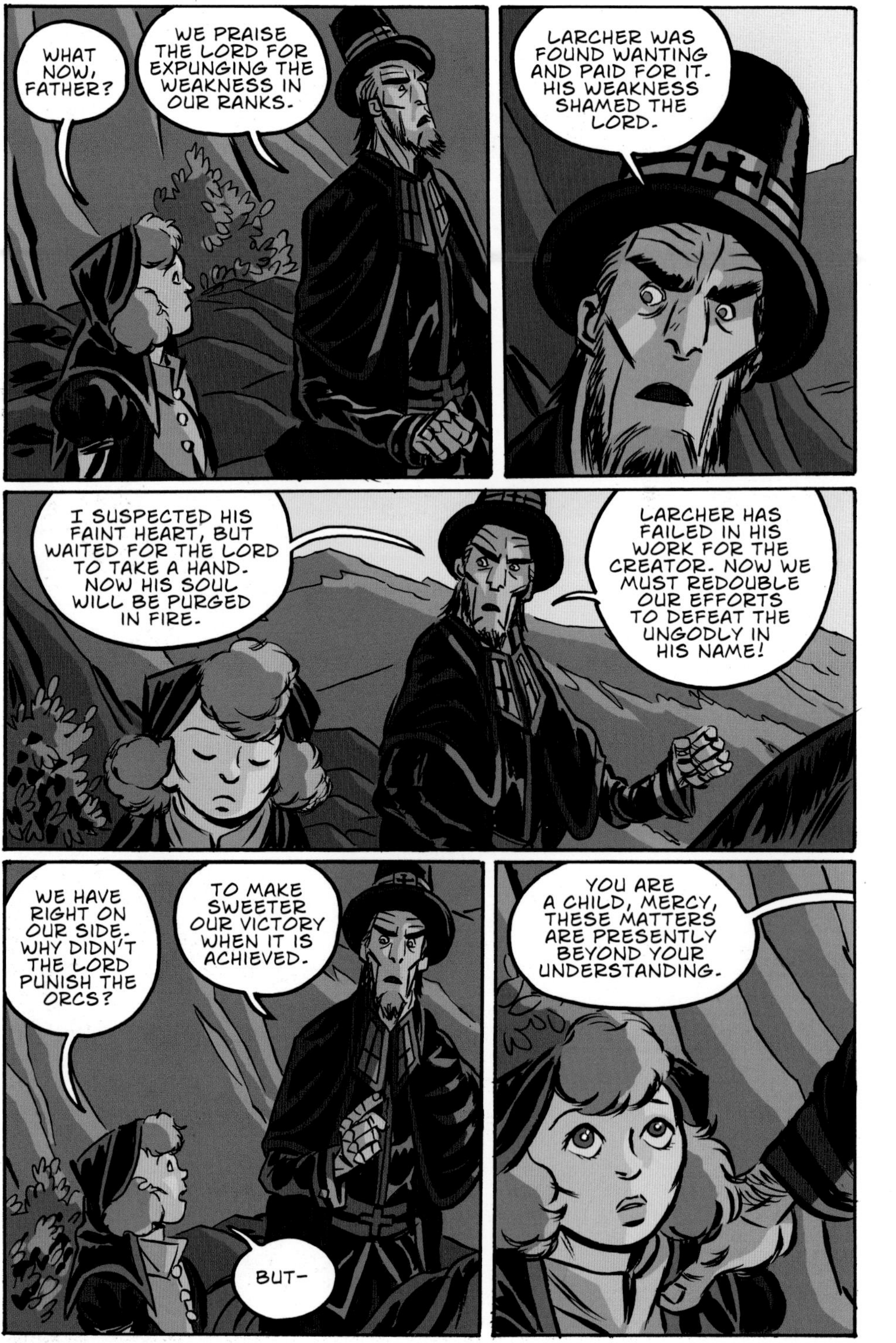

WHAT NOW, FATHER?
WE PRAISE THE LORD FOR EXPUNGING THE WEAKNESS IN OUR RANKS.
LARCHER WAS FOUND WANTING AND PAID FOR IT. HIS WEAKNESS SHAMED THE LORD.
I SUSPECTED HIS FAINT HEART, BUT WAITED FOR THE LORD TO TAKE A HAND. NOW HIS SOUL WILL BE PURGED IN FIRE.
LARCHER HAS FAILED IN HIS WORK FOR THE CREATOR. NOW WE MUST REDOUBLE OUR EFFORTS TO DEFEAT THE UNGODLY IN HIS NAME!
WE HAVE RIGHT ON OUR SIDE. WHY DIDN'T THE LORD PUNISH THE ORCS?
TO MAKE SWEETER OUR VICTORY WHEN IT IS ACHIEVED.
BUT-
YOU ARE A CHILD, MERCY, THESE MATTERS ARE PRESENTLY BEYOND YOUR UNDERSTANDING.

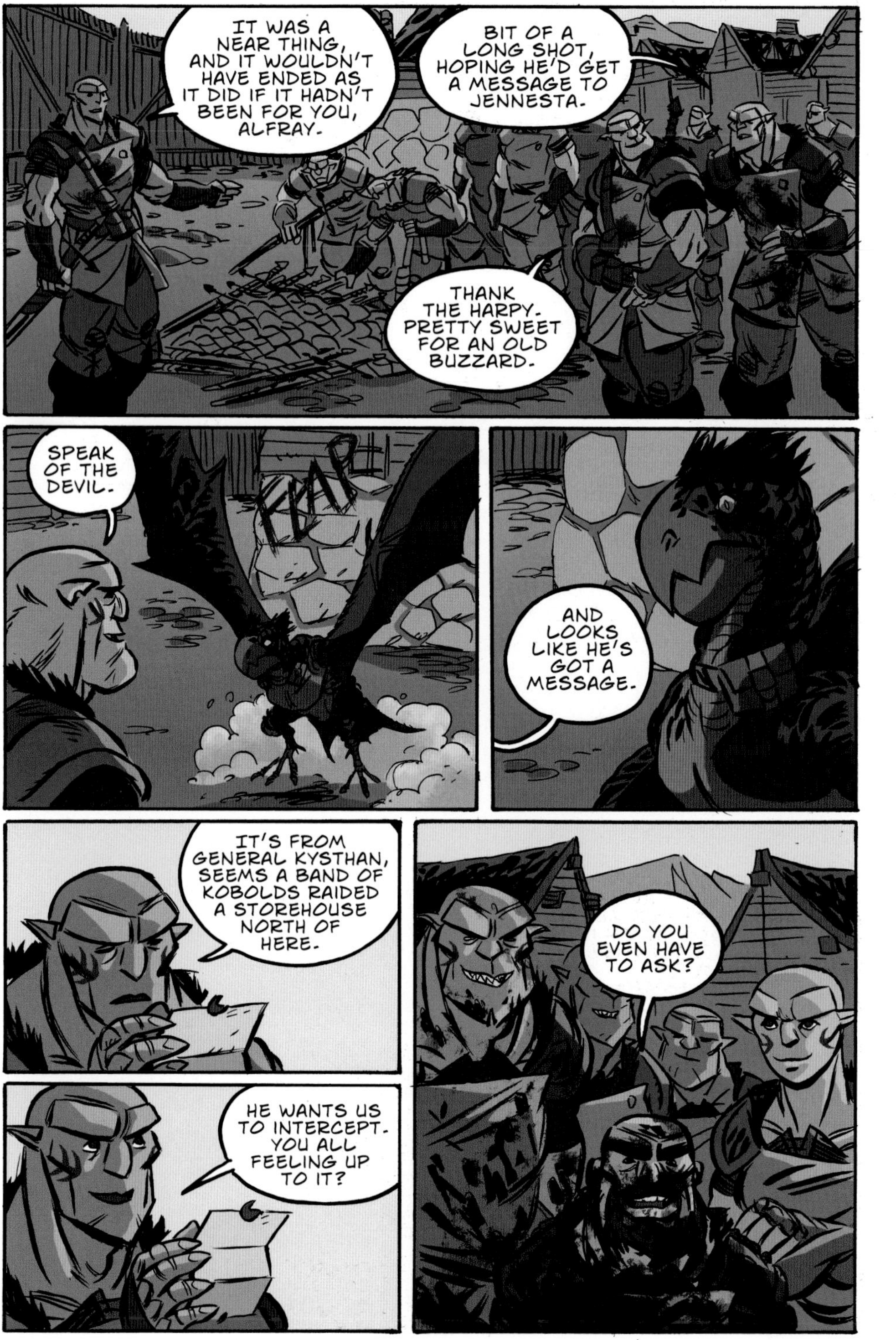
IT WAS A NEAR THING, AND IT WOULDN'T HAVE ENDED AS IT DID IF IT HADN'T BEEN FOR YOU, ALFRAY.
BIT OF A LONG SHOT, HOPING HE'D GET A MESSAGE TO JENNESTA.
THANK THE HARPY. PRETTY SWEET FOR AN OLD BUZZARD.
SPEAK OF THE DEVIL.
FLAP
AND LOOKS LIKE HE'S GOT A MESSAGE.
IT'S FROM GENERAL KYSTHAN, SEEMS A BAND OF KOBOLDS RAIDED A STOREHOUSE NORTH OF HERE.
HE WANTS US TO INTERCEPT. YOU ALL FEELING UP TO IT?
DO YOU EVEN HAVE TO ASK?

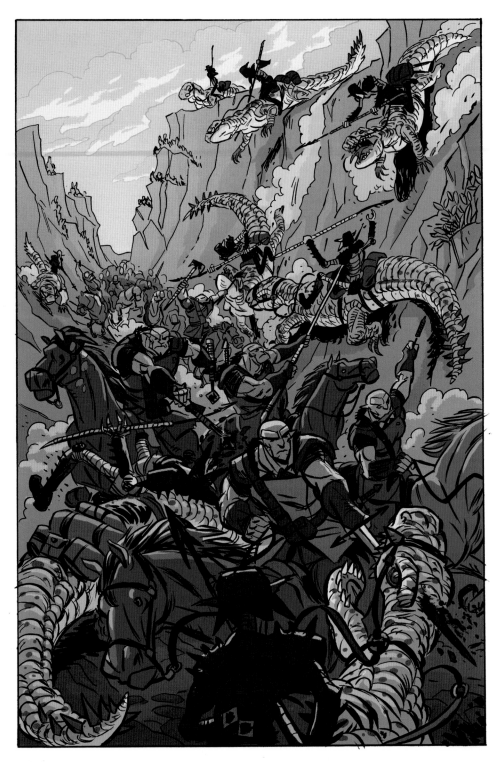

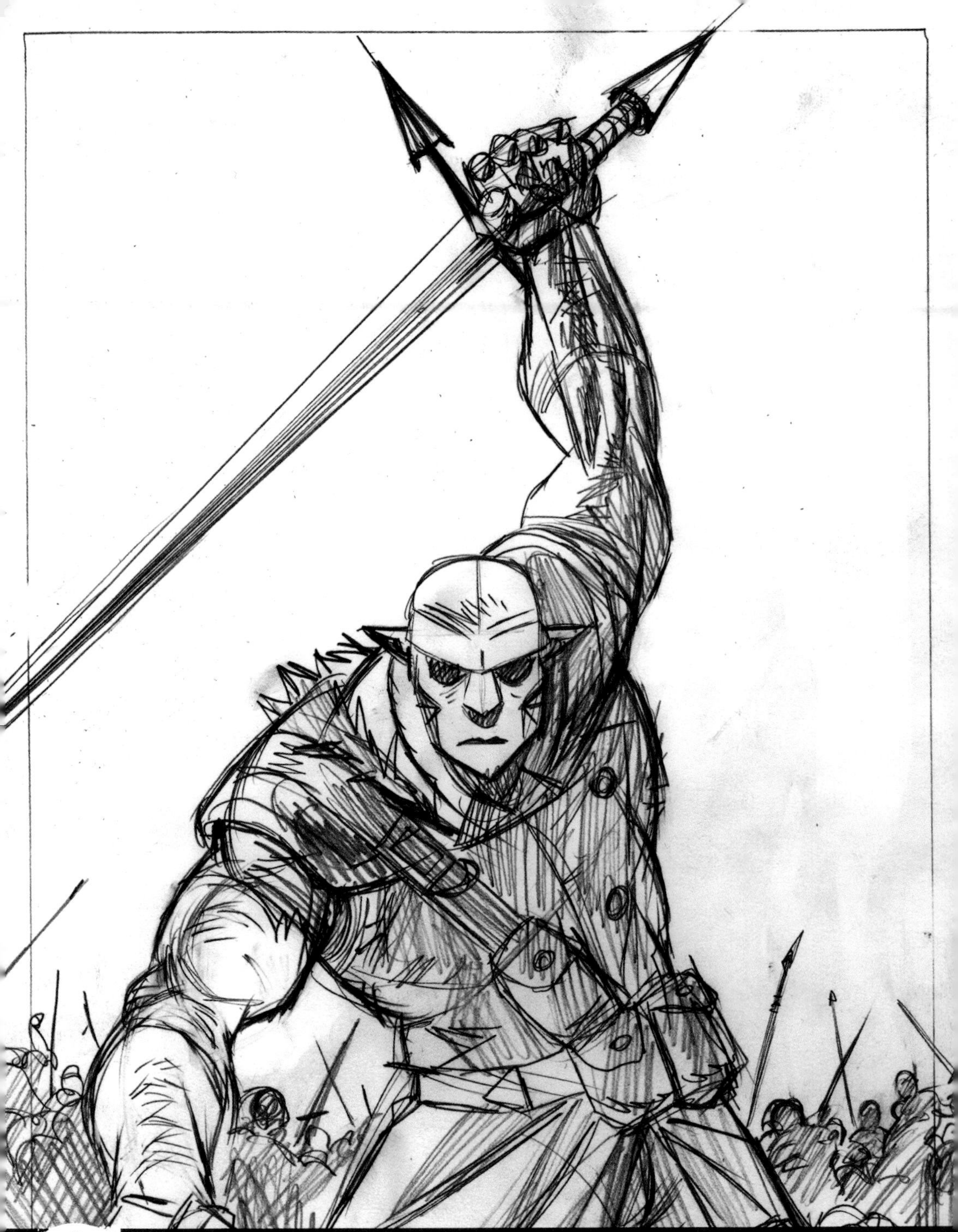

SKETCHBOOK

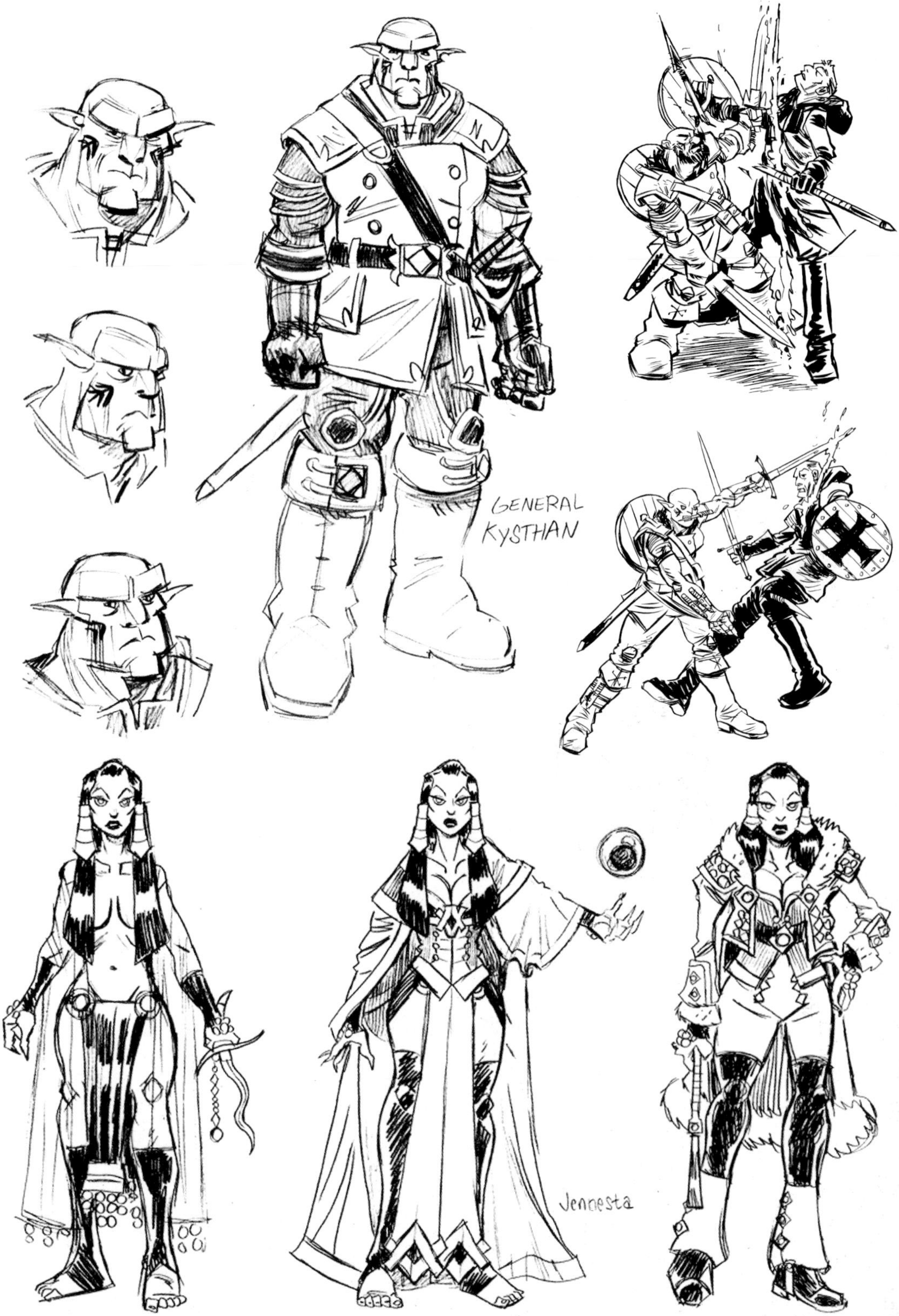
GENERAL KYSTHAN
Jennesta

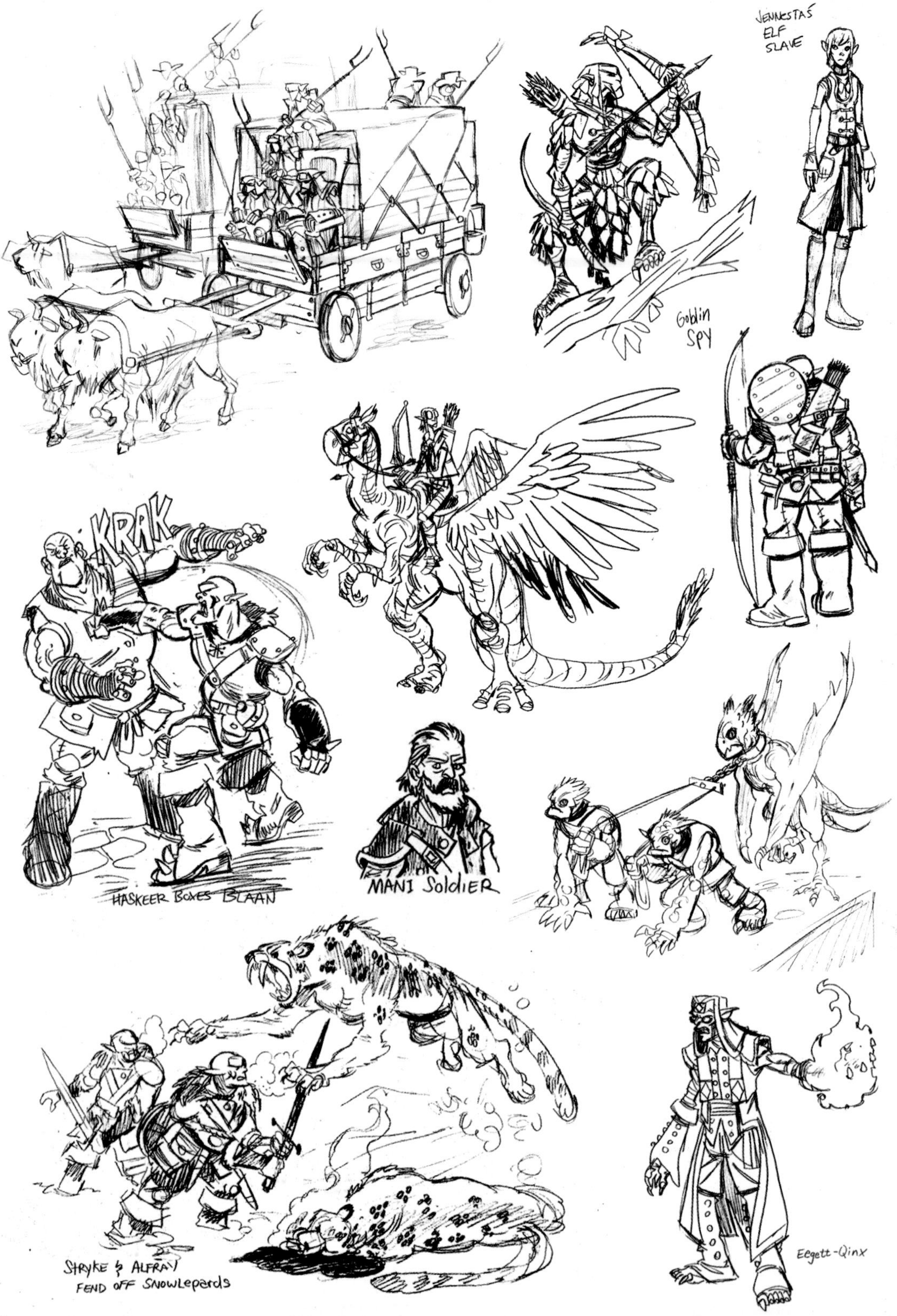
JENNESTA'S
ELF
SLAVE
Goblin
Spy
KRAK
HASKEER BOXES BLAAN
MANI Soldier
STRYKE & ALFRAY
FEND OFF SNOWLEPARDS
Eegett-Qinx